Advance Praise for *The Sincerest Form: Writing Fiction by Imitation*

"Hallelujah! Nicholas Delbanco has finally put into accessible form his well-known method for prodding his students to imitate their elders and betters. But he does more than suggest some very smart exercises; he has also isolated the most significant mysteries of technique into which so many disappear, never to emerge with readable prose, and has solicited the words of these 'master' authors to join their comments to his. The result is wise, often witty, and eminently usable. This is a book that honors the difficulty of good writing and believes its secrets can be shared by readers and writers who take an active (and often daring and entertaining) part in their own learning."

—Rosellen Brown, University of Houston

"In addition to a long and distinguished career as a first rate writer of fiction and nonfiction, Nicholas Delbanco has earned an enviable reputation as one of the most successful teachers of creative reading and writing in America. Here, in *The Sincerest Form,* this master craftsman brings together and shares with us the knowledge, practices, and, yes, the secrets gleaned from many years in the classroom. The result is a highly original and altogether indispensable guide for writers of all ages at all stages."

—George Garrett, Poet Laureate of Virginia

"Nicholas Delbanco is one of our country's finest fiction writers. He also happens to be one of our country's finest master teachers. The fusion of his talents in this instructive and delightful manual makes for an irresistible combination."

—Alan Cheuse, National Public Radio book critic

"Imitation is something we writers have always practiced, though we never wanted to admit it for fear of not being original . . . It's wonderful for this text to have the stories as well as exercises . . . I love the notes. This is what makes Delbanco's text very special. Great stuff and inspiring . . . This is going to be a very useful text for both students and instructors."

—Helena Viramontes, Cornell University

"*The Sincerest Form* offers a rich, representative anthology and a handful of possibilities for the fiction writing classroom. The imitation premise, though singular in drive, acts as a rudder to steer our reading through a diversity of stories, highlighting various key elements, tactics, and stylistics signatures along the way . . . it could provide a steady platform, a jumping off point into the reading and writing of fiction, and perhaps room in which

to develop the wings to carry us away. And, as Delbanco says, the premise is fun. I look forward to having this text in the future! Bravo to Delbanco."

—Katrina Roberts, Whitman College

"A great anthology, a good read, and a good sourcebook for narrative techniques and ideas. The selection of authors is superb. From minimalism to magical realism to high postmodernism, this book has examples for every kind of student and writerly interest. I like Professor Delbanco's emphasis on imitation because, let's face it, he is correct when he states that we all learn by imitating the world around us, even in writing."

—David Stevens, Seton Hall University

"I would suggest this book with enthusiasm to colleagues because of its inclusiveness, because of the usefulness of its exercises, and particularly because of those passages in which the writers talk about their writing process."

—Diane McPherson, Ithaca College

"Very appealing . . . The idea of using imitation as a primary tool for teaching creative writing to beginning students is a really good one because it emphasizes the need to read extensively in order to learn how to write."

—Maud Casey, Illinois Wesleyan University

"I think Delbanco's text could be more helpful than most anything else out there could be . . . I will adopt this book. What he teaches writers will make them better analysts and writers, too, because he shows them the tension that vibrates between deliberateness, self-awareness, and unconscious creativity, as well as how that tension vibrates within and for every writer."

—William B. Miller, George Mason University

"A unique approach. The stylistic devices are workable and insightful. The story selections are excellent. The chapters are [on the] students' level, and I like the easy, clear, personal tone."

—Louis Gallo, Radford University

"A good and valuable book—there's nothing like it I can think of out there. The book's emphasis on style is something I'm very interested in using in my courses, and would find useful. I like the range of authors Delbanco uses; I also appreciate the breakdown of devices. The tone is eloquent, tight, and succinct . . . the student samples are excellent."

—Anne Panning, SUNY Brockport

The Sincerest Form

Writing Fiction by Imitation

Nicholas Delbanco
University of Michigan

Boston   Burr Ridge, IL   Dubuque, IA   Madison, WI   New York
San Francisco   St. Louis   Bangkok   Bogotá   Caracas   Kuala Lumpur
Lisbon   London   Madrid   Mexico City   Milan   Montreal   New Delhi
Santiago   Seoul   Singapore   Sydney   Taipei   Toronto

Higher Education

THE SINCEREST FORM: WRITING FICTION BY IMITATION

Published by McGraw-Hill, an imprint of The McGraw-Hill Companies, Inc., 1221 Avenue of the Americas, New York, NY 10020. Copyright © 2004 by The McGraw-Hill Companies, Inc. All rights reserved. No part of this publication may be reproduced or distributed in any form or by any means, or stored in a database or retrieval system, without the prior written consent of The McGraw-Hill Companies, Inc., including, but not limited to, in any network or other electronic storage or transmission, or broadcast for distance learning.

1 2 3 4 5 6 7 8 9 0 FGR / FGR 0 9 8 7 6 5 4 3

ISBN 0-07-241471-5

Vice president and Editor-in-chief: *Thalia Dorwick*
Publisher: *Steve Debow*
Executive editor: *Lisa Moore*
Developmental editor: *Anne Stameshkin*
Marketing manager: *David S. Patterson*
Senior media producer: *Todd Vaccaro*
Production editor: *Brett Coker*
Senior production supervisor: *Richard DeVitto*
Design manager and cover designer: *Cassandra Chu*
Interior designer: *Linda M. Robertson*
Art editor: *Cristin Yancey*
Photo researcher: *Natalia Peschiera*
Manuscript editor: *Patricia Ohlenroth*
Compositor: *TBH Typecast, Inc.*
Typeface: *10/12 Minion*
Paper: *45# New Era Matte*
Printer and binder: *Quebecor World Fairfield*

Library of Congress Cataloging-in-Publication Data
Delbanco, Nicholas.
    The sincerest form: writing fiction by imitation / by Nicholas Delbanco
        p.   cm.
    ISBN 0-07-241471-5
    1. English language—Rhetoric—Problems, exercises, etc.
    2. Fiction—Technique—Problems, exercises, etc.   3. Creative writing—Problems, exercises, etc.   4. College readers. I. Title.

PE1408.D435 2003
808.3—dc21
                                                                2003054076

The Internet addresses listed in the text were accurate at the time of publication. The inclusion of a Web site does not indicate an endorsement by the authors or McGraw-Hill Higher Education, and McGraw-Hill does not guarantee the accuracy of the information presented at these sites.

www.mhhe.com

To My Students

Contents

PART II
An Anthology 273

(A short story by each of the following authors, with ten exercises attached)

Please visit the website at *www.mhhe.com/delbanco* for Additional Exercises
(Advanced Level Exercises for further study)

How to Use This Book

When someone asks me, on a train or plane, what I do for a living, I rarely answer, "Write." Every well-meaning stranger—the taxicab driver, the lawyer or bartender—is convinced he or she has a story to tell, and all it takes to be a writer is the time they don't happen to have. There are, in fact, many stories to tell and it may well be that each of us could become—over time—a published author. But no one starts from scratch and completes a marathon and no one writes a book of fiction without working up to it first. If I introduced myself to a brain surgeon or a ballerina and said, "Hey, let me borrow that scalpel or those toe-shoes; I've never tried an operation or a pirouette before but it looks easy enough," they'd throw me (let's hope) out of the hospital or boot me off the stage . . .

Our trade has tools; our craft requires practice. In the chapter that follows—"Theory and Practice"—I'll talk about the larger intention and not-so-buried purpose of one way of entering the world of words. But these introductory pages are intended as a user's manual, and they should function as a road map to what will be shared terrain. It's an overview only, of course; the devil's in the details, and this is a bare-bones summary of the bulk of what's to come. Still, it may help you to know how this book has been structured, and why.

About the Authors

The Sincerest Form has twelve chapters, twelve examples of close reading. The specific genre or "form" under examination is that of short prose fiction, composed in this country and in the twentieth century. Each chapter starts with a brief summary of the individual author's career. I don't include in these summaries what our writers like for breakfast or prefer to drive or wear; biographical data is useful, but only up to a point. Most of our authors are alive; four—Carver,

Hemingway, Malamud, and O'Connor—are dead. Most are producing new and changed work, and it would be counterproductive as well as misleading to say that the story we study is the single thing they've written you should read. On the website for this book, *www.mhhe.com/delbanco,* you can find the bibliography—the full list of titles, in chronological order—of the twelve writers here included. May your appetite grow with the feeding; may you hunger as readers for more.

Approaches

At the beginning of each chapter I print a short statement by the writer as to what he or she hopes to achieve. Sometimes these assertions derive from interviews, sometimes they come out of essays, sometimes from a letter to a friend. But they should serve to focus attention on a particular problem the writer confronts and, in the writing, tries to solve. It's a way of establishing rules of the game and therefore how to compete. Baseball and basketball and bowling—to name only three sports that start with a "B"—each require a spherical, hand-held object for the player to pick up and throw. Then and there similarity ends. When we look at Andrea Barrett or John Barth or Charles Baxter, therefore, we'll be looking at three different ways to play the game of composition, and the quotes and questions that accompany each story establish some opening rules. I'll try, I mean, to indicate a *way* of reading the work here printed: what to focus on and look for in the text.

The Stories

The bulk of every chapter consists of the story itself. This is right and proper. What these authors have produced is more important, truly, than what I have to say about them; if nothing else, this book provides an anthology of recent and excellent prose. But it's worth repeating that what we'll look at is the iceberg's tip—only a very small sampling of a particular genre (the short story) written in a particular country (the United States of America) and in a particular time (the twentieth century). As one of our authors famously wrote, "The dignity of movement of an iceberg is due to only one-eighth of it being above water." Ernest Hemingway suggests a reader ought to scrutinize what's not immediately obvious and keep an eye out for depths.

Notes on Craft and Context

In the "Notes on Craft and Context" section I focus on the enterprise of composition and how an artist sets and solves an issue—the aesthetic strategy entailed. I won't pretend my own experience of writing is irrelevant here; as the author of twenty books of fiction and nonfiction I think I understand—or ought to by now—some of the problems we face and some of the choices we make. At every stage (and even if only half-consciously) a writer makes decisions, constructing a checklist of questions: *was that parenthesis useful; should I use short or long sentences here, elaborate images or flat declarative prose, dialogue or stream-of-consciousness; what about those semicolons as opposed to the serial comma; is this going on too long and does it need to be clarified, amplified, cut; is it a mistake to have end-rhymed those last two three-syllable words, and what am I doing and why am I doing it and should I continue or stop?*

The nature of that set of choices—our half-conscious questions and answers—is what we mean by "aesthetic strategy." And it holds just as true in other art forms also; it's the way a composer decides on a major or a minor key, an actor picks an accent, or a sculptor chooses metal or marble or wood.

Imitation

To comprehend such strategies, it helps to try to copy them. This is the premise as well as promise of *The Sincerest Form;* if you understand the way another's story has been built you can set about building your own. At the end of every other chapter I reproduce examples of student prose—work produced in classes I taught at the University of Michigan—in order to show what can be achieved by way of imitation. To do so for all twelve chapters would be to extend these pages needlessly as well as to stifle invention; these samples are a way of pointing out the way. So after you have read the story and talked about it in class or in private, turn your hand to the "Exercises" section and try to get *inside* that process of decision-making; try to see why *this* word has been italicized for emphasis and not that one instead.

Following Your Own Lead

No first word or sentence is impossible. You are the literal lords of your created domain. (Some first sentences are admittedly more inviting than others; the reader may choose to stop reading after the opening phrase.) By the second sentence, however, we have fewer possibilities; we begin to need to follow our own lead. A story that starts from a first-person, present-tense vantage would dizzy the reader if it shifted to third person and the past tense on the next page; one that starts in Zimbabwe had better not move to Rhode Island in the second phrase. And if the writer chooses such disjunction, then the third sentence somehow ought to indicate that this particular story will be told from shifting vantage points. This holds just as true for dialogue as for descriptive prose. If a character's way of expressing herself is, "I ain't sure I love you," she can't use the alternative, "Arabella's in dubiety with reference to hate." The game we invite our readers to join has a coherent system, and we should not cheat nor alter the rules as we play.

I do not mean that every story must be linear or that the reader should be able to fathom it by the first paragraph's end. Any situation worth exploring is progressively revealed. But if we understand a woman to be forty we should not learn ten pages later that she's twenty-two; if we're told—authoritatively— Tom has been a murderer we should not find at story's end that it was really Harry or Dick. (A murder mystery has many possible suspects, of course, and part of the pleasure of reading in that genre is a guessing game: *who really done it*, and why. The writer tries to fool us, to make us change our minds, but that's very different from changing the identity of the actual killer halfway through.)

So the process of delimiting continues throughout the piece; the third sentence follows the second as the second did the first. The thirtieth follows the twenty-ninth, excluding what once might have been. And there should be, ideally, only one possible last line. Of the infinite range of possibilities with which the writer began, he or she is left with a single legitimate closure—all others being foreclosed.

Applications, Connections, and Exercises

Attached to each selection are ten exercises—more than any single student could possibly accomplish in the course of a semester. These are intended as signposts, not the road itself. The points raised by the "Applications and Connections" sections can be viewed—to extend the "driving" metaphor—as a set of traffic signs. Here's where you should yield or slow or stop; here's an intersection; here's a scenic overview or detour; here's a congested area or rest area or a place where the bridge may freeze first. I mean by these admittedly inexact comparisons to suggest there are ways to *think* about the stories that will help you follow the rules of the road and navigate the exercises that come next; the "Applications and Connections" section should help us get inside the mind-set of the author and emulate it via imitation. The journey, not arrival, matters, and this is where we start.

It should be admitted also that any student who could perform even a large proportion of these writing tasks would be so preternaturally gifted as to have no need of this textbook at all. Typically, I would expect you to choose two or three exercises from every set of ten. You may prefer to compose an exercise or two of your own, or to write your own short story in the spirit of the prose you've just been reading. I want to repeat, as suggested above, that there's *logic* involved in the work of the imagination, but it's not the sort of logic that arithmetic entails. There aren't, in short, a series of problems for which there is only one answer or a single correct solution; the more the merrier . . .

The Approach: Variations on a Theme

My working assumption is that to work through these pages will take a semester, not a year. A second set of twelve texts is appended as anthology, so that the teacher and student may apply these strategies of imitation to other examples of short prose fiction—or simply pick and choose. It's in the spirit of our subject, after all, that there should be variations on a theme; you may want to spend three weeks on one of the authors or one week on three.

Our sequence of a dozen stories is neither alphabetical nor chronological but thematic. To the best of my ability, I have separated out the topics in order to focus, turn by turn, on specific matters of craft. But this is of course a false schematic; *all* writers use dialogue and descriptive prose and dramatic encounters "in scene." You can't say, "*A* does only *B*" or "*X* is only interested in *Y*." It's therefore a matter of proportion and emphasis: In the chapter on Lorrie Moore, for example, we'll focus on her use of wit; in the chapter on Bernard Malamud, the process of revision, though the former scrupulously revises her prose and the latter can be humorous. So we'll look at topics turn by turn in the hope that, having completed *The Sincerest Form,* we may see a work of fiction steadily and whole.

Teaching Imitation

I first taught a version of this course more than twenty years ago at Bennington College in Vermont, to twenty undergraduates. I have taught similar texts and much the same procedure to MFA in creative writing students at Columbia University and the University of Michigan, as well as to a mixed cohort of graduate and undergraduate students. Recently I taught an intensive workshop in "Imitations" to fifty adults in San Francisco; this winter I'm teaching it again to English majors in Ann Arbor. In every instance—whether dealing with undergraduates, graduate students, or summer session enrollees—I've been delighted by the quality of work produced as well as the quality of the discussions in class.

Advanced Exercises

The website that accompanies this book, *www.mhhe.com/delbanco,* contains a number of advanced exercises in imitation. Once the ingredients of composition have been separated out, it's a pleasure to mix them together and create a stew of styles. This requires an advanced and not beginning level of technique, and the writer should be encouraged to seek his or her own comfort level. Here too I have appended examples of my students' work, and here too the work is impressive. (The website includes several such cross-pollinating efforts: "Oedipus Rex," as told by Ford Madox Ford or James Joyce's *Ulysses* by A.A. Milne.) I haven't, for obvious reasons, reprinted work that fails to grasp the principles of imitation—but in my years of teaching such failure has been rare. More students have near-perfect pitch than a tin ear. So what's reprinted in these pages, though excellent, is representative: the best of a very good lot.

Generally the exercises go from simple to complex, but that's a rule to which there are many exceptions; it's not possible beforehand to gauge the gift of mimicry. Some of you may find dialogue easy and descriptive language hard; others may find the reverse. Some feel at ease with the first-person, present-tense narrative voice; others prefer the past third. So the teacher might well urge the student to write a short story by Tim O'Brien with characters by Flannery O'Connor, or vice-versa; write a scene by Raymond Carver set in Jamaica Kincaid's Antigua; write an argument in Bharati Mukherjee's kitchen as revised by Richard Ford. Write two hundred additional exercises for a volume still to come.

Practice Makes a Better Practitioner

I have carried with me now for years the notion of writers as artisans, or artists engaged in a guild. My model is that of the medieval guild, with its compelling triad of apprentice, then journeyman laborer, then master craftsman—the last attained after a lifetime's study and practice of the craft. That writing *is* a craft as well as art is something all accomplished authors take to be self-evident. Every professor professes it; every student studies it. Practice makes, if not perfect, a better practitioner; if we swing a baseball bat or golf club forty thousand times in order to improve our game, why not hone the skills of imitation, too?

Acknowledgments

This book has been a long time a'borning. I have been a teacher now for more than thirty-five years and for more than half of them have consciously deployed the tactics here described. In those years and decades I have worked with many students, but almost by definition taught no one not in the room. This, then, is an effort, to put in writing what was conceived of as discussion, and I want to acknowledge at the outset that ours has been a collective effort; it would and could not have happened without that exchange of opinion which is the pith and marrow of a teacher's life. To my students past, present, and future, I dedicate the book.

My first public description of the value of imitation appeared in the *New York Times* in their "Writers on Writing" column in the summer of 1999. That article was titled "From Echoes Emerge Original Voices" and it piqued the interest of the editor of what would become *The Sincerest Form*, Sarah Touborg. Whereas the gratitude expressed above is general, her name should be specific; without her canny and attentive encouragement this book would not exist. Lisa Moore has been responsible for bringing the book to completion, and Anne Stameshkin at McGraw-Hill proved tireless in tending to the details of the project; I owe her many thanks. Patricia Ohlenroth copyedited this manuscript with the kind of rigorous attention every author dreams of and very few receive. Lewis Lapham and Ben Metcalf of *Harpers* magazine also encouraged the project; my essay "In Praise of Imitation" (July 2002) came to fruition under their supportive watch, and an adapted version thereof serves as my introduction. As always, my agent Gail Hochman of Brandt & Hochman has been indispensable to both process and result.

Marvin Parnes of the University of Michigan's Office of Research Development and Administration supported the project with an open-handed generosity that continues to inspirit; colleagues and friends too numerous to name have read and reviewed what I wrote.

My sincerest thanks to all the reviewers who read and responded to various drafts of the manuscript:

Maud Casey, Illinois Wesleyan University
Louis Gallo, Radford University
Bernard Kaplan, University of Delaware
Diane McPherson, Ithaca College
William Miller, George Mason University
Anne Panning, SUNY Brockport
Katrina Roberts, Whitman College
Rocco Versaci, Palomar College
Helena Maria Viramontes, Cornell University

One of my students in the MFA Program at the University of Michigan deserves particular mention. Valerie Laken was a member of the cohort I taught in the fall of 1999 and—as the last exercise in the project's website will indicate—brilliantly engaged by the spirit of the enterprise and adept at learned play. I asked her to work with me on *The Sincerest Form;* to my great relief and the book's great advantage, she agreed. She joined me the next year as graduate assistant in an undergraduate class whose syllabus largely prefigured this table of contents; we have worked together on the project since. From the mechanics of transcription to the specifics of ascription—legwork at which she's fleeter footed—Ms. Laken has been splendid; she wrote précis of several of the chapters, compiled the glossary, shored up my enthusiasm when it flagged, and proved these strategies are best when shared. I know no better definition of the rewards of teaching than to acknowledge how much I've been taught; to each and all, my thanks.

Theory and Practice: An Introduction

This book deals with imitation, and in the spirit of praise. Both in theory and in practice the gift of imitation is, I think, a useful one. The habit begins in the cradle; we copy what we watch. That delighted codger lifting arms and clapping hands while a grandchild does the same is teaching by repeated gesture: *How big is baby? So-o-o big!* We learn by the example of others to walk and dress and brush our teeth and play tennis or the violin; it's how we learn to spell and drive and swim. It's the way we first acquire language and, later, languages. *How does the cow go? Moo-Moo!* In every act of reading there's an agreement, however unspoken, that we follow where the author leads; the very act of printing books consists of repetition. And if what we study is writing, it's surely how we learn to write; all writers read all the time.

Often this process of replication is unconscious or only partly conscious. We hear a phrase and repeat it; we memorize the lines of a joke or ceremony or play. Those authors we admire have a habit of seeing, of *saying* the world, and when we lift our heads from the world of the page, we're likely to see as they saw. The human race reproduces itself, as do snow leopards and snow peas; the Human Genome Project undertakes to map that process of transmission: how and why. What these pages will attempt to show is how the writer writes, and why, and knowledge of that process will help shape the reader's response. This book is intended for apprentices as well as for those far advanced in the trade; we all are members—readers and writers, students and teachers—of a single guild.

Sweeping assertions, brave claims. They need some spelling out.

Here are a set of definitions from a series of dictionaries of the word "imitation" as such. My sources are, in order, *Webster's New Collegiate Dictionary, The American Heritage Dictionary of the English Language,* and *The Oxford English Dictionary;* what they have in common is, it seems to me, distrust.

1. An imitating; a copying.
2. That which is made or produced as a copy; an artificial likeness.

3. Properly, a literary work designed to reproduce the style or manner of another author.

4. Biol. Mimicry.

5. Something derived or copied from an original.

6. Music. The repetition of a phrase or sequence often with variations in key, rhythm, and voice.

7. A thing made to look like something else, which it is not; a counterfeit.

8. Made (of less costly material) in imitation of a real or genuine article or substance.

As the fourth of these brief definitions suggests, the act of mimicry is well established in nature. The coat of mountain goats and skin tint of chameleons blend in with the rock face or leaf. A mockingbird borrows its song. But we'll deal in *The Sincerest Form* not so much with mimicry in the biological sense as in the second of the eight definitions above: "a copy; an artificial likeness."

In music and the visual arts, "strict" or "free" repetition is common; both ear and eye acknowledge variations on a theme. We salute the work of others in a musical arrangement or a composition structured as a predecessor painted it; this process of "quotation" is familiar. In museums all over the country there's someone bent over an easel, doing their best to reproduce what's framed and on the wall. The techniques of mimicry—and its silent partner, mime—prove crucial to the actor's craft, taking stage center on stage.

In most forms of performance, indeed, we take such skills for granted—and personal expressiveness may even be a mistake. The members of a dance troupe must follow their choreographer's lead, moving in trained unison, and woe betide that member of the string section of an orchestra who chooses an exotic bowing. To be singled out while joining in a chorus is to risk correction; when you march you should do so in step.

I'm not suggesting here that protective coloration need be drab, or that not to be noticed is best. But for many centuries and in many different cultural contexts the standard of imitation and close reproduction held sway. It was how to learn a trade. An apprentice in a studio would have mixed paint for years or cleaned the varnish rags and swept wood shavings from the floor for what must have felt like forever; only slowly and under supervision might the young artisan approach the canvas or the cabinet itself. The French instrument maker J. B. Vuillaume took his pattern for violins and violoncellos unabashedly from his much-admired predecessor Antonio Stradivari. This is not forgery so much as emulation, a willing admission that others have gone this way before.

Nor is mimicry confined to craftsmanship and the creative or performing arts. In middle age we find ourselves repeating what our parents said; as candidates for political office we recite slogans time after time while pounding the pavement for votes. At the ticket counter or the fast food take-out line the dictates of efficiency make a virtue out of "sameness"; the entire profit-system of the industrial age is based on uniformity. Component parts must be inter-changeable and therefore identical in manufactured products; you can't im-provise the size of a conveyor belt or gear. To a greater or lesser degree, it would seem, *all* ritual observances partake of repetition. Religion thrives on it; so do those who practice medicine or soldiering or law.

So why should we exempt the art of fiction from, as *Webster's* describes it, "An imitating; a copying"? We've grown so committed as a culture to the ideal of originality that the writer who admits to working in the mode and manner of another writer will likely stand accused of being second-rate. But to imitate is not to be derivative; it's simply to admit we derive from what was accom-plished by others. In our pursuit of self-expression, we've forgotten the old adage that "There's nothing new under the sun."

In this regard at least the early authors had it easier, had fewer doubts. They would have found nothing shameful in prescribed subjects or in avoiding the first-person pronoun. Since the story was a constant one—how Troy was burned, how Rome was built—the apprentice could focus on style. A copyist must pay the kind of close attention to the model that a counterfeiter does, and though such results may not be art they are, when successful, real proof of technique.

It's possible, in other words, that the problem is not what to write but how to write it, and that style itself can be predetermined, not something we need to invent. Originality is rare indeed, not subject to instruction, and in any case it's not the focus of *The Sincerest Form*. Still, I expect that—having imitated and absorbed the voices here represented—the student's own authentic voice will start to sound. As the English novelist Edward Bulwer-Lytton (1803–1873) once wrote: "Imitation, if noble and general, insures the best hope of originality."

The title of this book itself is an imitation. The famous phrase to which the phrase refers is "Imitation is the sincerest form of flattery." If asked, nine readers out of ten would recite the line as I've transcribed it. But they would be wrong. The actual quotation, according to Bartlett's—who got it right—comes from a book of aphorisms called *The Lacon*, by George Caleb Colton (1780–1832). The line he wrote and none of us remember is "Imitation is the sincer-est of flattery." Colton himself makes no mention of form.

But by the alchemy of a collective consciousness, "form" enters in never-theless. The sentence seems to need it, and not merely for the sake of the extra added syllable. Always implicit in the idea of copying, "form" here becomes explicit. And although its author has been long forgotten, the line he didn't write is widely quoted now.

The third word of our title is more important than the first—a definite article—or the second—a superlative. Without that third word, the noun "form," the first two words convey little or nothing. Neither "the" nor "the sin-cerest" would make sense alone. The article and adjective both modify their subject, and the focus of these pages is on attributes of "form."

Back to our second word. "Sincerity" and "fiction" are, on the face of it, strange bedfellows; as writers we weave fantasies and hope to be believed. We make up situations and invent characters whole cloth in order to persuade the reader of our imagined truth. If art is mimesis—a Greek word meaning imitation of reality—then it's done with smoke and mirrors and twenty-six letters in an agreed-on sequence; we pretend that there's a world within the word. The alphabet is merely a convention, after all, and so are the rules of grammar and spacing: What law of nature has ordained that "the" not be spelled "eht"? Or, come to that, XXY?

Such matters of convention—of recognized shared pretense—lie at the root of **modernism,** of postmodernism when acknowledged; the artist grows self-conscious while wielding pen or brush. In recent years the ideal of realism or "a mirror held to nature" has been much modified; the artificial nature of the act of copying has been, in and of itself, stressed. To be "sincere" or "more sincere" or "sincerest" is still to lie for a living, and even the confessional author has to shape his or her tale. So there's an appropriate irony in the widespread addition of "form" to Colton's phrase: it's a quasi-quotation, half-truth.

What George Colton described, it should be clear, was neither insincerity nor flattery's forked tongue. There are several forms of flattery in which the tongue is lodged in cheek or where the courtier does not mean the praise brought forth in court. But the "sincerest" of flattery admits of no such irony or hypocritical double-dealing and must be taken at face value. Colton meant the desire to emulate, and we imitate what we admire.

This need not, however, always be the case. There's a variety of humor in which the critic or the comic is making fun of what he or she impersonates; think of those comedians who copy the mannerisms of valley girls or presidents, and it's obvious that imitation need not always be sincere. Parody and **caricature** rely on just such exaggeration. Take a signature component part—a nose, an accent, a way of wearing suits or skirts—and blow it up out of proportion: the part represents the whole. (Some of our exercises will be parodic in this manner, making use of disproportion.) One sure way to get a laugh—or irritate the model in a game most children play—is simply to repeat. *One sure way to get a laugh—or irritate the model in a game most children play—is simply to repeat. One sure way to get a laugh*—until we cry "Enough!"

And this perhaps explains some negative connotations of the word "imitation" itself. The American ideals of "rugged individuality" and "independence" stand in opposition to what we're told we have become, a nation of "conformists." Often we compare an imitation unfavorably to the original; often we call it counterfeit or mass-produced or fraud. In the worst-case academic scenario—unacknowledged quotation—we call it *plagiarism;* in the business scenario it's *copyright infringement* or *intellectual property theft.* A "copycat's" booed and not cheered. A "camp follower" cannot by definition be the leader of the pack. So imitation may be seen as stealing or second-rank invention or, at the least, uninspired; it's a pejorative term.

But those legions who impersonate Elvis do so almost as an act of worship; similarly most of those who copy do so in the spirit of praise. They mean to compliment not insult the model reproduced. When mimicry's sincere, it does connote respect; Colton meant what he wrote, and he's right. Our selections of prose fiction are, though various, consistent in this: They each will reward imitation. They each are "the real thing."

At this forward-facing moment and start of the millennium, it seems we've acquired the Janus-faced habit of also looking back. (Janus is the two-faced god who gave his name to January: Poised at the turning of the year, he sees both ways at once.) Michael Cunningham's prize-winning book, *The Hours,* is an extended act of imitation; he enters the world both of a modern-day Clarissa Dalloway and her creator, Virginia Woolf. *Shakespeare in Love* is highly allusive, a good-humored tip of the cap to the language of Elizabethan England; its jokes require knowledge of the great plays and playwright it spoofs. Patrick O'Brian's Aubrey and Maturin novels constitute an almost uninterrupted foray into the imaginative discourse of a world at war 200 years ago, and large swatches of the story pay homage to Jane Austen or borrow from naval accounts. And these are just a small sampling; present examples abound.

This year there'll be another "Faux Faulkner" contest in Oxford, Mississippi, and there are more Hemingway look-alike and write-alike contests than one can shake a fishing rod or rifle at. There's the "Bulwer-Lytton" contest, in which we're invited to write as badly as possible—to bottom, as it were, his famous opening phrase, "It was a dark and stormy night." Think also of the tasks of translation or dubbing; the translator fails when he or she places a personal stamp on the text rendered; the dubber fails as soon as you notice how good a job's being done.

Imitation is, as well, a time-honored practice in verse. Robert Lowell used precisely that word to describe his own effort of translation from languages he read only a little and sometimes not at all. His book *Imitations* (1962) is a series of original poems inspired by and freely rendering the work of other poets. We call a sonnet "Petrarchan" or "Shakespearean" in honor of those who popularized the particular rhyme scheme and stanzaic pattern; we write in the "Miltonic" or "Spenserian" or "Eliotic" mode. The poet William Butler Yeats called apprenticeship a "singing school," and much of his own verse deploys traditional forms. Emily Dickinson and Walt Whitman—two widely admired "originals" of the nineteenth century—have influenced modern practitioners in direct lines of descent. I can imagine a companion book on how to read and write poetry and improve the skills of **prosody** via conscious copying. (My anecdotal sense of the matter, indeed, is that poets routinely use imitation as a **pedagogical device.**) But here, in *The Sincerest Form,* we'll restrict ourselves to prose.

Whether the genre be poetry or prose fiction, however, one task of the writing teacher is to point out antecedents: "Tom, you might want to look at what Dick did with this **plot device.** Harriet, you might (re)read the novel by *X*, which your *Y* appears to follow." More often than not the student has no notion that it's been tried before. Often the apprentice has not seen the model he or she has somehow come to imitate, and there's a way in which such ignorance is bliss. It's a precondition, nearly, of the engaged imagination; when you dream your way into the world of your work you have to forget what you know. Still, Ezra Pound's great injunction, "Make it new," predicates some knowledge of what was yesterday's news.

Therefore what I'm proposing may appear original—innovative in the classroom, experimental in its emphases—but it's an ancient technique. Memorization, copying, recitation in unison, transcribing whole passages verbatim: all these systems of instruction were established centuries ago. In the Palmer method of learning handwriting or the Suzuki method of learning a musical instrument such a system of "mimicry" continues. It isn't a question of inventing the wheel but watching it turn on a time-honored track; the exercises that follow are, I think, inventive, but they're in the spirit of a tradition that has served long and well. These pages too are Janus-faced; the revolution they advance is a "back to basics," close reading of the text.

One more aspect of this project and what mimicry suggests. Sincere imitation takes time. Too often in the contemporary classroom the written text is relegated to the sideline—as a springboard for discussion, an occasion for debate, a soapbox or a whipping boy; too rarely does the student get to perform what used to be called close analysis or pay sustained attention to the author's language as such. That process of sustained attention is necessary here. You cannot copy what you glance at nor remember what you speed read nor repeat what you half heard; the reason one writer chooses semicolons, or another elects an apposite comma, or a third prefers the absence of standard punctuation marks, has a great deal to do with the worldview expressed, and a complex or compound sentence or parenthetical observation (such as the one we're engaged in) will represent a different way of looking at the linkages of things—the way the past impinges on the present as does the present on the future in an unbroken line of descent or argument if represented with a dash—than does a simple or short. Or a sentence that isn't one, such as this and the succeeding one word. Sentence. Our anthology of authors represents a sampling only of the great range of fiction written in English in the twentieth century, and they have been chosen to represent variety. They have one thing in common, however: each of them merits close study. Each will teach an aspect of technique.

Let me close by repeating—copying out—why I believe this methodology works. Imitation is deep-rooted as a form of cultural transmission; we tell our old stories again and again. The bard-in-training had to memorize long histories verbatim, saying or singing what others had sung. In the oral-formulaic tradition, indeed, the system *required* retentiveness; you listened to your master's tale until you could recite, say, *The Odyssey* or *Beowulf* for the next generation.

As recently as Shakespeare's time, the plays were remembered, not written down; what we have of *Romeo and Juliet* or *Hamlet* is largely what the playwright's colleagues *heard*. Rote learning—the recital of poems or multiplication tables in class—has been discredited as a teaching technique, but it did have its points. By now this assertion itself must seem repetitive, but it's worth repeating: all artists who borrow or adapt a form—*all* artists, in effect—engage in imitation all the time.

Back, therefore, to the basics. Imitation is the route—not perhaps the only route, but a well-traveled one—to authenticity. To copy *Moby-Dick* or *Endymion* verbatim is to come nearer to great artistry than we will on our own. And even if there be a young Melville or Keats among us, that writer's self-awareness will be aided by close study of a predecessor's work.

In the last analysis—and at the end of each exercise set—each reader and writer must set out alone. There the aim is earned originality, not mimicry. But here's the final reason for a course of imitations: As these chapters indicate, it's fun.

PART I

Reading and Imitating the Master Stylists

CHAPTER 1

PLOT AND STRUCTURE:
The Art of the Echo

ANDREA BARRETT, "The Behavior of the Hawkweeds"

■ **WRITER'S VIEW:** *In "The Behavior of the Hawkweeds," there was a wonderful story from history I wanted to tell. And I didn't just want to set it in the past, so I asked, How can I braid it into a contemporary story and then make the two comment on each other in some way that is possibly fruitful or useful? How can I make that Mendel story mean not only what it meant then, but also mean something in our time? . . . So I thought: Okay, take the material, but now invent somebody else who's living a related life, and see if you can make the invented story and the real story talk to each other, and see what happens with the two characters side by side. (Interview with Marian Ryan,* The Writer's Chronicle *32. 3 [Dec. 1999])*

Andrea Barrett was born in Boston, Massachusetts, in 1954; she attended Union College in Schenectady, where she studied biology and graduated in 1974. Her early training in and exposure to the sciences provides a context for the 1996 National Book Award winning *Ship Fever and Other Stories.* Among her additional honors are the Guggenheim Fellowship and the "genius award," the MacArthur Fellowship. Her other works of fiction, in order of appearance, include *Lucid Stars* (1988), *Secret Harmonies* (1989), *The Middle Kingdom* (1991), *The Forms of Water* (1993), *The Voyage of the Narwhal* (1998), and *Servants of the Map* (2002).

The idea of scientific exploration—both intellectual and literal—is a constant in her work. Naturalists, geographers, armchair travelers, geneticists, and doctors have peopled Barrett's pages from the start. In each she combines a researched situation with a formal sense of structure, and in the following story she links the present to the past both implicitly and explicitly. This thematic linkage is what we will focus on: the way the parts reflect upon each other and two **narratives** connect.

A rule of Euclidean logic is that the sum of the parts must always be precisely equal to the whole. But art can complicate this old assumption—as does modern mathematics—and make the whole somehow larger than its separate components. Note the way the two main narratives have been joined together in "The Behavior of the Hawkweeds"; neither would function quite so successfully alone. In visual terms this might be called a "repeating form," in aural terms an "echo" or "sympathetic vibration," but the paired stories of Mendel and Antonia are stronger because linked.

One other thing to notice is the relative simplicity of **diction;** the author/speaker's language is straightforward and unmannered. Antonia uses few striking **images** or shocking turns of phrase. But this serves to emphasize the value of "scientific" terms; they lend impersonal authority to the situation here. The hawkweeds themselves are an exception to the genetic rule; they confound expectation and behave unpredictably till understood. "'*Hieracium,*' Tati said. 'That is their real name. It comes from the Greek word for hawk. The juice from the stem is supposed to make your vision very sharp.'"

Andrea Barrett's vision is sharp indeed; she watches her prey like a hawk.

The Behavior of the Hawkweeds

For thirty years, until he retired, my husband stood each fall in front of his sophomore genetics class and passed out copies of Gregor Mendel's famous paper on the hybridization of edible peas. This paper was a model of clarity, Richard told his students. It represented everything that science should be.

Richard paced in front of the chalkboard, speaking easily and without notes. Like the minor evolutionist Robert Chambers, he had been born hexadactylic; he was sensitive about his left hand, which was somewhat scarred from the childhood operation that had removed his extra finger. And so, although Richard gestured freely, he used only his right hand and kept his left in his pocket. From the back of the room, where I sat when I came each fall to hear him lecture, I could watch the students listen to him.

After he passed out the paper, Richard told the students his first, conventional version of Gregor Mendel's life. Mendel, he said, grew up in a tiny village in the northwestern corner of Moravia, which was then a part of the Hapsburg Empire and later became part of Czechoslovakia. When he was twenty-one, poor and desperate for further education, he entered the Augustinian monastery in the capital city of Brunn, which is now called Brno. He studied science and later taught at a local high school. In 1856, at the age of thirty-four, he began his experiments in the hybridization of the edible pea. For his laboratory he used a little strip of garden adjoining the monastery wall.

Over the next eight years Mendel performed hundreds of experiments on thousands of plants, tracing the ways in which characteristics were passed through generations. Tall and short plants, with white or violet flowers; peas that were wrinkled or smooth; pods that were arched or constricted around the seeds. He kept meticulous records of his hybridizations in order to write the paper the students now held in their hands. On a clear, cold evening in 1865, he read the first part of this paper to his fellow members of the Brunn Society for the Study of Natural Science. About forty men were present, a few professional scientists and many serious amateurs. Mendel read to them for an hour, describing his experiments and demonstrating the invariable ratios with which traits appeared in his hybrids. A month later, at the Society's next meeting, he presented the theory he'd formulated to account for his results.

Right there, my husband said, right in that small, crowded room, the science of genetics was born. Mendel knew nothing of genes or chromosomes or DNA, but he'd discovered the principles that made the search for those things possible.

"Was there applause?" Richard always asked at this point. "Was there a great outcry of approval or even a mutter of disagreement?" A rhetorical question; the students knew better than to answer.

"There was not. The minutes of that meeting show that no questions were asked and no discussion took place. Not one person in that room understood the significance of what Mendel had presented. A year later, when the paper was published, no one noticed it."

The students looked down at their papers and Richard finished his story quickly, describing how Mendel went back to his monastery and busied himself with other things. For a while he continued to teach and to do other experiments; he raised grapes and fruit trees and all kinds of flowers, and he kept bees. Eventually he was elected abbot of his monastery, and from that time until his death he was occupied with his administrative duties. Only in 1900 was his lost paper rediscovered and his work appreciated by a new generation of scientists.

When Richard reached this point, he would look toward the back of the room and catch my eye and smile. He knew that I knew what was in store for the students at the end of the semester. After they'd read the paper and survived the labs where fruit flies bred in tubes and displayed the principles of

Mendelian inheritance, Richard would tell them the other Mendel story. The one I told him, in which Mendel is led astray by a condescending fellow scientist and the behavior of the hawkweeds. The one in which science is not just unappreciated, but bent by loneliness and longing.

I had a reason for showing up in that classroom each fall, and it was not just that I was so dutiful, so wifely. Richard was not the one who introduced Mendel into my life.

When I was a girl, during the early years of the Depression, my grandfather, Anton Vaculik, worked at a nursery in Niskayuna, not far from where Richard and I still live in Schenectady. This was not the only job my grandfather had ever had, but it was the one he liked the best. He had left Moravia in 1891 and traveled to the city of Bremen with his pregnant wife. From there he'd taken a boat to New York and then another to Albany. He'd meant to journey on to one of the large Czech settlements in Minnesota or Wisconsin, but when my mother was born six weeks early he settled his family here instead. A few other Czech families lived in the area, and one of those settlers hired my grandfather to work in a small factory that made mother-of-pearl buttons for women's blouses.

Later, after he learned more English, he found the nursery job that he liked so much. He worked there for thirty years; he was so skilled at propagating plants and grafting trees that his employers kept him on part-time long past the age when he should have retired. Everyone at the nursery called him Tony, which sounded appropriately American. I called him Tati, a corruption of *tatínek,* which is Czech for "dad" and was what my mother called him. I was named Antonia after him.

We were never hungry when I was young, we were better off than many, but our daily life was a web of small economies. My mother took in sewing, making over jackets and mending pants; when she ironed she saved the flat pieces for last, to be pressed while the iron was cooling and the electricity was off. My father's wages had been cut at the GE plant and my older brothers tried to help by scrounging for odd jobs. I was the only idle member of the family, and so on weekends and during the summer my mother sometimes let me go with Tati. I loved it when Tati put me to work.

At the nursery there were fields full of fruit trees, peach and apple and pear, and long, low, glass houses full of seedlings. I followed Tati around and helped him as he transplanted plants or worked with his sharp, curved knife and his grafting wax. I sat next to him on a tall wooden stool, holding his forceps or the jar of methylated spirits as he emasculated flowers. While we worked he talked, which is how I learned about his early days in America.

The only time Tati frowned and went silent was when his new boss appeared. Sheldon Hardy, the old chief horticulturalist, had been our friend; he was Tati's age and had worked side by side with Tati for years, cutting scions and whip-grafting fruit trees. But in 1931, the year I was ten, Mr. Hardy had a heart attack and went to live with his daughter in Ithaca. Otto Leiniger descended on us shortly after that, spoiling part of our pleasure every day.

Leiniger must have been in his late fifties. He lost no time telling Tati that he had a master's degree from a university out west, and it was clear from his white lab coat and the books in his office that he thought of himself as a scholar. In his office he sat at a big oak desk, making out lists of tasks for Tati with a fancy pen left over from better days; once he had been the director of an arboretum. He tacked the lists to the propagating benches, where they curled like shavings of wood from the damp, and when we were deep in work he'd drift into the glass house and hover over us. He didn't complain about my presence, but he treated Tati like a common laborer. One day he caught me alone in a greenhouse filled with small begonias we'd grown from cuttings.

Tati had fitted a misting rose to a pot small enough for me to handle, and I was watering the tiny plants. It was very warm beneath the glass roof. I was wearing shorts and an old white shirt of Tati's, with nothing beneath it but my damp skin; I was only ten. There were benches against the two side walls and another, narrower, propagating bench running down the center of the house. On one side of this narrow bench I stood on an overturned crate to increase my reach, bending to mist the plants on the far side. When I looked up Leiniger was standing across from me. His face was round and heavy, with dark pouches beneath his eyes.

"You're a good little helper," he said. "You help your grandpapa out." Tati was in the greenhouse next door, examining a new crop of fuchsias.

"I like it here," I told Leiniger. The plants beneath my hands were Rex begonias, grown not for their flowers but for their showy, ruffled leaves. I had helped Tati pin the mother leaves to the moist sand and then transplant the babies that rooted from the ribs.

Leiniger pointed at the row of begonias closest to him, farthest from me. "These seem a little dry," he said. "Over here."

I didn't want to walk around the bench and stand by his side. "You can reach," he said. "Just lean over a little farther."

I stood up on my toes and bent across the bench, stretching the watering pot to reach those farthest plants. Leiniger flushed. "That's right," he said thickly. "Lean towards me."

Tati's old white shirt gaped at the neck and fell away from my body when I bent over. I stretched out my arm and misted the begonias. When I straightened I saw that Leiniger's face was red and that he was pressed against the wooden bench.

"Here," he said, and he made a shaky gesture at another group of plants to the right of him. "These here, these are also very dry."

I was afraid of him, and yet I also wanted to do my job and feared that any sloppiness on my part might get Tati in trouble. I leaned over once again, the watering pot in my hand. This time Leiniger reached for my forearm with his thick fingers. "Not those," he said, steering my hand closer to the edge of the bench, which he was still pressed against. "These."

Just as the pot brushed the front of his lab coat, Tati walked in. I can imagine, now, what that scene must have looked like to him. Me bent over that narrow bench, my toes barely touching the crate and the white shirt hanging down like a sheet to the young begonias below; Leiniger red-faced, sweating, grinding into the wooden bench. And his hand, that guilty hand, forcing me towards him. I dropped the pot when I heard Tati shout my name.

Who can say what Leiniger had in mind? To Tati it must have looked as though Leiniger was dragging me across the begonias to him. But Leiniger was just a lonely old man and it seems possible to me, now, that he wanted only the view down my shirt and that one small contact with the skin of my inner arm. Had Tati not entered the greenhouse just then, nothing more might have happened.

But Tati saw the worst in what was there. He saw that fat hand on my arm and those eyes fixed on my childish chest. He had a small pruning knife in his hand. When he called my name and I dropped the pot, Leiniger clamped down on my arm. As I was tearing myself away, Tati flew over and jabbed his knife into the back of Leiniger's hand.

"*Německy!*" he shouted. "*Prase!*"

Leiniger screamed and stumbled backward. Behind him was the concrete block on which I stood to water the hanging plants, and that block caught Leiniger below the knees. He went down slowly, heavily, one hand clutching the wound on the other and a look of disbelief on his face. Tati was already reaching out to catch him when Leiniger cracked his head against a heating pipe.

But of course this is not what I told Richard. When we met, just after the war, I was working at the GE plant that had once employed my father and Richard was finishing his thesis. After my father died I had dropped out of junior college; Richard had interrupted his Ph.D. program to join the Navy, where he'd worked for three years doing research on tropical fungi. We both had a sense of urgency and a need to make up for lost time. During our brief courtship, I told Richard only the things that I thought would make him love me.

On our second date, over coffee and Italian pastries, I told Richard that my grandfather had taught me a little about plant breeding when I was young, and that I was fascinated by genetics. "Tati lived with us for a while, when I was a girl," I said. "He used to take me for walks through the empty fields of Niska-yuna and tell me about Gregor Mendel. I still know a pistil from a stamen."

"Mendel's my hero," Richard said. "He's always been my ideal of what a scientist should be. It's not so often I meet a woman familiar with his work."

"I know a lot about him," I said. "What Tati told me—you'd be surprised." I didn't say that Tati and I had talked about Mendel because we couldn't stand to talk about what we'd both lost.

Tati slept in my room during the months before the trial; he was released on bail on the condition that he leave his small house in Rensselaer and stay with us. I slept on the couch in the living room and Leiniger lay unconscious in the Schenectady hospital. We were quiet, Tati and I. No one seemed to want to talk to us. My brothers stayed away from the house as much as possible and my father worked long hours. My mother was around, but she was so upset by what had happened that she could hardly speak to either Tati or myself. The most she could manage to do was to take me aside, a few days after Tati's arrival, and say, "What happened to Leiniger wasn't your fault. It's an old-country thing, what's between those men."

She made me sit with her on the porch, where she was turning mush-rooms she'd gathered in the woods and laid out to dry on screens. Red, yellow, violet, buff. Some pieces were drier than others. While she spoke she moved from screen to screen, turning the delicate fragments.

"What country?" I said. "What are you talking about?"

"Tati is Czech," my mother said. "Like me. Mr. Leiniger's family is German, from a part of Moravia where only Germans live. Tati and Mr. Leiniger don't like each other because of things that happened in the Czech lands a long time ago."

"Am I Czech, then?" I said. "This happened because I am Czech?"

"You're American," my mother said. "American first. But Tati hates Ger-mans. He and Leiniger would have found some way to quarrel even if you hadn't been there." She told me a little about the history of Moravia, enough to help me understand how long the Czechs and Germans had been quarreling. And she told me how thrilled Tati had been during the First World War, when the Czech and Slovak immigrants in America had banded together to contribute funds to help in the formation of an independent Czechoslovak state. When she was a girl, she said, Tati and her mother had argued over the donations Tati made and the meetings he attended.

But none of this seemed important to me. In the greenhouse, a policeman had asked Tati what had happened, and Tati had said, "I stuck his hand with my knife. But the rest was an accident—he tripped over that block and fell."

"Why?" the policeman had said. "Why did you do that?"

"My granddaughter," Tati had said. "He was . . . feeling her."

The policeman had tipped my chin up with his hand and looked hard at me. "Is that right?" he'd asked. And I had nodded dumbly, feeling both very guilty and very important. Now my mother was telling me that I was of no consequence.

"Am *I* supposed to hate Germans?" I asked.

A few years later, when Tati was dead and I was in high school and Hitler had dismembered Czechoslovakia, my mother would become loudly anti-German. But now all she said was, "No. Mr. Leiniger shouldn't have bothered you, but he's only one man. It's not right to hate everyone with a German last name."

"Is that what Tati does?"

"Sometimes."

I told my mother what Tati had shouted at Leiniger, repeating the foreign sounds as best as I could. My mother blushed. "*Německy* means 'German,'" she said reluctantly. "*Prase* means 'pig.' You must never tell anyone you heard your grandfather say such things."

I did not discuss this conversation with Tati. All during that fall, but especially after Leiniger died, I'd come home from school to find Tati waiting for me on the porch, his knobby walking stick in his hands and his cap on his head. He wanted to walk, he was desperate to walk. My mother wouldn't let him leave the house alone but she seldom found the time to go out with him; my brothers could not be bothered. And so Tati waited for me each afternoon like a restless dog.

While we walked in the fields and woods behind our house, we did not talk about what had happened in the greenhouse. Instead, Tati named the ferns and mosses and flowers we passed. He showed me the hawkweeds—Canada hawkweed, spotted hawkweed, poor-Robin's hawkweed. Orange hawkweed, also called devil's paintbrush, creeping into abandoned fields. The plants had long stems, rosettes of leaves at the base, small flowerheads that resembled dandelions. Once Tati opened my eyes to them I realized they were everywhere.

"*Hieracium*," Tati said. "That is their real name. It comes from the Greek word for hawk. The juice from the stem is supposed to make your vision very sharp." They were weeds, he said: extremely hardy. They grew wherever the soil was too poor to support other plants. They were related to asters and daisies and dahlias—all plants I'd seen growing at the nursery—but also to thistles and burdocks. I should remember them, he said. They were important. With his own eyes he had watched the hawkweeds ruin Gregor Mendel's life.

Even now this seems impossible: how could I have known someone of an age to have known Mendel? And yet it was true: Tati had grown up on the outskirts of Brno, the city where Mendel spent most of his life. In 1866, when they first met, there was cholera in Brno, and Prussian soldiers were passing through after the brief and nasty war. Tati was ten then, and those things didn't interest him. He had scaled the white walls of the Augustinian monastery of St. Thomas one afternoon, for a lark. As he'd straddled the wall he'd seen a plump, short-legged man with glasses looking up at him.

"He looked like my mother's uncle," Tati said. "A little bit."

Mendel had held out a hand and helped Tati jump down from the wall. Around him were fruit trees and wild vines; in the distance he saw a clocktower and a long, low building. Where Tati had landed, just where his feet touched ground, there were peas. Not the thousands of plants that would have been there at the height of Mendel's investigations, but still hundreds of plants clinging to sticks and stretched strings.

The place was magical, Tati said. Mendel showed him the tame fox he tied up during the day but allowed to run free at night, the hedgehogs and the hamsters and the mice he kept, the beehives and the cages full of birds. The two of them, the boy and the middle-aged man, made friends. Mendel taught Tati most of his horticultural secrets and later he was responsible for getting him a scholarship to the school where he taught. But Tati said that the first year of their friendship, before the hawkweed experiments, was the best. He and Mendel, side by side, had opened pea flowers and transferred pollen with a camel-hair brush.

On the last day of 1866, Mendel wrote his first letter to Carl Nägeli of Munich, a powerful and well-known botanist known to be interested in hybridization. He sent a copy of his pea paper along with the letter, hoping

Nägeli might help it find the recognition it deserved. But he also, in his letter, mentioned that he had started a few experiments with hawkweeds, which he hoped would confirm his results with peas.

Nägeli was an expert on the hawkweeds, and Tati believed that Mendel had only mentioned them to pique Nägeli's interest in his work. Nägeli didn't reply for several months, and when he finally wrote back he said almost nothing about the peas. But he was working on the hawkweeds himself, and he proposed that Mendel turn his experimental skills to them. Mendel, desperate for recognition, ceased to write about his peas and concentrated on the hawkweeds instead.

"Oh, that Nägeli!" Tati said. "Month after month, year after year, I watched Mendel writing his long, patient letters and getting no answer or slow answers or answers off the point. Whenever Nägeli wrote to Mendel, it was always about the hawkweeds. Later, when I learned why Mendel's experiments with them hadn't worked, I wanted to cry."

The experiments that had given such tidy results with peas gave nothing but chaos with hawkweeds, which were very difficult to hybridize. Experiment after experiment failed; years of work were wasted. The inexplicable behavior of the hawkweeds destroyed Mendel's belief that the laws of heredity he'd worked out with peas would be universally valid. By 1873, Mendel had given up completely. The hawkweeds, and Nägeli behind them, had convinced him that his work was useless.

It was bad luck, Tati said. Bad luck in choosing Nägeli to help him, and in letting Nägeli steer him toward the hawkweeds. Mendel's experimental technique was fine, and his laws of heredity were perfectly true. He could not have known—no one knew for years—that his hawkweeds didn't hybridize in rational ways because they frequently formed seeds without fertilization. "Parthenogenesis," Tati told me—a huge, knobby word that I could hardly get my mouth around. Still, it sounds to me like a disease. "The plants grown from seeds formed this way are exact copies of the mother plant, just like the begonias we make from leaf cuttings."

Mendel gave up on science and spent his last years, after he was elected abbot, struggling with the government over the taxes levied on his monastery. He quarreled with his fellow monks; he grew bitter and isolated. Some of the monks believed he had gone insane. In his quarters he smoked heavy cigars and gazed at the ceiling, which he'd had painted with scenes of saints and fruit trees, beehives and scientific equipment. When Tati came to visit him, his conversation wandered.

Mendel died in January 1884, on the night of Epiphany, confused about the value of his scientific work. That same year, long after their correspondence had ceased, Nägeli published an enormous book summarizing all his years of work. Although many of his opinions and observations seemed to echo Mendel's work with peas, Nägeli made no mention of Mendel or his paper.

That was the story I told Richard. Torn from its context, stripped of the reasons why it was told, it became a story about the beginnings of Richard's discipline. I knew that Richard would have paid money to hear it, but I gave it to him as a gift.

"And your grandfather saw all that?" he said. This was later on in our courtship; we were sitting on a riverbank, drinking Manhattans that Richard had mixed and enjoying the cold spiced beef and marinated vegetables and lemon tart I had brought in a basket. Richard liked my cooking quite a bit. He liked me too, but apparently not enough; I was longing for him to propose but he still hadn't said a word. "Your grandfather saw the letters," he said. "He watched Mendel assembling data for Nägeli. That's remarkable. That's extraordinary. I can't believe the things you know."

There was more, I hinted. What else did I have to offer him? Now it seems to me that I had almost everything: youth and health and an affectionate temperament; the desire to make a family. But then I was more impressed than I should have been by Richard's education.

"More?" he said.

"There are some papers," I said. "That Tati left behind."

Of course I was not allowed in the courtroom, I was much too young. After Leiniger died, the date of the trial was moved forward. I never saw Tati sitting next to the lawyer my father had hired for him; I never saw a judge or a jury and never learned whether my testimony might have helped Tati. I never even learned whether, in that long-ago time, the court would have accepted the testimony of a child, because Tati died on the evening before the first day of the trial.

He had a stroke, my mother said. In the night she heard a loud, garbled cry and when she ran into the room that had once been mine she found Tati tipped over in bed, with his head hanging down and his face dark and swollen. Afterwards, after the funeral, when I came home from school I no longer went on walks through the woods and fields. I did my homework at the kitchen table and then I helped my mother around the house. On weekends I no longer went to the nursery.

Because there had been no trial, no one in town learned of my role in Leiniger's death. There had been a quarrel between two old men, people thought, and then an accident. No one blamed me or my family. I was able to go through school without people pointing or whispering. I put Tati out of my mind, and with him the nursery and Leiniger, Mendel and Nägeli, and the behavior of the hawkweeds. When the war came I refused to listen to my mother's rantings. After my father died she went to live with one of my married brothers, and I went off on my own. I loved working in the factory, I felt very independent.

Not until the war was over and I met Richard did I dredge up the hawkweed story. Richard's family had been in America for generations and seemed to have no history; that was one of the things that drew me to him. But after our picnic on the riverbank I knew for sure that part of what drew him to me was the way I was linked so closely to other times and places. I gave Richard the yellowed sheets of paper that Tati had left in an envelope for me.

This is a draft of one of Mendel's letters to Nägeli, Tati had written, on a note attached to the manuscript. *He showed it to me once, when he was feeling sad. Later he gave it to me. I want you to have it.*

Richard's voice trembled when he read that note out loud. He turned the pages of Mendel's letter slowly, here and there reading a line to me. The letter was an early one, or perhaps even the first. It was all about peas.

Richard said, "I can't believe I'm holding this in my hand."

"I could give it to you," I said. In my mind this seemed perfectly reasonable. Mendel had given the letter to Tati, the sole friend of his last days; then Tati had passed it to me, when he was no longer around to protect me himself. Now it seemed right that I should give it to the man I wanted to marry.

"To me?" Richard said. "You would give it to me?"

"Someone who appreciates it should have it."

Richard cherished Tati's letter like a jewel. We married, we moved to Schenectady, Richard got a good job at the college, and we had our two daughters. During each of my pregnancies Richard worried that our children might inherit his hexadactyly, but Annie and Joan were both born with regulation fingers and toes. I stayed home with them, first in the apartment on Union Street and then later, after Richard's promotion, in the handsome old house on campus that the college rented to us. Richard wrote papers and served on committees; I gave monthly dinners for the departmental faculty, weekly coffee hours for favored students, picnics for alumni on homecoming weekends. I managed that sort of thing rather well: it was a job, if an unpaid one, and it was expected of me.

Eventually our daughters grew up and moved away. And then, when I was nearly fifty, after Richard had been tenured and won his awards and grown almost unbearably self-satisfied, there came a time when the world went gray on me for the better part of a year.

I still can't explain what happened to me then. My doctor said it was hormones, the beginning of my change of life. My daughters, newly involved with the women's movement, said my years as a housewife had stifled me and that I needed a career of my own. Annie, our oldest, hemmed and hawed and finally asked me if her father and I were still sharing a bed; I said we were but didn't have the heart to tell her that all we did was share it. Richard said I needed more exercise and prescribed daily walks in the college gardens, which were full of exotic specimen trees from every corner of the earth.

He was self-absorbed, but not impossible; he hated to see me suffer. And I suppose he also wanted back the wife who for years had managed his household so well. But I could no longer manage anything. All I knew was that I felt old, and that everything had lost its savor. I lay in the windowseat in our bedroom with an afghan over my legs, watching the students mass and swirl and separate in the quad in front of the library.

This was 1970, when the students seemed to change overnight from pleasant boys into uncouth and hairy men. Every week brought a new protest. Chants and marches and demonstrations; bedsheets hanging like banners from the dormitory windows. The boys who used to come to our house for tea dressed in blue blazers and neatly pressed pants now wore vests with dangling fringes and jeans with holes in them. And when I went to Richard's genetics class that fall, to listen to his first Mendel lecture, I saw that the students gazed out the window while he spoke or tipped back in their chairs with their feet on the desks: openly bored, insubordinate. A girl encased in sheets of straight blond hair—there were girls in class, the college had started admitting them—interrupted Richard mid-sentence and said, "But what's the *relevance* of this? Science confined to the hands of the technocracy produces nothing but destruction."

Richard didn't answer her, but he hurried through the rest of his lecture and left the room without looking at me. That year, he didn't give his other Mendel lecture. The students had refused to do most of the labs; there was no reason, they said, why harmless fruit flies should be condemned to death just to prove a theory that everyone already acknowledged as true. Richard said they didn't deserve to hear about the hawkweeds. They were so dirty, so destructive, that he feared for the safety of Mendel's precious letter.

I was relieved, although I didn't say that; I had no urge to leave my perch on the windowseat and no desire to hear Richard repeat that story again. It seemed to me then that he told it badly. He muddled the dates, compressed the years, identified himself too closely with Mendel and painted Nägeli as too black a villain. By then I knew that he liked to think of himself as another Mendel, unappreciated and misunderstood. To me he looked more like another Nägeli. I had seen him be less than generous to younger scientists struggling to establish themselves. I had watched him pick, as each year's favored student, not the brightest or most original but the most agreeable and flattering.

That year all the students seemed to mutate, and so there was no favorite student, no obsequious well-dressed boy to join us for Sunday dinner or cocktails after the Wednesday seminars. As I lay in my windowseat, idly addressing envelopes and stuffing them with reprints of Richard's papers, I hardly noticed that the house was emptier than usual. But at night, when I couldn't sleep, I rose from Richard's side and went down to the couch in the living room, where I lay midway between dream and panic. I heard Tati's voice then, telling me about Mendel. I heard Mendel, frantic over those hawkweeds, trying out draft after draft of his letters on the ears of an attentive little boy who sat in a garden next to a fox. *Highly esteemed sir, your honor, I beg you to allow me to submit for your kind consideration the results of these experiments.* How humble Mendel had been in his address, and yet how sure of his science. How kind he had been to Tati.

Some nights I grew very confused. Mendel and Nägeli, Mendel and Tati; Tati and Leiniger, Tati and me. Pairs of men who hated each other and pairs of friends passing papers. A boy I saw pruning shrubs in the college garden turned into a childish Tati, leaping over a white wall. During a nap I dreamed of Leiniger's wife. I had seen her only once; she had come to Tati's funeral. She stood in the back of the church in a brown dress flecked with small white leaves, and when my family left after the service she turned her face from us.

That June, after graduation, Sebastian Dunitz came to us from his lab in Frankfurt. He and Richard had been corresponding and they shared common research interests; Richard had arranged for Sebastian to visit the college for a year, working with Richard for the summer on a joint research project and then, during the fall and spring semesters, as a teaching assistant in the departmental laboratories. He stayed with us, in Annie's old bedroom, but he was little trouble. He did his own laundry and cooked his own meals except when we asked him to join us.

Richard took to Sebastian right away. He was young, bright, very well-educated; although speciation and evolutionary relationships interested him more than the classical Mendelian genetics Richard taught, his manner toward Richard was clearly deferential. Within a month of his arrival, Richard was telling me how, with a bit of luck, a permanent position might open up for his new protegé. Within a month of his arrival, I was up and about, dressed in bright colors, busy cleaning the house from basement to attic and working in the garden. It was nice to have some company around.

Richard invited Sebastian to a picnic dinner with us on the evening of the Fourth of July. This was something we'd done every year when the girls were growing up; we'd let the custom lapse but Richard thought Sebastian might enjoy it. I fried chicken in the morning, before the worst heat of the day; I dressed tomatoes with vinegar and olive oil and chopped fresh basil and I made potato salad and a chocolate cake. When dusk fell, Richard and I gathered a blanket and the picnic basket and our foreign guest and walked to the top of a rounded hill not far from the college grounds. In the distance, we could hear the band that preceded the fireworks.

"This is wonderful," Sebastian said. "Wonderful food, a wonderful night. You have both been very kind to me."

Richard had set a candle in a hurricane lamp in the center of our blanket, and in the dim light Sebastian's hair gleamed like a helmet. We all drank a lot of the sweet white wine that Sebastian had brought as his offering. Richard lay back on his elbows and cleared his throat, surprising me when he spoke.

"Did you know," he said to Sebastian, "that I have an actual draft of a letter that Gregor Mendel wrote to the botanist Nägeli? My dear Antonia gave it to me."

Sebastian looked from me to Richard and back. "Where did you get such a thing?" he asked. "How . . . ?"

Richard began to talk, but I couldn't bear to listen to him tell that story badly one more time. "My grandfather gave it to me," I said, interrupting Richard. "He knew Mendel when he was a little boy." And without giving Richard a chance to say another word, without even looking at the hurt and puzzlement I knew must be on his face, I told Sebastian all about the behavior of the hawkweeds. I told the story slowly, fully, without skipping any parts. In the gathering darkness I moved my hands and did my best to make Sebastian see the wall and the clocktower and the gardens and the hives, the spectacles on Mendel's face and Tati's bare feet. And when I was done, when my words hung in the air and Sebastian murmured appreciatively, I did something I'd never done before, because Richard had never thought to ask the question Sebastian asked.

"How did your grandfather come to tell you that?" he said. "It is perhaps an unusual story to tell a little girl."

"It gave us something to talk about," I said. "We spent a lot of time together, the fall that I was ten. He had killed a man—accidentally, but still the man was dead. He lived with us while we were waiting for the trial."

Overhead, the first fireworks opened into blossoms of red and gold and green. "Antonia," Richard said, but he caught himself. In front of Sebastian he would not admit that this was something his wife of twenty-five years had never told him before. In the light of the white cascading fountain above us I could see him staring at me, but all he said was, "An amazing story, isn't it? I used to tell it to my genetics students every year, but this fall everything was so deranged—I left it out, I knew they wouldn't appreciate it."

"Things are different," Sebastian said. "The world is changing." He did not ask me how it was that my grandfather had killed a man.

The pace and intensity of the fireworks increased, until all of them seemed to be exploding at once; then there was one final crash and then silence and darkness. I had been rude, I knew. I had deprived Richard of one of his great pleasures simply for the sake of hearing that story told well once.

We gathered up our blanket and basket and walked home quietly. The house was dark and empty. In the living room I turned on a single light and then went to the kitchen to make coffee; when I came in with the tray the men were talking quietly about their work. "I believe what we have here is a *Rassenkreis*," Sebastian said, and he turned to include me in the conversation. In his short time with us, he had always paid me the compliment of assuming I understood his and Richard's work. "A German word," he said. "It means 'race-circle'—it is what we call it when a species spread over a large area is broken into a chain of subspecies, each of which differs slightly from its neighbors. The neighboring subspecies can interbreed, but the subspecies at the two ends of the chain may be so different that they cannot. In the population that Richard and I are examining. . . ."

"I am very tired," Richard said abruptly. "If you'll excuse me, I think I'll go up to bed."

"No coffee?" I said.

He looked at a spot just beyond my shoulder, as he always did when he was upset. "No," he said. "Are you coming?"

"Soon," I said.

And then, in that dim room, Sebastian came and sat in the chair right next to mine. "Is Richard well?" he said. "Is something wrong?"

"He's fine. Only tired. He's been working hard."

"That was a lovely story you told. When I was a boy, at university, our teachers did not talk about Nägeli, except to dismiss him as a Lamarckian. They would skip from Mendel's paper on the peas to its rediscovery, later. Nägeli's student, Correns, and Hugo de Vries—do you know about the evening primroses and de Vries?"

I shook my head. We sat at the dark end of the living room, near the stairs and away from the windows. Still, occasionally, came the sound of a renegade firecracker.

"No? You will like this."

But before he could tell me his anecdote I leaned toward him and rested my hand on his forearm. His skin was as smooth as a flower. "Don't tell me any more science," I said. "Tell me about yourself."

There was a pause. Then Sebastian pulled his arm away abruptly and stood up. "Please," he said. "You're an attractive woman, still. And I am flattered. But it's quite impossible, anything between us." His accent, usually almost imperceptible, thickened with those words.

I was grateful for the darkness that hid my flush. "You misunderstood," I said. "I didn't mean . . ."

"Don't be embarrassed," he said. "I've seen the way you watch me when you think I am not looking. I appreciate it."

A word came back to me, a word I thought I'd forgotten. "*Prase,*" I muttered.

"What?" he said. Then I heard a noise on the stairs behind me, and a hand fell on my shoulder. I reached up and felt the knob where Richard's extra finger had once been.

"Antonia," Richard said. His voice was very gentle. "It's so late—won't you come up to bed?" He did not say a word to Sebastian; upstairs, in our quiet room, he neither accused me of anything nor pressed me to explain the mysterious comment I'd made about my grandfather. I don't know what he said later to Sebastian, or how he arranged things with the Dean. But two days later Sebastian moved into an empty dormitory room, and before the end of the summer he was gone.

Německy, prase; secret words. I have forgotten almost all the rest of Tati's language, and both he and Leiniger have been dead for sixty years. Sebastian Dunitz is back in Frankfurt, where he has grown very famous. The students study molecules now, spinning models across their computer screens and splicing the genes of one creature into those of another. The science of genetics is utterly changed and Richard has been forgotten by everyone. Sometimes I wonder where we have misplaced our lives.

Of course Richard no longer teaches. The college retired him when he turned sixty-five, despite his protests. Now they trot him out for dedications and graduations and departmental celebrations, along with the other emeritus professors who haunt the library and the halls. Without his class, he has no audience for his treasured stories. Instead he corners people at the dim, sad ends of parties when he's had too much to drink. Young instructors, too worried about their jobs to risk being impolite, turn their ears to Richard like flowers. He keeps them in place with a knobby hand on a sleeve or knee as he talks.

When I finally told him what had happened to Tati, I didn't really tell him anything. Two old men had quarreled, I said. An immigrant and an immigrant's son, arguing over some plants. But Tati and Leiniger, Richard decided, were Mendel and Nägeli all over again; surely Tati identified with Mendel and cast Leiniger as another Nägeli? Although he still doesn't know of my role in the accident, somehow the equation he's made between these pairs of men allows him to tell his tale with more sympathy, more balance. As he talks he looks across the room and smiles at me. I nod and smile back at him, thinking of Annie, whose first son was born with six toes on each foot.

Sebastian sent me a letter the summer after he left us, in which he finished the story I'd interrupted on that Fourth of July. The young Dutch botanist Hugo de Vries, he wrote, spent his summers searching the countryside for new species. One day, near Hilversum, he came to an abandoned potato field glowing strangely in the sun. The great evening primrose had been cultivated in a small bed in a nearby park; the plants had run wild and escaped into the field, where they formed a jungle as high as a man. From 1886 through 1888, de Vries made thousands of hybridization experiments with them, tracing the persistence of mutations. During his search for a way to explain his results, he uncovered Mendel's paper and found that Mendel had anticipated all his theories. Peas and primroses, primroses and peas, passing their traits serenely through generations.

I still have this letter, as Richard still has Mendel's. I wonder, sometimes, what Tati would have thought of all this. Not the story about Hugo de Vries, which he probably knew, but the way it came to me in a blue airmail envelope, from a scientist who meant to be kind. I think of Tati when I imagine Sebastian composing his answer to me.

Because it was an answer, of sorts; in the months after he left I mailed him several letters. They were, on the surface, about Mendel and Tati, all I recalled of their friendship. But I'm sure Sebastian read them for what they were. In 1906, Sebastian wrote, after Mendel's work was finally recognized, a small museum was opened in the Augustinian monastery. Sebastian visited it, when he passed through Brno on a family holiday.

"I could find no trace of your Tati," he wrote. "But the wall is still here, and you can see where the garden was. It's a lovely place. Perhaps you should visit someday."

Notes on Craft and Context

On Point of View in Structure

This is a deceptively simple tale, and its complicated structure merits close attention. Utilizing the first-person past tense, the **narrator** seems casual about her recollections. It's almost as though she's telling a story to the listener/audience while they wander through the fields, as she herself had done with her grandfather "Tati" years before. There's an anecdotal feel to the telling, an offhand digressiveness to this account of a life—an elderly person's ramble down memory lane. "The Behavior of the Hawkweeds" is much more tightly organized, however, than might appear at first reading.

On Characterization in Structure

Let's look—for a single example—at the way Richard's worry about his hexadactyly seems to be needless; the couple's daughters are born "normally." And yet, in a story about genetics—about predisposition and patterning—it's unsurprising that their grandson "was born with six toes on each foot." Notice also how Richard hides his "abnormal" hand in the lecture room, concerned about his image, but in the climactic **scene** near story's end he places his hand on Antonia's shoulder and leaves it in full view. He has become a protective presence, a man more alert to his wife's feelings than at first we believed.

On Theme in Structure

More elaborately, consider the close parallel of the confrontation between Leiniger and the young Antonia, then—many years later and in another context—the scene between Antonia and Sebastian Dunitz. In both encounters the disappointed elder party engages in erotically charged contact with youth; the word "*prase*" (pig) is spoken in both. *Německy, prase* are secret, half-understood and half-forgotten words, and that they should surface from Antonia's subconscious makes the parallel circumstance clear. Both scenes are interrupted by a third party—in the former instance "Tati," in the latter Richard. Leiniger is a fifty-odd-year-old German confronted by a Czech with a knife in his hand; Antonia, of Czech extraction, is in her fifties when she reaches out to the young German scholar. The roles are, however, reversed.

These criss-crossing parallels are made explicit elsewhere in the story. Richard self-pityingly compares himself to a misunderstood Gregor Mendel, and the patterned pairings of Mendel and Nägeli with "Tati" and Leiniger are unavoidable—even to the number of syllables in the names of the antagonists ("Mendel" and "Tati" have two syllables each, "Nägeli" and "Leiniger" are tri-syllabic.) "Tati and Leiniger, Richard decided, were Mendel and Nägeli all over again; surely Tati identified with Mendel and cast Leiniger as another Nägeli?"

On Theme in Plot

Antonia's intelligence is, however, more subtle than that of her husband, and the story of Mendel's disappointment—which she cannot bear to hear him tell so badly—is not so much black-and-white as a compound of the two: that grayness which overtakes her in the time of her collapse. There are at least two sides to every action, alternative versions of truth; Nägeli's not a "double-dyed" villain nor was Leiniger necessarily prevented from assaulting a young girl by her grandfather's intervention: "Had Tati not entered the greenhouse just then, nothing more might have happened."

In a story about genetics the way that history repeats itself—or very slightly alters—this expansiveness over the course of generations seems an appropriate theme. Antonia's first words ("For thirty years, until he retired, my husband") suggest that we'll be in the world of this narrative not for a single scene but, as it were, the long haul. And this permits the author to provide an historical overview; the women's liberation movement, though not fore-grounded in the picture, forms a part of the cultural background, as do scien-tific advances and the way a present course of study can displace the past: "The students study molecules now, spinning models across their computer screens and splicing the genes of one creature into those of another. The science of genetics is utterly changed . . ."

"The Behavior of the Hawkweeds" declares its principal subject by the end of the **opening beat.** There are two parallel versions of Mendel's history, and the one that the narrator will focus on has to do with "loneliness and longing." This **doubling pattern** occurs throughout, and the contemporary story becomes a variation on the **theme** of the historical case. Even the cherished let-ters from Mendel have their parallel in the letters Antonia sends Sebastian, and the letter from the now "very famous" scientist with which the story ends.

On Time Span: The Structure of Plot

Notice, also, the long reach of memory—the way this first-person narrative permits us to link distant antecedents with the contemporary world. The tem-

poral span—from Antonia as a ten-year-old to the seventy-year-old who nar-
rates the tale, from the time of Mendel's old age to that of Tati—is quite considerable, a long historical arc. "Even now this seems impossible: how could I
have known someone of an age to have known Mendel?" Antonia asks herself
and, by extension, the reader. Tati met Mendel in 1866; Mendel lived from 1824
to 1884. Antonia was born in 1921 and fifty when the societal shift of the sev-
enties precipitates the **crisis** with Richard and Sebastian Dunitz; in 1991, when
she tells the story, she herself is seventy years old. So the action of the narrative
spans 125 years, and by implication its extent is greater still—Mendel's discov-
eries antedated his meeting with Tati; Antonia's grandchild will continue with
the legacy, etc.

On Plot and Structure: Putting It Together

A less scientific way to ask all this is, perhaps, "Which came first, the chicken or
the egg?" Do you think the author wanted to tell the story of a seventy-year-old
lady and her academic husband or the story of Abbot Mendel, the geneticist,
and his bad luck with the "behavior" of self-generating hawkweeds? How do
the two parts connect so as to make a whole? It's important here to separate the
"known" facts from the invented story, and Andrea Barrett is scrupulous as to
the distinction. In a letter to this editor she draws the dividing line:

> **WRITER'S VIEW:** *If the students ask what's "real" in the story—*
> *-All the facts about Mendel and his work and his life, as far as I've been*
> *able to determine them; I never bend facts like this when I'm working with*
> *historical figures. Not in this story, not elsewhere; I know some people do and*
> *often for good reason, but it makes me queasy, and I don't.*
> *-The physical detail of the college, which is basically Union College,*
> *where I went to school.*
> *-The sights and smells of a greenhouse, as best as I could remember;*
> *I worked in one for a while, right after college.*
> *-But neither Tati nor Antonia, nor Richard nor Sebastian. Antonia I*
> *invented because someone had to tell the story; Richard just tagged along*
> *with her; Tati truly emerged from the air—I needed him; without him the*
> *story would have had neither plot nor shape. Sebastian grew sideways out of*
> *Nägeli (another historical figure). Once the structure of the story started to*
> *reveal itself, and I realized the contemporary figures either were, or fanta-*
> *sized that they were, analogues to the historical ones, Sebastian was neces-*
> *sary to complete the set. (Letter to Nicholas Delbanco, 5 Sept. 2000)*

On History and Invention

Such a blend of fact and fiction has grown to be widely accepted; it no doubt
played a part in *The Odyssey* and *The Iliad*. Some of what Homer reported on
would have been collective knowledge, some his own interpretation of the past.

Shakespeare's version of *King Richard III* or *King Henry V* bears only a kissing cousin resemblance to the historical record, but the power of the playwright's language has made the former a villain, the latter a hero forever. We take it almost for granted that an author departs from the historical occasion and invents information at will. But changing the known facts is, as it were, another story, and this particular author is unwilling to do so; if she knows that it was raining on the day and place in question then the sun can't shine.

The poet Marianne Moore wonderfully described her art as "imaginary gardens with real toads in them." But this prose writer reverses the terms, placing her imagined characters in a real garden; as Sebastian informs Antonia, "I could find no trace of your Tati . . . But the wall is still here . . ." Sebastian, Antonia, and Tati exist only in the artifact of "The Behavior of the Hawkweeds"; Mendel's garden and his research did in fact exist. This is a seamless blend of an actual historical record and an invented story line, and the latter derives its force from the former. For, finally, this is less an **anecdote** about Gregor Mendel's scientific reputation than a short story about a disappointed woman who finds life almost unbearable in late middle age. Yet one of the reasons she does so is because of the secret she's carried for years, a history of "loneliness and longing." And in this sense the parallel stories become concentric circles instead, one tale inside the other and spreading out with a ripple effect so that Mendel's failed experiment is an emblem of her failure too. Or, as Antonia puts it, "Sometimes I wonder where we have misplaced our lives."

> WRITER'S VIEW: *. . . I am always interested in the way stories are told and the uses we make of stories, and the fact that all history is a process of making narrative, whether we acknowledge it or not, and that all narratives have consequences, whether we acknowledge them or not. Lies have consequences, histories have consequences, anecdotes have consequences, even jokes have consequences. Stories mean something, and the ways they're shared mean something. The ways we pass them to each other, truly or falsely, are very interesting to me. If there's a place I repeat myself most in my work, I think that's it. There's something epistemological about storytelling. It's the way we know each other, the way we know ourselves, the way we know the world. It's also the way we don't know: the way the world is kept from us, the way we're kept from knowledge about ourselves, the way we're kept from understanding other people. (Interview with Marian Ryan,* The Writer's Chronicle *32. 3 [Dec. 1999])*

At the end of this first chapter and before the first section of "Applications and Connections," I think it might be useful to establish a ground rule or three. To begin with, it should be admitted that this is a difficult story to "imitate," and that issues of structure such as those on which we've focused are much harder to copy than issues of **style.** As suggested above, this author's diction (or that of her first-person narrator, Antonia) is nearly transparent; it has no **verbal tics** or eccentricities such as those we'll notice in the next story by John Barth. This first set of imitations is conceived by way of pointing out the intricacies of composition and not with the expectation that the young writer will produce "The Behavior of the Hawkweeds: A Sequel." It's more a matter here of entering into the spirit of a story than trying to reproduce it; how does the past affect the present, how do two versions of a single tale make it more than the sum of its parts?

Here as in the other chapters the exercises should function as a kind of menu from which the reader can choose. No one should attempt all ten; no one should feel a failure if their own chosen exercise stretches a muscle that's not at full strength. The effect will be cumulative, not instantaneous, and partial success is the most one can hope for in the writing process. This holds true for the "advanced" as well as the apprentice author; writing's not like tic-tac-toe, a game whose rules, once grasped, are boringly predictable (start with an X in the middle and you won't lose, start with a Y in the corner and you may not win). It is guesswork and challenge always, not a puzzle we set just to solve.

When I asked Andrea Barrett to describe her own learning curve with this work of fiction, she put it as follows:

> ▓ **WRITER'S VIEW:** *-What else? I dislike writing first-person narratives and seldom do; I didn't again, after this, until a story I published last year called "Theories of Rain."*
>
> *-I was writing this and "Soroche" at the same time, though one was in an earlier stage than the other; I remember going back and forth between late drafts of "Soroche" and early drafts of this and (this is embarrassing but true) thinking that "Soroche" (which seems to me now by far the lesser story) was the real story, the story I should really be working on; why was this other story intruding, why was I writing about Mendel when I wanted to be writing about Darwin? For some time I thought the Mendel material —which came first, long before there were the characters of Antonia, or Tati —was just a way of my avoiding work on "Soroche" . . . Similarly, when Antonia arrived I viewed her first with relief (oh, good, I don't have to write any more about Mendel and Moravia, neither of which I know much about) and then with suspicion (is she another way I am avoiding the real material, which is about Mendel?)**

---

*"Soroche" is a short story and "Ship Fever" a novella in the same collection as "The Behavior of the Hawkweeds." The former deals with Charles Darwin and Jemmy Button, a displaced native, the latter with an epidemic among Irish immigrants quarantined in Canada. The "Linnaeus story" concerns the death of the great classifier; it's called "The English Pupil" and also included in *Ship Fever and Other Stories*.

-I don't know if the students will be familiar with the other stories of "Ship Fever" . . . A person might be able to see the progression of a timid and not-very-skilled writer learning a little bit about certain narrative approaches: in "Soroche," clumsily incorporating, into an essentially contemporary story, shards of an anecdote about an historical figure (Darwin). In "Behavior," a more even-handed intertwining of two strands, one contemporary and one historical. And after that (take off the water-wings, jump into the pool) the full plunge into material fully distanced from the world I "know": the Linnaeus story, "Ship Fever" itself . . .

▨ Applications and Connections

- While writing—or after completing—the first draft of a story, chart its events, both shown and recalled, on a time line. Seeing a physical measure of the number of hours, days, or years between events—when certain characters find out about something, meet one another, etc.—helps make the story's **plot** and structure more tangible. This exercise may seem quantitative, but it is a clear way to see if anything is missing, inconsistent, or simply in the wrong order.
- Consider how "The Behavior of the Hawkweeds" would differ if it were told strictly in chronological order, and in the omniscient third person. Altering the **structure**—the order in which you reveal events—or the **point of view** of a story shifts both focus and emphasis. Mixing and matching orders, points of view, and narrators will help you find the appropriate fit. And through the process of trying different combinations and seeing things through a number of different lenses, you will discover more about your characters and their **backstory**—events that happened in the past and off the page.
- How, in their various ways, have Richard, Antonia, Nägeli, Tati, and Sebastian blended fact and fiction in their own lives and dramatized/paralleled/glorified/demonized/identified with people they never knew? When writing a fictional story rooted in fact, be aware that you as the writer are susceptible to approaching your "real" subject in all of these ways. Your story will—and should—take its own approach, as you give your characters free rein to judge and misunderstand each other; however, be careful to honor what makes the real story true.

▨ Exercises

1. Write a letter that Mendel sends to Nägeli.
2. Write the letters that Antonia sends to Sebastian, and flesh out his response.

3. Describe Richard's lecture from the point of view of:
   a. a girl who has a crush on him.
   b. a boy who has to take the course for credit and couldn't care less.
   c. a junior colleague who wants him to retire.

4. Have Tati tell the young Antonia about the behavior of the hawkweeds, why Mendel fell into that trap. Have him teach her instead about the propagation of peas.

5. Write a scene in which Antonia goes to visit her grandchildren, carrying a copy of Willa Cather's *My Antonia* and trying to explain to them about her own childhood in a greenhouse.

6. Have Richard, in retirement, buttonhole the dean at a cocktail party— where he, Richard, drinks too much—and explain why he should no longer be emeritus but should be allowed to teach.

7. Write the confrontation between Richard and Sebastian that results in the latter's departure; then imagine a parallel scene between Sebastian thirty years later and his own student apprentice.

8. Have the German acolyte reciprocate Antonia's advances; let them become lovers; write the conversation, then the scene. Do this from Sebastian's point of view.

9. Transpose any memory from Antonia's childhood into the third person; compare.

10. Write your own short story on the theme of "loneliness and longing" from either the first-person point of view or the third-person narrative vantage. Then explain why you chose which.

CHAPTER 2

A PRIMER FOR NARRATIVE STYLES:
Self-Reflexive Fiction and the World within the Word

JOHN BARTH, "Lost in the Funhouse"

▦ **WRITER'S VIEW:** *Of what one can't make sense, one may make art.* (Once upon a Time *[Boston: Little, Brown, 1994]*)

John Barth was born in Cambridge, Maryland, on May 27, 1930, and—though he has traveled widely and spent his teaching career else-where—lives in that region still. Much of his fiction—from *The Sot-Weed Factor*, in 1960, to *Coming Soon!!!*, in 2001—describes the world of the Chesapeake Bay; indeed *Sabbatical: A Romance* (1982), *Tidewater Tales: A Novel* (1987), and *The Last Voyage of Somebody the Sailor* (1991) take place on the water as such. His first two novels, *The Floating Opera* (1956) and *The End of the Road* (1958) also are set on the Maryland shore, as are a large number of his stories. It's fair to say—Barth says so repeatedly—that this is his heart's geography and the constant landscape of his freely ranging imagination; he doubles back, repeats himself, revises and sets sail once more.

Of the living authors in this anthology—Carver, Hemingway, Malamud and O'Connor all died in the twentieth century—Barth is the senior citizen. This comes as a surprise, somehow, since his books continue to be youthful, playful: comic extravaganzas from first to final page. As he writes in the story "Anomyiad": "I examined our tongue, the effects wrought in it by minstrels old and new and how it might speak eloquentest for me. I considered the fashion in art and ideas, how perhaps to enlist their aid in escaping their grip."

And though much of his work is tradition based, honoring such eighteenth-century yarn spinners as Laurence Sterne, more of it is thoroughly modern and experimental. Wit runs riot; high-spirited word games abound; this "tide-tongued" (Barth's phrase) bard keeps his tongue lodged firmly in cheek.

John Barth taught at Pennsylvania State University, University Park, then at SUNY/Buffalo, and for most of his career at Johns Hopkins University in Baltimore, where he is now Emeritus Alumni Centennial Professor of English and Creative Writing. His works of fiction, in addition to those referred to above, include *Giles Goat-Boy* (1966), *Lost in the Funhouse: Fiction for Print, Tape, Live Voice* (1968), *Chimera* (1973), *Letters* (1979), *Once upon a Time: A Floating Opera* (1994), and *On with the Story* (1996). His critical and self-critical essays are perhaps the best guides to his own work; they have been collected twice as *The Friday Book: Essays and Other Nonfiction* (1984) and *Further Fridays: Essays, Lectures, and Other Nonfiction* (1995).

A member of the American Academy and Institute of Arts and Letters and the American Academy of Arts and Sciences, he has won the National Book Award (for *Chimera*), the F. Scott Fitzgerald Award for outstanding achievement in American literature (1997), the PEN/Malamud Award for Excellence in the Short Story (1998), the Lannan Foundation Lifetime Achievement Award (1998), and the Enoch Pratt Society Lifetime Achievement in Letters Award in 1999.

It is as a practitioner of **"metafiction"** or **"postmodernism"** that Barth has been most celebrated or—in some instances—attacked. These terms describe the writer's conviction that art consists of artifice, that the reader must interact with the text (its multiple puns, labyrinthine plots, and literary jokes) and that the text itself must announce its own construction. His is a world of words. In a crucial essay called "The Literature of Exhaustion" (1967), Barth proclaimed the ascendancy of the **self-conscious artist**—by which he meant such authors as Beckett, Borges, and Nabokov (and, by explicit extension, himself) who admitted to the sleight-of-hand and manipulation at work in *mimesis,* or "imitation of reality." Instead of an attempt to hold a "mirror up to nature" the artist admits to the technical nature of the task, the arbitrary arrangement of sentences and fashioned style—inviting us as readers to examine the mirror itself. "After which I add on behalf of the rest of us it might be conceivable to rediscover validly the artifices of language and literature—such far-out notions as grammar, punctuation . . . even characterization! Even *plot*—if one goes about it the right way, aware of what one's predecessors have been up to."

Much of Barth's more recent work deals with cyberspace and hypertext, all of it self-conscious. Here is the title tale from the collection *Fiction for Print, Tape, Live Voice.*

Lost in the Funhouse

For whom is the funhouse fun? Perhaps for lovers. For Ambrose it is *a place of fear and confusion.* He has come to the seashore with his family for the holiday, *the occasion of their visit is Independence Day, the most important secular holiday of the United States of America.* A single straight underline is the manuscript mark for italic type, *which in turn* is the printed equivalent to oral emphasis of words and phrases as well as the customary type for titles of complete works, not to mention. Italics are also employed, in fiction stories especially, for "outside," intrusive, or artificial voices, such as radio announcements, the texts of telegrams and newspaper articles, et cetera. They should be used *sparingly.* If passages originally in roman type are italicized by someone repeating them, it's customary to acknowledge the fact. *Italics mine.*

Ambrose was "at that awkward age." His voice came out high-pitched as a child's if he let himself get carried away; to be on the safe side, therefore, he moved and spoke with *deliberate calm* and *adult gravity.* Talking soberly of unimportant or irrelevant matters and listening consciously to the sound of your own voice are useful habits for maintaining control in this difficult interval. *En route* to Ocean City he sat in the back seat of the family car with his brother Peter, age fifteen, and Magda G_____, age fourteen, a pretty girl an exquisite young lady, who lived not far from them on B_____ Street in the town of D_____, Maryland. Initials, blanks, or both were often substituted for proper names in nineteenth-century fiction to enhance the illusion of reality. It is as if the author felt it necessary to delete the names for reasons of tact or legal liability. Interestingly, as with other aspects of realism, it is an *illusion* that is being enhanced, by purely artificial means. Is it likely, does it violate the principle of verisimilitude, that a thirteen-year-old boy could make such a sophisticated observation? A girl of fourteen is *the psychological coeval* of a boy of fifteen or sixteen; a thirteen-year-old boy, therefore, even one precocious in some other respects, might be three years *her emotional junior.*

Thrice a year—on Memorial, Independence, and Labor Days—the family visits Ocean City for the afternoon and evening. When Ambrose and Peter's father was their age, the excursion was made by train, as mentioned in the novel *The 42nd Parallel* by John Dos Passos. Many families from the same neighborhood used to travel together, with dependent relatives and often with Negro servants; schoolfuls of children swarmed through the railway cars; everyone shared everyone else's Maryland fried chicken, Virginia ham, deviled eggs, potato salad, beaten biscuits, iced tea. Nowadays (that is, in 19__, the year of our story) the journey is made by automobile—more comfortably and quickly though without the extra fun though without the *camaraderie* of a general excursion. It's all part of the deterioration of American life, their father declares; Uncle Karl supposes that when the boys take *their* families to Ocean City for the holidays they'll fly in Autogiros. Their mother, sitting in the middle of the front seat like Magda in the second, only with her arms on the seat-back behind the men's shoulders, wouldn't want the good old days back again, the steaming trains and stuffy long dresses; on the other hand she can do without Autogiros, too, if she has to become a grandmother to fly in them.

Description of physical appearance and mannerisms is one of several standard methods of characterization used by writers of fiction. It is also important to "keep the senses operating"; when a detail from one of the five senses, say visual, is "crossed" with a detail from another, say auditory, the reader's imagination is oriented to the scene, perhaps unconsciously. This procedure may be compared to the way surveyors and navigators determine their positions by two or more compass bearings, a process known as triangulation. The brown hair on Ambrose's mother's forearms gleamed in the sun like. Though right-handed, she took her left arm from the seat-back to press the dashboard cigar lighter for Uncle Karl. When the glass bead in its handle glowed red, the lighter was ready for use. The smell of Uncle Carl's cigar smoke reminded one of. The fragrance of the ocean came strong to the picnic ground where they always stopped for lunch, two miles inland from Ocean City. Having to pause for a full hour almost within sound of the breakers was difficult for Peter and Ambrose when they were younger; even at their present age it was not easy to keep their anticipation, *stimulated by the briny spume,* from turning into short temper. The Irish author James Joyce, in his unusual novel entitled *Ulysses,* now available in this country, uses the adjectives *snot-green* and *scrotum-tightening* to describe the sea. Visual, auditory, tactile, olfactory, gustatory. Peter and Ambrose's father, while steering their black 1936 LaSalle sedan with one hand, could with the other remove the first cigarette from a white pack of Lucky Strikes and, more remarkably, light it with a match forefingered from its book and thumbed against the flint paper without being detached. The matchbook cover merely advertised U. S. War Bonds and Stamps. A fine metaphor, simile, or other figure of speech, in addition to its obvious "first-order" relevance to the thing it describes, will be seen upon reflection to have a second order of significance: it may be drawn from the *milieu* of the action, for example, or be particularly appropriate to the sensibility of the narrator, even hinting to the reader things of which the narrator is unaware; or it may cast further and subtler lights upon the thing it describes, sometimes ironically qualifying the more evident sense of the comparison.

To say that Ambrose's and Peter's mother was *pretty* is to accomplish nothing; the reader may acknowledge the proposition, but his imagination is not engaged. Besides, Magda was also pretty, yet in an altogether different way. Although she lived on B_____ Street she had very good manners and did better than average in school. Her figure was very well developed for her age. Her right hand lay casually on the plush upholstery of the seat, very near Ambrose's left leg, on which his own hand rested. The space between their legs, between her right and his left leg, was out of the line of sight of anyone sitting on the other side of Magda, as well as anyone glancing into the rearview mirror. Uncle Karl's face resembled Peter's—rather, vice versa. Both had dark hair and eyes, short husky statures, deep voices. Magda's left hand was probably in a similar position on her left side. The boy's father is difficult to describe; no particular feature of his appearance or manner stood out. He wore glasses and was principal of a T_____ County grade school. Uncle Karl was a masonry contractor.

Although Peter must have known as well as Ambrose that the latter, because of his position in the car, would be the first to see the electrical towers of the power plant at V_____, the halfway point of their trip, he leaned forward and slightly toward the center of the car and pretended to be looking for them through the flat pinewoods and tuckahoe creeks along the highway. For as long as the boys could remember, "looking for the Towers" had been a feature of the first half of their excursions to Ocean City, "looking for the standpipe" of the second. Though the game was childish, their mother preserved the tradition of rewarding the first to see the Towers with a candy bar or piece of fruit. She insisted now that Magda play the game; the prize, she said, was "something hard to get nowadays." Ambrose decided not to join in; he sat far back in his seat. Magda, like Peter, leaned forward. Two sets of straps were discernible through the shoulders of her sun dress; the inside right one, a brassiere-strap, was fastened or shortened with a small safety pin. The right armpit of her dress, presumably the left as well, was damp with perspiration. The simple strategy for being first to espy the Towers, which Ambrose had understood by the age of four, was to sit on the right-hand side of the car. Whoever sat there, however, had also to put up with the worst of the sun, and so Ambrose, without mentioning the matter, chose sometimes the one and sometimes the other. Not impossibly Peter had never caught on to the trick, or thought that his brother hadn't simply because Ambrose on occasion preferred shade to a Baby Ruth or tangerine.

The shade-sun situation didn't apply to the front seat, owing to the windshield; if anything the driver got more sun, since the person on the passenger side not only was shaded below by the door and dashboard but might swing down his sunvisor all the way too.

"Is that them?" Magda asked. Ambrose's mother teased the boys for letting Magda win, insinuating that "somebody [had] a girlfriend." Peter and Ambrose's father reached a long thin arm across their mother to butt his cigarette in the dashboard ashtray, under the lighter. The prize this time for seeing the Towers first was a banana. Their mother bestowed it after chiding their father for wasting a half-smoked cigarette when everything was so scarce. Magda, to take the prize, moved her hand from so near Ambrose's that he could have touched it as though accidentally. She offered to share the prize, things like that were so hard to find; but everyone insisted it was hers alone. Ambrose's mother sang an iambic trimeter couplet from a popular song, femininely rhymed:

"What's good is in the Army;
What's left will never harm me."

Uncle Karl tapped his cigar ash out the ventilator window; some particles were sucked by the slipstream back into the car through the rear window on the passenger side. Magda demonstrated her ability to hold a banana in one hand and peel it with her teeth. She still sat forward; Ambrose pushed his glasses back onto the bridge of his nose with his left hand, which he then negligently let fall to the seat cushion immediately behind her. He even permitted the single hair, gold, on the second joint of his thumb to brush the fabric of her skirt. Should she have sat back at that instant, his hand would have been caught under her.

Plush upholstery prickles uncomfortably through gabardine slacks in the July sun. The function of the *beginning* of a story is to introduce the principal characters, establish their initial relationships, set the scene for the main action, expose the background of the situation if necessary, plant motifs and foreshadowings where appropriate, and initiate the first complication or whatever of the "rising action." Actually, if one imagines a story called "The Funhouse," or "Lost in the Funhouse," the details of the drive to Ocean City don't seem especially relevant. The *beginning* should recount the events between Ambrose's first sight of the funhouse early in the afternoon and his entering it with Magda and Peter in the evening. The *middle* would narrate all relevant events from the time he goes in to the time he loses his way; middles have the double and contradictory function of delaying the climax while at the same time preparing the reader for it and fetching him to it. Then the *ending* would tell what Ambrose does while he's lost, how he finally finds his way out, and what everybody makes of the experience. So far there's been no real dialogue, very little sensory detail, and nothing in the way of a *theme*. And a long time has gone by already without anything happening; it makes a person wonder. We haven't even reached Ocean City yet: we will never get out of the funhouse.

The more closely an author identifies with the narrator, literally or metaphorically, the less advisable it is, as a rule, to use the first-person narrative viewpoint. Once three years previously the young people *aforementioned* played Niggers and Masters in the backyard; when it was Ambrose's turn to be Master and theirs to be Niggers Peter had to go serve his evening papers; Ambrose was afraid to punish Magda alone, but she led him to the white-washed Torture Chamber between the woodshed and the privy in the Slaves Quarters; there she knelt sweating among bamboo rakes and dusty Mason jars, pleadingly embraced his knees, and while bees droned in the lattice as if on an ordinary summer afternoon, purchased clemency at a surprising price set by herself. Doubtless she remembered nothing of this event; Ambrose on the other hand seemed unable to forget the least detail of his life. He even recalled how, standing beside himself with awed impersonality in the reeky heat, he'd stared the while at an empty cigar box in which Uncle Karl kept stone-cutting chisels: beneath the words *El Producto*, a laureled, loose-toga'd lady regarded the sea from a marble bench; beside her, forgotten or not yet turned to, was a five-stringed lyre. Her chin reposed on the back of her right hand; her left depended negligently from the bench-arm. The lower half of scene and lady was peeled away; the words examined by _____ were inked there into the wood. Nowadays cigar boxes are made of pasteboard. Ambrose wondered what Magda would have done, Ambrose wondered what Magda would do when she sat back on his hand as he resolved she should. Be angry. Make a teasing joke of it. Give no sign at all. For a long time she leaned forward, playing cow-poker with Peter against Uncle Karl and Mother and watching for the first sign of Ocean City. At nearly the same instant, picnic ground and Ocean City stand-pipe hove into view; an Amoco filling station on their side of the road cost Mother and Uncle Karl fifty cows and the game; Magda bounced back, clapping her right hand on Mother's right arm; Ambrose moved clear "in the nick of time."

At this rate our hero, at this rate our protagonist will remain in the fun-house forever. Narrative ordinarily consists of alternating dramatization and summarization. One symptom of nervous tension, paradoxically, is repeated and violent yawning; neither Peter nor Magda nor Uncle Karl nor Mother reacted in this manner. Although they were no longer small children, Peter and Ambrose were each given a dollar to spend on boardwalk amusements in addition to what money of their own they'd brought along. Magda too, though she protested she had ample spending money. The boys' mother made a little scene out of distributing the bills; she pretended that her sons and Magda were small children and cautioned them not to spend the sum too quickly or in one place. Magda promised with a merry laugh and, having both hands free, took the bill with her left. Peter laughed also and pledged in a falsetto to be a good boy. His imitation of a child was not clever. The boys' father was tall and thin, balding, fair-complexioned. Assertions of that sort are not effective; the reader may acknowledge the proposition, but. We should be much farther along than we are; something has gone wrong; not much of this preliminary rambling seems relevant. Yet everyone begins in the same place; how is it that most go along without difficulty but a few lose their way?

"Stay out from under the boardwalk," Uncle Karl growled from the side of his mouth. The boys' mother pushed his shoulder *in mock annoyance.* They were all standing before Fat May the Laughing Lady who advertised the funhouse. Larger than life, Fat May mechanically shook, rocked on her heels, slapped her thighs while recorded laughter—uproarious, female—came amplified from a hidden loudspeaker. It chuckled, wheezed, wept; tried in vain to catch its breath; tittered, groaned, exploded raucous and anew. You couldn't hear it without laughing yourself, no matter how you felt. Father came back from talking to a Coast-Guardsman on duty and reported that the surf was spoiled with crude oil from tankers recently torpedoed offshore. Lumps of it, difficult to remove, made tarry tidelines on the beach and stuck on swimmers. Many bathed in the surf nevertheless and came out speckled; others paid to use a municipal pool and only sunbathed on the beach. We would do the latter. We would do the latter. We would do the latter.

Under the boardwalk, matchbook covers, grainy other things. What is the story's theme? Ambrose is ill. He perspires in the dark passages; candied apples-on-a-stick, delicious-looking, disappointing to eat. Funhouses need men's and ladies' rooms at intervals. Others perhaps have also vomited in corners and corridors; may even have had bowel movements liable to be stepped in in the dark. The word *fuck* suggests suction and/or and/or flatulence. Mother and Father; grandmothers and grandfathers on both sides; great-grandmothers and great-grandfathers on four sides, et cetera. Count a generation as thirty years: in approximately the year when Lord Baltimore was granted charter to the province of Maryland by Charles I, five hundred twelve

women—English, Welsh, Bavarian, Swiss—of every class and character, received into themselves the penises the intromittent organs of five hundred
twelve men, ditto, in every circumstance and posture, to conceive the five hundred twelve ancestors of the two hundred fifty-six ancestors of the et cetera et
cetera et cetera et cetera et cetera et cetera et cetera et cetera of the author, of
the narrator, of this story, *Lost in the Funhouse.* In alleyways, ditches, canopy
beds, pinewoods, bridal suites, ship's cabins, coach-and-fours, coaches-and-
four, sultry toolsheds; on the cold sand under boardwalks, littered with *El Producto* cigar butts, treasured with Lucky Strike cigarette stubs, Coca-Cola caps,
gritty turds, cardboard lollipop sticks, matchbook covers warning that A Slip of
the Lip Can Sink a Ship. The shluppish whisper, continuous as seawash round
the globe, tidelike falls and rises with the circuit of dawn and dusk.

Magda's teeth. She *was* left-handed. Perspiration. They've gone all the way,
through, Magda and Peter, they've been waiting for hours with Mother and
Uncle Karl while Father searches for his lost son; they draw french-fried potatoes from a paper cup and shake their heads. They've named the children
they'll one day have and bring to Ocean City on holidays. Can spermatozoa
properly be thought of as male animalcules when there are no female spermatozoa? They grope through hot, dark windings, past Love's Tunnel's fearsome
obstacles. Some perhaps lose their way.

Peter suggested then and there that they do the funhouse; he had been
through it before, so had Magda, Ambrose hadn't and suggested, his voice
cracking on account of Fat May's laughter, that they swim first. All were chuckling, couldn't help it; Ambrose's father, Ambrose's and Peter's father came up
grinning like a lunatic with two boxes of syrup-coated popcorn, one for
Mother, one for Magda; the men were to help themselves. Ambrose walked on
Magda's right; being by nature left-handed, she carried the box in her left hand.
Up front the situation was reversed.

"What are you limping for?" Magda inquired of Ambrose. He supposed in
a husky tone that his foot had gone to sleep in the car. Her teeth flashed. "Pins
and needles?" It was the honeysuckle on the lattice of the former privy that
drew the bees. Imagine being stung there. How long is this going to take?

The adults decided to forgo the pool; but Uncle Karl insisted they change
into swimsuits and do the beach. "He wants to watch the pretty girls," Peter
teased, and ducked behind Magda from Uncle Karl's pretended wrath. "You've
got all the pretty girls you need right here," Magda declared, and Mother said:
"Now that's the gospel truth." Magda scolded Peter, who reached over her
shoulder to sneak some popcorn. "Your brother and father aren't getting any."

Uncle Karl wondered if they were going to have fireworks that night, what with the shortages. It wasn't the shortages, Mr. M_____ replied; Ocean City had fireworks from pre-war. But it was too risky on account of the enemy submarines, some people thought.

"Don't seem like Fourth of July without fireworks," said Uncle Karl. The inverted tag in dialogue writing is still considered permissible with proper names or epithets, but sounds old-fashioned with personal pronouns. "We'll have 'em again soon enough," predicted the boys' father. Their mother declared she could do without fireworks: they reminded her too much of the real thing. Their father said all the more reason to shoot off a few now and again. Uncle Karl asked *rhetorically* who needed reminding, just look at people's hair and skin.

"The oil, yes," said Mrs. M_____.

Ambrose had a pain in his stomach and so didn't swim but enjoyed watching the others. He and his father burned red easily. Magda's figure was exceedingly well developed for her age. She too declined to swim, and got mad, and became angry when Peter attempted to drag her into the pool. She always swam, he insisted; what did she mean not swim? Why did a person come to Ocean City?

"Maybe I want to lay here with Ambrose," Magda teased.

Nobody likes a pedant.

"Aha," said Mother. Peter grabbed Magda by one ankle and ordered Ambrose to grab the other. She squealed and rolled over on the beach blanket. Ambrose pretended to help hold her back. Her tan was darker than even Mother's and Peter's. "Help out, Uncle Karl!" Peter cried. Uncle Karl went to seize the other ankle. Inside the top of her swimsuit, however, you could see the line where the sunburn ended and, when she hunched her shoulders and squealed again, one nipple's auburn edge. Mother made them behave themselves. "*You* should certainly know," she said to Uncle Karl. Archly. "That when a lady says she doesn't feel like swimming, a gentleman doesn't ask questions." Uncle Karl said excuse *him;* Mother winked at Magda; Ambrose blushed; stupid Peter kept saying "Phooey on *feel like!*" and tugging at Magda's ankle. Then even he got the point, and cannonballed with a holler into the pool.

"I swear," Magda said, in mock *in feigned* exasperation.

The diving would make a suitable literary symbol. To go off the high board you had to wait in a line along the poolside and up the ladder. Fellows tickled girls and goosed one another and shouted to the ones at the top to hurry up, or razzed them for bellyfloppers. Once on the springboard some took a great while posing or clowning or deciding on a dive or getting up their nerve; others ran right off. Especially among the younger fellows the idea was

to strike the funniest pose or do the craziest stunt as you fell, a thing that got harder to do as you kept on and kept on. But whether you hollered *Geronimo!* or *Sieg heil!*, held your nose or "rode a bicycle," pretended to be shot or did a perfect jacknife or changed your mind halfway down and ended up with nothing, it was over in two seconds, after all that wait. Spring, pose, splash. Spring, neat-o, splash. Spring, aw fooey, splash.

The grown-ups had gone on; Ambrose wanted to converse with Magda; she was remarkably well developed for her age; it was said that that came from rubbing with a turkish towel, and there were other theories. Ambrose could think of nothing to say except how good a diver Peter was, who was showing off for her benefit. You could pretty well tell by looking at their bathing suits and arm muscles how far along the different fellows were. Ambrose was glad he hadn't gone in swimming, the cold water shrank you up so. Magda pretended to be uninterested in the diving; she probably weighed as much as he did. If you knew your way around in the funhouse like your own bedroom, you could wait until a girl came along and then slip away without ever getting caught, even if her boyfriend was right with her. She'd think *he* did it! It would be better to be the boyfriend, and act outraged, and tear the funhouse apart.

Not act; *be.*

"He's a master diver," Ambrose said. In feigned admiration. "You really have to slave away at it to get that good." What would it matter anyhow if he asked her right out whether she remembered, even teased her with it as Peter would have?

There's no point in going farther; this isn't getting anybody anywhere; they haven't even come to the funhouse yet. Ambrose is off the track, in some new or old part of the place that's not supposed to be used; he strayed into it by some one-in-a-million chance, like the time the roller-coaster car left the tracks in the nineteen-teens against all the laws of physics and sailed over the boardwalk in the dark. And they can't locate him because they don't know where to look. Even the designer and operator have forgotten this other part, that winds around on itself like a whelk shell. That winds around the right part like the snakes on Mercury's caduceus. Some people, perhaps, don't "hit their stride" until their twenties, when the growing-up business is over and women appreciate other things besides wisecracks and teasing and strutting. Peter didn't have one-tenth the imagination *he* had, not one-tenth. Peter did this naming-their-children thing as a joke, making up names like Aloysius and Murgatroyd, but Ambrose knew *exactly* how it would feel to be married and have children of your own, and be a loving husband and father, and go comfortably to work in the mornings and to bed with your wife at night, and wake

up with her there. With a breeze coming through the sash and birds and mockingbirds singing in the Chinese-cigar trees. His eyes watered, there aren't enough ways to say that. He would be quite famous in his line of work. Whether Magda was his wife or not, one evening when he was wise-lined and gray at the temples he'd smile gravely, at a fashionable dinner party, and remind her of his youthful passion. The time they went with his family to Ocean City; the *erotic fantasies* he used to have about her. How long ago it seemed, and childish! Yet tender, too, *n'est-ce pas?* Would she have imagined that the world-famous whatever remembered how many strings were on the lyre on the bench beside the girl on the label of the cigar box he'd stared at in the toolshed at age ten while she, age eleven. Even then he had felt *wise beyond his years;* he'd stroked her hair and said in his deepest voice and correctest English, as to a dear child: "I shall never forget this moment."

But though he had breathed heavily, groaned as if ecstatic, what he'd really felt throughout was an odd detachment, as though someone else were Master. Strive as he might to be transported, he heard his mind take notes upon the scene: *This is what they call* passion. *I am experiencing it.* Many of the digger machines were out of order in the penny arcades and could not be repaired or replaced for the duration. Moreover the prizes, made now in USA, were less interesting than formerly, pasteboard items for the most part, and some of the machines wouldn't work on white pennies. The gypsy fortune-teller machine might have provided a foreshadowing of the climax of this story if Ambrose had operated it. It was even dilapidateder than most: the silver coating was worn off the brown metal handles, the glass windows around the dummy were cracked and taped, her kerchiefs and silks long-faded. If a man lived by himself, he could take a department-store mannequin with flexible joints and modify her in certain ways. *However:* by the time he was that old he'd have a real woman. There was a machine that stamped your name around a white-metal coin with a star in the middle: *A_____I.* His son would be the second, and when the lad reached thirteen or so he would put a strong arm around his shoulder and tell him calmly: "It is perfectly normal. We have all been through it. IT will not last forever." Nobody knew how to be what they were right. He'd smoke a pipe, teach his son how to fish and softcrab, assure him he needn't worry about himself. Magda would certainly give, Magda would certainly yield a great deal of milk, although guilty of occasional solecisms. It don't taste so bad. Suppose the lights came on now!

The day wore on. You think you're yourself, but there are other persons in you. Ambrose gets hard when Ambrose doesn't want to, *and obversely.*

Ambrose watches them disagree; Ambrose watches him watch. In the funhouse mirror-room you can't see yourself go on forever, because no matter how you stand, your head gets in the way. Even if you had a glass periscope, the image of your eye would cover up the thing you really wanted to see. The police will come; there'll be a story in the papers. That must be where it happened. Unless he can find a surprise exit, an unofficial backdoor or escape hatch opening on an alley, say, and then stroll up to the family in front of the funhouse and ask where everybody's been; *he's* been out of the place for ages. That's just where it happened, in that last lighted room: Peter and Magda found the right exit; he found one that you weren't supposed to find and strayed off into the works somewhere. In a perfect funhouse you'd be able to go only one way, like the divers off the high-board; getting lost would be impossible; the doors and halls would work like minnow traps or the valves in veins.

On account of German U-boats, Ocean City was "browned out": street-lights were shaded on the seaward side; shopwindows and boardwalk amusement places were kept dim, not to silhouette tankers and Liberty-ships for torpedoing. In a short story about Ocean City, Maryland, during World War II, the author could make use of the image of sailors on leave in the penny arcades and shooting galleries, sighting through the crosshairs of toy machine guns at swastika'd subs, while out in the black Atlantic a U-boat skipper squints through his periscope at real ships outlined by the glow of penny arcades. After dinner the family strolled back to the amusement end of the boardwalk. The boys' father had burnt red as always and was masked with Noxzema, a minstrel in reverse. The grown-ups stood at the end of the boardwalk where the Hurricane of '33 had cut an inlet from the ocean to Assawoman Bay.

"Pronounced with a long *o*," Uncle Karl reminded Magda with a wink. His shirt sleeves were rolled up; Mother punched his brown biceps with the arrowed heart on it and said his mind was naughty. Fat May's laugh came suddenly from the funhouse, as if she'd just got the joke; the family laughed too at the coincidence. Ambrose went under the boardwalk to search for out-of-town matchbook covers with the aid of his pocket flashlight; he looked out from the edge of the North American continent and wondered how far their laughter carried over the water. Spies in rubber rafts; survivors in lifeboats. If the joke had been beyond his understanding, he could have said: *"The laughter was over his head."* And let the reader see the serious wordplay on second reading.

He turned the flashlight on and then off at once even before the woman whooped. He sprang away, heart athud, dropping the light. What had the man grunted? Perspiration drenched and chilled him by the time he scrambled up to the family. "See anything?" his father asked. His voice wouldn't come; he shrugged and violently brushed sand from his pants legs.

"Let's ride the old flying horses!" Magda cried. I'll never be an author. It's been forever already, everybody's gone home, Ocean City's deserted, the ghost-crabs are trickling across the beach and down the littered cold streets. And the empty halls of clapboard hotels and abandoned funhouses. A tidal wave; an enemy air raid; a monster-crab swelling like an island from the sea. *The inhabitants fled in terror.* Magda clung to his trouser leg; he alone knew the maze's secret. "He gave his life that we might live," said Uncle Karl with a scowl of pain, as he. The fellow's hands had been tattooed; the woman's legs, the woman's fat white legs had. *An astonishing coincidence.* He yearned to tell Peter. He wanted to throw up for excitement. They hadn't even chased him. He wished he were dead.

One possible ending would be to have Ambrose come across another lost person in the dark. They'd match their wits together against the funhouse, struggle like Ulysses past obstacle after obstacle, help and encourage each other. Or a girl. By the time they found the exit they'd be closest friends, sweethearts if it were a girl; they'd know each other's inmost souls, be bound together *by the cement of shared adventure;* then they'd emerge into the light and it would turn out that his friend was a Negro. A blind girl. President Roosevelt's son. Ambrose's former archenemy.

Shortly after the mirror room he'd groped along a musty corridor, his heart already misgiving him at the absence of phosphorescent arrows and other signs. He'd found a crack of light—not a door, it turned out, but a seam between the plyboard wall panels—and squinting up to it, espied a small old man, *in appearance not unlike* the photographs at home of Ambrose's late grandfather, nodding upon a stool beneath a bare, speckled bulb. A crude panel of toggle- and knife-switches hung beside the open fuse box near his head; elsewhere in the little room were wooden levers and ropes belayed to boat cleats. At the time, Ambrose wasn't lost enough to rap or call; later he couldn't find that crack. Now it seemed to him that he'd possibly dozed off for a few minutes somewhere along the way; certainly he was exhausted from the afternoon's sunshine and the evening's problems; he couldn't be sure he hadn't dreamed part or all of the sight. Had an old black wall fan droned like bees and shimmied two flypaper streamers? Had the funhouse operator—gentle, somewhat sad and tired-appearing, in expression not unlike the photographs at home of Ambrose's late Uncle Konrad—murmured in his sleep? Is there really such a person as Ambrose, or is he a figment of the author's imagination? Was it Assawoman Bay or Sinepuxent? Are there other errors of fact in this fiction? Was there another sound besides the little slap slap of thigh on ham, like water sucking at the chine-boards of a skiff?

When you're lost, the smartest thing to do is stay put till you're found, hollering if necessary. But to holler guarantees humiliation as well as rescue; keeping silent permits some saving of face—you can act surprised at the fuss when your rescuers find you and swear you weren't lost, if they do. What's more you might find your own way yet, *however belatedly.*

"Don't tell me your foot's still asleep!" Magda exclaimed as the three young people walked from the inlet to the area set aside for ferris wheels, carrousels, and other carnival rides, they having decided in favor of the vast and ancient merry-go-round instead of the funhouse. What a sentence, everything was wrong from the outset. People don't know what to make of him, he doesn't know what to make of himself, he's only thirteen, *athletically and socially inept,* not astonishingly bright, but there are antennae; he has . . . some sort of receivers in his head; things speak to him, he understands more than he should, the world winks at him through its objects, grabs grinning at his coat. Everybody else is in on some secret he doesn't know; they've forgotten to tell him. Through simple *procrastination* his mother put off his baptism until this year. Everyone else had it done as a baby; he'd assumed the same of himself, as had his mother, so she claimed, until it was time for him to join Grace Methodist-Protestant and the oversight came out. He was mortified, but pitched sleepless through his private catechizing, intimidated by the ancient mysteries, a thirteen-year-old would never say that, resolved to experience conversion like St. Augustine. When the water touched his brow and Adam's sin left him, he contrived by a strain like defecation to bring tears into his eyes— but felt nothing. There was some simple, radical difference about him; he hoped it was genius, feared it was madness, devoted himself to amiability and inconspicuousness. Alone on the seawall near his house he was seized by the terrifying transports he'd thought to find in toolshed, in Communion-cup. The grass was alive! The town, the river, himself, were not imaginary; time roared in his ears like wind; the world was *going on!* This part ought to be dramatized. The Irish author James Joyce once wrote. Ambrose M_____ is going to scream.

There is no *texture of rendered sensory detail,* for one thing. The faded distorting mirrors beside Fat May; the impossibility of choosing a mount when one had but a single ride on the great carrousel; the *vertigo attendant on his recognition* that Ocean City was worn out, the place of fathers and grandfathers, straw-boatered men and parasoled ladies survived by their amuse-ments. Money spent, the three paused at Peter's insistence beside Fat May to watch the girls get their skirts blown up. The object was to tease Magda, who said: "I swear, Peter M_____, you've got a one-track mind! Amby and me aren't *interested* in such things." In the tumbling-barrel, too, just inside the Devil's-mouth entrance to the funhouse, the girls were upended and their boyfriends and others could see up their dresses if they cared to. Which was the whole point, Ambrose realized. Of the entire funhouse! If you looked around, you noticed that almost all the people on the boardwalk were paired off into cou-ples except the small children; in a way, that was the whole point of Ocean City! If you had X-ray eyes and could see everything going on at that instant under the boardwalk and in all the hotel rooms and cars and alleyways, you'd realize that all that normally *showed*, like restaurants and dance halls and clothing and test-your-strength machines, was merely preparation and intermission. Fat May screamed.

Because he watched the goings-on from the corner of his eye, it was Ambrose who spied the half-dollar on the boardwalk near the tumbling-barrel. Losers weepers. The first time he'd heard some people moving through a corri-dor not far away, just after he'd lost sight of the crack of light, he'd decided not to call to them, for fear they'd guess he was scared and poke fun; it sounded like roughnecks; he'd hoped they'd come by and he could follow in the dark with-out their knowing. Another time he'd heard just one person, unless he imag-ined it, bumping along as if on the other side of the plywood; perhaps Peter coming back for him, or Father, or Magda lost too. Or the owner and operator of the funhouse. He'd called out once, as though merrily: "Anybody know where the heck we are?" But the query was too stiff, his voice cracked, when the sounds stopped he was terrified: maybe it was a queer who waited for fellows to get lost, or a longhaired filthy monster that lived in some cranny of the fun-house. He stood rigid for hours it seemed like, scarcely respiring. His future was shockingly clear, in outline. He tried holding his breath to the point of unconsciousness. There ought to be a button you could push to end your life absolutely without pain; disappear in a flick, like turning out a light. He would push it instantly! He despised Uncle Karl. But he despised his father too, for not being what he was supposed to be. Perhaps his father hated *his* father, and so on, and his son would hate him, and so on. Instantly!

Naturally he didn't have nerve enough to ask Magda to go through the funhouse with him. With incredible nerve and to everyone's surprise he invited Magda, quietly and politely, to go through the funhouse with him. "I warn you,

I've never been through it before," he added, *laughing easily;* "but I reckon we can manage somehow. The important thing to remember, after all, is that it's meant to be a *fun*house; that is, a place of amusement. If people really got lost or injured or too badly frightened in it, the owner'd go out of business. There'd even be lawsuits. No character in a work of fiction can make a speech this long without interruption or acknowledgment from the other characters."

Mother teased Uncle Karl: "Three's a crowd, I always heard." But actually Ambrose was relieved that Peter now had a quarter too. Nothing was what it looked like. Every instant, under the surface of the Atlantic Ocean, millions of living animals devoured one another. Pilots were falling in flames over Europe; women were being forcibly raped in the South Pacific. His father should have taken him aside and said: "There is a simple secret to getting through the fun-house, as simple as being first to see the Towers. Here it is. Peter does not know it; neither does your Uncle Karl. You and I are different. Not surprisingly, you've often wished you weren't. Don't think I haven't noticed how unhappy your childhood has been! But you'll understand, when I tell you, why it had to be kept secret until now. And you won't regret not being like your brother and your uncle. *On the contrary!*" If you knew all the stories behind all the people on the boardwalk, you'd see that *nothing* was what it looked like. Husbands and wives often hated each other; parents didn't necessarily love their children; et cetera. A child took things for granted because he had nothing to compare his life to and everybody acted as if things were as they should be. Therefore each saw himself as the hero of the story, when the truth might turn out to be that he's the villain, or the coward. And there wasn't one thing you could do about it!

Hunchbacks, fat ladies, fools—that no one chose what he was was unbear-able. In the movies he'd meet a beautiful young girl in the funhouse; they'd have hairs-breadth escapes from real dangers; he'd do and say the right things; she also; in the end they'd be lovers; their dialogue lines would match up; he'd be perfectly at ease; she'd not only like him well enough, she'd think he was *marvelous;* she'd lie awake thinking about *him,* instead of vice versa—the way *his* face looked in different lights and how he stood and exactly what he'd said —and yet that would be only one small episode in his wonderful life, among many many others. Not a *turning point* at all. What had happened in the tool-shed was nothing. He hated, he loathed his parents! One reason for not writing a lost-in-the-funhouse story is that either everybody's felt what Ambrose feels, in which case it goes without saying, or else no normal person feels such things, in which case Ambrose is a freak. "Is anything more tiresome, in fiction, than the problems of sensitive adolescents?" And it's all too long and rambling, as if the author. For all a person knows the first time through, the end could be just around any corner; perhaps, *not impossibly* it's been within reach any number of times. On the other hand he may be scarcely past the start, with everything yet to get through, an intolerable idea.

Fill in: His father's raised eyebrows when he announced his decision to do the funhouse with Magda. Ambrose understands now, but didn't then, that his father was wondering whether he knew what the funhouse was *for*—especially since he didn't object, as he should have, when Peter decided to come along too. The ticket-woman, witchlike, mortifying him when inadvertently he gave her his name-coin instead of the half-dollar, then unkindly calling Magda's attention to the birthmark on his temple: "Watch out for him, girlie, he's a marked man!" She wasn't even cruel, he understood, only vulgar and insensitive. Somewhere in the world there was a young woman with such splendid understanding that she'd see him entire, like a poem or story, and find his words so valuable after all that when he confessed his apprehensions she would explain why they were in fact the very things that made him precious to her . . . and to Western Civilization! There was no such girl, the simple truth being. Violent yawns as they approached the mouth. Whispered advice from an old-timer on a bench near the barrel: "Go crabwise and ye'll get an eyeful without upsetting!" Composure vanished at the first pitch: Peter hollered joyously, Magda tumbled, shrieked, clutched her skirt; Ambrose scrambled crabwise, tight-lipped with terror, was soon out, watched his dropped name-coin slide among the couples. Shamefaced he saw that to get through expeditiously was not the point; Peter feigned assistance in order to trip Magda up, shouted "I see Christmas!" when her legs went flying. The old man, his latest betrayer, cacked approval. A dim hall then of black-thread cobwebs and recorded gibber: he took Magda's elbow to steady her against revolving discs set in the slanted floor to throw your feet out from under, and explained to her in a calm, deep voice his theory that each phase of the funhouse was triggered either automatically, by a series of photoelectric devices, or else manually by operators stationed at peepholes. But he lost his voice thrice as the discs unbalanced him; Magda was anyhow squealing; but at one point she clutched him about the waist to keep from falling, and her right cheek pressed for a moment against his belt-buckle. Heroically he drew her up, it was his chance to clutch her close as if for support and say: "I love you." He even put an arm lightly about the small of her back before a sailor-and-girl pitched into them from behind, sorely treading his left big toe and knocking Magda asprawl with them. The sailor's girl was a string-haired hussy with a loud laugh and light blue drawers; Ambrose realized that he wouldn't have said "I love you" anyhow, and was smitten with self-contempt. How much better it would be to be that common sailor! A wiry little Seaman 3rd, the fellow squeezed a girl to each side and stumbled hilarious into the mirror room, closer to Magda in thirty seconds than Ambrose had got in thirteen years. She giggled at something the fellow said to Peter; she drew her hair from her eyes with a movement so womanly it struck Ambrose's heart; Peter's smacking her backside then seemed particularly coarse. But Magda made a pleased indignant face and cried, "All right for *you,* mister!" and pursued Peter into the maze without a backward glance. The sailor followed after, leisurely, drawing his girl against his hip; Ambrose understood not only that they were all so relieved to be rid of his burdensome company that they didn't even notice his absence, but that he himself shared their relief. Stepping from the treacherous passage at last into the mirror-maze, he saw once again, more clearly than ever, how readily he deceived himself into supposing he was a person. He even foresaw, wincing at his dreadful self-knowledge, that he would repeat the deception, at ever-rarer intervals, all his wretched life, so fearful were the alternatives. Fame, madness, suicide; perhaps all three. It's not believable that so young a boy could articulate that reflection, and in fiction the merely true must always yield to the plausible. Moreover, the symbolism is in places heavy-footed. Yet Ambrose M_____ understood, as few adults do, that the famous loneliness of the great was no popular myth but a general truth—furthermore, that it was as much cause as effect.

All the preceding except the last few sentences is exposition that should've been done earlier or interspersed with the present action instead of lumped together. No reader would put up with so much with such *prolixity.* It's interesting that Ambrose's father, though presumably an intelligent man (as indicated by his role as grade-school principal), neither encouraged nor discouraged his sons at all in any way—as if he either didn't care about them or cared all right but didn't know how to act. If this fact should contribute to one of them's becoming a celebrated but wretchedly unhappy scientist, was it a good thing or not? He too might someday face the question; it would be useful to know whether it had tortured his father for years, for example, or never once crossed his mind.

In the maze two important things happened. First, our hero found a name-coin someone else had lost or discarded: *AMBROSE,* suggestive of the famous lightship and of his late grandfather's favorite dessert, which his mother used to prepare on special occasions out of coconut, oranges, grapes, and what else. Second, as he wondered at the endless replication of his image in the mirrors, second, as he *lost himself in the reflection* that the necessity for an observer makes perfect observation impossible, better make him eighteen at least, yet that would render other things unlikely, he heard Peter and Magda chuckling somewhere together in the maze. "Here!" "No, here!" they shouted to each other; Peter said, "Where's Amby?" Magda murmured. "Amb?" Peter called. In a pleased, friendly voice. He didn't reply. The truth was, his brother was a *happy-go-lucky youngster* who'd've been better off with a regular brother of his own, but who seldom complained of his lot and was generally cordial. Ambrose's throat ached; there aren't enough different ways to say that. He stood quietly while the two young people giggled and thumped through the glittering maze, hurrah'd their discovery of its exit, cried out in joyful alarm at what next beset them. Then he set his mouth and followed after, as he supposed, took a wrong turn, strayed into the pass *wherein he lingers yet.*

The action of conventional dramatic narrative may be represented by a diagram called Freitag's Triangle:

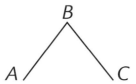

or more accurately by a variant of that diagram:

in which *AB* represents the exposition, *B* the introduction of conflict, *BC* the "rising action," complication, or development of the conflict, *C* the climax, or turn of the action, *CD* the dénouement, or resolution of the conflict. While there is no reason to regard this pattern as an absolute necessity, like many other conventions it became conventional because great numbers of people over many years learned by trial and error that it was effective; one ought not to forsake it, therefore, unless one wishes to forsake as well the effect of drama or has clear cause to feel that deliberate violation of the "normal" pattern can better can better effect that effect. This can't go on much longer; it can go on forever. He died telling stories to himself in the dark; years later, when that vast unsuspected area of the funhouse came to light, the first expedition found his skeleton in one of its labyrinthine corridors and mistook it for part of the entertainment. He died of starvation telling himself stories in the dark; but unbeknownst unbeknownst to him, an assistant operator of the funhouse, happening to overhear him, crouched just behind the plyboard partition and wrote down his every word. The operator's daughter, an exquisite young woman with a figure unusually well developed for her age, crouched just behind the partition and transcribed his every word. Though she had never laid eyes on him, she recognized that here was one of Western Culture's truly great imaginations, the eloquence of whose suffering would be an inspiration to unnumbered. And her heart was torn between her love for the misfortunate young man (yes, she loved him, though she had never laid though she knew him only—but how well!—through his words, and the deep, calm voice in which he spoke them) between her love et cetera and her womanly intuition that only in suffering and isolation could he give voice et cetera. Lone dark dying. Quietly she kissed the rough plyboard, and a tear fell upon the page. Where she had written in shorthand *Where she had written in shorthand* Where she had written in shorthand *Where she* et cetera. A long time ago we should have passed the apex of Freitag's Triangle and made brief work of the *dénouement;* the plot doesn't rise by meaningful steps but winds upon itself, digresses, retreats, hesitates, sighs, collapses, expires. The climax of the story must be its protagonist's discovery of a way to get through the funhouse. But he has found none, may have ceased to search.

What relevance does the war have to the story? Should there be fireworks outside, or not?

Ambrose wandered, languished, dozed. Now and then he fell into his habit of rehearsing to himself the unadventurous story of his life, narrated from the third-person point of view, from his earliest memory parenthesis of maple leaves stirring in the summer breath of tidewater Maryland end of parenthesis to the present moment. Its principal events, on this telling, would appear to have been *A, B, C,* and *D.*

He imagined himself years hence, successful, married, at ease in the world, the trials of his adolescence far behind him. He has come to the seashore with his family for the holiday: how Ocean City has changed! But at one seldom at one ill-frequented end of the boardwalk a few derelict amusements survive from times gone by: the great carrousel from the turn of the century, with its monstrous griffins and mechanical concert band; the roller coaster rumored since 1916 to have been condemned; the mechanical shooting gallery in which only the image of our enemies changed. His own son laughs with Fat May and wants to know what a funhouse is; Ambrose hugs the sturdy lad close and smiles around his pipestem at his wife.

The family's going home. Mother sits between Father and Uncle Karl, who teases him good-naturedly who chuckles over the fact that the comrade with whom he'd fought his way shoulder to shoulder through the funhouse had turned out to be a blind Negro girl—to their mutual discomfort, as they'd opened their souls. But such are the walls of custom, which even. Whose arm is where? How must it feel. He dreams of a funhouse vaster by far than any yet constructed; but by then they may be out of fashion, like steamboats and excursion trains. Already quaint and seedy: the draperied ladies on the frieze of the carrousel are his father's father's moonchecked dreams; if he thinks of it more he will vomit his apple-on-a-stick.

He wonders: will he become a regular person? Something has gone wrong; his vaccination didn't take; at the Boy-Scout initiation campfire he only pretended to be deeply moved, as he pretends to this hour that it is not so bad after all in the funhouse, and that he has a little limp. How long will it last? He envisions a truly astonishing funhouse, incredibly complex yet utterly controlled from a great central switchboard like the console of a pipe organ. Nobody had enough imagination. He could design such a place himself, wiring and all, and he's only thirteen years old. He would be its operator: panel lights would show what was up in every cranny of its cunning of its multifarious vastness; a switch-flick would ease this fellow's way, complicate that's, to balance things out; if anyone seemed lost or frightened, all the operator had to do was.

He wishes he had never entered the funhouse. But he has. Then he wishes he were dead. But he's not. Therefore he will construct funhouses for others and be their secret operator—though he would rather be among the lovers for whom funhouses are designed.

Notes on Craft and Context

On Form and Language in Style

This comic tale is **episodic** yet sequential; it begins at the beginning and stops at journey's end. Yet its author delights in **digression**, and getting there is more than half the fun. For the funhouse itself is a labyrinth, an all-encompassing structure, and within it the reader and Ambrose/author will be both found and lost. Barth is the proprietor of this amusement park, and our ticket of admission is the willingness to play; here is a game with a new set of rules, and they are established early on. Let's look at the opening beat:

> For whom is the funhouse fun? Perhaps for lovers. For Ambrose it is *a place of fear and confusion.* He has come to the seashore with his family for the holiday, *the occasion of their visit is Independence Day, the most important secular holiday of the United States of America.* A single straight underline is the manuscript mark for italic type, *which in turn* is the printed equivalent to oral emphasis of words and phrases as well as the customary type for titles of complete works, not to mention. Italics are also employed, in fiction stories especially, for "outside," intrusive, or artificial voices, such as radio announcements, the texts of telegrams and newspaper articles, et cetera. They should be used *sparingly.* If passages originally in roman type are italicized by someone repeating them, it's customary to acknowledge the fact. *Italics mine.*

The first sentence is both formal and informal—a question asked of the reader with a certain rhetorical stiffness ("For whom . . .") and a hint of repetition ("funhouse fun"); imagine how the mood would alter if the author had written instead, "Which folks like amusement parks?" or "Who *really enjoys* a funhouse?" The three-word second sentence provides a partial answer; again the style uses the formal "perhaps" as opposed to the colloquial "maybe," but the sentence fragment is informal, as though the author has been talking to himself. In the third sentence the first proper noun, "Ambrose," tells us we're meeting the story's chief character and these people aren't called Dick or Jane. This sense of something out of the ordinary is reinforced by the italicized *"it is a place of fear and confusion,"* as well as the ensuing definition of Independence Day. Note that within the first four lines we've been provided with "when, where, and why" the story takes place, but it's already clear that we will advance by indirection and pause to digress; Barth describes his own description in terms of the mechanics of representation and throws in a lexical primer: *this is how it's done.* By the end of the first paragraph the author addresses the reader in first person (*"Italics mine."*), and throughout the tale to follow we will never quite lose sight of him—winking, offering useful or parenthetical **"asides,"** ducking around the edge of the page while we hurry to catch up. (It's hard not to imitate Barth while discussing him. Notice, for example, how this "parenthetical 'aside'" takes place in a parenthesis, and how—if we define art as serious play—the fiction's opening question has to do with "fun.")

On Theme in Style

In the story's final sentence, that particular notion of serious play comes full circle: "Therefore he will construct funhouses for others and be their secret operator—though he would rather be among the lovers for whom funhouses are designed." The "he" is Ambrose and, by extension, his author, that not-so "secret operator" who has designed the tale. Those who are doomed to witness and not participate in "fun" take solace in the very act of witnessing what others do unthinkingly and well. The artist, in effect, can never be Peter or Magda but can write for them nevertheless. Though "he wishes he had never entered the funhouse" and "wishes he were dead"—how seriously, one wonders?—he's inside it and alive. This is a paradox that Barth returns to often; Ambrose consoles himself for his inability to be song's subject by having composed the song itself. In verbal terms it's the equivalent of "eating cake and having it too"; descriptive language *lasts*.

The poet Dylan Thomas says much the same in "In My Craft or Sullen Art":

> In my craft or sullen art
> Exercised in the still night
> When only the moon rages
> And the lovers lie abed
> With all their griefs in their arms,
> I labor by singing light
> Not by ambition or bread
> Or the strut and trade of charms
> On the ivory stages
> But for the common wages
> Of their most secret heart.
>
> Not for the proud man apart
> From the raging moon I write
> On these spindrift pages
> Nor for the towering dead
> With their nightingales and psalms
> But for the lovers, their arms
> Round the griefs of the ages,
> Who pay no praise or wages
> Nor heed my craft or art.

Author as Character, Character as Author

Dylan Thomas uses the first-person pronoun explicitly, but Barth is more cagey in "Lost in the Funhouse." As befits a story with so many mirrors and such pleasure in illusion, a one-to-one equivalence between young Ambrose and his middle-aged inventor would be too simple by half. We need not conclude, for example, that Barth had a girlfriend called—or recalled as—Magda, or that he went with his family to this particular amusement park on this particular day. Indeed, the entire presentation of the memory suggests the opposite—that this is an act of imagination and not autobiography. The initiation into manhood that Magda gave Ambrose ("purchased clemency at a surprising price set by herself") takes place well before the present action, so the initiation rite here described has more to do with artistic awareness than sex. This is a story about the making of a story, and when its author moans, "I'll never be an author," we're entitled to doubt that as well.

On Fiction about Fiction

While a magician performs magic tricks, the running commentary is meant to provide distraction for the audience, so that those who watch the performance can't see up his sleeves or her hat. By contrast, here the "patter" is the perform-ance itself; Barth's discussion of the stuff of fiction is the story's central **action,** its thematic point. He acts, in effect, as his own teacher—making comments on the text produced, suggesting general rules of narration or specific alternate strategies and offering reactions to his own just-printed prose. We read both the draft and its revisions, or, to shift the **metaphor,** we watch a dramatic encounter both from the hall and the wings. This sense of the writer as per-former/impresario is essential to the modern sensibility and quintessential to postmodernism ("quintessence" meaning literally one-fifth of the "essence" and therefore irreducible); Ambrose is a puppet and Barth the puppeteer.

Fiction itself is a relatively recent **genre**—at least by comparison with poetry or drama. It came into vogue in English in the eighteenth century— there are earlier examples elsewhere—and has flourished since. Although this is a rule to which there are many exceptions, the dominant mode of the genre has been **realistic:** a report on society, its individuals and classes, its challenges and patterns of behavior. The great previous practitioners of fiction written in English—from Samuel Richardson and Charles Dickens to Herman Melville and Joseph Conrad—did not hesitate to use a wide-ranging cast of **characters;** they wrote of squires, lawyers, sailors, engineers. Often, as in the novels of Jane Austen, Henry James, or Virginia Woolf, the central figure was independently wealthy and had no need of work. But we've grown more leery nowadays of border crossing and inauthenticity; as of the twentieth century the artist increasingly writes about artists, the author makes of his characters authors, and now we have books about books.

This is what I mean by the "self-reflexive" artifact, the mirror held up not so much to nature as to the mirror itself. Look at the protagonists of the next two short stories, "Fenstad's Mother" and "A Small, Good Thing," and you'll see how much more "realistic" they are, how much less visible their creators in each paragraph and page. From the very beginning of "Lost in the Funhouse" and all through the pages that follow we read a running commentary on what works or fails to in the story—though often the despairing assertion of failure masks the text's success. Of a hundred such examples, let me cite just one:

> So far there's been no real dialogue, very little sensory detail, and nothing in the way of a *theme.* And a long time has gone by already without any-

thing happening; it makes a person wonder. We haven't even reached Ocean City yet: we will never get out of the funhouse.

The more closely an author identifies with the narrator, literally or metaphorically, the less advisable it is, as a rule, to use the first-person narrative viewpoint.

Who's the narrator who wonders here; who's the "I" of "We"? And though there's a first-person observer implicit from the story's first sentence, it's explicit only rarely and then for the sake of the comic aside: the writer takes a pratfall while winking at the reader and dusts himself off and goes on.

"Lost in the Funhouse" as a Primer for Narrative Styles

One other aspect to note of Barth's prose is its wonderful suppleness, the range of diction he here employs. From the highest to the lowest common denominator, this is a handbook of rhetorics and primer for narrative styles. In casual asides such as "Losers weepers" or "I'll never be an author" or the lines of dialogue—for a story so lengthy there's little spoken utterance—the author uses everyday language and standard colloquial speech. But he's not above the use of terms such as **"solecism"** (an ungrammatical combination of words in a sentence) or **"prolixity"** (unduly verbose and long-winded) to describe Magda's way of talking and then his narrator's dismissive aside: "Nobody loves a pedant!"

This is, in short, a way of taking both parts in a comic argument—of putting on the page what its author disavows. It's perfectly clear to the reader that Magda flirts with Peter, not Ambrose, but Ambrose is too self-absorbed to get the story right. There are aspects of this entertainment that suggest a bedroom **farce** or even a **burlesque.** People are always opening the wrong door or staring at their own reflections in a misleading mirror; what Ambrose *fails* to see is just as vivid to the reader as what he in fact observes. The sexual hijinks and suggestiveness—in other fictions by this author they occupy stage center—are characteristic of Barth. He's turn by turn bawdy and sly.

On Self-Reflexive Imitation

And here's the final point to make about **self-reflexive fiction:** it imitates itself. Barth's entire project—over nearly fifty years of published prose—is a grid of criss-crossed referents, a doubling and quadrupling back over constantly shifting ground. His characters from book to book refer to their previous incarnations; they appear as matched pairs and sometimes as literal twins. From the shortest of his short stories to *Letters,* a nearly eight-hundred-page **epistolary novel,** the subject of his body of work is the work as such. To get addicted to this world of words is to become obsessive; every year on his birthday the author hears from a nationwide fan club, the Society for the Celebration of Barthomania. "In the beginning was the word" might serve as apt conclusion for our study of this comic bard; let's give him the final word too.

▓ **WRITER'S VIEW:** *Suppose you are a writer by vocation—a "print-oriented bastard," as the McLuhanites call us—and you feel, for example, that the novel, if not narrative literature generally, if not the printed word altogether, has by this hour of the world just about shot its bolt, as Leslie Fiedler and others maintain. I'm inclined to agree, with reservations and hedges. Literary forms certainly have histories and historical contingencies, and it may well be that the novel's time as a major art form is up, as the "times" of classical tragedy, Italian and German grand opera, or the sonnet-sequence came to be. No necessary cause for alarm in this at all, except perhaps to certain novelists, and one way to handle such a feeling might be to write a novel about it. Whether historically the novel expires or persists as a major art form seems immaterial to me; if enough writers and critics feel apocalyptical about it, their feeling becomes a considerable cultural fact, like the feeling that Western civilization, or the world, is going to end rather soon. If you take a bunch of people out into the desert and the world didn't end, you'd come home shamefaced, I imagine; but the persistence of an art form doesn't invalidate work created in the comparable apocalyptic ambience. That is one of the fringe benefits of being an artist instead of a prophet. There are others. If you happened to be Vladimir Nabokov, you might address that felt ultimacy by writing* Pale Fire, *a fine novel by a learned pedant, in the form of a pedantic commentary on a poem invented for the purpose. If you were Borges you might write* Labyrinths: *fictions by a learned librarian in the form of footnotes, as he describes them, to imaginary or hypothetical books. And I'll add that if you were the author of this paper, you'd have written something like* The Sot-Weed Factor *or* Giles Goat-Boy: *novels which imitate the form of the Novel, by an author who imitates the role of Author.* (The Friday Book *"The Literature of Exhaustion,"* [New York: Putnam, 1984])

▓ Applications and Connections

- Almost every writer, at one point or another, will write about the act of writing itself. After all, we are always being told to write what we know, and, alternately, to stretch our imagination. Writing is always double-edged—the familiar and the completely new at once. Is Barth's story more about writing a story or about a boy who gets lost in a funhouse?
- Consider how stylistic contrasts contribute to the story's humor. How does style influence mood, **characterization,** and even plot?
- In "Lost in the Funhouse" it's sometimes difficult to distinguish the author from the narrator and the narrator from the protagonist. Consider how you would define each of these roles generally, and then find places in the story where they overlap. In your own stories be aware that these relationships exist regardless of whether or not the story draws the reader's attention to it.

You as author have an inescapable autobiographical investment in your story; pieces of you and what you have witnessed and researched will surface everywhere.

Exercises

1. Tell Magda's version of what happened in the car and barn and funhouse: as it happened, or the next day, or twenty years thereafter.

2. Describe, as Barth might, what the couple underneath the boardwalk do and see. Describe it from the pair's shared point of view.

3. Write a love poem to Magda, in Ambrose's diction; then the limerick Peter might taunt her with. Which does she prefer?

4. Deploy (as in this instance) the parenthesis as a way of describing (or, if you prefer, transcribing) the family picnic on the beach (or perhaps that evening, when returned home), and then allow the sentences to trail off to. Finality. Get rid of the apposite comma and the dependent clause.

5. Substituting "circus" for "funhouse," reimagine any three pages of Barth and write your own version.

6. "The more closely an author identifies with the narrator, literally or metaphorically, the less advisable it is, as a rule, to use the first-person narrative viewpoint." Transform that paragraph and the one that precedes it into the first person.

7. "Visual, auditory, tactile, olfactory, gustatory." Take these five senses and describe the ticket taker at the funhouse according to each sense.

8. What does Uncle Karl see Magda doing with Peter and say that he saw that evening—to the sailor and his girlfriend—in the bar?

9. Write a newspaper article about a German submarine found washed up on the Maryland beach. Consider whether its commander surrendered willingly, how they tracked him to the funhouse, and what he said when caught.

10. Write your own story of first love and loss, but using Barth's techniques.

Examples of Student Work

(*Editor's Note:* Here follow—for the sake of brevity—two first paragraphs of two separate student efforts to deploy Barth's techniques. They are both written tongue-in-cheek and, to my mind, with verbal and imaginative flair. Indeed, my students' responsiveness to Barth's stylistic pyrotechnics took me by—happy!—surprise; this seemed a difficult set of exercises but, almost without exception, the written response to the challenge was inventive and up to the task. As with the responses, later, to the work of Lorrie Moore it may be that the element of comedy helps; there's a no-holds-barred feel to the act of imitation here.)

Genevieve Kolasa, EXERCISE 4

The family and co. (abbreviation for "company") have arrived at **Z___Beach** just outside **D___City**. Ambrose, feeling slightly carsick or possibly excited (he's still new to the thrills of puberty), cautiously rises out of the backseat (but not without sneaking a peek down Magda's sundress). For as long as Ambrose can remember, his parents have brought him and Peter to the aforementioned beach for (what his mother calls) a *picnic (italics mine)*. **pic-nic, (bold not mine)** pik'nik, n. *(italics not mine)*. An outdoor pleasure excursion, usually one with a meal carried along and shared by the participants; *colloq. (italics not mine)* a pleasurable or easy experience or undertaking. The arm and shank sections of pork shoulder, sold fresh, pickled, or cured and smoked; also **pic-nick shoul-der (bold not mine)**—*v.i. picnicked, picnicking. (italics not mine)* To have or take part in a picnic. -**pick-nick-er,** n. (according to Noah Webster). And not unlike most English speakers, Ambrose was unaware of the fact that he could have **picnic** without having a **picnic** but while still being considered as **picnicking** *(n.)* or as a **picknicker** *(n)*. Of course Ambrose has his mind (and eyes) on another matter than the diversity of the English language. Just at that moment, Magda insert parenthesis who was very well developed for her age insert parenthesis sat down at the picnic table directly across from our main character . . .

Erin Hockenberry, EXERCISE 10

For whom is a summer vacation a vacation? Perhaps for small children. For Ellen it is a time of constant observation and strenuous attention to detail. For two and a half months she has spent her day planning and plotting plotting and planning. Placing two identical words one right after the other while typing on a computer drives the spellchecker nuts. The red squiggly line that it places under the second repetition of the word is meant to function as an alert system to those who temporarily become stuck in a word rut. It is the computer's way of reminding you that your attempts at humor and originality are frowned upon by the modern language association.

CHAPTER 3

CHARACTER AND THE EPIPHANIC MOMENT:
Learning to Reveal the Hidden

CHARLES BAXTER, "Fenstad's Mother"

▓ **WRITER'S VIEW:** *Stories bring characters together, too, mixed and matched, sometimes pushing them toward each other like chaperons who see to it that the diffident seventh graders in dancing class are suddenly, and against all expectations, in one another's arms.* (Burning Down the House: Essays on Fiction *[Saint Paul: Graywolf Press, 1997]).*

Charles Baxter was born on May 13, 1947, in Minneapolis, Minnesota; he graduated from Macalester College and received a PhD in English literature from SUNY/Buffalo. Although he transcends the label of "regional author," Baxter has lived and worked for most of his life in the Midwest; he taught at Wayne State University in Detroit, at the University of Michigan in Ann Arbor and is now adjunct professor at the University of Minnesota. The experience of teaching composition in night classes at Wayne State provided a context for "Fenstad's Mother," and his novel *The Feast of Love,* a finalist for the National Book Award in 2000, takes place in the town of Ann Arbor. His fourth novel, *Saul and Patsy,* takes place in Five Oaks, Michigan—a fictional small town that provides the landscape for much of Baxter's fiction and fires his imagination as does the Chesapeake Bay for John Barth.

Charles Baxter has published two additional novels, *First Light* (1987) and *Shadow Play* (1993), a book of poems, *Imaginary Paintings* (1989), and a book of essays on fiction, *Burning Down the House* (1997). He has been the editor or coeditor of several volumes of contemporary prose. It is as a short story writer, however, that he earned his reputation as one of the premier voices of American literature. His fourth collection of short stories, *Believers,* appeared in 1997; his three previous collections of stories are *Harmony of the World* (winner of the Associated Writing Programs competition in 1984), *Through the Safety Net* (1986), and *A Relative Stranger* (1990), of which "Fenstad's Mother" comprises the opening beat. His work has been widely anthologized. He has received a J. S. Guggenheim Fellowship and an Award in Literature from the American Academy of Arts and Letters.

The title of the collection—"a relative stranger"—establishes its tone. Not so much a pun as a doubling and even self-contradictory phrase, the title suggests that we can be distant from those we hold most dear; so too "Fenstad's Mother" indicates we will meet a woman whose relation to her son, and his to her, proves central to the tale. Is the main character here Fenstad or his mother; will she take stage center from his point of view?

Charles Baxter reports that this is not the first piece he composed for *A Relative Stranger,* but when it came time to assemble the whole he placed this story first. "Fenstad's Mother" shows the writer's pervasive concern with ordinary people oscillating between happiness and grief, proximity and distance; his characters possess a kind of muted eloquence and—to continue with this list of opposites—stressed calm. One way to read what follows is with an eye for **"epiphany,"** that moment when something hidden is revealed. In the context of religion the term means "showing forth"; in the artistic context—as first established by James Joyce in his book *Dubliners*—"epiphany" suggests that we—both as characters and readers—begin to see more clearly what once had been obscured.

Fenstad's Mother

On Sunday morning after communion Fenstad drove across town to visit his mother. Behind the wheel, he exhaled with his hand flat in front of his mouth to determine if the wine on his breath could be detected. He didn't think so. Fenstad's mother was a lifelong social progressive who was amused by her son's churchgoing, and, wine or no wine, she could guess where he had been. She had spent her life in the company of rebels and deviationists, and she recognized all their styles.

Passing a frozen pond in the city park, Fenstad slowed down to watch the skaters, many of whom he knew by name and skating style. From a distance they were dots of color ready for flight, frictionless. To express grief on skates seemed almost impossible, and Fenstad liked that. He parked his car on a residential block and took out his skates from the back seat, where he kept them all winter. With his fingertips he touched the wooden blade guards, thinking of the time. He checked his watch; he had fifteen minutes.

Out on the ice, still wearing his churchy Sunday-morning suit, tie, and overcoat, but now circling the outside edge of the pond with his bare hands in his overcoat pockets, Fenstad admired the overcast sky and luxuriated in the brittle cold. He was active and alert in winter but felt sleepy throughout the summer. He passed a little girl in a pink jacket, pushing a tiny chair over the ice. He waved to his friend Ann, an off-duty cop, practicing her twirls. He waved to other friends. Without exception they waved back. As usual, he was impressed by the way skates improved human character.

Twenty minutes later, in the doorway of her apartment, his mother said, "Your cheeks are red." She glanced down at his trousers, damp with melted snow. "You've been skating." She kissed him on the cheek and turned to walk into her living room. "Skating after church? Isn't that some sort of doctrinal error?"

"It's just happiness," Fenstad said. Quickly he checked her apartment for any signs of memory loss or depression. He found none and immediately felt relief. The apartment smelled of soap and Lysol, the signs of an old woman who wouldn't tolerate nonsense. Out on her coffee table, as usual, were the letters she was writing to her congressman and to political dictators around the globe. Fenstad's mother pleaded for enlightened behavior and berated the dictators for their bad political habits.

She grasped the arm of the sofa and let herself down slowly. Only then did she smile. "How's your soul, Harry?" she asked. "What's the news?"

He smiled back and smoothed his hair. Martin Luther King's eyes locked into his from the framed picture on the wall opposite him. In the picture King was shaking hands with Fenstad's mother, the two of them surrounded by smiling faces. "My soul's okay, Ma," he said. "It's a hard project. I'm always working on it." He reached down for a chocolate-chunk cookie from a box on top of the television. "Who brought you these?"

"Your daughter Sharon. She came to see me on Friday." Fenstad's mother tilted her head at him. "You *want* to be a good person, but she's the real article. Goodness comes to her without any effort at all. She says you have a new girlfriend. A pharmacist this time. Susan, is it?" Fenstad nodded. "Harry, why does your generation always have to find the right person? Why can't you learn to live with the wrong person? Sooner or later everyone's wrong. Love isn't the most important thing, Harry, far from it. Why can't you see that? I still don't comprehend why you couldn't live with Eleanor." Eleanor was Fenstad's ex-wife. They had been divorced for a decade, but Fenstad's mother hoped for a reconciliation.

"Come on, Ma," Fenstad said. "Over and done with, gone and gone." He took another cookie.

"You live with somebody so that you're living with *somebody,* and then you go out and do the work of the world. I don't understand all this pickiness about lovers. In a pinch anybody'll do, Harry, believe me."

On the side table was a picture of her late husband, Fenstad's mild, middle-of-the-road father. Fenstad glanced at the picture and let the silence hang between them before asking, "How are you, Ma?"

"I'm all right." She leaned back in the sofa, whose springs made a strange, almost human groan. "I want to get out. I spend too much time in this place in January. You should expand my horizons. Take me somewhere."

"Come to my composition class," Fenstad said. "I'll pick you up at dinnertime on Tuesday. Eat early."

"They'll notice me," she said, squinting. "I'm too old."

"I'll introduce you," her son said. "You'll fit right in."

Fenstad wrote brochures in the publicity department of a computer company during the day, and taught an extension English-composition class at the downtown campus of the state university two nights a week. He didn't need the money; he taught the class because he liked teaching strangers and because he enjoyed the sense of hope that classrooms held for him. This hopefulness and didacticism he had picked up from his mother.

On Tuesday night she was standing at the door of the retirement apartment building, dressed in a dark blue overcoat—her best. Her stylishness was belied slightly by a pair of old fuzzy red earmuffs. Inside the car Fenstad noticed that she had put on perfume, unusual for her. Leaning back, she gazed out contentedly at the nighttime lights.

"Who's in this group of students?" she asked. "Working-class people, I hope. Those are the ones you should be teaching. Anything else is just a career."

"Oh, they work, all right." He looked at his mother and saw, as they passed under a streetlight, a combination of sadness and delicacy in her face. Her usual mask of tough optimism seemed to be deserting her. He braked at a red light and said, "I have a hairdresser and a garage mechanic and a housewife, a Mrs. Nelson, and three guys who're sanitation workers. Plenty of others. One guy you'll really like is a young black man with glasses who sits in the back row and reads *Workers' Vanguard* and Bakunin during class. He's brilliant. I don't know why he didn't test out of this class. His name's York Follette, and he's—"

"I want to meet him," she said quickly. She scowled at the moonlit snow. "A man with ideas. People like that have gone out of my life." She looked over at her son. "What I hate about being my age is how *nice* everyone tries to be. I was never nice, but now everybody is pelting me with sugar cubes." She opened her window an inch and let the cold air blow over her, ruffling her stiff gray hair.

When they arrived at the school, snow had started to fall, and at the other end of the parking lot a police car's flashing light beamed long crimson rays through the dense flakes. Fenstad's mother walked deliberately toward the door, shaking her head mistrustfully at the building and the police. Approaching the steps, she took her son's hand. "I liked the columns on the old buildings," she said, "the old university buildings, I mean. I liked Greek Revival better than this Modernist-bunker stuff." Inside, she blinked in the light at the smooth, waxed linoleum floors and cement-block walls. She held up her hand to shade her eyes. Fenstad took her elbow to guide her over the snow melting in puddles in the entryway. "I never asked you what you're teaching tonight."

"Logic," Fenstad said.

"Ah." She smiled and nodded. "Dialectics!"

"Not quite. Just logic."

She shrugged. She was looking at the clumps of students standing in the glare of the hallway, drinking coffee from paper cups and smoking cigarettes in the general conversational din. She wasn't used to such noise: she stopped in the middle of the corridor underneath a wall clock and stared happily in no particular direction. With her eyes shut she breathed in the close air, smelling of wet overcoats and smoke, and Fenstad remembered how much his mother had always liked smoke-filled rooms, where ideas fought each other, and where some of those ideas died.

"Come on," he said, taking her hand again. Inside Fenstad's classroom six people sat in the angular postures of pre-boredom. York Follette was already in the back row, his copy of *Workers' Vanguard* shielding his face. Fenstad's mother headed straight for him and sat down in the desk next to his. Fenstad saw them shake hands, and in two minutes they were talking in low, rushed murmurs. He saw York Follette laugh quietly and nod. What was it that blacks saw and appreciated in his mother? They had always liked her—written to her, called her, checked up on her—and Fenstad wondered if they recognized something in his mother that he himself had never been able to see.

At seven thirty-five most of the students had arrived and were talking to each other vigorously, as if they didn't want Fenstad to start and thought they could delay him. He stared at them, and when they wouldn't quiet down, he made himself rigid and said, "Good evening. We have a guest tonight." Immediately the class grew silent. He held his arm out straight, indicating with a flick of his hand the old woman in the back row. "My mother," he said. "Clara Fenstad." For the first time all semester his students appeared to be paying attention: they turned around collectively and looked at Fenstad's mother, who smiled and waved. A few of the students began to applaud; others joined in. The applause was quiet but apparently genuine. Fenstad's mother brought herself slowly to her feet and made a suggestion of a bow. Two of the students sitting in front of her turned around and began to talk to her. At the front of the class Fenstad started his lecture on logic, but his mother wouldn't quiet down. This was a class for adults. They were free to do as they liked.

Lowering his head and facing the blackboard, Fenstad reviewed problems in logic, following point by point the outline set down by the textbook: *post hoc* fallacies, false authorities, begging the question, circular reasoning, *ad hominem* arguments, all the rest. Explaining these problems, his back turned, he heard sighs of boredom, boldly expressed. Occasionally he glanced at the back of the room. His mother was watching him carefully, and her face was expressing all the complexity of dismay. Dismay radiated from her. Her disappointment wasn't personal, because his mother didn't think that people as individuals were at fault for what they did. As usual, her disappointed hope was located in history and in the way people agreed with already existing histories.

She was angry with him for collaborating with grammar. She would call it unconsciously installed authority. Then she would find other names for it.

"All right," he said loudly, trying to make eye contact with someone in the room besides his mother, "let's try some examples. Can anyone tell me what, if anything, is wrong with the following sentence? 'I, like most people, have a unique problem.'"

The three sanitation workers, in the third row, began to laugh. Fenstad caught himself glowering and singled out the middle one.

"Yes, it is funny, isn't it?"

The man in the middle smirked and looked at the floor. "I was just thinking of my unique problem."

"Right," Fenstad said. "But what's wrong with saying, 'I, like most people, have a unique problem'?"

"Solving it?" This was Mrs. Nelson, who sat by the window so that she could gaze at the tree outside, lit by a streetlight. All through class she looked at the tree as if it were a lover.

"Solving what?"

"Solving the problem you have. What is the problem?"

"That's actually not what I'm getting at," Fenstad said. "Although it's a good *related* point. I'm asking what might be wrong logically with that sentence."

"It depends," Harold Robinson said. He worked in a service station and sometimes came to class wearing his work shirt with his name tag, HAROLD, stitched into it. "It depends on what your problem is. You haven't told us your problem."

"No," Fenstad said, "my problem is *not* the problem." He thought of Alice in Wonderland and felt, physically, as if he himself were getting small. "Let's try this again. What might be wrong with saying that most people have a unique problem?"

"You shouldn't be so critical," Timothy Melville said. "You should look on the bright side, if possible."

"What?"

"He's right," Mrs. Nelson said. "Most people have unique problems, but many people do their best to help themselves, such as taking night classes or working at meditation."

"No doubt that's true," Fenstad said. "But why can't most people have a unique problem?"

"Oh, I disagree," Mrs. Nelson said, still looking at her tree. Fenstad glanced at it and saw that it was crested with snow. It *was* beautiful. No wonder she looked at it. "I believe that most people do have unique problems. They just shouldn't talk about them all the time."

"Can anyone," Fenstad asked, looking at the back wall and hoping to see something there that was not wall, "can anyone give me an example of a unique problem?"

"Divorce," Barb Kjellerud said. She sat near the door and knitted during class. She answered questions without looking up. "Divorce is unique."

"No, it isn't!" Fenstad said, failing in the crucial moment to control his voice. He and his mother exchanged glances. In his mother's face for a split second was the history of her compassionate, ambivalent attention to him. "Divorce is not unique." He waited to calm himself. "It's everywhere. Now try again. Give me a unique problem."

Silence. "This is a trick question," Arlene Hubbly said. "I'm sure it's a trick question."

"Not necessarily. Does anyone know what *unique* means?"

"One of a kind," York Follette said, gazing at Fenstad with dry amusement. Sometimes he took pity on Fenstad and helped him out of jams. Fenstad's mother smiled and nodded.

"Right," Fenstad crowed, racing toward the blackboard as if he were about to write something. "So let's try again. Give me a unique problem."

"You give *us* a unique problem," one of the sanitation workers said. Fenstad didn't know whether he'd been given a statement or a command. He decided to treat it as a command.

"All right," he said. He stopped and looked down at his shoes. Maybe it *was* a trick question. He thought for ten seconds. Problem after problem presented itself to him. He thought of poverty, of the assaults on the earth, of the awful complexities of love. "I can't think of one," Fenstad said. His hands went into his pockets.

"That's because problems aren't personal," Fenstad's mother said from the back of the room. "They're collective." She waited while several students in the class sat up and nodded. "And people must work together on their solutions." She talked for another two minutes, taking the subject out of logic and putting it neatly in politics, where she knew it belonged.

The snow had stopped by the time the class was over. Fenstad took his mother's arm and escorted her to the car. After letting her down on the passenger side and starting the engine, he began to clear the front windshield. He didn't have a scraper and had forgotten his gloves, so he was using his bare hands. When he brushed the snow away on his mother's side, she looked out at him, surprised, a terribly aged Sleeping Beauty awakened against her will.

Once the car had warmed up, she was in a gruff mood and repositioned herself under the seat belt while making quiet but aggressive remarks. The sight of the new snow didn't seem to calm her. "Logic," she said at last. "That wasn't logic. Those are just rhetorical tactics. It's filler and drudgery."

"I don't want to discuss it now."

"All right. I'm sorry. Let's talk about something more pleasant."

They rode together in silence. Then she began to shake her head. "Don't take me home," she said. "I want to have a spot of tea somewhere before I go back. A nice place where they serve tea, all right?"

He parked outside an all-night restaurant with huge front plate-glass windows; it was called Country Bob's. He held his mother's elbow from the car to the door. At the door, looking back to make sure that he had turned off his headlights, he saw his tracks and his mother's in the snow. His were separate footprints, but hers formed two long lines.

Inside, at the table, she sipped her tea and gazed at her son for a long time. "Thanks for the adventure, Harry. I do appreciate it. What're you doing in class next week? Oh, I remember. How-to papers. That should be interesting."

"Want to come?"

"Very much. I'll keep quiet next time, if you want me to."

Fenstad shook his head. "It's okay. It's fun having you along. You can say whatever you want. The students loved you. I knew you'd be a sensation, and you were. They'd probably rather have you teaching the class than me."

He noticed that his mother was watching something going on behind him, and Fenstad turned around in the booth so that he could see what it was. At first all he saw was a woman, a young woman with long hair wet from snow and hanging in clumps, talking in the aisle to two young men, both of whom were nodding at her. Then she moved on to the next table. She spoke softly. Fenstad couldn't hear her words, but he saw the solitary customer to whom she was speaking shake his head once, keeping his eyes down. Then the woman saw Fenstad and his mother. In a moment she was standing in front of them.

She wore two green plaid flannel shirts and a thin torn jacket. Like Fenstad, she wore no gloves. Her jeans were patched, and she gave off a strong smell, something like hay, Fenstad thought, mixed with tar and sweat. He looked down at her feet and saw that she was wearing penny loafers with no socks. Coins, old pennies, were in both shoes; the leather was wet and cracked. He looked in the woman's face. Under a hat that seemed to collapse on either side of her head, the woman's face was thin and chalk-white except for the fatigue lines under her eyes. The eyes themselves were bright blue, beautiful, and crazy. To Fenstad, she looked desperate, percolating slightly with insanity, and he was about to say so to his mother when the woman bent down toward him and said, "Mister, can you spare any money?"

Involuntarily, Fenstad looked toward the kitchen, hoping that the manager would spot this person and take her away. When he looked back again, his mother was taking her blue coat off, wriggling in the booth to free her arms from the sleeves. Stopping and starting again, she appeared to be stuck inside the coat; then she lifted herself up, trying to stand, and with a quick, quiet groan slipped the coat off. She reached down and folded the coat over and held it toward the woman. "Here," she said. "Here's my coat. Take it before my son stops me."

"Mother, you can't." Fenstad reached forward to grab the coat, but his mother pulled it away from him.

When Fenstad looked back at the woman, her mouth was open, showing several gray teeth. Her hands were outstretched, and he understood, after a moment, that this was a posture of refusal, a gesture saying no, and that the woman wasn't used to it and did it awkwardly. Fenstad's mother was standing and trying to push the coat toward the woman, not toward her hands but lower, at waist level, and she was saying, "Here, here, here, here." The sound, like a human birdcall, frightened Fenstad, and he stood up quickly, reached for his wallet, and removed the first two bills he could find, two twenties. He grabbed the woman's chapped, ungloved left hand.

"Take these," he said, putting the two bills in her icy palm, "for the love of God, and please go."

He was close to her face. Tonight he would pray for her. For a moment the woman's expression was vacant. His mother was still pushing the coat at her, and the woman was unsteadily bracing herself. The woman's mouth was open, and her stagnant-water breath washed over him. "I know you," she said. "You're my little baby cousin."

"Go away, please," Fenstad said. He pushed at her. She turned, clutching his money. He reached around to put his hands on his mother's shoulders. "Ma," he said, "she's gone now. Mother, sit down. I gave her money for a coat." His mother fell down on her side of the booth, and her blue coat rolled over on the bench beside her, showing the label and the shiny inner lining. When he looked up, the woman who had been begging had disappeared, though he could still smell her odor, an essence of wretchedness.

"Excuse me, Harry," his mother said. "I have to go to the bathroom."

She rose and walked toward the front of the restaurant, turned a corner, and was out of sight. Fenstad sat and tried to collect himself. When the waiter came, a boy with an earring and red hair in a flattop, Fenstad just shook his head and said, "More tea." He realized that his mother hadn't taken off her earmuffs, and the image of his mother in the ladies' room with her earmuffs on gave him a fit of uneasiness. After getting up from the booth and following the path that his mother had taken, he stood outside the ladies'-room door and, when no one came in or out, he knocked. He waited for a decent interval. Still hearing no answer, he opened the door.

His mother was standing with her arms down on either side of the first sink. She was holding herself there, her eyes following the hot water as it poured from the tap around the bright porcelain sink down into the drain, and she looked furious. Fenstad touched her and she snapped toward him.

"Your logic!" she said.

He opened the door for her and helped her back to the booth. The second cup of tea had been served, and Fenstad's mother sipped it in silence. They did not converse. When she had finished, she said, "All right. I do feel better now. Let's go."

At the curb in front of her apartment building he leaned forward and kissed her on the cheek. "Pick me up next Tuesday," she said. "I want to go back to that class." He nodded. He watched as she made her way past the security guard at the front desk; then he put his car into drive and started home.

That night he skated in the dark for an hour with his friend, Susan, the pharmacist. She was an excellent skater; they had met on the ice. She kept late hours and, like Fenstad, enjoyed skating at night. She listened attentively to his story about his mother and the woman in the restaurant. To his great relief she recommended no course of action. She listened. She didn't believe in giving advice, even when asked.

The following Tuesday, Fenstad's mother was again in the back row next to York Follette. One of the fluorescent lights overhead was flickering, which gave the room, Fenstad thought, a sinister quality, like a debtors' prison or a refuge for the homeless. He'd been thinking about such people for the entire week. For seven days now he had caught whiffs of the woman's breath in the air, and one morning, Friday, he thought he caught a touch of the rotten-celery smell on his own breath, after a particularly difficult sales meeting.

Tonight was how-to night. The students were expected to stand at the front of the class and read their papers, instructing their peers and answering questions if necessary. Starting off, and reading her paper in a frightened monotone, Mrs. Nelson told the class how to bake a cheese soufflé. Arlene Hubbly's paper was about mushroom hunting. Fenstad was put off by the introduction. "The advantage to mushrooms," Arlene Hubbly read, "is that they are delicious. The disadvantage to mushrooms is that they can make you sick, even die." But then she explained how to recognize the common shaggy mane by its cylindrical cap and dark tufts; she drew a model on the board. She warned the class against the *Clitocybe illudens,* the Jack-o'-Lantern. "Never eat a mushroom like this one or *any* mushroom that glows in the dark. Take heed!" she said, fixing her gaze on the class. Fenstad saw his mother taking rapid notes. Harold Ronson, the mechanic, reading his own prose painfully and slowly, told the class how to get rust spots out of their automobiles. Again Fenstad noticed his mother taking notes. York Follette told the class about the proper procedures for laying down attic insulation and how to know when enough was enough, so that a homeowner wouldn't be robbed blind, as he put it, by the salesmen, in whose ranks he had once counted himself.

Barb Kjellerud had brought along a cassette player, and told the class that her hobby was ballroom dancing; she would instruct them in the basic waltz.

She pushed the play button on the tape machine, and "Tales from the Vienna Woods" came booming out. To the accompaniment of the music she read her paper, illustrating, as she went, how the steps were to be performed. She danced alone in front of them, doing so with flair. Her blond hair swayed as she danced, Fenstad noticed. She looked a bit like a contestant in a beauty contest who had too much personality to win. She explained to the men the necessity of leading. Someone had to lead, she said, and tradition had given this responsibility to the male. Fenstad heard his mother snicker.

When Barb Kjellerud asked for volunteers, Fenstad's mother raised her hand. She said she knew how to waltz and would help out. At the front of the class she made a counterclockwise motion with her hand, and for the next minute, sitting at the back of the room, Fenstad watched his mother and one of the sanitation workers waltzing under the flickering fluorescent lights.

"What a wonderful class," Fenstad's mother said on the way home. "I hope you're paying attention to what they tell you."

Fenstad nodded. "Tea?" he asked.

She shook her head. "Where're you going after you drop me off?"

"Skating," he said. "I usually go skating. I have a date."

"With the pharmacist? In the dark?"

"We both like it, Ma." As he drove, he made an all-purpose gesture. "The moon and the stars," he said simply.

When he left her off, he felt unsettled. He considered, as a point of courtesy, staying with her a few minutes, but by the time he had this idea he was already away from the building and was headed down the street.

He and Susan were out on the ice together, skating in large circles, when Susan pointed to a solitary figure sitting on a park bench near the lake's edge. The sky had cleared; the moon gave everything a cold, fine-edged clarity. When Fenstad followed the line of Susan's finger, he saw at once that the figure on the bench was his mother. He realized it simply because of the way she sat there, drawn into herself, attentive even in the winter dark. He skated through the uncleared snow over the ice until he was standing close enough to speak to her. "Mother," he said, "what are you doing here?"

She was bundled up, a thick woolen cap drawn over her head, and two scarves covering much of her face. He could see little other than the two lenses of her glasses facing him in the dark. "I wanted to see you two," she told him. "I thought you'd look happy, and you did. I like to watch happiness. I always have."

"How can you see us? We're so far away."

"That's how I saw you."

This made no sense to him, so he asked, "How'd you get here?"

"I took a cab. That part was easy."

"Aren't you freezing?"

"I don't know. I don't know if I'm freezing or not."

He and Susan took her back to her apartment as soon as they could get their boots on. In the car Mrs. Fenstad insisted on asking Susan what kind of safety procedures were used to ensure that drugs weren't smuggled out of pharmacies and sold illegally, but she didn't appear to listen to the answer, and by the time they reached her building, she seemed to be falling asleep. They helped her up to her apartment. Susan thought that they should give her a warm bath before putting her into bed, and, together, they did. She did not protest. She didn't even seem to notice them as they guided her in and out of the bath.

Fenstad feared that his mother would catch some lung infection, and it turned out to be bronchitis, which kept her in her apartment for the first three weeks of February, until her cough went down. Fenstad came by every other day to see how she was, and one Tuesday, after work, he went up to her floor and heard piano music: an old recording, which sounded much-played, of the brightest and fastest jazz piano he had ever heard—music of superhuman brilliance. He swung open the door to her apartment and saw York Follette sitting near his mother's bed. On the bedside table was a small tape player, from which the music poured into the room.

Fenstad's mother was leaning back against the pillow, smiling, her eyes closed.

Follette turned toward Fenstad. He had been talking softly. He motioned toward the tape machine and said, "Art Tatum. It's a cut called 'Battery Bounce.' Your mother's never heard it."

"Jazz, Harry," Fenstad's mother said, her eyes still closed, not needing to see her son. "York is explaining to me about Art Tatum and jazz. Next week he's going to try something more progressive on me." Now his mother opened her eyes. "Have you ever heard such music before, Harry?"

They were both looking at him. "No," he said, "I never heard anything like it."

"This is my unique problem, Harry." Fenstad's mother coughed and then waited to recover her breath. "I never heard enough jazz." She smiled. "What glimpses!" she said at last.

After she recovered, he often found her listening to the tape machine that York Follette had given her. She liked to hear the Oscar Peterson Trio as the sun set and the lights of evening came on. She now often mentioned glimpses. Back at home, every night, Fenstad spoke about his mother in his prayers of remembrance and thanksgiving, even though he knew she would disapprove.

◼ Notes on Craft and Context

On Plot in Characterization

Before we consider how carefully this story has been built, let's look at what appear to be loose ends. Near action's end Fenstad's mother, sitting at the pond's black edge, watches her son skate—with Susan—because "I thought you'd look happy, and you did. I like to watch happiness. I always have." We may conclude that she's no longer angry at him for having left his wife a decade earlier; she knows he must move on. From the repeated early references to Fenstad's daughter, Sharon, we expect the girl to make an appearance—if only to demonstrate, by interaction with her father, what sort of parent he is. But real life is rarely so neat or symmetrical; the "well-made" story can fail to represent that slipshod thing, reality. What brings York Follette to Clara's apartment, for example, is a conversation we don't hear. So there's a sense of life lived elsewhere, *off the page.*

Note also how the unexpressed acquires more importance than that which is discussed. It's like skipping the cracks in a pavement or trying not to think about the word "rhinoceros"; suddenly what matters are the pavement cracks or the word "rhinoceros" itself. Early on, Fenstad—called "Harry" by his mother though "Fenstad" by everyone else—examines his mother's apartment; her first name is used only once in this story, when he introduces her as "Clara Fenstad" to the members of the class. He hunts for "any signs of memory loss or depression." Though he "found none," the issue of her possible senility is raised at the beginning of the action and never quite dismissed. For most of the story "Fenstad's mother" seems to be lucid, clear-sighted, but there's a brilliant allusion to Alzheimer's in the description of her walk. One of the symptoms of "memory loss or depression" is a shuffling, foot-dragging, straight-ahead gait, and when mother and son walk together in snow, "His were separate footprints, but hers formed two long lines."

Too, the older woman's decision to sit in the cold dark is reckless and self-endangering; she shows no more concern for comfort than when, earlier, she tried to give away her own warm coat. Fenstad and Susan recognize the risk she takes, and only their quick intervention, as well as the warm bath they give her back in the apartment, prevents what might have been a lethal chill. Characteristically, she has acted on impulse—taking a taxi to the lake in order to see her son happy—and that impulse imposes a burden on others; it was, as Clara says, the "easy" part.

Counterpointed Characterization: Protagonist and Antagonist

This principled opposition of the two principal characters (**protagonist** and **antagonist**) is announced in the opening lines. Fenstad is a church-going citizen who retains at least the outer trappings of faith; "tonight he would pray" for the outcast woman in the coffee shop and, at the story's conclusion, for his mother in "remembrance and thanksgiving, even though he knew she would disapprove." When she asks him, not quite jokingly, "How's your soul," his mother acknowledges his interest in the spiritual life; she, by contrast, sees things in terms of politics, and would no doubt agree with Karl Marx that "Religion is the opiate of the people."

In a letter to this editor Charles Baxter recalls knowing such women when he was a child: old-time Socialists of the north country who wrote letters to dictators and congressmen, convinced the world would change. He remembers a friend of the family who asked him, "Charley, what are your great plans?" When he responded, "I don't have any," she said, "You should be ashamed." This passionate commitment to the collective as opposed to individual well-being is one of the gulfs between generations—a distance that becomes most clear in the restaurant, though it reverses standard expectation as to the politics of youth and age. When confronted with the crazed panhandling derelict, Fenstad's first reaction is to call the manager; his mother's instinct is to offer up her coat.

A story that spent two pages in lingering detail while a son bathes his aging mother would skirt the sentimental. So too would a story that insisted on the generosity of Clara Fenstad's instinctual response to the beggar woman while dismissing the "blood money" offered by her son. Baxter's approach is more subtle; he takes both sides at once. As in any familial argument between "relative strangers," his characters represent weakness *and* strength; their opposition is not black and white but shaded gradations of gray. In an essay called "**Counterpointed Characterization**" (*Burning Down the House,* 132), the author suggests, "The habit of human contrast, like any path of knowing, carries with it all the dangers of stereotyping and easy categorization. Gossip is usually vicious and inaccurate . . . All the same, I keep thinking of music: character as melody and counter-melody . . ."

The Epiphanic Moment

The encounter with the begging woman is this story's pivot point, the fulcrum on which the plot turns. Baxter pulls no punches; the woman reeks, she has "stagnant-water breath" and "he could still smell her odor, an essence of wretchedness." We as readers might choose to question Fenstad's perception that "she looked desperate, percolating slightly with insanity," but when she says "I know you. You're my little baby cousin," there would seem to be no doubt the woman is deranged. (Compare this scene with the lethal encounter with a madman in Flannery O'Connor's "A Good Man Is Hard to Find" and you can see how essentially benign is Baxter's vision, how subtle his discussion of the attributes of faith. Fenstad's conversion, after all, is not from unbeliever to believer, but rather from someone who stays at a safe remove from misery to someone "thinking about such people for the entire week.") When Susan "recommended no course of action," it comes as a "great relief"; there's no obvious moral or morality here, just a clear unblinking vision of the gulf between his mother's reproachful "Your logic!" and Fenstad's effort to deal with her dismissive scorn.

Humor and Dialogue in Characterization

There's considerable if understated humor in the classroom sequences, a tongue-in-cheek description of Fenstad's hapless attempt to enlighten the adults he's trying to teach. Both in the **dialogue** and commentary ("She was angry with him for collaborating with grammar"), the author invites us to share in the fun. The discussion of "a unique problem" edges up to slapstick, a comic back-and-forth of misunderstanding and loss of verbal precision. Then Fenstad fails "in the crucial moment to control his voice. He and his mother exchanged glances. In his mother's face for a split second was the history of her compassionate, ambivalent attention to him." It remains for the enigmatic York Follette to set things straight; "*unique* means . . . One of a kind."

Music—or, as the author puts it, "melody and counter-melody"—has a part to play in the story's ending. York Follette undertakes to teach his teacher's mother the history of jazz, and she takes true pleasure in his generous instruction. "What glimpses!" may well be the defining phrase of Baxter's artistic strategy; he lets the reader "glimpse" the world of Art Tatum and Oscar Peterson, just as earlier he'd offered a quick look at classroom "problems in logic . . . *post hoc* fallacies, false authorities, begging the question, circular reasoning, *ad hominem* arguments, all the rest."

Extras: Allusions in Characterization

Buried, too, or half-submerged are literary **allusions**. One character is called Timothy Melville—a cap tip to the great nineteenth-century American writer; another, Arlene Hubbly, is named after a character in a Raymond Carver story. The crucial scene in the restaurant alludes to a tale by the Russian Nicolai Gogol called, appropriately enough, "The Overcoat." The conversations that Fenstad and his mother engage in are serious, freighted with meaning—but they don't feel heavy-handed or clamorous with rhetoric; this author rarely calls attention to himself. Note the way that long and complex sentences alternate with simple and brief ones; note how this story's title has been made more human and less abstract than would have been "Composition," the working title of an early draft. When we first meet Fenstad he goes skating by himself; when we watch him again on the ice he holds Susan—"an excellent skater"—in his outstretched arms.

Life off the Page: Development of Minor Characters

Even such secondary figures as Mrs. Nelson, Harold Robinson, and Barb Kjellerud suggest lives lived outside of class; though their purpose in these scenes may merely be to fill the room, the reader feels that each of them could star in their own story if seen steadily and whole. "What glimpses" we are given may be comic but never condescending; the writer turns his readers into witnesses *and* jury, presenting us with both sides of the argument at once.

On Real Characters

For there's no such thing as bravery or beauty or intelligence without at least a constituent part of cowardice, ugliness, stupidity—or at least there's no such thing in realistic fiction. In the context of a fairy tale or **allegory,** a character may be wholly good or wholly evil; in the context of a Charles Baxter short story a character's a complicated mix of each and both. It is this tension between opposites that lends dimension to each of the people in the aptly titled *A Relative Stranger,* as well as to the action and interaction between them. These characters remain enigmatic and surprising—which is to say, alive.

> ■ **WRITER'S VIEW:** *"Fenstad's Mother" grew out of an earlier story-draft called "Composition," which concerned a night class in English composition, with a fugitive white-collar teacher and his blue-collar students. The professor, an earlier version of Fenstad, kept losing his composure. As it developed, the story seemed comic but not particularly resonant, and it did not seem to be about much of anything except superficial misunderstandings. It needed some shadows, some darkening-agent.*
>
> *Thinking over the story, I happened to remember one occasion when I was visiting my aunt, who lived in Minneapolis; before I arrived at her house, she had been writing a letter to General Pinochet, berating him. She showed me the letter. This memory in turn led me to think of the old-time Socialist women I had known in the Twin Cities, and that, in turn, made me think of dramatic situations in which a progressive or radical parent comes into conflict with a more conservative son or daughter.*
>
> *Armed with this counterpointed characterization between Fenstad and his mother, I went back to work on the story, trying to stay, in point of view, very close to Fenstad without giving him away. The story's situation and submerged conflict are triangulated and brought to the surface by the appearance of the panhandling woman in the restaurant. The change in Fenstad happens very quickly and almost invisibly, in the scene in which he and his girlfriend give his mother a bath.*

The story contains several opposing sets of images: freezing cold exteriors and hot interiors, darkness and light, isolation and community. Cold, darkness, and isolation gradually give way to their opposites as the story goes on, though they do not leave the stage entirely. I wanted the style and the language to be relatively transparent, except for the examples of logic Fenstad uses in his classroom, and in the scene in the restaurant, where all the idioms seem ready to spiral out of control. Even in realism, madness and misery must always have a place on the stage. (Letter to Nicholas Delbanco, 27 Aug. 2001)

Applications and Connections

- What is it, in your opinion, that makes a character—a principal or a minor one—real? Is it something universal in his experience, something quirky about her, the way he responds to another character, a line of dialogue (or inner monologue), the way she wears her hat? Re-read "Fenstad's Mother" and make a mark by the first sentence where you feel each character comes to life. What different techniques does Baxter employ?
- Most stories contain a turning point, a moment when a leading character comes to a realization that changes him or her. Although this moment is often sudden—an epiphany—it is not solely the result of the **catalyst** that causes it. How does Baxter set the stage for this epiphanic moment? What details has he offered about Fenstad and his mother that make this moment both believable and resonant? Conversely, what kinds of details would make an epiphany inevitable and **anticlimactic?** What is the difference between a **climax** and an epiphany?
- To give your own characters a sense of life lived "off the page," ask yourself questions about everyone who steps onto it. While you don't need to (and probably shouldn't) include every detail of a character's history in the text of the story, having a sense of those details makes both your character and your story as a whole more believable. Some of the exercises below prompt you to explore what's happening off the page, to major and minor characters, in "Fenstad's Mother."

Exercises

1. If this story had been called "Fenstad's Father," what would change? "Fenstad's Sister"? "Fenstad's Second-Cousin Twice-Removed"?

2. "To express grief on skates seemed possible, and Fenstad liked to do so." Write the scene of how he skates and what grief he tries to express.

3. Have Fenstad's mother talk to York Follette about the class, while listening to jazz; re-create their conversation. Then have Follette tell his sister what he did that night.

4. Tell the story of Fenstad's mother's marriage and what happened to her husband; how does she solace herself in her privacy and how afflicted with Alzheimer's is Clara in actual fact?

5. Have Susan meet Eleanor at the A&P checkout line; have them go out for coffee together and discuss their romantic and marital woes.

6. Try to "give an example of a unique problem." Make Harry the subject or object of the problem; then explain why he "can't think of one."

7. " . . . she was in a gruff mood and repositioned herself under the seat belt while making quiet but aggressive remarks. The sight of the new snow didn't seem to calm her." Flesh out, for two pages, the drive and the scene.

8. Have Harold Robinson and Timothy Melville go ballroom dancing with Mrs. Nelson and Barb Kjellerud; have them discuss that week's class.

9. During a coffee break in the publicity department of the computer company he works for, Fenstad makes a political speech. What does he say and to whom?

10. Write a short story called "What glimpses!" in the third person, then the first.

CHAPTER 4

DIALOGUE:
Minimalism and the Monologue

RAYMOND CARVER, "A Small, Good Thing"

■ **WRITER'S VIEW:** *Every great or even every very good writer makes the world over according to his own specifications . . . It's akin to style, what I'm talking about, but it isn't style alone. It is the writer's particular and unmistakable signature on everything he writes. It is his world and no other. This is one of the things that distinguishes one writer from another. Not talent. There's plenty of that around. But a writer who has some special way of looking at things and who gives artistic expression to that way of looking: that writer may be around for a time. ("On Writing," Fires [London: Picador Press, 1986])*

© 2003 by Jill Krementz

Raymond Carver was born in Clatskanie, Oregon, in 1939, and raised in Yakima, Washington, where his father worked in a sawmill. His parents struggled to get by in the bleak years following the Depression, and Carver spent many years struggling as well—working odd jobs, drinking heavily, and going bankrupt twice. He married in 1957 and moved to California with his wife and daughter, then began taking courses part-time at Chico State College. There Carver commenced the study of writing in earnest and developed a lasting friendship with his teacher, the writer John Gardner. Eventually, Carver transferred to Humboldt State College and began publishing his stories and poems in small literary journals. In 1963 he received a fellowship to the Iowa Writer's Workshop for a year, and in 1967 his story, "Will You Please Be Quiet, Please?" was published in *The Best American Short Stories* collection.

Carver would receive that honor again many times, as well as others, but he continued to struggle to find enough money and time to support his family and his vocation. "I used to go out and sit in the car and try to write something on a pad on my knee," he once told an interviewer. "After years of working crap jobs and raising kids and trying to write, I realized I needed to write things I could finish and be done with in a hurry" ("The Art of Fiction LXXVI," interview by Mona Simpson, *The Paris Review* 88 [1983]). This sense of urgency may explain why he never completed a novel, but published only poems and short stories. Even within these shorter forms, Carver was notable for his spare, minimalist approach.

Look again at the second sentence of the "Writer's View": "It's akin to style, what I'm talking about, but it isn't style alone." Carver is *writing,* not *talking* here, but the offhand, conversational quality of such a formulation—"what I'm talking about"—is characteristic of his prose; he makes the reader feel like a good buddy in a bar, and the complexities of style are masked by simple diction. If Barth invites us, everywhere, to *notice* what he's up to as author, Carver takes the opposite tack and asks us to take it for granted: "There's plenty of that around."

His first book of poems, *Near Klamath,* appeared in 1968 and his first short-story collection, *Will You Please Be Quiet, Please?* in 1976. Carver received a National Book Award nomination for that work, and followed it with the collection, *What We Talk about When We Talk about Love* (1981). His next two collections of stories, *Cathedral* (1984) and *Where I'm Calling From* (1988), were each nominated for the Pulitzer Prize. Carver's other books of poetry include *Where Water Comes Together with Other Water* (1985), *Ultramarine* (1986), and *A New Path to the Waterfall* (1989). *Fires* (1986) is a collection of essays—including a tribute to Gardner—as well as poems and stories. Several of Carver's stories, including "A Small, Good Thing," were used by director Robert Altman as the basis for the 1993 film *Short Cuts.*

For a variety of reasons Carver felt his life was divided in two and that the dividing point came in 1977, the year he gave up drinking. Thereafter, his career flourished, and he was able to live off the proceeds of his writing, teaching, and fellowships, such as the Guggenheim and the Mildred and Harold Strauss Living Award. He also divorced his wife and began a new partnership with the writer Tess Gallagher, whom he later married. In 1987 Carver was diagnosed with lung cancer. He died on August 2, 1988.

A Small, Good Thing

Saturday afternoon she drove to the bakery in the shopping center. After looking through a loose-leaf binder with photographs of cakes taped onto the pages, she ordered chocolate, the child's favorite. The cake she chose was decorated with a space ship and launching pad under a sprinkling of white stars, and a planet made of red frosting at the other end. His name, SCOTTY, would be in green letters beneath the planet. The baker, who was an older man with a thick neck, listened without saying anything when she told him the child would be eight years old next Monday. The baker wore a white apron that looked like a smock. Straps cut under his arms, went around in back and then to the front again, where they were secured under his heavy waist. He wiped his hands on his apron as he listened to her. He kept his eyes down on the photographs and let her talk. He let her take her time. He'd just come to work and he'd be there all night, baking, and he was in no real hurry.

She gave the baker her name, Ann Weiss, and her telephone number. The cake would be ready on Monday morning, just out of the oven, in plenty of time for the child's party that afternoon. The baker was not jolly. There were no pleasantries between them, just the minimum exchange of words, the necessary information. He made her feel uncomfortable, and she didn't like that. While he was bent over the counter with the pencil in his hand, she studied his coarse features and wondered if he'd ever done anything else with his life besides be a baker. She was a mother and thirty-three years old, and it seemed to her that everyone, especially someone the baker's age—a man old enough to be her father—must have children who'd gone through this special time of cakes and birthday parties. There must be that between them, she thought. But he was abrupt with her—not rude, just abrupt. She gave up trying to make friends with him. She looked into the back of the bakery and could see a long, heavy wooden table with aluminum pie pans stacked at one end; and beside the table a metal container filled with empty racks. There was an enormous oven. A radio was playing country-Western music.

The baker finished printing the information on the special order card and closed up the binder. He looked at her and said, "Monday morning." She thanked him and drove home.

On Monday morning, the birthday boy was walking to school with another boy. They were passing a bag of potato chips back and forth and the birthday boy was trying to find out what his friend intended to give him for his birthday that afternoon. Without looking, the birthday boy stepped off the curb at an intersection and was immediately knocked down by a car. He fell on his side with his head in the gutter and his legs out in the road. His eyes were closed, but his legs moved back and forth as if he were trying to climb over something. His friend dropped the potato chips and started to cry. The car had gone a hundred feet or so and stopped in the middle of the road. The man in the driver's seat looked back over his shoulder. He waited until the boy got unsteadily to his feet. The boy wobbled a little. He looked dazed, but okay. The driver put the car into gear and drove away.

The birthday boy didn't cry, but he didn't have anything to say about anything either. He wouldn't answer when his friend asked him what it felt like to be hit by a car. He walked home, and his friend went on to school. But after the birthday boy was inside his house and was telling his mother about it—she sitting beside him on the sofa, holding his hands in her lap, saying, "Scotty, honey, are you sure you feel all right, baby?" thinking she would call the doctor anyway—he suddenly lay back on the sofa, closed his eyes, and went limp. When she couldn't wake him up, she hurried to the telephone and called her husband at work. Howard told her to remain calm, remain calm, and then he called an ambulance for the child and left for the hospital himself.

Of course, the birthday party was cancelled. The child was in the hospital with a mild concussion and suffering from shock. There'd been vomiting, and his lungs had taken in fluid which needed pumping out that afternoon. Now he simply seemed to be in a very deep sleep—but no coma, Dr. Francis had emphasized, no coma, when he saw the alarm in the parents' eyes. At eleven o'clock that night, when the boy seemed to be resting comfortably enough after the many X-rays and the lab work, and it was just a matter of his waking up and coming around, Howard left the hospital. He and Ann had been at the hospital with the child since that afternoon, and he was going home for a short while to bathe and change clothes. "I'll be back in an hour," he said. She nodded. "It's fine," she said. "I'll be right here." He kissed her on the forehead, and they touched hands. She sat in the chair beside the bed and looked at the child. She was waiting for him to wake up and be all right. Then she could begin to relax.

Howard drove home from the hospital. He took the wet, dark streets very fast, then caught himself and slowed down. Until now, his life had gone smoothly and to his satisfaction—college, marriage, another year of college for the advanced degree in business, a junior partnership in an investment firm. Fatherhood. He was happy and, so far, lucky—he knew that. His parents were still living, his brothers and his sister were established, his friends from college had gone out to take their places in the world. So far, he had kept away from any real harm, from those forces he knew existed and that could cripple or bring down a man if the luck went bad, if things suddenly turned. He pulled into the driveway and parked. His left leg began to tremble. He sat in the car for a minute and tried to deal with the present situation in a rational manner.

Scotty had been hit by a car and was in the hospital, but he was going to be all right. Howard closed his eyes and ran his hand over his face. He got out of the car and went up to the front door. The dog was barking inside the house. The telephone rang and rang while he unlocked the door and fumbled for the light switch. He shouldn't have left the hospital, he shouldn't have. "Goddamn it!" he said. He picked up the receiver and said, "I just walked in the door!"

"There's a cake here that wasn't picked up," the voice on the other end of the line said.

"What are you saying?" Howard asked.

"A cake," the voice said. "A sixteen-dollar cake."

Howard held the receiver against his ear, trying to understand. "I don't know anything about a cake," he said. "Jesus, what are you talking about?"

"Don't hand me that," the voice said.

Howard hung up the telephone. He went into the kitchen and poured himself some whiskey. He called the hospital. But the child's condition remained the same; he was still sleeping and nothing had changed there. While water poured into the tub, Howard lathered his face and shaved. He'd just stretched out in the tub and closed his eyes when the telephone rang again. He hauled himself out, grabbed a towel, and hurried through the house, saying, "Stupid, stupid," for having left the hospital. But when he picked up the receiver and shouted, "Hello!" there was no sound at the other end of the line. Then the caller hung up.

He arrived back at the hospital a little after midnight. Ann still sat in the chair beside the bed. She looked up at Howard, and then she looked back at the child. The child's eyes stayed closed, the head was still wrapped in bandages. His breathing was quiet and regular. From an apparatus over the bed hung a bottle of glucose with a tube running from the bottle to the boy's arm.

"How is he?" Howard said. "What's all this?" waving at the glucose and the tube.

"Dr. Francis's orders," she said. "He needs nourishment. He needs to keep up his strength. Why doesn't he wake up, Howard? I don't understand, if he's all right."

Howard put his hand against the back of her head. He ran his fingers through her hair. "He's going to be all right. He'll wake up in a little while. Dr. Francis knows what's what."

After a time, he said, "Maybe you should go home and get some rest. I'll stay here. Just don't put up with this creep who keeps calling. Hang up right away."

"Who's calling?" she asked.

"I don't know who, just somebody with nothing better to do than call up people. You go on now."

She shook her head. "No," she said, "I'm fine."

"Really," he said. "Go home for a while, and then come back and spell me in the morning. It'll be all right. What did Dr. Francis say? He said Scotty's going to be all right. We don't have to worry. He's just sleeping now, that's all."

A nurse pushed the door open. She nodded at them as she went to the bedside. She took the left arm out from under the covers and put her fingers on the wrist, found the pulse, then consulted her watch. In a little while, she put the arm back under the covers and moved to the foot of the bed, where she wrote something on a clipboard attached to the bed.

"How is he?" Ann said. Howard's hand was a weight on her shoulder. She was aware of the pressure from his fingers.

"He's stable," the nurse said. Then she said, "Doctor will be in again shortly. Doctor's back in the hospital. He's making rounds right now."

"I was saying maybe she'd want to go home and get a little rest," Howard said. "After the doctor comes," he said.

"She could do that," the nurse said. "I think you should both feel free to do that, if you wish." The nurse was a big Scandinavian woman with blond hair. There was the trace of an accent in her speech.

"We'll see what the doctor says," Ann said. "I want to talk to the doctor. I don't think he should keep sleeping like this. I don't think that's a good sign." She brought her hand up to her eyes and let her head come forward a little. Howard's grip tightened on her shoulder, and then his hand moved up to her neck, where his fingers began to knead the muscles there.

"Dr. Francis will be here in a few minutes," the nurse said. Then she left the room.

Howard gazed at his son for a time, the small chest quietly rising and falling under the covers. For the first time since the terrible minutes after Ann's telephone call to him at his office, he felt a genuine fear starting in his limbs. He began shaking his head. Scotty was fine, but instead of sleeping at home in his own bed, he was in a hospital bed with bandages around his head and a tube in his arm. But this help was what he needed right now.

Dr. Francis came in and shook hands with Howard, though they'd just seen each other a few hours before. Ann got up from the chair. "Doctor?"

"Ann," he said and nodded. "Let's just first see how he's doing," the doctor said. He moved to the side of the bed and took the boy's pulse. He peeled back one eyelid and then the other. Howard and Ann stood beside the doctor and watched. Then the doctor turned back the covers and listened to the boy's heart and lungs with his stethoscope. He pressed his fingers here and there on the abdomen. When he was finished, he went to the end of the bed and studied the chart. He noted the time, scribbled something on the chart, and then looked at Howard and Ann.

"Doctor, how is he?" Howard said. "What's the matter with him exactly?"

"Why doesn't he wake up?" Ann said.

The doctor was a handsome, big-shouldered man with a tanned face. He wore a three-piece blue suit, a striped tie, and ivory cufflinks. His gray hair was combed along the sides of his head, and he looked as if he had just come from a concert. "He's all right," the doctor said. "Nothing to shout about, he could be better, I think. But he's all right. Still, I wish he'd wake up. He should wake up pretty soon." The doctor looked at the boy again. "We'll know some more in a couple of hours, after the results of a few more tests are in. But he's all right, believe me, except for the hairline fracture of the skull. He does have that."

"Oh, no," Ann said.

"And a bit of a concussion, as I said before. Of course, you know he's in shock," the doctor said. "Sometimes you see this in shock cases. This sleeping."

"But he's out of any real danger?" Howard said. "You said before he's not in a coma. You wouldn't call this a coma, then—would you, doctor?" Howard waited. He looked at the doctor.

"No, I don't want to call it a coma," the doctor said and glanced over at the boy once more. "He's just in a very deep sleep. It's a restorative measure the body is taking on its own. He's out of any real danger, I'd say that for certain, yes. But we'll know more when he wakes up and the other tests are in," the doctor said.

"It's a coma," Ann said. "Of sorts."

"It's not a coma yet, not exactly," the doctor said. "I wouldn't want to call it coma. Not yet, anyway. He's suffered shock. In shock cases, this kind of reaction is common enough; it's a temporary reaction to bodily trauma. Coma. Well, coma is a deep, prolonged unconsciousness, something that could go on for days, or weeks even. Scotty's not in that area, not as far as we can tell. I'm certain his condition will show improvement by morning. I'm betting that it will. We'll know more when he wakes up, which shouldn't be long now. Of course, you may do as you like, stay here or go home for a time. But by all means feel free to leave the hospital for a while if you want. This is not easy, I know." The doctor gazed at the boy again, watching him, and then he turned to Ann and said, "You try not to worry, little mother. Believe me, we're doing all that can be done. It's just a question of a little more time now." He nodded at her, shook hands with Howard again, and then he left the room.

Ann put her hand over the child's forehead. "At least he doesn't have a fever," she said. Then she said, "My God, he feels so cold, though. Howard? Is he supposed to feel like this? Feel his head."

Howard touched the child's temples. His own breathing had slowed. "I think he's supposed to feel this way right now," he said. "He's in shock, remember? That's what the doctor said. The doctor was just in here. He would have said something if Scotty wasn't okay."

Ann stood there a while longer, working her lip with her teeth. Then she moved over to her chair and sat down.

Howard sat in the chair next to her chair. They looked at each other. He wanted to say something else and reassure her, but he was afraid, too. He took her hand and put it in his lap, and this made him feel better, her hand being there. He picked up her hand and squeezed it. Then he just held her hand. They sat like that for a while, watching the boy and not talking. From time to time, he squeezed her hand. Finally, she took her hand away.

"I've been praying," she said.

He nodded.

She said, "I almost thought I'd forgotten how, but it came back to me. All I had to do was close my eyes and say, 'Please God, help us—help Scotty,' and then the rest was easy. The words were right there. Maybe if you prayed, too," she said to him.

"I've already prayed," he said. "I prayed this afternoon—yesterday afternoon, I mean—after you called, while I was driving to the hospital. I've been praying," he said.

"That's good," she said. For the first time, she felt they were together in it, this trouble. She realized with a start that, until now, it had only been happening to her and to Scotty. She hadn't let Howard into it, though he was there and needed all along. She felt glad to be his wife.

The same nurse came in and took the boy's pulse again and checked the flow from the bottle hanging above the bed.

In an hour, another doctor came in. He said his name was Parsons, from Radiology. He had a bushy mustache. He was wearing loafers, a Western shirt, and a pair of jeans.

"We're going to take him downstairs for more pictures," he told them. "We need to do some more pictures, and we want to do a scan."

"What's that?" Ann said. "A scan?" She stood between this new doctor and the bed. "I thought you'd already taken all your X-rays."

"I'm afraid we need some more," he said. "Nothing to be alarmed about. We just need some more pictures, and we want to do a brain scan on him."

"My God," Ann said.

"It's perfectly normal procedure in cases like this," this new doctor said. "We just need to find out for sure why he isn't back awake yet. It's normal medical procedure, and nothing to be alarmed about. We'll be taking him down in a few minutes," this new doctor said.

In a little while, two orderlies came into the room with a gurney. They were black-haired, dark-complexioned men in white uniforms, and they said a few words to each other in a foreign tongue as they unhooked the boy from the tube and moved him from his bed to the gurney. Then they wheeled him from the room. Howard and Ann got on the same elevator. Ann gazed at the child. She closed her eyes as the elevator began its descent. The orderlies stood at either end of the gurney without saying anything, though once one of the men made a comment to the other in their own language, and the other man nodded slowly in response.

Later that morning, just as the sun was beginning to lighten the windows in the waiting room outside the X-ray department, they brought the boy out and moved him back up to his room. Howard and Ann rode up on the elevator with him once more, and once more they took up their places beside the bed.

They waited all day, but still the boy did not wake up. Occasionally, one of them would leave the room to go downstairs to the cafeteria to drink coffee and then, as if suddenly remembering and feeling guilty, get up from the table and hurry back to the room. Dr. Francis came again that afternoon and examined the boy once more and then left after telling them he was coming along and could wake up at any minute now. Nurses, different nurses from the night before, came in from time to time. Then a young woman from the lab knocked and entered the room. She wore white slacks and a white blouse and carried a little tray of things which she put on the stand beside the bed. Without a word to them, she took blood from the boy's arm. Howard closed his eyes as the woman found the right place on the boy's arm and pushed the needle in.

"I don't understand this," Ann said to the woman.

"Doctor's orders," the young woman said. "I do what I'm told. They say draw that one, I draw. What's wrong with him, anyway?" she said. "He's a sweetie."

"He was hit by a car," Howard said. "A hit-and-run."

The young woman shook her head and looked again at the boy. Then she took her tray and left the room.

"Why won't he wake up?" Ann said. "Howard? I want some answers from these people."

Howard didn't say anything. He sat down again in the chair and crossed one leg over the other. He rubbed his face. He looked at his son and then he settled back in the chair, closed his eyes, and went to sleep.

Ann walked to the window and looked out at the parking lot. It was night, and cars were driving into and out of the parking lot with their lights on. She stood at the window with her hands gripping the sill, and knew in her heart that they were into something now, something hard. She was afraid, and her teeth began to chatter until she tightened her jaws. She saw a big car stop in front of the hospital and someone, a woman in a long coat, get into the car. She wished she were that woman and somebody, anybody, was driving her away from here to somewhere else, a place where she would find Scotty waiting for her when she stepped out of the car, ready to say *Mom* and let her gather him in her arms.

In a little while, Howard woke up. He looked at the boy again. Then he got up from the chair, stretched, and went over to stand beside her at the window. They both stared out at the parking lot. They didn't say anything. But they seemed to feel each other's insides now, as though the worry had made them transparent in a perfectly natural way.

The door opened and Dr. Francis came in. He was wearing a different suit and tie this time. His gray hair was combed along the sides of his head, and he looked as if he had just shaved. He went straight to the bed and examined the boy. "He ought to have come around by now. There's just no good reason for this," he said. "But I can tell you we're all convinced he's out of any danger. We'll just feel better when he wakes up. There's no reason, absolutely none, why he shouldn't come around. Very soon. Oh, he'll have himself a dilly of a headache when he does, you can count on that. But all of his signs are fine. They're as normal as can be."

"It is a coma, then?" Ann said.

The doctor rubbed his smooth cheek. "We'll call it that for the time being, until he wakes up. But you must be worn out. This is hard. I know this is hard. Feel free to go out for a bite," he said. "It would do you good. I'll put a nurse in here while you're gone if you'll feel better about going. Go and have yourselves something to eat."

"I couldn't eat anything," Ann said.

"Do what you need to do, of course," the doctor said. "Anyway, I wanted to tell you that all the signs are good, the tests are negative, nothing showed up at all, and just as soon as he wakes up he'll be over the hill."

"Thank you, doctor," Howard said. He shook hands with the doctor again. The doctor patted Howard's shoulder and went out.

"I suppose one of us should go home and check on things," Howard said. "Slug needs to be fed, for one thing."

"Call one of the neighbors," Ann said. "Call the Morgans. Anyone will feed a dog if you ask them to."

"All right," Howard said. After a while, he said, "Honey, why don't *you* do it? Why don't you go home and check on things, and then come back? It'll do you good. I'll be right here with him. Seriously," he said. "We need to keep up our strength on this. We'll want to be here for a while even after he wakes up."

"Why don't *you* go?" she said. "Feed Slug. Feed yourself."

"I already went," he said. "I was gone for exactly an hour and fifteen minutes. You go home for an hour and freshen up. Then come back."

She tried to think about it, but she was too tired. She closed her eyes and tried to think about it again. After a time, she said, "Maybe I *will* go home for a few minutes. Maybe if I'm not just sitting right here watching him every second, he'll wake up and be all right. You know? Maybe he'll wake up if I'm not here. I'll go home and take a bath and put on clean clothes. I'll feed Slug. Then I'll come back."

"I'll be right here," he said. "You go on home, honey. I'll keep an eye on things here." His eyes were bloodshot and small, as if he'd been drinking for a long time. His clothes were rumpled. His beard had come out again. She touched his face, and then she took her hand back. She understood he wanted to be by himself for a while, not have to talk or share his worry for a time. She picked her purse up from the nightstand, and he helped her into her coat.

"I won't be gone long," she said.

"Just sit and rest for a little while when you get home," he said. "Eat something. Take a bath. After you get out of the bath, just sit for a while and rest. It'll do you a world of good, you'll see. Then come back," he said. "Let's try not to worry. You heard what Dr. Francis said."

She stood in her coat for a minute trying to recall the doctor's exact words, looking for any nuances, any hint of something behind his words other than what he had said. She tried to remember if his expression had changed any when he bent over to examine the child. She remembered the way his features had composed themselves as he rolled back the child's eyelids and then listened to his breathing.

She went to the door, where she turned and looked back. She looked at the child, and then she looked at the father. Howard nodded. She stepped out of the room and pulled the door closed behind her.

She went past the nurses' station and down to the end of the corridor, looking for the elevator. At the end of the corridor, she turned to her right and entered a little waiting room where a Negro family sat in wicker chairs. There was a middle-aged man in a khaki shirt and pants, a baseball cap pushed back on his head. A large woman wearing a housedress and jeans, hair done in dozens of little braids, lay stretched out in one of the chairs smoking a cigarette, her legs crossed at the ankles. The family swung their eyes to Ann as she entered the room. The little table was littered with hamburger wrappers and Styrofoam cups.

"Franklin," the large woman said as she roused herself. "Is it about Franklin?" Her eyes widened. "Tell me now, lady," the woman said. "Is it about Franklin?" She was trying to rise from her chair, but the man had closed his hand over her arm.

"Here, here," he said. "Evelyn."

"I'm sorry," Ann said. "I'm looking for the elevator. My son is in the hospital, and now I can't find the elevator."

"Elevator is down that way, turn left," the man said as he aimed a finger.

The girl drew on her cigarette and stared at Ann. Her eyes were narrowed to slits, and her broad lips parted slowly as she let the smoke escape. The Negro woman let her head fall on her shoulder and looked away from Ann, no longer interested.

"My son was hit by a car," Ann said to the man. She seemed to need to explain herself. "He has a concussion and a little skull fracture, but he's going to be all right. He's in shock now, but it might be some kind of coma, too. That's what really worries us, the coma part. I'm going out for a little while, but my husband is with him. Maybe he'll wake up while I'm gone."

"That's too bad," the man said and shifted in the chair. He shook his head. He looked down at the table, and then he looked back at Ann. She was still standing there. He said, "Our Franklin, he's on the operating table. Somebody cut him. Tried to kill him. There was a fight where he was at. At this party. They say he was just standing and watching. Not bothering nobody. But that don't mean nothing these days. Now he's on the operating table. We're just hoping and praying, that's all we can do now." He gazed at her steadily.

Ann looked at the girl again, who was still watching her, and at the older woman, who kept her head down, but whose eyes were now closed. Ann saw the lips moving silently, making words. She had an urge to ask what those words were. She wanted to talk more with these people who were in the same kind of waiting she was in. She was afraid, and they were afraid. They had that in common. She would have liked to have said something else about the accident, told them more about Scotty, that it had happened on the day of his birthday, Monday, and that he was still unconscious. Yet she didn't know how to begin. She stood looking at them without saying anything more.

She went down the corridor the man had indicated and found the elevator. She waited a minute in front of the closed doors, still wondering if she was doing the right thing. Then she put out her finger and touched the button.

She pulled into the driveway and cut the engine. She closed her eyes and leaned her head against the wheel for a minute. She listened to the ticking sounds the engine made as it began to cool. Then she got out of the car. She could hear the dog barking inside the house. She went to the front door, which was unlocked. She went inside and turned on lights and put on a kettle of water for tea. She opened some dogfood and fed Slug on the back porch. The dog ate in hungry little smacks. It kept running into the kitchen to see that she was going to stay. As she sat down on the sofa with her tea, the telephone rang.

"Yes!" she said as she answered. "Hello!"

"Mrs. Weiss," a man's voice said. It was five o'clock in the morning, and she thought she could hear machinery or equipment of some kind in the background.

"Yes, yes! What is it?" she said. "This is Mrs. Weiss. This is she. What is it, please?" She listened to whatever it was in the background. "Is it Scotty, for Christ's sake?"

"Scotty," the man's voice said. "It's about Scotty, yes. It has to do with Scotty, that problem. Have you forgotten about Scotty?" the man said. Then he hung up.

She dialed the hospital's number and asked for the third floor. She demanded information about her son from the nurse who answered the telephone. Then she asked to speak to her husband. It was, she said, an emergency.

She waited, turning the telephone cord in her fingers. She closed her eyes and felt sick at her stomach. She would have to make herself eat. Slug came in from the back porch and lay down near her feet. He wagged his tail. She pulled at his ear while he licked her fingers. Howard was on the line.

"Somebody just called here," she said. She twisted the telephone cord. "He said it was about Scotty," she cried.

"Scotty's fine," Howard told her. "I mean, he's still sleeping. There's been no change. The nurse has been in twice since you've been gone. A nurse or else a doctor. He's all right."

"This man called. He said it was about Scotty," she told him.

"Honey, you rest for a little while, you need the rest. It must be that same caller I had. Just forget it. Come back down here after you've rested. Then we'll have breakfast or something."

"Breakfast," she said. "I don't want any breakfast."

"You know what I mean," he said. "Juice, something. I don't know. I don't know anything, Ann. Jesus, I'm not hungry, either. Ann, it's hard to talk now. I'm standing here at the desk. Dr. Francis is coming again at eight o'clock this morning. He's going to have something to tell us then, something more definite. That's what one of the nurses said. She didn't know any more than that. Ann? Honey, maybe we'll know something more then. At eight o'clock. Come back here before eight. Meanwhile, I'm right here and Scotty's all right. He's still the same," he added.

"I was drinking a cup of tea," she said, "when the telephone rang. They said it was about Scotty. There was a noise in the background. Was there a noise in the background on that call you had, Howard?"

"I don't remember," he said. "Maybe the driver of the car, maybe he's a psychopath and found out about Scotty somehow. But I'm here with him. Just rest like you were going to do. Take a bath and come back by seven or so, and we'll talk to the doctor together when he gets here. It's going to be all right, honey. I'm here, and there are doctors and nurses around. They say his condition is stable."

"I'm scared to death," she said.

She ran water, undressed, and got into the tub. She washed and dried quickly, not taking the time to wash her hair. She put on clean underwear, wool slacks, and a sweater. She went into the living room, where the dog looked up at her and let its tail thump once against the floor. It was just starting to get light outside when she went out to the car.

She drove into the parking lot of the hospital and found a space close to the front door. She felt she was in some obscure way responsible for what had happened to the child. She let her thoughts move to the Negro family. She remembered the papers, and the teenaged girl staring at her as she drew on her cigarette. "Don't have children," she told the girl's image as she entered the front door of the hospital. "For God's sake, don't."

She took the elevator up to the third floor with two nurses who were just going on duty. It was Wednesday morning, a few minutes before seven. There was a page for a Dr. Madison as the elevator doors slid open on the third floor. She got off behind the nurses, who turned in the other direction and continued the conversation she had interrupted when she'd gotten into the elevator. She walked down the corridor to the little alcove where the Negro family had been waiting. They were gone now, but the chairs were scattered in such a way that it looked as if people had just jumped up from them the minute before. The tabletop was cluttered with the same cups and papers, the ashtray was filled with cigarette butts.

She stopped at the nurses' station. A nurse was standing behind the counter, brushing her hair and yawning.

"There was a Negro boy in surgery last night," Ann said. "Franklin was his name. His family was in the waiting room. I'd like to inquire about his condition."

A nurse who was sitting at a desk behind the counter looked up from a chart in front of her. The telephone buzzed and she picked up the receiver, but she kept her eyes on Ann.

"He passed away," said the nurse at the counter. The nurse held the hair-brush and kept looking at her. "Are you a friend of the family or what?"

"I met the family last night," Ann said. "My own son is in the hospital. I guess he's in shock. We don't know for sure what's wrong. I just wondered about Franklin, that's all. Thank you." She moved down the corridor. Elevator doors the same color as the walls slid open and a gaunt, bald man in white pants and white canvas shoes pulled a heavy cart off the elevator. She hadn't noticed these doors last night. The man wheeled the cart out into the corridor and stopped in front of the room nearest the elevator and consulted a clip-board. Then he reached down and slid a tray out of the cart. He rapped lightly on the door and entered the room. She could smell the unpleasant odors of warm food as she passed the cart. She hurried on without looking at any of the nurses and pushed open the door to the child's room.

Howard was standing at the window with his hands behind his back. He turned around as she came in.

"How is he?" she said. She went over to the bed. She dropped her purse on the floor beside the nightstand. It seemed to her she had been gone a long time. She touched the child's face. "Howard?"

"Dr. Francis was here a little while ago," Howard said. She looked at him closely and thought his shoulders were bunched a little.

"I thought he wasn't coming until eight o'clock this morning," she said quickly.

"There was another doctor with him. A neurologist."

"A neurologist," she said.

Howard nodded. His shoulders were bunching, she could see that. "What'd they say, Howard? For Christ's sake, what'd they say? What is it?"

"They said they're going to take him down and run more tests on him, Ann. They think they're going to operate, honey. Honey, they *are* going to operate. They can't figure out why he won't wake up. It's more than just shock or concussion, they know that much now. It's in his skull, the fracture, it has something, something to do with that, they think. So they're going to operate. I tried to call you, but I guess you'd already left the house."

"Oh, God," she said. "Oh, please, Howard, please," she said, taking his arms.

"Look!" Howard said. "Scotty! Look, Ann!" He turned her toward the bed.

The boy had opened his eyes, then closed them. He opened them again now. The eyes stared straight ahead for a minute, then moved slowly in his head until they rested on Howard and Ann, then traveled away again.

"Scotty," his mother said, moving to the bed.

"Hey, Scott," his father said. "Hey, son."

They leaned over the bed. Howard took the child's hand in his hands and began to pat and squeeze the hand. Ann bent over the boy and kissed his forehead again and again. She put her hands on either side of his face. "Scotty, honey, it's Mommy and Daddy," she said. "Scotty?"

The boy looked at them, but without any sign of recognition. Then his mouth opened, his eyes scrunched closed, and he howled until he had no more air in his lungs. His face seemed to relax and soften then. His lips parted as his last breath was puffed through his throat and exhaled gently through the clenched teeth.

The doctors called it a hidden occlusion and said it was a one-in-a-million circumstance. Maybe if it could have been detected somehow and surgery undertaken immediately, they could have saved him. But more than likely not. In any case, what would they have been looking for? Nothing had shown up in the tests or in the X-rays.

Dr. Francis was shaken. "I can't tell you how badly I feel. I'm so very sorry, I can't tell you," he said as he led them into the doctors' lounge. There was a doctor sitting in a chair with his legs hooked over the back of another chair, watching an early-morning TV show. He was wearing a green delivery-room outfit, loose green pants and green blouse, and a green cap that covered his hair. He looked at Howard and Ann and then looked at Dr. Francis. He got to his feet and turned off the set and went out of the room. Dr. Francis guided Ann to the sofa, sat down beside her, and began to talk in a low, consoling voice. At one point, he leaned over and embraced her. She could feel his chest rising and falling evenly against her shoulder. She kept her eyes open and let him hold her. Howard went into the bathroom, but he left the door open. After a violent fit of weeping, he ran water and washed his face. Then he came out and sat down at the little table that held a telephone. He looked at the telephone as though deciding what to do first. He made some calls. After a time, Dr. Francis used the telephone.

"Is there anything else I can do for the moment?" he asked them.

Howard shook his head. Ann stared at Dr. Francis as if unable to comprehend his words.

The doctor walked them to the hospital's front door. People were entering and leaving the hospital. It was eleven o'clock in the morning. Ann was aware of how slowly, almost reluctantly, she moved her feet. It seemed to her that Dr. Francis was making them leave when she felt they should stay, when it would be more the right thing to do to stay. She gazed out into the parking lot and then turned around and looked back at the front of the hospital. She began shaking her head. "No, no," she said. "I can't leave him here, no." She heard herself say that and thought how unfair it was that the only words that came out were the sort of words used on TV shows where people were stunned by violent or sudden deaths. She wanted her words to be her own. "No," she said, and for some reason the memory of the Negro woman's head lolling on the woman's shoulder came to her. "No," she said again.

"I'll be talking to you later in the day," the doctor was saying to Howard. "There are still some things that have to be done, things that have to be cleared up to our satisfaction. Some things that need explaining."

"An autopsy," Howard said.

Dr. Francis nodded.

"I understand," Howard said. Then he said, "Oh, Jesus. No, I don't understand, doctor. I can't, I can't. I just can't."

Doctor Francis put his arm around Howard's shoulders. "I'm sorry, God, how I'm sorry." He let go of Howard's shoulders and held out his hand. Howard looked at the hand, and then he took it. Dr. Francis put his arms around Ann once more. He seemed full of some goodness she didn't understand. She let her head rest on his shoulder, but her eyes stayed open. She kept looking at the hospital. As they drove out of the parking lot, she looked back at the hospital.

At home, she sat on the sofa with her hands in her coat pockets. Howard closed the door to the child's room. He got the coffee-maker going and then he found an empty box. He had thought to pick up some of the child's things that were scattered around the living room. But instead he sat down beside her on the sofa, pushed the box to one side, and leaned forward, arms between his knees. He began to weep. She pulled his head over into her lap and patted his shoulder. "He's gone," she said. She kept patting his shoulder. Over his sobs, she could hear the coffee-maker hissing in the kitchen. "There, there," she said tenderly. "Howard, he's gone. He's gone and now we'll have to get used to that. To being alone."

In a little while, Howard got up and began moving aimlessly around the room with the box, not putting anything into it, but collecting some things together on the floor at one end of the sofa. She continued to sit with her hands in her coat pockets. Howard put the box down and brought coffee into the living room. Later, Ann made calls to relatives. After each call had been placed and the party had answered, Ann would blurt out a few words and cry for a minute. Then she would quietly explain, in a measured voice, what had happened and tell them about arrangements. Howard took the box out to the garage, where he saw the child's bicycle. He dropped the box and sat down on the pavement beside the bicycle. He took hold of the bicycle awkwardly so that it leaned against his chest. He held it, the rubber pedal sticking into his chest. He gave the wheel a turn.

Ann hung up the telephone after talking to her sister. She was looking up another number when the telephone rang. She picked it up on the first ring.

"Hello," she said, and she heard something in the background, a humming noise. "Hello!" she said. "For God's sake," she said. "Who is this? What is it you want?"

"Your Scotty, I got him ready for you," the man's voice said. "Did you forget him?"

"You evil bastard!" she shouted into the receiver. "How can you do this, you evil son of a bitch?"

"Scotty," the man said. "Have you forgotten about Scotty?" Then the man hung up on her.

Howard heard the shouting and came in to find her with her head on her arms over the table, weeping. He picked up the receiver and listened to the dial tone.

Much later, just before midnight, after they had dealt with many things, the telephone rang again.

"You answer it," she said. "Howard, it's him, I know." They were sitting at the kitchen table with coffee in front of them. Howard had a small glass of whiskey beside his cup. He answered on the third ring.

"Hello," he said. "Who is this? Hello! Hello!" The line went dead. "He hung up," Howard said. "Whoever it was."

"It was him," she said. "That bastard. I'd like to kill him," she said. "I'd like to shoot him and watch him kick," she said.

"Ann, my God," he said.

"Could you hear anything?" she said. "In the background? A noise, machinery, something humming?"

"Nothing, really. Nothing like that," he said. "There wasn't much time. I think there was some radio music. Yes, there was a radio going, that's all I could tell. I don't know what in God's name is going on," he said.

She shook her head. "If I could, could get my hands on him." It came to her then. She knew who it was. Scotty, the cake, the telephone number. She pushed the chair away from the table and got up. "Drive me down to the shopping center," she said. "Howard."

"What are you saying?"

"The shopping center. I know who it is who's calling. I know who it is. It's the baker, the son-of-a-bitching baker, Howard. I had him bake a cake for Scotty's birthday. That's who's calling. That's who has the number and keeps calling us. To harass us about that cake. The baker, that bastard."

They drove down to the shopping center. The sky was clear and stars were out. It was cold, and they ran the heater in the car. They parked in front of the bakery. All of the shops and stores were closed, but there were cars at the far end of the lot in front of the movie theater. The bakery windows were dark, but when they looked through the glass they could see a light in the back room and, now and then, a big man in an apron moving in and out of the white, even light. Through the glass, she could see the display cases and some little tables with chairs. She tried the door. She rapped on the glass. But if the baker heard them, he gave no sign. He didn't look in their direction.

They drove around behind the bakery and parked. They got out of the car. There was a lighted window too high up for them to see inside. A sign near the back door said THE PANTRY BAKERY, SPECIAL ORDERS. She could hear faintly a radio playing inside and something creak—an oven door as it was pulled down? She knocked on the door and waited. Then she knocked again, louder. The radio was turned down and there was a scraping sound now, the distinct sound of something, a drawer, being pulled open and then closed.

Someone unlocked the door and opened it. The baker stood in the light and peered out at them. "I'm closed for business," he said. "What do you want at this hour? It's midnight. Are you drunk or something?"

She stepped into the light that fell through the open door. He blinked his heavy eyelids as he recognized her. "It's you," he said.

"It's me," she said. "Scotty's mother. This is Scotty's father. We'd like to come in."

The baker said, "I'm busy now. I have work to do."

She had stepped inside the doorway anyway. Howard came in behind her. The baker moved back. "It smells like a bakery in here. Doesn't it smell like a bakery in here, Howard?"

"What do you want," the baker said. "Maybe you want your cake? That's it, you decided you want your cake. You ordered a cake, didn't you?"

"You're pretty smart for a baker," she said. "Howard, this is the man who's been calling us." She clenched her fists. She stared at him fiercely. There was a deep burning inside her, an anger that made her feel larger than herself, larger than either of these men.

"Just a minute here," the baker said. "You want to pick up your three-day-old cake? That it? I don't want to argue with you, lady. There it sits over there, getting stale. I'll give it to you for half of what I quoted you. No. You want it? You can have it. It's no good to me, no good to anyone now. It cost me time and money to make that cake. If you want it, okay, if you don't, that's okay, too. I have to get back to work." He looked at them and rolled his tongue behind his teeth.

"More cakes," she said. She knew she was in control of it, of what was increasing in her. She was calm.

"Lady, I work sixteen hours a day in this place to earn a living," the baker said. He wiped his hands on his apron. "I work night and day in here, trying to make ends meet." A look crossed Ann's face that made the baker move back and say, "No trouble, now." He reached to the counter and picked up a rolling pin with his right hand and began to tap it against the palm of his other hand. "You want the cake or not? I have to get back to work. Bakers work at night," he said again. His eyes were small, mean-looking, she thought, nearly lost in the bristly flesh around his cheeks. His neck was thick with fat.

"I know bakers work at night," Ann said. "They make phone calls at night, too. You bastard," she said.

The baker continued to tap the rolling pin against his hand. He glanced at Howard. "Careful, careful," he said to Howard.

"My son's dead," she said with a cold, even finality. "He was hit by a car Monday morning. We've been waiting with him until he died. But, of course, you couldn't be expected to know that, could you? Bakers can't know every-thing—can they, Mr. Baker? But he's dead. He's dead, you bastard!" Just as sud-denly as it had welled in her, the anger dwindled, gave way to something else, a dizzy feeling of nausea. She leaned against the wooden table that was sprinkled with flour, put her hands over her face, and began to cry, her shoulders rocking back and forth. "It isn't fair," she said. "It isn't, isn't fair."

Howard put his hand at the small of her back and looked at the baker. "Shame on you," Howard said to him. "Shame."

The baker put the rolling pin back on the counter. He undid his apron and threw it on the counter. He looked at them, and then he shook his head slowly. He pulled a chair out from under the card table that held papers and receipts, an adding machine, and a telephone directory. "Please sit down," he said. "Let me get you a chair," he said to Howard. "Sit down now, please." The baker went into the front of the shop and returned with two little wrought-iron chairs. "Please sit down, you people."

Ann wiped her eyes and looked at the baker. "I wanted to kill you," she said. "I wanted you dead."

The baker had cleared a space for them at the table. He shoved the adding machine to one side, along with the stacks of notepaper and receipts. He pushed the telephone directory onto the floor, where it landed with a thud. Howard and Ann sat down and pulled their chairs up to the table. The baker sat down, too.

"Let me say how sorry I am," the baker said, putting his elbows on the table. "God alone knows how sorry. Listen to me. I'm just a baker. I don't claim to be anything else. Maybe once, maybe years ago, I was a different kind of human being. I've forgotten, I don't know for sure. But I'm not any longer, if I ever was. Now I'm just a baker. That don't excuse my doing what I did, I know. But I'm deeply sorry. I'm sorry for your son, and sorry for my part in this," the baker said. He spread his hands out on the table and turned them over to reveal his palms. "I don't have any children myself, so I can only imagine what you must be feeling. All I can say to you now is that I'm sorry. Forgive me, if you can," the baker said. "I'm not an evil man, I don't think. Not evil, like you said on the phone. You got to understand what it comes down to is I don't know how to act anymore, it would seem. Please," the man said, "let me ask you if you can find it in your hearts to forgive me?"

It was warm inside the bakery. Howard stood up from the table and took off his coat. He helped Ann from her coat. The baker looked at them for a minute and then nodded and got up from the table. He went to the oven and turned off some switches. He found cups and poured coffee from an electric coffee-maker. He put a carton of cream on the table, and a bowl of sugar.

"You probably need to eat something," the baker said. "I hope you'll eat some of my hot rolls. You have to eat and keep going. Eating is a small, good thing in a time like this," he said.

He served them warm cinnamon rolls just out of the oven, the icing still runny. He put butter on the table and knives to spread the butter. Then the baker sat down at the table with them. He waited. He waited until they each took a roll from the platter and began to eat. "It's good to eat something," he said, watching them. "There's more. Eat up. Eat all you want. There's all the rolls in the world in here."

They ate rolls and drank coffee. Ann was suddenly hungry, and the rolls were warm and sweet. She ate three of them, which pleased the baker. Then he began to talk. They listened carefully. Although they were tired and in anguish, they listened to what the baker had to say. They nodded when the baker began to speak of loneliness, and of the sense of doubt and limitation that had come to him in his middle years. He told them what it was like to be childless all these years. To repeat the days with the ovens endlessly full and endlessly empty. The party food, the celebrations he'd worked over. Icing knuckle-deep. The tiny wedding couples stuck into cakes. Hundreds of them, no, thousands by now. Birthdays. Just imagine all those candles burning. He had a necessary trade. He was a baker. He was glad he wasn't a florist. It was better to be feeding people. This was a better smell anytime than flowers.

"Smell this," the baker said, breaking open a dark loaf. "It's a heavy bread, but rich." They smelled it, then he had them taste it. It had the taste of molasses and coarse grains. They listened to him. They ate what they could. They swallowed the dark bread. It was like daylight under the fluorescent trays of light. They talked on into the early morning, the high, pale cast of light in the windows, and they did not think of leaving.

▦ Notes on Craft and Context

On Economy in Language and Dialogue

Even a quick look at Raymond Carver's short story titles reveals much about his approach to language and storytelling. From "Tell the Women We're

Going" to "Why Don't You Dance?" or "The Third Thing that Killed My Father Off," his narrator deploys the first-person colloquial voice. Overwhelmingly, his characters are ordinary people using ordinary language, and Carver allows them, in effect, to speak as though the reader eavesdrops while they tell their tales. His stories, particularly the earlier ones, unfold rapidly "in scene," with a great deal of dialogue and very little introspection or authorial interference. There's comedy here also, though the characters in "A Small, Good Thing" are anything but lighthearted. Often the narration seems improvisational, even digressive, with a "that reminds me" quality that's casual seeming yet clear; nonetheless, the point of view is all-knowing or omniscient. The rhetoric is simple yet painstakingly precise.

As Carver's student Jay McInerney observes:

> Carver's language was unmistakably like Hemingway's—the simplicity and clarity, the repetitions, the nearly conversational rhythms, the precision of physical description. But Carver completely dispensed with the romantic egoism that made the Hemingway idiom such an awkward model for other writers in the late twentieth century. The cafés and *pensiones* and battlefields of Europe were replaced by trailer parks and apartment complexes, the glamorous occupations by dead-end jobs. The trout in Carver's streams were apt to be pollution-deformed mutants. The good *vin du pays* was replaced by cheap gin, the romance of drinking by the dull grind of full-time alcoholism. ("Raymond Carver: A Still, Small Voice," *New York Times Book Review,* 6 Aug. 1989)

Hemingway's emphasis on economy and things unsaid is everywhere apparent in this more recent writer's work. (We will study the technique of narrative restraint closely in chapter 6; it overstates the case to call Carver Hemingway's disciple, but there's no doubt he "imitated" his predecessor's strategies for dialogue and descriptive prose.) As is the case with Hemingway, some of Carver's most remarkable stories are no more than a few pages long; they have in common a close focus on the commonplace. And while the stories may seem improvised at first glance, each successive reading reveals how tightly constructed they are. In the spring of 1978, he told an interviewer, "Everything is important in a story, every word, every punctuation mark. I believe very much in economy in fiction. Some of my stories . . . were three times as long in their first drafts" ("Echoes of Our Own Lives," interview with David Koehne, *Daily Iowan,* 18 April 1978).

On Expansion as Revision

Despite this emphasis on paring back work through revision, however, "A Small, Good Thing" represents the opposite kind of endeavor. Though the phrasing itself is minimalist, the story has been much expanded from its original version. In the 1981 collection, *What We Talk about When We Talk about*

Love, Carver published an early **précis** of this fiction, "The Bath," which is only nine pages long. Both versions contain the same events: a cake is ordered; a boy is hit by a car; his parents are tormented by calls from the baker as they wait for their son to wake up. "The Bath," however, is a truncated piece, both in terms of style and structure. The final scene of "The Bath," which occurs when Ann leaves Scotty (asleep, but alive) for a few hours to go home for a bath, reads in its entirety as follows:

> She pulled into the driveway. The dog ran out from behind the house. He ran in circles on the grass. She closed her eyes and leaned her head against the wheel. She listened to the ticking of the engine.
>
> She got out of the car and went to the door. She turned on lights and put on water for tea. She opened a can and fed the dog. She sat down on the sofa with her tea.
>
> The telephone rang.
>
> "Yes!" she said. "Hello!" she said.
>
> "Mrs. Weiss," a man's voice said.
>
> "Yes," she said. "This is Mrs. Weiss. Is it about Scotty?" she said.
>
> "Scotty," the voice said. "It is about Scotty," the voice said. "It has to do with Scotty, yes."

Fleshing Out a Story

"The Bath" ends abruptly, mysteriously. The reader doesn't know if Scotty will live or die, and Scotty's parents don't know who is calling them. There is considerable distance between the reader and Ann Weiss: *We* may presume the call is coming from the baker, but Ann cannot. The primary function of the **episode,** therefore, is neither to connect the reader to the Weiss family in the midst of **tragedy** nor to make possible an understanding of the baker and his lonely life, but rather to emphasize with absolute finality this more universal, cruel predicament: in the midst of one family's tragedy, the rest of the world goes about its business with indifference. In "The Bath" Carver allows for no resolution of that predicament, no "small, good thing" to console its characters after this "big, bad" event.

A few years later, however, Carver reconsidered. "I wrote the story and I didn't go far enough with it," he said ("As Raymond Carver Muses, His Stature Grows," interview with Jim Naughton, *Post-Standard* [Syracuse, NY] 23 Nov. 1982). He meant by this, it would seem, not merely that the story required more time and space, but also that the thematic content—its moral resonance —should be enlarged. In the second version of this story, Carver did more than just take the ending a few scenes further, allowing Ann and Howard Weiss to confront and be comforted by the baker; he also substantially expanded and fleshed out each scene along the way. Why?

"The Bath" is a perfect exercise in **minimalism.** Since the story seems geared to express a harsh, universal truth, the characters are pared back to the bare essentials. In many ways they seem more like generic **types** than individuals. The first scene of "The Bath," though functionally identical to that of its successor, differs in a few key ways from "A Small, Good Thing."

> Saturday afternoon the mother drove to the bakery in the shopping center. After looking through a loose-leaf binder with photographs of cakes taped onto the pages, she ordered chocolate, the child's favorite. The cake she chose was decorated with a spaceship and a launching pad under a sprinkling of white stars. The name SCOTTY would be iced on in green as if it were the name of the spaceship.
>
> The baker listened thoughtfully when the mother told him Scotty would be eight years old. He was an older man, this baker, and he wore a curious apron, a heavy thing with loops that went under his arms and around his back and then crossed in front again where they were tied in a very thick knot. He kept wiping his hands on the front of the apron as he listened to the woman, his wet eyes examining her lips as she studied the samples and talked.
>
> He let her take her time. He was in no hurry.
>
> The mother decided on the spaceship cake, and then she gave the baker her name and her telephone number. The cake would be ready Monday morning, in plenty of time for the party Monday afternoon. This was all the baker was willing to say. No pleasantries, just this small exchange, the barest information, nothing that was not necessary.

On Character: Names and Distance

Notice the way in which the characters are handled with labels here; their nomenclature is categorical. While in "A Small, Good Thing" Carver never names "the baker" and generally refers to Scotty only as "the child," at least the mother is called "she" in the first line, identifying her as a character more central to the narration than either the baker or Scotty. In the second version she offers her full name in the first scene, and that name is used descriptively by the narrator throughout. In "The Bath," however, Ann remains almost without exception "the mother" or "the wife." This may seem unimportant, but in writing, just as in life, the names we use for people indicate our degree of intimacy, and in "The Bath" Carver is holding his characters at arm's length. The last line of the passage could serve as an **aesthetic or artistic credo**: "No pleasantries, just this small exchange, the barest information, nothing that was not necessary." What better way to summarize the minimalist mode?

On Point of View and Distance

Consider, too, the point of view offered by the line, "He let her take her time. He was in no hurry." Is this a shift into the baker's point of view? Is it the mother's observation about the baker's manner? Or is it simply an objective, omniscient point of view, unattached to any particular character? Overall, this third strategy seems to be Carver's prevailing vantage in "The Bath"; when he says "this baker" he suggests familiarity, but it is a dispassionate one, a distanced intimacy. Only rarely does the narrator go inside a character's head to reveal thought or emotion. The objective witness reports on what can be seen and heard in each scene; there's little editorial interpolation or invention, and "He was in no hurry" hides as much as it reveals. Imagine, therefore, how out of place the following lines (from the second paragraph of "A Small, Good Thing") would be in the first scene of "The Bath": "She was a mother and thirty-three years old, and it seemed to her that everyone, especially someone the baker's age—a man old enough to be her father—must have children who'd gone through this special time of cakes and birthday parties. There must be that between them, she thought."

Passages like this one, however, play an integral role in the construction of the expanded tale. In the story's later version Carver still relies primarily on an unattached, **objective point of view,** but he does allow the reader access to the consciousness of his central characters. Often these brief forays into a character's thought processes stand out, both because they represent a slight shift in perspective, and because they tend to occur at pivotal points in the action, representing moments of emotional intensity. In this instance, the entry into Ann's thoughts prefigures what will become a central feature of the story: the potential for connection between Ann and the baker at tale's end.

On the Selection of Details

When the three main characters agree to share a meal—when the baker offers Mr. and Mrs. Weiss the consolation of "a small, good thing" and they remain in his kitchen, there's something sacramental in the act of breaking bread. It's worth noting also here that the names Ann and Howard Weiss suggest the family is Jewish, but the name of "the birthday boy," Scotty—whether his given name or nickname—is secular, hard to pin down; these people are neither observant Jews nor Catholics. "Jesus" and "God" are invoked repeatedly but in offhand conversation ("For God's sake," or "Oh, Jesus") and when the parents pray, they do so in a line or two, offstage. While this story is never overtly religious, the grieving couple nonetheless partakes of proffered comfort in a way that approaches communion and therefore at least the hint of resurrection: something has been born again during this shared meal.

On Dialogue and Monologue

Even as he probed more deeply into his characters' lives and minds, moving beneath the surface of what his characters merely *did* and *said,* Carver's focus remained on the common and the colloquial. His men and women were, in a way, still speaking for themselves, but the shift was away from dialogue and towards monologue. Consider the following passage—another entry into a character's consciousness:

Howard drove home from the hospital. He took the wet, dark streets very fast, then caught himself and slowed down. Until now, his life had gone smoothly and to his satisfaction—college, marriage, another year of college for the advanced degree in business, a junior partnership in an investment firm. Fatherhood. He was happy and, so far, lucky—he knew that. His parents were still living, his brothers and his sister were established, his friends from college had gone out to take their places in the world. So far, he had kept away from any real harm, from those forces he knew existed and that could cripple or bring down a man if the luck went bad, if things suddenly turned. He pulled into the driveway and parked. His left leg began to tremble. He sat in the car for a minute and tried to deal with the present situation in a rational manner. Scotty had been hit by a car and was in the hospital, but he was going to be all right. Howard closed his eyes and ran his hand over his face. He got out of the car and went up to the front door.

This is, technically speaking, an **interior monologue.** The narrative consciousness shifts, in the third sentence, from an unattached, objective perspective into Howard's own thoughts. But notice how this strategy, most often associated with the impressionistic writing of Joyce or Woolf, remains, in Carver's hands, a thoroughly concrete experience. While Joyce's Molly Bloom (the faithless wife in *Ulysses*) muses to herself, "who is in your mind now tell me who are you thinking of who is it tell me his name who tell me who the German Emperor is," Carver's Howard Weiss dazedly catalogues his advanced degree and junior partnership. Notice, too, how Carver shifts back out of Howard's thoughts midstream to report on the physical developments of the scene: "He pulled into the driveway and parked. His left leg began to tremble." With this detail of the trembling leg Carver marries the intangible to the tangible. Howard's fear, his need to reassure himself can only be expressed, in Carver's world, through action: bare physical gesture and facts.

> ▧ **WRITER'S VIEW:** *It's possible, in a poem or short story, to write about commonplace things and objects using commonplace but precise language and to endow those things—a chair, a window curtain, a fork, a stone, a woman's earring—with immense, even startling power. It is possible to write a line of seemingly innocuous dialogue and have it send a chill along the reader's spine . . . That's the kind of writing that most interests me . . . That's all we have, finally, the words, and they had better be the right ones, with the punctuation in the right places so that they can best say what they are meant to say. If the words are heavy with the writer's own unbridled emotions, or if they are imprecise and inaccurate for some other reason—if the words are in any way blurred—the reader's eyes will slide right over them and nothing will be achieved. ("On Writing")*

On Evoking Emotional Intensity through Restraint

There is, in Carver's language, a constant stoicism and emotion held in check even while his people endure the most disastrous events. All this emphasis on the concrete can make his characters, if not their creator, seem dispassionate, aloof. Yet it may be that Carver's understated style allowed him to tackle ideas for short stories that were uncommonly extreme. In these fictions, yes, a boy can get hit by a car on his birthday and—though the chances are "one in a million"—die. Notice, however, how another family **catastrophe** proceeds along parallel lines. Near the midpoint of the story we read, "'Franklin,' the large woman said as she roused herself. 'Is it about Franklin?'" and a few pages later learn that he has died. This makes the repeated phrase, "It's about Scotty" all the more replete with menace and predictive: no happy ending here.

It is a dark, unsettling vision, and in another writer's hands a similar story could quickly turn to **melodrama.** Yet "a small, good thing" does offer the sort of consolation denied the parents in "The Bath"; that "they did not think of leaving"—the revision's final line—means they take comfort together against the outer dark. What Carver manages, through his unflinching presentation of the things people do and say and endure, is to construct stories of an emotional intensity that is *almost* inexpressible.

Applications and Connections

- Consider the thematic undertones in this story's dialogue. What kinds of miscommunications are conveyed through what is said—or not said? Dialogue is often at its best when it shows the ways in which communication fails, when two characters are speaking about two entirely different things. Why is this?
- Read the story aloud to hear the dialogue. What makes it so believable, so natural? When writing your own dialogue, ask yourself, does this sound like the way people really talk? Does this sound like something my character would say? Of course not all characters speak as simply as those in a "A Small, Good Thing." Dialogue between the erudite or long-winded, between children, between nonnative speakers, would in each instance sound different. However, what could you take from Carver's use of dialogue that would be universally applicable?
- When Carver revised and expanded "The Bath" into "A Small, Good Thing," he raised the story's emotional stakes by fleshing out almost every scene and character. However, reading "A Small, Good Thing," do you find any sentimentality, any wasted words, any scenes or descriptions that could be omitted? Minimalism is a difficult art because—as in "The Bath"—it can be taken too far; it can leave the reader watching the story from behind a glass

window. Be aware when you are paring down that sometimes you may have to go farther with something. If the theme enlarges, some details must follow suit.

Exercises

1. Have the "hit-and-run driver" stop and offer assistance. Compose the speech he gives to the parents when he brings Scotty home.

2. Describe the husband's workplace; have Howard call his boss and ask for a "personal day."

3. Write the baker's phone calls from his own perspective; explain how he looks at the cake, then waits for Mrs. Weiss, then works himself into a rage.

4. Add three more pages to story's end; what happens when they go home?

5. Cut three pages from story's end; rewrite the conclusion after "The baker, that bastard."

6. Write Scotty's dying fantasia; what does he dream in his coma, what presents do his friends bring to the nonexistent party, what will his teachers say next day?

7. Send a letter from "Ray" to a writer friend explaining why "I felt I needed to rewrite 'The Bath' and call it 'A Small, Good Thing.'"

8. Have Ann tell her new lover—who will become her second husband—why the marriage fell apart.

9. Have Dr. Francis, next morning at the gym, tell a colleague what went wrong in Scotty's case.

10. "Don't have children . . . For God's sake don't." Write your own story called "A Big, Bad Thing" and use this quote as epigraph.

Examples of Student Work

(*Editor's Note:* One of the ways to consider the rules of composition—in a painting or song as well as a short story—is to look at what can be easily added or cut out. Exercise 3 suggests that we could spend more time in the baker's consciousness; exercise 4 suggests that the story could continue for three additional pages. But even though these two students did a fine job with Carver's diction, it's clear that this sort of amplification is beside the point; there's nothing useful to add. The author would no doubt have cut each of the following additions; Carver stops where his own story must.)

Dena Zamore, EXERCISE 3

```
Sunday afternoon, she came into the bakery. After looking
through the loose-leaf binder, she ordered a chocolate
```

cake to be made for Monday morning. The cake she chose
was decorated with a space ship and launching pad under
a sprinkling of white stars, and a planet made of red
frosting at the other end. She talked on about the boy.
His name, Scotty, would be in green letters beneath the
planet.

The baker did not concern himself with the lives of
his customers. He just baked the cakes. He knew his cakes
made people happy and this made him feel good, but he was
never particularly interested in the business of others.
He kept his eyes down on the photographs of the cakes and
let her talk. Let her take her time. This is how he
operated. He made the cakes. He let his customers talk
and talk, but once he had taken the order, he didn't
really listen nor care to. He knew the cake he was to
make. He knew her name, Ann Weiss, and her telephone
number. He knew to have the cake ready for her Monday
morning.

On Monday morning, early, the baker was putting the
finishing touches on the cakes he was to have ready. He
was up early as usual. At nine, he unlocked the doors to
let the customers in. One by one, throughout the day,
people came in to place orders or to pick up previously
made orders. The morning orders were picked up. The
afternoon orders were picked up. The early evening orders
were picked up. The Weiss order stayed on the rack. . . .

Ray Howell, EXERCISE 4

They were silent as they finally pulled back into the
driveway at home. The whole world seemed quiet. It was
Thursday, Howard remembered. He would be expected at the
office in a couple of hours. He tried to think of what he
would do at work, tried to think of the project that he
had been working on before everything had gone all wrong.
He tried to picture his desk the last time he saw it, but
he couldn't focus. Everything seemed so distant.

He looked across the car at his wife. She was staring
straight ahead, her eyes blank. She looked emptier than
he had ever seen her. So tired. Howard remembered how she
had looked on the day they were married. She had smiled,
glowed like a sunrise under her veil. She had been
brimming with youthful innocence and hope. He had loved
her very, very much. Howard wondered what she was
thinking about now.

He reached across the car, over the gearshift console,
and touched her gently on the knee. She jumped as if he
had touched her with a red-hot poker. "Are we home?" she

asked. Yes, Howard replied. They had been sitting in the driveway for at least five minutes. The windows were beginning to fog up with their breathing. "Oh," she said, and got out of the car.

Howard fumbled with the keys at the front door. Inside, the house was dim. It smelled faintly of wool . . .

CHAPTER 5

THEME AND THE
SELECTION OF DETAIL:
Writing Up Close and at a Distance

RICHARD FORD, "Communist"

■ **WRITER'S VIEW:** *Influence seems different from imitation, which is conscious and concerted, whereas the former can be conscious, unconscious, subtle, profound, small or large, but usually comes to bear in the performance of original work. Thus, Hemingway was influenced by Turgenev; Chekhov was influenced (admittedly) by Pushkin; Carver was influenced (admittedly) by John Gardner and (grudgingly and unadmittedly) by Hemingway. We are influenced by all that we read, sometimes obviously, sometimes invisibly, sometimes unwittingly, sometimes helpfully, sometimes not. Indeed, to write at all—a story or a novel or a villanelle—means that we are influenced by those practices and practitioners who have come before us and whose work we've read. (Letter to Nicholas Delbanco, 20 Feb. 2001)*

Richard Ford was born in 1944; he was raised in Jackson, Mississippi, and Little Rock, Arkansas. His father had a heart attack when Ford was eight and died when his son was sixteen. Thereafter the writer's life would be one of near-constant motion. An only child, he has no children; he and his wife make their homes in New Orleans, Maine, and Montana; he has lived for lengthy periods in California, Michigan, New Jersey, and in France. Ford has committed, as he puts it, "random acts of journalism" and has taught at institutions such as Harvard, Northwestern, Princeton, and the University of Michigan—but the single through-line of his peripatetic career has been the commitment to prose.

His first novel, *A Piece of My Heart*, appeared in 1976; since then he has published, in chronological succession, *The Ultimate Good Luck, The*

Sportswriter, Rock Springs (the short story collection in which "Communist" is included), the brief novel *Wildlife, Independence Day, Women with Men,* and, in 2002, *A Multitude of Sins. Independence Day* is the only novel ever to have been accorded both the Pulitzer Prize and the Pen/Faulkner award. His reputation, in America and abroad, has grown continually; no list of this generation of writers would fail to include Richard Ford.

The protagonists of his stories are restless, questing, intelligent, young or middle-aged men, most often adrift and alone; his characteristic first-person narrative mode links action with meditation. Note in the pages that follow the span of years between the hunting trip and the tale told later about it: a quarter of a century divides the incidents of "Communist" from the account and retrospect itself. The narrator looks back upon a crucial encounter of his youth and from a present vantage attempts to make sense of the past. It's not so much an occasion for regret as a mapping of the road not taken, a cold-eyed consideration of what might have been.

Another striking detail is the one-word title, "Communist." Since the end of the Cold War and the collapse of the Soviet Union the term is less inflammatory, but in the period evoked it aroused both distrust and suspicion. Ford means to alert the reader to the world beyond the local landscape and to yoke a larger political context to this story of one young man's experience of beauty and his initiation into adult argument; somehow the fight between Glen Baxter and his mother becomes an emblem of opposed beliefs and warring systems too. This single titular word, therefore—Ford often uses a single term in summary of the subjects of his stories—provides both point and **counterpoint**; it's both variation and theme.

Communist

My mother once had a boyfriend named Glen Baxter. This was in 1961. We—my mother and I—were living in the little house my father had left her up the Sun River, near Victory, Montana, west of Great Falls. My mother was thirty-two at the time. I was sixteen. Glen Baxter was somewhere in the middle, between us, though I cannot be exact about it.

We were living then off the proceeds of my father's life insurance policies, with my mother doing some part-time waitressing work up in Great Falls and going to the bars in the evenings, which I know is where she met Glen Baxter. Sometimes he would come back with her and stay in her room at night, or she would call up from town and explain that she was staying with him in his little place on Lewis Street by the GN yards. She gave me his number every time, but I never called it. I think she probably thought that what she was doing was terrible, but simply couldn't help herself. I thought it was all right, though. Regular life it seemed, and still does. She was young, and I knew that even then.

Glen Baxter was a Communist and liked hunting, which he talked about a lot. Pheasants. Ducks. Deer. He killed all of them, he said. He had been to Vietnam as far back as then, and when he was in our house he often talked about shooting the animals over there—monkeys and beautiful parrots—using military guns just for sport. We did not know what Vietnam was then, and Glen, when he talked about that, referred to it only as "the Far East." I think now he must've been in the CIA and been disillusioned by something he saw or found out about and been thrown out, but that kind of thing did not matter to us. He was a tall, dark-eyed man with short black hair, and was usually in a good humor. He had gone halfway through college in Peoria, Illinois, he said, where he grew up. But when he was around our life he worked wheat farms as a ditcher, and stayed out of work winters and in the bars drinking with women like my mother, who had work and some money. It is not an uncommon life to lead in Montana.

What I want to explain happened in November. We had not been seeing Glen Baxter for some time. Two months had gone by. My mother knew other men, but she came home most days from work and stayed inside watching television in her bedroom and drinking beers. I asked about Glen once, and she said only that she didn't know where he was, and I assumed they had had a fight and that he was gone off on a flyer back to Illinois or Massachusetts, where he said he had relatives. I'll admit that I liked him. He had something on his mind always. He was a labor man as well as a Communist, and liked to say that the country was poisoned by the rich, and strong men would need to bring it to life again, and I liked that because my father had been a labor man, which was why we had a house to live in and money coming through. It was also true that I'd had a few boxing bouts by then—just with town boys and one with an Indian from Choteau—and there were some girlfriends I knew from that. I did not like my mother being around the house so much at night, and I wished Glen Baxter would come back, or that another man would come along and entertain her somewhere else.

At two o'clock on a Saturday, Glen drove up into our yard in a car. He had had a big brown Harley-Davidson that he rode most of the year, in his black-and-red irrigators and a baseball cap turned backwards. But this time he had a car, a blue Nash Ambassador. My mother and I went out on the porch when he stopped inside the olive trees my father had planted as a shelter belt, and my mother had a look on her face of not much pleasure. It was starting to be cold in earnest by then. Snow was down already onto the Fairfield Bench, though on this day a Chinook was blowing, and it could as easily have been spring, though the sky above the Divide was turning over in silver and blue clouds of winter.

"We haven't seen you in a long time, I guess," my mother said coldly.

"My little retarded sister died," Glen said, standing at the door of his old car. He was wearing his orange VFW jacket and canvas shoes we called wino shoes, something I had never seen him wear before. He seemed to be in a good humor. "We buried her in Florida near the home."

"That's a good place," my mother said in a voice that meant she was a wronged party in something.

"I want to take this boy hunting today, Aileen," Glen said. "There's snow geese down now. But we have to right away, or they'll be gone to Idaho by tomorrow."

"He doesn't care to go," my mother said.

"Yes I do," I said, and looked at her.

My mother frowned at me. "Why do you?"

"Why does he need a reason?" Glen Baxter said and grinned.

"I want him to have one, that's why." She looked at me oddly. "I think Glen's drunk, Les."

"No, I'm not drinking," Glen said, which was hardly ever true. He looked at both of us, and my mother bit down on the side of her lower lip and stared at me in a way to make you think she thought something was being put over on her and she didn't like you for it. She was very pretty, though when she was mad her features were sharpened and less pretty by a long way. "All right, then I don't care," she said to no one in particular. "Hunt, kill, maim. Your father did that too." She turned to go back inside.

"Why don't you come with us, Aileen?" Glen was smiling still, pleased.

"To do what?" my mother said. She stopped and pulled a package of cigarettes out of her dress pocket and put one in her mouth.

"It's worth seeing."

"See dead animals?" my mother said.

"These geese are from Siberia, Aileen," Glen said. "They're not like a lot of geese. Maybe I'll buy us dinner later. What do you say?"

"Buy with what?" my mother said. To tell the truth, I didn't know why she was so mad at him. I would've thought she'd be glad to see him. But she just suddenly seemed to hate everything about him.

"I've got some money," Glen said. "Let me spend it on a pretty girl tonight."

"Find one of those and you're lucky," my mother said, turning away toward the front door.

"I already found one," Glen Baxter said. But the door slammed behind her, and he looked at me then with a look I think now was helplessness, though I could not see a way to change anything.

My mother sat in the backseat of Glen's Nash and looked out the window while we drove. My double gun was in the seat between us beside Glen's Belgian pump, which he kept loaded with five shells in case, he said, he saw something beside the road he wanted to shoot. I had hunted rabbits before, and had ground-sluiced pheasants and other birds, but I had never been on an actual hunt before, one where you drove out to some special place and did it formally. And I was excited. I had a feeling that something important was about to happen to me, and that this would be a day I would always remember.

My mother did not say anything for a long time, and neither did I. We drove up through Great Falls and out the other side toward Fort Benton, which was on the benchland where wheat was grown.

"Geese mate for life," my mother said, just out of the blue, as were driving. "I hope you know that. They're special birds."

"I know that," Glen said in the front seat. "I have every respect for them."

"So where were you for three months?" she said. "I'm only curious."

"I was in the Big Hole for a while," Glen said, "and after that I went to Douglas, Wyoming."

"What were you planning to do there?" my mother asked.

"I wanted to find a job, but it didn't work out."

"I'm going to college," she said suddenly, and this was something I had never heard about before. I turned to look at her, but she was staring out her window and wouldn't see me.

"I knew French once," Glen said. "*Rosé*'s pink. *Rouge*'s red." He glanced at me and smiled. "I think that's a wise idea, Aileen. When are you going to start?"

"I don't want Les to think he was raised by crazy people all his life," my mother said.

"Les ought to go himself," Glen said.

"After I go, he will."

"What do you say about that, Les?" Glen said, grinning.

"He says it's just fine," my mother said.

"It's just fine," I said.

Where Glen Baxter took us was out onto the high flat prairie that was disked for wheat and had high, high mountains out to the east, with lower heart-break hills in between. It was, I remember, a day for blues in the sky, and down in the distance we could see the small town of Floweree, and the state highway running past it toward Fort Benton and the Hi-line. We drove out on top of the prairie on a muddy dirt road fenced on both sides, until we had gone about three miles, which is where Glen stopped.

"All right," he said, looking up in the rearview mirror at my mother. "You wouldn't think there was anything here, would you?"

"*We're* here," my mother said. "You brought us here."

"You'll be glad though," Glen said, and seemed confident to me. I had looked around myself but could not see anything. No water or trees, nothing that seemed like a good place to hunt anything. Just waste land. "There's a big lake out there, Les," Glen said. "You can't see it now from here because it's low. But the geese are there. You'll see."

"It's like the moon out here, I recognize that," my mother said, "only it's worse. She was staring out at the flat wheatland as if she could actually see something in particular, and wanted to know more about it. "How'd you find this place?"

"I came once on the wheat push," Glen said.

"And I'm sure the owner told you just to come back and hunt anytime you like and bring anybody you wanted. Come one, come all. Is that it?"

"People shouldn't own land anyway," Glen said. "Anybody should be able to use it."

"Les, Glen's going to poach here," my mother said. "I just want you to know that, because that's a crime and the law will get you for it. If you're a man now, you're going to have to face the consequences."

"That's not true," Glen Baxter said, and looked gloomily out over the steering wheel down the muddy road toward the mountains. Though for myself I believed it was true, and didn't care. I didn't care about anything at that moment except seeing geese fly over me and shooting them down.

"Well, I'm certainly not going out there," my mother said. "I like towns better, and I already have enough trouble."

"That's okay," Glen said. "When the geese lift up you'll get to see them. That's all I wanted. Les and me'll go shoot them, won't we, Les?"

"Yes," I said, and I put my hand on my shotgun, which had been my father's and was heavy as rocks.

"Then we should go on," Glen said, "or we'll waste our light."

We got out of the car with our guns. Glen took off his canvas shoes and put on his pair of black irrigators out of the trunk. Then we crossed the barbed wire fence, and walked out into the high, tilled field toward nothing. I looked back at my mother when we were still not so far away, but I could only see the small, dark top of her head, low in the backseat of the Nash, staring and thinking what I could not then begin to say.

On the walk toward the lake, Glen began talking to me. I had never been alone with him, and knew little about him except what my mother said—that he drank too much, or other times that he was the nicest man she had ever known in the world and that someday a woman would marry him, though she didn't think it would be her. Glen told me as we walked that he wished he had finished college, but that it was too late now, that his mind was too old. He said he had liked the Far East very much, and that people there knew how to teach each other, and that he would go back some day but couldn't go now. He said also that he would like to live in Russia for a while and mentioned the names of people who had gone there, names I didn't know. He said it would be hard at first, because it was so different, but that pretty soon anyone would learn to like it and wouldn't want to live anywhere else, and that Russians treated Americans who came to live there like kings. There were Communists everywhere now, he said. You didn't know them, but they were there. Montana had a large number, and he was in touch with all of them. He said that Communists were always in danger and that he had to protect himself all the time. And when he said that he pulled back his VFW jacket and showed me the butt of a pistol he had stuck under his shirt against his bare skin. "There are people who want to kill me right now," he said, "and I would kill a man myself if I thought I had to." And we kept walking. Though in a while he said, "I don't think I know much about you, Les. But I'd like to. What do you like to do?"

"I like to box," I said. "My father did it. It's a good thing to know."

"I suppose you have to protect yourself too," Glen said.

"I know how to," I said.

"Do you like to watch TV," Glen asked, and smiled.

"Not much."

"I love to," Glen said. "I could watch it instead of eating if I had one."

I looked out straight ahead over the green tops of sage that grew to the edge of the disked field, hoping to see the lake Glen said was there. There was an airishness and a sweet smell that I thought might be the place we were going, but I couldn't see it. "How will we hunt these geese?" I said.

"It won't be hard," Glen said. "Most hunting isn't even hunting. It's only shooting. And that's what this will be. In Illinois you would dig holes in the ground and hide and set out your decoys. Then the geese come to you, over and over again. But we don't have time for that here." He glanced at me. "You have to be sure the first time here."

"How do you know they're here now," I asked. And I looked toward the Highwood Mountains twenty miles away, half in snow and half dark blue at the bottom. I could see the little town of Floweree then, looking shabby and dimly lighted in the distance. A red bar sign shone. A car moved slowly away from the scattered buildings.

"They always come November first," Glen said.

"Are we going to poach them?"

"Does it make any difference to you," Glen asked.

"No, it doesn't."

"Well then, we aren't," he said.

We walked then for a while without talking. I looked back once to see the Nash far and small in the flat distance. I couldn't see my mother, and I thought that she must've turned on the radio and gone to sleep, which she always did, letting it play all night in her bedroom. Behind the car the sun was nearing the rounded mountains southwest of us, and I knew that when the sun was gone it would be cold. I wished my mother had decided to come along with us, and I thought for a moment of how little I really knew her at all.

Glen walked with me another quarter-mile, crossed another barbed wire fence where sage was growing, then went a hundred yards through wheatgrass and spurge until the ground went up and formed a kind of long hillock bunker built by a farmer against the wind. And I realized the lake was just beyond us. I could hear the sound of a car horn blowing and a dog barking all the way down in the town, then the wind seemed to move and all I could hear then and after then were geese. So many geese, from the sound of them, though I still could not see even one. I stood and listened to the high-pitched shouting sound, a sound I had never heard so close, a sound with size to it—though it was not loud. A sound that meant great numbers and that made your chest rise and your shoulders tighten with expectancy. It was a sound to make you feel separate from it and everything else, as if you were of no importance in the grand scheme of things.

"Do you hear them singing," Glen asked. He held his hand up to make me stand still. And we both listened. "How many do you think, Les, just hearing?"

"A hundred," I said. "More than a hundred."

"Five thousand," Glen said. "More than you can believe when you see them. Go see."

I put down my gun and on my hands and knees crawled up the earthwork through the wheatgrass and thistle, until I could see down to the lake and see the geese. And they were there, like a white bandage laid on the water, wide and long and continuous, a white expanse of snow geese, seventy yards from me, on the bank, but stretching far onto the lake, which was large itself—a half-mile across, with thick tules on the far side and wild plums farther and the blue mountain behind them.

"Do you see that big raft?" Glen said from below me, in a whisper.

"I see it," I said, still looking. It was such a thing to see, a view I had never seen and have not since.

"Are any on the land?" he said.

"Some are in the wheatgrass," I said, "but most are swimming."

"Good," Glen said. "They'll have to fly. But we can't wait for that now."

And I crawled backwards down the heel of land to where Glen was, and my gun. We were losing our light, and the air was purplish and cooling. I looked toward the car but couldn't see it, and I was no longer sure where it was below the lighted sky.

"Where do they fly to?" I said in a whisper, since I did not want anything to be ruined because of what I did or said. It was important to Glen to shoot the geese, and it was important to me.

"To the wheat," he said. "Or else they leave for good. I wish your mother had come, Les. Now she'll be sorry."

I could hear the geese quarreling and shouting on the lake surface. And I wondered if they knew we were here now. "She might be," I said with my heart pounding, but I didn't think she would be much.

It was a simple plan he had. I would stay behind the bunker, and he would crawl on his belly with his gun through the wheatgrass as near to the geese as he could. Then he would simply stand up and shoot all the ones he could close up, both in the air and on the ground. And when all the others flew up, with luck some would turn toward me as they came into the wind, and then I could shoot them and turn them back to him, and he would shoot them again. He could kill ten, he said, if he was lucky, and I might kill four. It didn't seem hard.

"Don't show them your face," Glen said. "Wait till you think you can touch them, then stand up and shoot. To hesitate is lost in this."

"All right," I said. "I'll try it."

"Shoot one in the head, and then shoot another one," Glen said. "It won't be hard. He patted me on the arm and smiled. Then he took off his VFW jacket and put it on the ground, climbed up the side of the bunker, cradling his shotgun in his arms, and slid on his belly into the dry stalks of yellow grass out of my sight.

Then, for the first time in that entire day, I was alone. And I didn't mind it. I sat squat down in the grass, loaded my double gun and took my other two shells out of my pocket to hold. I pushed the safety off and on to see that it was right. The wind rose a little, scuffed the grass and made me shiver. It was not the warm Chinook now, but a wind out of the north, the one geese flew away from if they could.

Then I thought about my mother, in the car alone, and how much longer I would stay with her, and what it might mean to her for me to leave. And I wondered when Glen Baxter would die and if someone would kill him, or whether my mother would marry him and how I would feel about it. And though I didn't know why, it occurred to me that Glen Baxter and I would not be friends when all was said and done, since I didn't care if he ever married my mother or didn't.

Then I thought about boxing and what my father had taught me about it. To tighten your fists hard. To strike out straight from the shoulder and never punch backing up. How to cut a punch by snapping your fist inwards, how to carry your chin low, and to step toward a man when he is falling so you can hit him again. And most important, to keep your eyes open when you are hitting in the face and causing damage, because you need to see what you're doing to encourage yourself, and because it is when you close your eyes that you stop hitting and get hurt badly. "Fly all over your man, Les," my father said. "When you see your chance, fly on him and hit him till he falls." That, I thought, would always be my attitude in things.

And then I heard the geese again, their voices in unison, louder and shouting, as if the wind had changed again and put all new sounds in the cold air. And then a *boom*. And I knew Glen was in among them and had stood up to shoot. The noise of geese rose and grew worse, and my fingers burned where I held my gun too tight to the metal, and I put it down and opened my fist to make the burning stop so I could feel the trigger when the moment came. *Boom*, Glen shot again, and I heard him shuck a shell, and all the sounds out beyond the bunker seemed to be rising—the geese, the shots, the air itself going up. *Boom*, Glen shot another time, and I knew he was taking his careful time to make his shots good. And I held my gun and started to crawl up the bunker so as not to be surprised when the geese came over me and I could shoot.

From the top I saw Glen Baxter alone in the wheatgrass field, shooting at a white goose with black tips of wings that was on the ground not far from him, but trying to run and pull into the air. He shot it once more, and it fell over dead with its wings flapping.

Glen looked back at me and his face was distorted and strange. The air around him was full of white rising geese and he seemed to want them all. "Behind you, Les," he yelled at me and pointed. "They're all behind you now." I looked behind me, and there were geese in the air as far as I could see, more than I knew how many, moving so slowly, their wings wide out and working calmly and filling the air with noise, though their voices were not as loud or as shrill as I had thought they would be. And they were so close! Forty feet, some of them. The air around me vibrated and I could feel the wind from their wings and it seemed to me I could kill as many as the times I could shoot—a hundred or a thousand—and I raised my gun, put the muzzle on the head of a white goose, and fired. It shuddered in the air, its wide feet sank below its belly, its wings cradled out to hold back air, and it fell straight down and landed with an awful sound, a noise a human would make, a thick, soft, *hump* noise. I looked up again and shot another goose, could hear the pellets hit its chest, but it didn't fall or even break its pattern for flying. *Boom,* Glen shot again. And then again. "Hey," I heard him shout, "Hey, hey." And there were geese flying over me, flying in line after line. I broke my gun and reloaded, and thought to myself as I did: I need confidence here. I need to be sure with this. I pointed at another goose and shot it in the head, and it fell the way the first one had, wings out, its belly down, and with the same thick noise of hitting. Then I sat down in the grass on the bunker and let geese fly over me.

By now the whole raft was in the air, all of it moving in a slow swirl above me and the lake and everywhere, finding the wind and heading out south in long wavering lines that caught the last sun and turned to silver as they gained a distance. It was a thing to see, I will tell you now. Five thousand white geese all in the air around you, making a noise like you have never heard before. And I thought to myself then: this is something I will never see again. I will never forget this. And I was right.

Glen Baxter shot twice more. Once he missed, but with the other he hit a goose flying away from him, and knocked it half falling and flying into the empty lake not far from shore, where it began to swim as though it was fine and make its noise.

Glen stood in the stubby grass, looking out at the goose, his gun lowered. "I didn't need to shoot that one, did I, Les?"

"I don't know," I said, sitting on the little knoll of land, looking at the goose swimming in the water.

"I don't know why I shoot 'em. They're so beautiful." He looked at me.

"I don't know either," I said.

"Maybe there's nothing else to do with them." Glen stared at the goose again and shook his head. "Maybe this is exactly what they're put on earth for."

I did not know what to say because I did not know what he could mean by that, though what I felt was embarrassment at the great numbers of geese there were, and a dulled feeling like a hunger because the shooting had stopped and it was over for me now.

Glen began to pick up his geese, and I walked down to my two that had fallen close together and were dead. One had hit with such an impact that its stomach had split and some of its inward parts were knocked out. Though the other looked unhurt, its soft white belly turned up like a pillow, its head and jagged bill-teeth, its tiny black eyes looking as they would if they were alive.

"What's happened to the hunters out here?" I heard a voice speak. It was my mother, standing in her pink dress on the knoll above us, hugging her arms. She was smiling though she was cold. And I realized that I had lost all thought of her in the shooting. "Who did all this shooting? Is this your work, Les?"

"No," I said.

"Les is a hunter, though, Aileen," Glen said. "He takes his time." He was holding two white geese by their necks, one in each hand, and he was smiling. He and my mother seemed pleased.

"I see you didn't miss too many," my mother said and smiled. I could tell she admired Glen for his geese, and that she had done some thinking in the car alone. "It *was* wonderful, Glen," she said. "I've never seen anything like that. They were like snow."

"It's worth seeing once, isn't it?" Glen said. "I should've killed more, but I got excited."

My mother looked at me then. "Where's yours, Les?"

"Here," I said and pointed to my two geese on the ground beside me.

My mother nodded in a nice way, and I think she liked everything then and wanted the day to turn out right and for all of us to be happy. "Six, then. You've got six in all."

"One's still out there," I said, and motioned where the one goose was swimming in circles on the water.

"Okay," my mother said and put her hand over her eyes to look. "Where is it?"

Glen Baxter looked at me then with a strange smile, a smile that said he wished I had never mentioned anything about the other goose. And I wished I hadn't either. I looked up in the sky and could see the lines of geese by the thousands shining silver in the light, and I wished we could just leave and go home.

"That one's my mistake there," Glen Baxter said and grinned. "I shouldn't have shot that one, Aileen. I got too excited."

My mother looked out on the lake for a minute, then looked at Glen and back again. "Poor goose." She shook her head. "How will you get it, Glen?"

"I can't get that one now," Glen said.

My mother looked at him. "What do you mean?"

"I'm going to leave that one," Glen said.

"Well, no. You can't leave one," my mother said. "You shot it. You have to get it. Isn't that a rule?"

"No," Glen said.

And my mother looked from Glen to me. "Wade out and get it, Glen," she said in a sweet way, and my mother looked young then, like a young girl, in her flimsy short-sleeved waitress dress and her skinny, bare legs in the wheatgrass.

"No." Glen Baxter looked down at his gun and shook his head. And I didn't know why he wouldn't go, because it would've been easy. The lake was shallow. And you could tell that anyone could've walked out a long way before it got deep, and Glen had on his boots.

My mother looked at the whiter goose, which was not more than thirty yards from the shore, its head up, moving in slow circles, its wings settled and relaxed so you could see the black tips. "Wade out and get it, Glenny, won't you, please?" she said. "They're special things."

"You don't understand the world, Aileen," Glen said. "This can happen. It doesn't matter."

"But that's so cruel, Glen," she said, and a sweet smile came on her lips.

"Raise up your own arms, 'Leeny," Glen said. "I can't see any angel's wings, can you, Les?" He looked at me, but I looked away.

"Then you go on and get it, Les," my mother said. "You weren't raised by crazy people." I started to go, but Glen Baxter suddenly grabbed me by my shoulder and pulled me back hard, so hard his fingers made bruises in my skin that I saw later.

"Nobody's going," he said. "This is over with now."

And my mother gave Glen a cold look then. "You don't have a heart, Glen," she said. "There's nothing to love in you. You're just a son of a bitch, that's all."

And Glen Baxter nodded at my mother, then, as if he understood something he had not understood before, but something that he was willing to know. "Fine," he said, "that's fine." And he took his big pistol out from against his belly, the big blue revolver I had only seen part of before and that he said protected him, and he pointed it out at the goose on the water, his arm straight away from him, and shot and missed. And then he shot and missed again. The goose made its noise once. And then he hit it dead, because there was no splash. And then he shot it three times more until the gun was empty and the goose's head was down and it was floating toward the middle of the lake where it was empty and dark blue. "Now who has a heart?" Glen said. But my mother was not there when he turned around. She had already started back to the car and was almost lost from sight in the darkness. And Glen smiled at me then and his face had a wild look on it. "Okay, Les?" he said.

"Okay," I said.

"There're limits to everything, right?"

"I guess so," I said.

"Your mother's a beautiful woman, but she's not the only beautiful woman in Montana." And I did not say anything. And Glen Baxter suddenly said, "Here," and he held the pistol out at me. "Don't you want this? Don't you want to shoot me? Nobody thinks they'll die. But I'm ready for it right now." And I did not know what to do then. Though it is true that what I wanted to do was to hit him, hit him as hard in the face as I could, and see him on the ground bleeding and crying and pleading for me to stop. Only at that moment he looked scared to me, and I had never seen a grown man scared before—though I have seen one since—and I felt sorry for him, as though he was already a dead man. And I did not end up hitting him at all.

A light can go out in the heart. All of this happened years ago, but I still can feel now how sad and remote the world was to me. Glen Baxter, I think now, was not a bad man, only a man scared of something he'd never seen before—something soft in himself—his life going a way he didn't like. A woman with a son. Who could blame him there? I don't know what makes people do what they do, or call themselves what they call themselves, only that you have to live someone's life to be the expert.

My mother had tried to see the good side of things, tried to be hopeful in the situation she was handed, tried to look out for us both, and it hadn't worked. It was a strange time in her life then and after that, a time when she had to adjust to being an adult just when she was on the thin edge of things. Too much awareness too early in life was her problem, I think.

And what I felt was only that I had somehow been pushed out into the world, into the real life then, the one I hadn't lived yet. In a year I was gone to hard-rock mining and no-paycheck jobs and not to college. And I have thought more than once about my mother saying that I had not been raised by crazy people, and I don't know what that could mean or what difference it could make, unless it means that love is a reliable commodity, and even that is not always true, as I have found out.

Late on the night that all this took place I was in bed when I heard my mother say, "Come outside, Les. Come and hear this." And I went out onto the front porch barefoot and in my underwear, where it was warm like spring, and there was a spring mist in the air. I could see the lights of the Fairfield Coach in the distance, on its way up to Great Falls.

And I could hear geese, white birds in the sky, flying. They made their high-pitched sound like angry yells, and though I couldn't see them high up, it seemed to me they were everywhere. And my mother looked up and said, "Hear them?" I could smell her hair wet from the shower. "They leave with the moon," she said. "It's still half wild out here."

And I said, "I hear them," and I felt a chill come over my bare chest, and the hair stood up on my arms the way it does before a storm. And for a while we listened.

"When I first married your father, you know, we lived on a street called Bluebird Canyon, in California. And I thought that was the prettiest street and the prettiest name. I suppose no one brings you up like your first love. You don't mind if I say that, do you?" She looked at me hopefully.

"No," I said.

"We have to keep civilization alive somehow." And she pulled her little housecoat together because there was a cold vein in the air, a part of the cold that would be on us the next day. "I don't feel part of things tonight, I guess."

"It's all right," I said.

"Do you know where I'd like to go?"

"No," I said. And I suppose I knew she was angry then, angry with life, but did not want to show me that.

"To the Straits of Juan de Fuca. Wouldn't that be something? Would you like that?"

"I'd like it," I said. And my mother looked off for a minute, as if she could see the Straits of Juan de Fuca out against the line of mountains, see the lights of things alive and a whole new world.

"I know you liked him," she said after a moment. "You and I both suffer fools too well."

"I didn't like him too much," I said. "I didn't really care."

"He'll fall on his face. I'm sure of that," she said. And I didn't say anything because I didn't care about Glen Baxter anymore, and was happy not to talk about him. "Would you tell me something if I asked you? Would you tell me the truth?"

"Yes," I said.

And my mother did not look at me. "Just tell the truth," she said.

"All right," I said.

"Do you think I'm still very feminine? I'm thirty-two years old now. You don't know what that means. But do you think I am?"

And I stood at the edge of the porch, with the olive trees before me, looking straight up into the mist where I could not see geese but could still hear them flying, could almost feel the air move below their white wings. And I felt the way you feel when you are on a trestle all alone and the train is coming, and you know you have to decide. And I said, "Yes, I do." Because that was the truth. And I tried to think of something else then and did not hear what my mother said after that.

And how old was I then? Sixteen. Sixteen is young, but it can also be a grown man. I am forty-one years old now, and I think about that time without regret, though my mother and I never talked in that way again, and I have not heard her voice now in a long, long time.

Notes on Craft and Context

Details: On Time Span

Let's start with the story's conclusion. We learn in the last paragraph that a full twenty-five years have elapsed between the time of telling and the events described. In the bulk of "Communist," Les—whose last name we never learn —is half the age of his mother Aileen—sixteen to thirty-two; at the present moment he's nine years older than she had been in 1961. It's possible—this is left intentionally ambiguous and unresolved—the closing phrase, "I have not heard her voice now in a long, long time" means Aileen is dead. Just as plausible, of course, is simple estrangement; the adult who relates this tale is very far removed from those he writes about. Glen Baxter's withdrawal is announced in the opening sentence: "My mother *once* had a boyfriend . . ." Note the use of the pluperfect tense here, as well as the word I've italicized, "once"; all this happened—as in the story's final phrase—"a long, long time" ago. Consider how radically different the action would feel if Ford used the present tense: "My mother *now* has a boyfriend . . ." And there's small doubt that at tale's end the "Communist" will leave the family again, this time for good. What happened on this particular day is—we are told repeatedly—important; what happens later is not so much unimportant as irrelevant.

Writing Up Close

Yet the story has great immediacy; the arrival of Glen Baxter and the car trip and hunt and resolution of the conflict are each recounted in vivid detail. When Les walks towards the lake, he doesn't yet know—in the "real time" of the story's telling—what he's about to see. The point of view is first-person past tense, but the present action compels our close attention, and the questions asked—though long since answered—retain their urgency. In some sense this demands a "willing suspension of disbelief"; no one can recall verbatim a conversation engaged in twenty-five years previously. The author therefore takes a kind of **dramatic license,** putting in quotation marks the dialogue he by necessity invents. It's important to note that this isn't an issue of personal history or the memoir, not a question of whether Richard Ford himself once went hunting with his pretty mother and her friend. There's no more reason to believe that Richard Ford is Les than to disbelieve that Charles Baxter is Fenstad or John Barth a boy like Ambrose because "Fenstad's Mother" and "Lost in the Funhouse" are told in the third person.

Writing at a Distance

Still, the narrative distance entailed by the first-person point of view is a matter of degree. By comparison with the "I" we come to know as Antonia in "The Behavior of the Hawkweeds," for example, the character of Les would seem more closely allied with the character of his author. Ford "throws" his voice less far. We have the sense as readers that the writer reconstructs not so much an actual event of his youth as a set of emotions experienced then; he's both very close to the action and aloof. One way we commonly put this is "If I knew then what I know now . . ." but everybody's present awareness includes experience acquired in the near or distant past. The narrator Ford puts on the page, an adolescent on the verge of manhood, would have to have had a photographic as well as phonographic memory to evoke with such precision what happened way back when.

Summary vs. Dialogue

The "indirect discourse" of Glen Baxter's speech about Vietnam and Communism—while the two men approach the lake—is closer to the mark. *"He told me about, and then we discussed"* is more plausibly the way Les would later on remember such a conversation. Yet fiction relies on scene and speech; the genuine encounters here cannot be handled in indirect discourse or as **summary.** We require dialogue in order to *see* what we *hear.* Just as we might well be bored by an extended monologue in which Glen Baxter repeats his experience of Southeast Asia, so would we be uninterested in the behavior of these characters if summarized. One way to read this story, indeed, is to look at the places where Ford compresses speech and where and when he lets his characters talk.

Details: On What's Left Unsaid

Another way of looking at this is to recognize how much of the "surrounding situation" has been **elided** or left out. What's said is less important, often, than what remains unsaid. There are only three speakers in these pages, but the cast of characters feels sizable. Aileen's other men, the folks she meets while waitressing or in the bar, Glen's other ladyfriends and his just-buried or possibly invented "little retarded sister," Les's girlfriends and boxing adversaries and dead father each play a role in the story, though none of them appear. The title, too, suggests a world beyond the circumscribed world of this house and small town. The memory of Vietnam and looming threat of wartime engagement and Glen's political convictions and real or imagined persecution and the dead father's insurance policies and the possibility of college for Aileen and Les—all these provide the background for the foregrounded action of what happened at "two o'clock on a Saturday" in November 1961. The world Les enters when he leaves Great Falls is, in effect, a present absence; his future has been circumscribed but not in detail described.

The Selection of Details

As writers—as human beings—we live in "valuative time." We focus on what matters to us and disregard what fails to; we engage in the act of artistic selection whenever we deal with a scene. "I only saw her for an hour, but it was worth it" is an example of valuative time; the twenty-three other hours of the day in question don't need to take time therefore space on the page. In a room full of people the one we desire is the one we pay attention to; in a war the single important adversary is the one we face. A story that included *everything* would be as dull as daily life, and an afternoon recounted with total attention to every subject and object would take months to write and afternoons to read. The world is a welter of details, and the tale teller's art consists of knowing which to pick.

In terms of narrative selection, therefore, this lengthy retrospect can serve a double purpose; it provides perspective and highlights what endures. Our vision blurs until suddenly we focus; our hearing dims until we hear a memorable line. And this is just as true for characters in fiction as for their creators and audience; certain moments *matter*, others don't. As readers we should ask ourselves, where are the "hot spots" of the story; what counts in the emotional reckoning here? For Les the vision of those massed airborne geese is crucial and not to be repeated; for Aileen it's that a wounded creature must not be abandoned to die. For Glen Baxter it's the admission of failure, the explosion of rage engendered when he empties his gun at the bird. In a story so full of anger suppressed and expressed—not so much during the hunt itself as in the fantasies of combat, boxing, persecution—it's doubly telling, somehow, that the final moment be an act of tenderness: mother and son in the dark.

On Details in Theme

What matters to Les, finally, is that he told the truth to his mother, that he found her "very feminine" and comforted her "at the edge of the porch" when she was unhappy and needed his support. She has just faced Glen Baxter down, publicly humiliating him, and knows she's lost her chance of marriage to the man. Consider, for example, how the whole **tone** of "Communist" would shift if the son's answer to the mother's question, "Do you think I'm still very feminine?" had been "No," instead of "Yes, I do." This affirmation is an act of generosity, "and I think about that time without regret."

And here is the moment preserved, the reason that a quarter of a century thereafter Les meditates upon and needs to tell his tale. A story that seems bleak, its human consolations sparse, becomes a record of kindness exchanged and—as Ford's friend Raymond Carver memorably put it in the short story we have just examined—"a small, good thing."

It's neither accidental nor merely a function of the alphabet that Carver, Ford and Hemingway follow each other sequentially here. From Carver to Ford to Hemingway there's a kind of artistic lineage and linkage, each to each. I mean by this not so much—though it's the case—that Ford and Carver were friends as that writers respond to each other. It helps, perhaps, to have personal familiarity with an author one admires but it's not of course essential; no writer alive has met Flaubert or Shakespeare and every living writer is nonetheless in their debt. So a son's white lie to his mother—that he still finds her "very feminine"—is related to the baker's proffered solace of fresh bread; they function in much the same way. "We have to keep civilization alive somehow," the mother says, and she and Les—though on the edge of wilderness and only for that fleeting shared moment—succeed.

On Setting in Theme

One other thing to notice is the beauty of the world evoked, the role that nature plays. A skein of American fiction and nonfiction has always been the **lyric** evocation of landscape, and this writer describes the countryside and snow geese with a naturalist's eye. A hunter's eye also, of course, but the way the men approach the lake could have been composed by Thoreau. There's a near ecstatic vision here that's quintessential Ford:

> By now the whole raft was in the air, all of it moving in a slow swirl above me and the lake and everywhere, finding the wind and heading out south in long wavering lines that caught the last sun and turned to silver as they gained a distance. It was a thing to see, I will tell you now. Five thousand

white geese all in the air around you, making a noise like you have never heard before. And I thought to myself then: this is something I will never see again. I will never forget this. And I was right.

In 1992 Richard Ford delivered the annual Hopwood Awards Lecture at the University of Michigan. One of the interesting aspects of this talk is how resolutely public it is, how collective are its concerns. The following paragraphs attach only indirectly to the short story "Communist," with its background of the CIA, Vietnam, and the political paranoia manifested by Glen Baxter. But Ford insists on the high moral calling of every act of witness, as well as on the way our public and private word worlds intersect. "Responsibility" is the signature word in this speech:

> ■ **WRITER'S VIEW:** *It is one of the privileges of being a writer, and likewise one of its high prices, that we intend the effect of what we write to be permanent, and accept responsibility for it . . .*
>
> *Art always thrives as some function of freedom, which isn't to say that oppression will kill it, only impede it, and deprive some of us of its generosity and its light. To accord others freedom is, however, not such a noteworthy virtue when you agree with what they're doing. It's only a great virtue when you agree to allow what you don't like. It is that odd, uneasy, vertiginous quality of art—that it may surprise you and tell you things you won't like to know—which makes it different from politics. And it is also this quality of art which makes it so fragile and precious and attractive . . .*
>
> *And so, to be better, I take that as my own premise: to exceed the limits of parochial experience in what I write; and to try, using my little freedoms, even occasionally moderating them, to represent mankind not so as to endear myself but so as to dignify it by insisting on its humanity and its complexity, its finality.*
>
> *And I try harder. I try to stay thoughtful of what is humanity's best self. If I diminish a character, make assaults on humankind in some way, I try eventually to replenish the account in other ways; and I don't part with a book unless I feel I've authorized every line. (Hopwood Awards Lecture, University of Michigan, 1992)*

■ Applications and Connections

- What would you say are the theme or themes in "Communist"? Are there specific lines of dialogue or narrative that express or hint at the theme(s)? How are the moral and **aesthetic** aspects of experience revealed in the details here? (Note: Something Ford wisely avoids is overexplicitness—not trusting the reader to understand a story, and in the process, overstating its theme.)
- In certain sections of the story many sentences in a row begin with "And". See, for instance, the second to last paragraph, beginning with "And I stood

at the edge of the porch . . ." as well as in the previous scene, "And my mother gave Glen a cold look then." What does the repetition of this conjunction accomplish? How does this stylistic choice affect the rhythm of the narrative?

• Because Ford writes at once up close and at a distance, the story has both an immediacy and a sense of perspective. How would "Communist" differ if written in the present tense, when Les is sixteen? If the story were written this way, what could the writer change—and how—to ensure "Communist" would still resonate thematically?

Exercises

1. Give Glen Baxter's account, either from a story of his own, or in dialogue with Aileen or Les, of exactly where he's been and what he's been up to in the past few months.

2. Rewrite the opening section, but set it in Chicago, Phoenix, or your own neighborhood.

3. Rewrite the long paragraph ("On the walk toward the lake, Glen began talking to me. I had never been alone with him . . . And when he said that he pulled back his VFW jacket and showed me the butt of a pistol he had stuck under his shirt against his bare skin.") all in dialogue, conveying the same information as Ford but without using any of his phrases from that passage. Why do you think Ford paraphrases here?

4. Write a scene in which Les tells Glen Baxter all about his father. Consider —and show—Glen's reactions. Consider why Ford leaves talk like this out of the story.

5. Expand the final paragraph; have Les tell us much more about his life now, at forty-one, and what has passed between then and now.

6. Describe the geese flying overhead in the voice of Barrett, Barth, Carver or any of the other authors in this text.

7. Write Aileen's encounter with the FBI, when they come to inquire the next morning about Baxter's whereabouts.

8. Have Les tell his first serious girlfriend what he thinks about marriage; have him tell his mother he won't go to college, and why.

9. Invent a fight—both physical and verbal—between Glen Baxter and Les.

10. "My mother had tried to see the good side of things, tried to be hopeful in the situation she was handed, tried to look out for us both, and it hadn't worked . . . Too much awareness too early in life was her problem, I think." Expand on this perception, and in Aileen's voice.

CHAPTER 6

COMPRESSION:
Prose as Architecture

ERNEST HEMINGWAY, "Chapter VII" and
"In Another Country"

■ **WRITER'S VIEW:** *The most essential gift for a good writer is a built-in, shock-proof shit detector. This is the writer's radar, and all great writers have had it. (Interview with Ernest Hemingway,* Writers at Work, *The Paris Review interview series, vol. 2)*

Ernest Hemingway (1899–1961) is perhaps the most influential American author of the twentieth century. He did more to define our artistic language than any of his contemporaries, and for years he seemed the image of "the great American writer." (I put that phrase in quotes because it's no more realistic than the idea of "the great American novel.") With the possible exception of William Faulkner, another Nobel Prize–winning laureate, Hemingway held the title—as he was fond of describing it—of writing's "heavyweight champ." The metaphor of the prizefighter is appropriate here; the man's imposing physical presence was as familiar as his prose, and even today there are furniture lines—Paris, Key West, Havana—that are supposed to confer upon their purchaser the famous Hemingway style. Although his personality and prose style no longer dominate the literary landscape, he remains a major figure in the history of American **prose,** and no anthology of short fiction would be complete without a sampling of his work.

Born in Oak Park, Illinois, he died—a suicide—in Ketchum, Idaho; this representative American figure spent, however, many years abroad. Much of his fiction takes place, as he put it, "In Another Country." His first novel, *The Sun Also Rises* (1926), deals with American expatriates in France and Spain; his novel *A Farewell to Arms* (1929) is set in Italy and Switzerland during the

First World War. *For Whom the Bell Tolls* (1940) takes as its topic the Spanish Civil War, and *The Old Man and the Sea* (1952) explores fishing waters off Cuba. In addition to these four, the novels and short story collections published during Hemingway's lifetime include *Three Stories and Ten Poems* (1923), *In Our Time* (1924), *The Torrents of Spring* (1926), *Men without Women* (1927), *Winner Take Nothing* (1933), *To Have and Have Not* (1937), and *Across the River and into the Trees* (1950). Trained as a newspaper reporter, Hemingway wrote nonfiction also; the accounts of his adventures include *Death in the Afternoon* (1932), *Green Hills of Africa* (1935), and *The Dangerous Summer* (1960).

Many more books have appeared since his death. First came a memoir of his early years in Paris titled *A Moveable Feast,* then several novels culled from work-in-progress: *The Island and the Stream, The Garden of Eden,* and *True at First Light* as well as a baker's dozen of reissued short story collections and letters and dispatches. Indeed, so enduring is this author's commercial success that his bibliography lists more volumes that have been published *after* his death than those he produced while alive.

In novels, short stories, and nonfiction alike, Hemingway celebrated the ideal of "grace under pressure" as a writing style. His characters are matadors and soldiers and big-game hunters; they are without exception tight-lipped and coolheaded in the face of danger. At their best they revel in *machismo,* at their worst they are merely *macho,* and their creator has often been accused—with, it must be admitted, some justice—of dealing in stereotype. His old people and children are cardboard cutouts and his women can look like cartoons. This author's heroes are wholly heroic, his cowards entirely cowardly, and though the "good guys" don't always win it's always clear which of his characters are pure and which corrupt. There's a strict moral regimen here, and a code of behavior—from drinking to hunting and fishing—that celebrates not so much restraint as self-control.

Hemingway distrusted fancy phrasing and abstract utterance. Brilliantly, in *A Farewell to Arms,* he makes the case for concrete speech. His protagonist, Frederick Henry, has come to understand the futility of sloganeering in wartime, and the risks of propaganda:

> I did not say anything. I was always embarrassed by the words sacred, glorious, and sacrifice and the expression in vain. We had heard them, sometimes standing in the rain almost out of earshot, so that only the shouted words came through, and had read them, on proclamations that were slapped up by billposters over other proclamations, now for a long time, and I had seen nothing sacred, and the things that were glorious had no glory and the sacrifices were like the stockyards at Chicago if nothing was done with the meat except to bury it. There were many words that you could not stand to hear and finally only the names of places had dignity. Certain numbers were the same way and certain dates and these with the

names of the places were all you could say and have them mean anything. Abstract words such as glory, honor, courage or hallow were obscene beside the concrete names of villages, the numbers of roads, the names of rivers, the numbers of regiments and the dates. (*A Farewell to Arms,* Scribner Paperback Fiction Edition [New York: Scribner, 1995])

In this chapter we will look at two examples of Hemingway's work. In both he cuts back the fat of language to a bare-bones skeleton; in both he strives for precision and conciseness, sticking—like the TV policeman in *Dragnet*—to "Just the facts, ma'am."

Here is one of his early descriptions of the expatriate experience, a story located in Italy during World War I.

Chapter VII

*W*hile the bombardment was knocking the trench to pieces at Fossalta, he lay very flat and sweated and prayed oh jesus christ get me out of here. Dear jesus please get me out. Christ please please please christ. If you'll only keep me from getting killed I'll do anything you say. I believe in you and I'll tell every one in the world that you are the only one that matters. Please please dear jesus. The shelling moved further up the line. We went to work on the trench and in the morning the sun came up and the day was hot and muggy and cheerful and quiet. The next night back at Mestre he did not tell the girl he went upstairs with at the Villa Rossa about Jesus. And he never told anybody.

▓ Notes on Craft and Context

On Compression and Style

This early example of the famous prose style comes from a series of very short stories and "chapters" titled *In Our Time*. Hemingway began his career as a newspaperman, where brevity and action-driven sentences are indispensable tools of the trade. He also apprenticed himself, though informally, to two great teachers of writing: Sherwood Anderson and Gertrude Stein. Both were engaged in stripping literary prose of all abstraction; both helped him cut and prune.

Here is Hemingway at his most concise. The language of this "Chapter" has a compression approaching simultaneity; a great deal happens in eight short lines. To call this paragraph a "Chapter" is to revise the notion of expansiveness and prove the modernist assertion that "Less is More." One could of course argue that even eight lines are a form of enlargement, and that these scenes expand upon the saying: "There are no atheists in foxholes." But that's an **aphorism**, a thing reduced to its bare minimum, and in fewer than 150 words we have an entire story sketched in if not fleshed out.

A wartime situation and its terror modulates—the bombing is severe, then stops; a man makes a promise and breaks it. The author accomplishes this with only one comma, after the first phrase of the first sentence, and many of the words themselves are repeated: *please please please.* The "signature" Hemingway sentence here, it would seem, is "We went to work on the trench and in the morning the sun came up and the day was hot and muggy and cheerful and quiet."

On Point of View in Style

First of all, who is this "We"? The author speaks in a **collective first person;** the members of the troop all go to work on the trench. Somehow, too, he manages to overhear what the nameless protagonist of the story (the soldier, "he") is praying to himself while under fire; although "he never told anybody" the narrator nonetheless knows. This is a form of **omniscience** or total authorial knowledge, but it's done quite quietly and calls no attention to itself.

On Word Choice and Syntax

Too, the four adjectives that modify the noun "day" partake of a similar **transposition;** "the day was hot and muggy and quiet" makes good descriptive sense, but "cheerful" is a kind of odd man out; it's the troops who are cheerful —having survived bombardment—not the day. Finally, Hemingway's use of the conjunction should be noted: "*and* in the morning the sun came up *and* the day was hot *and* muggy *and* cheerful *and* quiet" is called a paratactic construction; component parts of the sentence are linked by a conjunction (and, but, or, etc.) in a system that suggests they all belong together. There's no "subjugation" or "subordination," as in the standard rules of **syntax,** with its commas and dependent clauses; everything in Hemingway is equally important; every detail counts.

From first to final line this vignette feels hard-boiled and acid etched. The narrative's efficient and the manner of its telling brusque. What could have been examined in microscopic detail is telescoped instead. The author seems to say that nothing takes him by surprise, and sincerity is fleeting in a world at war or peace. He uses place-names ("only the names of places had dignity") to lend a kind of geographic specificity and factual accuracy to this piece of storytelling; even if we've never before heard of Fossalta or Mestre, the use of proper nouns helps situate the tale. Too, it makes the reader believe, if only by association, that such a place as the "Villa Rossa" is likely to exist.

One last detail—a daring one—to notice. The lowercase "jesus" reduces what would have been a respectful invocation of divinity to the kind of casual blasphemy that men use when distracted; it's common parlance under stress and very different from the uppercase "Jesus" of the next-to-last descriptive sentence. Even the orthography (grammar treating of letters and spelling) in the soldier's prayer reveals a state of mind.

And next, one of this author's masterpieces. Here too the setting and situation belong to the war, but Hemingway moves beyond the "stiff upper lip" and plumbs emotional depths.

In Another Country

In the fall the war was always there but we did not go to it any more. It was cold in the fall in Milan and the dark came very early. Then the electric lights came on, and it was pleasant along the streets looking in the windows. There was much game hanging outside the shops, and the snow powdered in the fur of the foxes and the wind blew their tails. The deer hung stiff and heavy and empty, and small birds blew in the wind and the wind turned their feathers. It was a cold fall and the wind came down from the mountains.

We were all at the hospital every afternoon, and there were different ways of walking across the town through the dusk to the hospital. Two of the ways were alongside canals, but they were long. Always, though, you crossed a bridge across a canal to enter the hospital. There was a choice of three bridges. On one of them a woman sold roasted chestnuts. It was warm, standing in front of her charcoal fire, and the chestnuts were warm afterward in your pocket. The hospital was very old and very beautiful, and you entered through a gate and walked across a courtyard and out a gate on the other side. There were usually funerals starting from the courtyard. Beyond the old hospital were the new brick pavilions, and there we met every afternoon and were all very polite and interested in what was the matter, and sat in the machines that were to make so much difference.

The doctor came up to the machine where I was sitting and said: "What did you like best to do before the war? Did you practice a sport?"

I said: "Yes, football."

"Good," he said. "You will be able to play football again better than ever."

My knee did not bend and the leg dropped straight from the knee to the ankle without a calf, and the machine was to bend the knee and make it move as in riding a tricycle. But it did not bend yet, and instead the machine lurched when it came to the bending part. The doctor said: "That will all pass. You are a fortunate young man. You will play football again like a champion."

In the next machine was a major who had a little hand like a baby's. He winked at me when the doctor examined his hand, which was between two leather straps that bounced up and down and flapped the stiff fingers, and said: "And will I too play football, captain-doctor?" He had been a very great fencer, and before the war the greatest fencer in Italy.

The doctor went to his office in a back room and brought a photograph which showed a hand that had been withered almost as small as the major's, before it had taken a machine course, and after was a little larger. The major held the photograph with his good hand and looked at it very carefully. "A wound?" he asked.

"An industrial accident," the doctor said.

"Very interesting, very interesting," the major said, and handed it back to the doctor.

"You have confidence?"

"No," said the major.

There were three boys who came each day who were about the same age I was. They were all three from Milan, and one of them was to be a lawyer, and one was to be a painter, and one had intended to be a soldier, and after we were finished with the machines, sometimes we walked back together to the Café Cova, which was next door to the Scala. We walked the short way through the communist quarter because we were four together. The people hated us because we were officers, and from a wine-shop some one called out, "A basso gli ufficiali!" as we passed. Another boy who walked with us sometimes and made us five wore a black silk handkerchief across his face because he had no nose then and his face was to be rebuilt. He had gone out to the front from the military academy and been wounded within an hour after he had gone into the front line for the first time. They rebuilt his face, but he came from a very old family and they could never get the nose exactly right. He went to South America and worked in a bank. But this was a long time ago, and then we did not any of us know how it was going to be afterward. We only knew then that there was always the war, but that we were not going to it any more.

We all had the same medals, except the boy with the black silk bandage across his face, and he had not been at the front long enough to get any medals. The tall boy with a very pale face who was to be a lawyer had been a lieutenant of Arditi and had three medals of the sort we each had only one of. He had lived a very long time with death and was a little detached. We were all a little detached, and there was nothing that held us together except that we met every afternoon at the hospital. Although, as we walked to the Cova through the tough part of town, walking in the dark, with light and singing come out of the wine-shops, and sometimes having to walk into the street when the men and women would crowd together on the sidewalk so that we would have had to jostle them to get by, we felt held together by there being something that had happened that they, the people who disliked us, did not understand.

We ourselves all understood the Cova, where it was rich and warm and not too brightly lighted, and noisy and smoky at certain hours, and there were always girls at the tables and the illustrated papers on a rack on the wall. The girls at the Cova were very patriotic, and I found that the most patriotic people in Italy were the café girls—and I believe they are still patriotic.

The boys at first were very polite about my medals and asked me what I had done to get them. I showed them the papers, which were written in very beautiful language and full of *fratellanza* and *abnegazione*, but which really said, with the adjectives removed, that I had been given the medals because I was an American. After that their manner changed a little toward me, although I was their friend against outsiders. I was a friend, but I was never really one of them after they had read the citations, because it had been different with them and they had done very different things to get their medals. I had been wounded, it was true; but we all knew that being wounded, after all, was really an accident. I was never ashamed of the ribbons, though, and sometimes, after the cocktail hour, I would imagine myself having done all the things they had done to get their medals; but walking home at night through the empty streets with the cold wind and all the shops closed, trying to keep near the street lights, I knew that I would never have done such things, and I was very much afraid to die, and often lay in bed at night by myself, afraid to die and wondering how I would be when I went back to the front again.

The three with the medals were like hunting-hawks; and I was not a hawk, although I might seem a hawk to those who had never hunted; they, the three, knew better and so we drifted apart. But I stayed good friends with the boy who had been wounded his first day at the front, because he would never know now how he would have turned out; so he could never be accepted either, and I liked him because I thought perhaps he would not have turned out to be a hawk either.

The major who had been the great fencer, did not believe in bravery, and spent much time while we sat in the machines correcting my grammar. He had complimented me on how I spoke Italian, and we talked together very easily. One day I had said that Italian seemed such an easy language to me that I could not take a great interest in it; everything was so easy to say. "Ah, yes," the major said. "Why, then, do you not take up the use of grammar?" So we took up the use of grammar, and soon Italian was such a difficult language that I was afraid to talk to him until I had the grammar straight in my mind.

The major came very regularly to the hospital. I do not think he ever missed a day, although I am sure he did not believe in the machines. There was a time when none of us believed in the machines, and one day the major said that it was all nonsense. The machines were new then and it was we who were to prove them. It was an idiotic idea, he said, "a theory like another." I had not learned my grammar, and he said I was a stupid impossible disgrace, and he was a fool to have bothered with me. He was a small man and he sat straight up in his chair with his right hand thrust into the machine and looked straight ahead at the wall while the straps thumped up and down with his fingers in them.

"What will you do when the war is over if it is over?" he asked me. "Speak grammatically!"

"I will go to the States."

"Are you married?

"No, but I hope to be."

"The more of a fool you are," he said. He seemed very angry. "A man must not marry."

"Why, Signor Maggiore?"

"Don't call me 'Signor Maggiore.'"

"Why must not a man marry?"

"He cannot marry. He cannot marry," he said angrily. "If he is to lose everything, he should not place himself in a position to lose that. He should not place himself in a position to lose. He should find things he cannot lose."

He spoke very angrily and bitterly, and looked straight ahead while he talked.

"But why should he necessarily lose it?"

"He'll lose it," the major said. He was looking at the wall. Then he looked down at the machine and jerked his little hand out from between the straps and slapped it hard against his thigh. "He'll lose it," he almost shouted. "Don't argue with me!" Then he called to the attendant who ran the machines. "Come and turn this damned thing off."

He went back into the other room for the light treatment and the massage. Then I heard him ask the doctor if he might use his telephone and he shut the door. When he came back into the room, I was sitting in another machine. He was wearing his cape and had his cap on, and he came directly toward my machine and put his arm on my shoulder.

"I am so sorry," he said, and patted me on the shoulder with his good hand. "I would not be rude. My wife has just died. You must forgive me."

"Oh—" I said, feeling sick for him. "I am *so* sorry."

He stood there biting his lower lip. "It is very difficult," he said. "I cannot resign myself."

He looked straight past me and out through the window. Then he began to cry. "I am utterly unable to resign myself," he said and choked. And then crying, his head up looking at nothing, carrying himself straight and soldierly, with tears on both his cheeks and biting his lips, he walked past the machines and out the door.

The doctor told me that the major's wife, who was very young and whom he had not married until he was definitely invalided out of the war, had died of pneumonia. She had been sick only a few days. No one expected her to die. The major did not come to the hospital for three days. Then he came at the usual hour, wearing a black band on the sleeve of his uniform. When he came back, there were large framed photographs around the wall, of all sorts of wounds before and after they had been cured by the machines. In front of the machine the major used were three photographs of hands like his that were completely restored. I do not know where the doctor got them. I always understood we were the first to use the machines. The photographs did not make much difference to the major because he only looked out of the window.

■ Notes on Craft and Context

On Tense and Point of View

The title of this story echoes a phrase in Christopher Marlowe's play *The Jew of Malta*—"But that was in another country, and besides the wench is dead." Though this story seems immediate and personally experienced, it's told in the past tense. The strategy is similar to the one we've just examined in the case of Richard Ford. We can't tell precisely how many years afterward the American narrator looks back at what happened, but it's clear he tells the tale at both a temporal and geographical remove ("But this was a long time ago, and then we did not any of us know how it was going to be afterward.") Here again—as in "Chapter VII"—the narrator says "We" and can speak with a collective voice, but a first-person and particularized "I" emerges as the tale goes on. The Major's wife—whom he clearly loves, and whom he has tried to protect by not marrying until "he was definitely invalided out of the war"—dies offstage. Yet a dismissive phrase such as "the wench is dead" would be too hard-boiled a tag line for the Major's loss. Although his soldier's discipline militates against it, the Major allows emotion ("with tears on both his cheeks and biting his lips") to enter strongly in. His own survival—when his young bride dies—seems too much to bear. He bears it nonetheless.

The first sentence is echoed roughly halfway through ("We only knew then that there was always the war, but that we were not going to it any more.") and in both cases the abstraction "war" is rendered as a concrete thing, a perpetual place somewhere else. The question of bravery troubles the narrator, and how brave he would have proved under continued fire, but it no longer troubles the Major, who had been a very great fencer and who has earned his promotions and made—in a phrase from *A Farewell to Arms*—his own and "a separate peace."

Will the Major's hand enlarge and the narrator's leg heal? Have those machines been used before; where do the photographs come from; are they photographs of normal hands "doctored" to look like those of the injured? Such questions are asked but not answered. The programmatic optimism of the doctor is like the propaganda of those who celebrate war and write citations for medals. It has scant basis in reality; reality is grim.

On Dialogue and Language

In these two selections we have not so far focused on one of Hemingway's signature achievements, his use of dialogue. Though there is spoken utterance in the **vignette** ("Please please dear jesus") the nameless "he" talks to himself. The working assumption of "In Another Country" is that everything is spoken in Italian and the author translates for his audience after the fact. The discussion of how to learn Italian is partly comic and wholly serious; speech—and by extension, writing—seems "easy" until "we took up the use of grammar" and precise utterance proves "difficult." Avoidance and indirection structures the way these soldiers talk; it's all the more moving, therefore, when the major reveals strong emotion near the story's end.

On Prose as Architecture

It bears repeating here that Hemingway was experimental—even avant garde—in his approach to prose. To prove the radical nature of his innovations we need only glance at writing about war and romance before he perfected his **craft.** In his short stories in particular—the novel by its very nature requires digression and subplot—Hemingway writes with impressive efficiency and no wasted word. When he claims "the **Baroque** is over," he means that ornamentation and extravagant detail will not be a feature of modern design; when he claims that "Prose is architecture, not interior decoration," he signals his interest in shape. What the major sees when he "looked out the window" is the landscape of T. S. Eliot's *The Wasteland*—a major poem of the period, also written in response to war—and that bleak landscape endures.

▓ **WRITER'S VIEW:** *Prose is architecture, not interior decoration, and the Baroque is over . . . A good writer should know as near everything as possible. Naturally he will not. A great enough writer seems to be born with* *knowledge. But he really is not; he has only been born with a quicker ratio to the passage of time than other men and without conscious application, and with an intelligence to accept or reject what is already presented as knowledge. There are some things which cannot be learned quickly, and time, which is all we have, must be paid heavily for their acquiring. They are the very simplest things and because it takes a man's life to know them the little new that each man gets from life is very costly and the only heritage he has to leave. Every novel which is truly written contributes to the total of knowledge which is there at the disposal of the next writer who comes, but the next writer must pay, always, a certain nominal percentage in experience to be able to understand and assimilate what is available as his birthright and what he must, in turn, take his departure from. If a writer of prose knows enough about what he is writing about he may omit things that he knows and the reader, if the writer is writing truly enough, will have a feeling of those things as strongly as though the writer had stated them. The dignity of movement of an iceberg is due to only one-eighth of it being above water.* (Death in the Afternoon *[New York: Scribner, 1932])*

This passage is perhaps the single most famous of Hemingway's pronouncements about art. Its final sentence suggests that, while we must study the surface, we also have to pay attention to the depths. What *can't* be seen is crucial to the structure of what's visible, and the way a story or novel is built—"Prose is architecture . . ."—will matter a great deal. The offhand-seeming utterance—"due to only one-eighth of it being" sounds very much like casual speech—belies or disguises the formal "dignity" of the aesthetic intention. He's burying his deep seriousness, in effect, the way the iceberg too has been submerged.

▩ Applications and Connections

- How is Hemingway's use of the paratactic, in both "Chapter VII" and "In Another Country," different from Ford's repetitive use of "And" as a sentence starter in "Communist"? How is it similar? When would you employ either or both of these techniques in a story?
- Compression, or trimming a story down to its bare bones, forces the writer to separate what is really important and necessary in a story from details that might be interesting but distract from—more than contribute to—the narrative. However, aiming for compression in a first draft might do more to limit than inspire. Prose is architecture, and builders need both a foundation —that no one will end up seeing—and a scaffolding that comes down when the structure is complete. The trick is to learn to distinguish building materi-

als from the building itself. How does Hemingway do this? What extra information does he seem to know about the characters or the plot, and why has he chosen not to include it?

- How are Hemingway's characters "in another country" metaphorically as well as literally? What role does the title play in the story, with its weight as both an allusion and an extended metaphor? Consider the titles of other stories in this book, such as "Fenstad's Mother," "Lost in the Funhouse," and "A Good Man Is Hard to Find." How and how much does each title inform the story that follows?

Exercises

1. Translate the full citation for the medals that our soldier earned: *Fratellanza* and *Abnegazione* mean, roughly, "brotherhood" and "sacrifice."

2. "Football" in Italy would have meant "soccer." Amplify the dialogue between the doctor and the wounded American, in which the latter tries to explain to the former the differences in the two games.

3. Write a scene where the soldier returns to America with (a) a wooden leg, (b) crutches, and (c) fully recovered and ready to play football again.

4. Write the scene in which the Major proposes to his young bride, then the telephone call in which he learns of her death.

5. Take a familiar location and describe it in Hemingway's terms.

6. Have the protagonist take one of the café girls upstairs in the Milan equivalent of the Villa Mestre, and have him try to talk to her about bravery and hawks while she discusses patriotism; do they or don't they make love?

7. Write a scene in which the boy from a very old family and with a rebuilt nose goes to work in a bank in South America; what does he tell his coworkers, and how does he describe his own time in the military academy, at the front, and in the hospital?

8. Write one of the funeral scenes at the hospital—"There were usually funerals starting from the courtyard"—and do it in Hemingway's style. Write the funeral—by contrast—of the Major's wife.

9. "He had complimented me on how I spoke Italian, and we talked together very easily. One day I had said that Italian seemed such an easy language to me that I could not take a great interest in it; everything was so easy to say. 'Ah, yes,' the major said. 'Why, then, do you not take up the use of grammar?' So we took up the use of grammar, and soon Italian was such a difficult language that I was afraid to talk to him until I had the grammar straight in my mind." Substitute "English" for "Italian" and apply it to the principles of *The Sincerest Form.*

10. Write your own story of love and injury and loss, but using Hemingway's diction and striving, too, for his tone.

▨ Examples of Student Work

(*Editor's Note:* The writer here transposes a scene in *A Farewell to Arms* from Europe in the First World War to Hong Kong in the winter of 1997–1998, during the heart of the Asian financial meltdown. Frank Harris shares at least the initials of his name with Hemingway's novel's protagonist, Frederick Henry, and Kate—from Morgan Stanley's Human Resources Office—is a version of the nurse Catherine Barkley. The transposition seems remarkably adept, including the way the author transliterates a foreign tongue—the pidgin English of the Italians now rendered as Chinese—and though this scene follows Chapter XX of *A Farewell to Arms* quite closely, it also works well by itself.)

Jess Row

One Sunday in the afternoon we went to the races. Bridget went too and Arthur Ko, the boy who had been in Peregrine Fixed Assets when the scandal fell and the company folded the same day. The girls put on their makeup after lunch while Ko and I stood on the balcony and read the past performances of the horses and the predictions in the paper. Ko checked his pager every five minutes and he did not care much about these races but read the racing paper constantly and kept track of all the horses for something to do. He said the horses were a terrible lot but they were the best we could do with the Invitational in two weeks. The owners were saving the good horses for the Invitational.

Ah-Leung liked him and gave him tips. Leung won on nearly every race but disliked to give tips because it brought down the prices. The racing was very crooked. Though the Jockey Club put up a good front only the clubhouse members heard the good tips and their runners who could be bribed but for a small fortune in American dollars. Leung's information was good but I hated to ask him because sometimes he did not answer, and always you could see it hurt him to tell you, but he felt obligated to tell us for some reason and he hated less to tell Ko. Ko's family had been hurt badly by the loss of income, a building deal in Toronto had broken up, and Leung had also suffered terrible losses in the market collapse and so he liked Ko. Leung never told his wife what horses he was playing and she won or lost, mostly lost, and talked on her mobile all the time.

We four drove through the tunnel to Happy Valley in
Ko's Jaguar convertible. It was a lovely day and we drove
along the green hillsides and the Repulse Bay beaches and
along the jetties east of Aberdeen and into the tunnel
past the sign that listed the number of accidents for the
year. There were villas with stucco walls and lines of
palms and banana and cypress and the water sparkling and
the humps of the outlying islands across the channel. We
could look across the water and see junks and sailboats
on the sparkling waves and the mountains of Lantau to the
north. There were many cars parking in the member's lot
and the men at the Gate let us in without cards because
Ko leaned over and said something quick and hard in
Cantonese about Ah-Leung. We left the car, bought racing
cards, and took the elevator to the clubhouse floor. The
carpet there was thick and deep and the windows were
polished so that we might have been outside, but the
members talked quietly and the waiters made no sound when
they walked. We went out onto the viewing balcony and saw
people that we knew and leaned over the rail and borrowed
binoculars to watch the horses.

The grooms led them in front of the grandstand one by
one, their heads down, and as each one passed its picture
appeared on the video screen with the name of the owner
and statistics and weight and pedigree. The horses' heads
bobbed as they walked and we could see the sweat rolling
off their flanks. The last one had a coat that shone like
gold and Ko swore the owner had it painted that color for
luck. No one believed him. The horse's name was Fat Choy:
lots of money. Ko said people would bet more on him with
that name and it was good luck even if he didn't win.
Kate said she didn't understand that kind of luck. But
later when were filling out our cards she and Bridget
filled out one for the one that the Racing Supplement said
would win and one for Fat Choy, who was thirty-five to
one. Ko gave the tickets and the money to one of the men
in tuxedos who took bets for the members and spoke to him
sharply in Cantonese again. It seemed he took no joy in
speaking his own language and I felt sorry about it.

We went up to Ah-Leung's table to watch the race.
He was eating hairy crabs with Mrs. Leung as we sat down.
As he talked he cracked open the legs of the crabs and
sucked out the meat and dropped the spent shells on the
tablecloth and a waiter gathered them up with a silver
rake. It was the season for hairy crabs and they had to
be eaten fresh or they would not be worth eating. The
race started very suddenly and the horses went around
once before we could see who was in front on the video

screen. They came past the grandstand with the gold horse well in front and on the turn he was running away from the others. We watched them on the final stretch and the jockey was nearly standing straight on his back and he finished three lengths ahead. He went past the grandstand and almost a quarter of the way around the track before the jockey reined him in and all the time Leung was cracking the shells of the crabs and eating them as if he could never be full. The crabs cost thirty American dollars apiece.

"Incredible," Kate said, doing the numbers on her Palm Pilot. "That's thirty-five hundred Hong Kong dollars for both of us. I should do this more often."

"You watch," Ko said. "When he goes past the grandstand, people want to touch him for luck."

"He's a beautiful horse," Kate said. "Did you bet on him, Mr. Leung?"

He nodded.

"I didn't," Mrs. Leung said. "Who you bet on?"

"Fat Choy."

"*Aiya*," she said and laughed. "Lots of money."

"Maybe he won't pay so much," Leung said.

"He's supposed to be thirty-five to one."

"Those are, ah, how you say—preliminary estimates," Leung said. "Right before they put more money on him, so odds change. He pay maybe three to one."

"They can't do that," Kate said. "Aren't the odds fixed?"

"Not when Li Ka-Shing is here," Leung said. "He put a lot of money in at the last minute." He had a high-pitched laugh.

"That's ridiculous. Then what's the point of racing?"

"Ah," Leung laughed again. "You know English saying. Who put gun to your head? You get maybe three hundred dollars, not so bad."

"It's a scam," Bridget said.

"Of course," said Kate, "we did have some insider information. But if you get the inside tip at least you should get the payoff, shouldn't you?"

"Let's go to the bar and get a drink and see what they pay," Ko said. We stood at the mahogany bar and watched the television screens with the numbers scrolling across the bottom. Li put up twenty on Fat Choy to win. That meant he paid less than even money on a ten-dollar bet.

(*Editor's Note:* This is a **parody** of Frederick Henry's plunge in the river in *A Farewell to Arms.* Having made "a separate peace," Henry must escape from those Italians who are planning to shoot him, and he does so in this fashion—though Ms. Stewart makes a joke of it. Note how the author's habit of repetition and **parataxis** is here exaggerated for comic effect; note how the weights in the boots recur and how the speaker sounds foolish rather than smart. Also, because this is parodic of the famous style, it's hard to tell when Ms. Stewart gets it wrong on purpose and when she's simply flat footed or, as it were, wet shod.

Leah Stewart

When I came up there was a log floating ahead of me in the water. It was a rough log and I reached it and held on. I got a splinter. Then there was another splinter. There were many splinters in my hand. I hid behind the log. I did not want to see the bank. On the bank there had been shots and carabinieri with hats that were called airplanes. Those hats reminded me of things that were wide. It was not hard to stay under with weights inside my boots.

The log swung in the current, and when I turned I could see the bank. Before I had not wanted to look at the bank. Now I looked at the bank. It seemed that it was going by very fast, and I was not moving in the wet and cold water. There was much wood in the stream, and I saw the boot of an Italian in the water. I saw many boots. It seemed that the water was very cold. The boots were coming toward me. I kept my head behind the log. I did not want to see the boots. I put my other hand on the log and I held onto it with both hands. There was no chance of seeing the shore now.

You do not know how long you are in a river when the current moves swiftly. It may be a very long time, but it might also be a very short time. It might be five minutes, but it might be more. The water was cold and wet and I was cold and wet and many things passed that were cold and wet also. I was lucky to have the log that I could keep both hands on and not see the shore when I did not want to and also look around and see the shore if I did want to, if the shore could be seen. I hoped I would see the shore coming closer soon. I had had enough of the water and my stomach hurt. I wanted to take my pants off, but decided I would not be able to get my boots off. Pants are hard to take off over boots, and it would be difficult to take my boots off because they were in the water and the water was making the knots in my boot laces tight and wet. It would be bad if I landed and I had no boots. I had to get to Mestre someway, and it seemed that I might have to walk. The log could go no further once I reached the shore.

The log and I were floating more slowly than we had
been floating before. The shore was very close. The shore
was so close that I could reach out and touch the twigs
on the willow bush. My knees were in the mud and my
stomach was in the mud and we were floating so slowly then
that we might as well have not been floating at all. I
could see the bush, but I could not stand up out of the
mud because of my boots. I thought I might lie in the mud
all day because of my boots. They were heavy and I held
onto the log with both hands and thought about it. It had
never occurred to me in the river that I might lie in the
mud all day. I felt muddy and wet in my pants and boots
and I waited for the wet feeling to pass but it did not
pass and I was still muddy and wet. I pulled myself up
onto the log and took off my boots and took out the
weights. Then I waded out of the water and up the
slippery bank. I rested and it seemed that I would slide
down the slippery bank into the river. I went up the bank
some more and rested again. There was rain and I was
already wet.

SETTING:
Perception, Place, and Displacement

BHARATI MUKHERJEE, "The Management of Grief"

■ WRITER'S VIEW: *The immigrants in my stories go through extreme transformations in America and at the same time they alter the country's appearance and psychological make-up.* ("An Interview with Bharati Mukherjee," The Massachusetts Review, *29.4 [1988]*)

Bharati Mukherjee was born in 1940 in Calcutta, India. She graduated from the University of Calcutta, then received an MA in English and Ancient Indian Culture from the University of Baroda; she earned both her master's degree in fine arts and a doctorate in English and comparative literature from the University of Iowa. Much of her work contrasts life in India with life in the United States—or, as in "The Management of Grief," Canada. This peripatetic author makes use of her travels to furnish locale; New York state—to take a single example—offers such settings as Flushing, Poughkeepsie, and Buffalo, where her short and long fictions take place. Mukherjee has taught creative writing at Columbia and New York universities, Skidmore College, Queens College and elsewhere. In 1990 she joined the faculty at the University of California, Berkeley.

She and her husband Clark Blaise met while they were graduate students at the University of Iowa's Writers Workshop. Married two years later on their lunch hour—a far cry from the elaborate ritual for Bengali brides—they collaborated on a book that stressed their disparate perceptions during a visit to her parental home in India: *Days and Nights in Calcutta* (1977). In most such cases "partners" share their drafts and finished texts; this is a memoir about shared events written turn by turn from the two points of view. *The Sorrow and the Terror: The Haunting Legacy of the Air India Tragedy* (1987) is a second book of nonfiction composed with Blaise; Mukherjee has published two other works of nonfiction: *Political Culture and Leadership in India* (1991) and *Regionalism in Indian Perspective* (1992).

These titles suggest both the range and focus of her attention. She rejects such delimiting descriptions of her work as those that come with hyphens ("Bengali-Indian-American"), those that come as categories ("women of color") or those that come with aesthetic constraints. Minimalism, she writes in the *New York Times Book Review* of Aug. 28, 1988, is "designed to keep anyone out with too much story to tell." In part perhaps because such labels are so easy to affix, she prefers the hard work of self-definition.

> **WRITER'S VIEW:** *I maintain that I am an American writer of Indian origin, not because I'm ashamed of my past, not because I'm betraying or distorting my past, but because my whole adult life has been lived here, and I write about the people who are immigrants going through the process of making a home here . . . I write in the tradition of immigrant experience rather than nostalgia and expatriation. That is very important. I am saying that the luxury of being a U.S. citizen for me is that I can define myself in terms of things like my politics, my sexual orientation or my education. My affiliation with readers should be on the basis of what they want to read, not in terms of my ethnicity or my race. ("Bharati Mukherjee," by Nicholas A. Basbanes)*

It is as a writer of fiction that she stakes her principal claim. Ms. Mukherjee won the National Book Critics Circle Award in fiction for *The Middleman and Other Stories,* becoming the first naturalized American citizen to receive that honor. Her novels include *The Tiger's Daughter* (1972), *Wife* (1975), *Jasmine* (1989), *The Holder of the World* (1993), *Leave It to Me* (1997), and *Desirable Daughters* (2002); her short story collections are *Darkness (1985)* and *The Middleman and Other Stories* (1988), which includes "The Management of Grief."

This writer's representative central figure is a young woman torn between cultures—not so much adrift between as doubly anchored by them. Her protagonists possess the kind of double vision that provides self-knowledge, but it can at first confuse. Whether the women are Indians in North America or Americans in the subcontinent, the clash of tradition and expectation powers Mukherjee's plots. The protagonists of *Jasmine* and *Leave It to Me* have a ferocity and lethal potential derived in seeming-equal parts from Indian **mythology** and American sociopathology; revenge is a motivating factor often for these characters, although the source of the insult to be avenged shifts from book to book. What's constant in Bharati Mukherjee's work is the search for identity and personal freedom, a description of women at risk.

Here is a story that deals with both individual and collective risk—what can and can't be saved.

The Management of Grief

A woman I don't know is boiling tea the Indian way in my kitchen. There are a lot of women I don't know in my kitchen, whispering, and moving tactfully. They open doors, rummage through the pantry, and try not to ask me where things are kept. They remind me of when my sons were small, on Mother's Day or when Vikram and I were tired, and they would make big, sloppy omelets. I would lie in bed pretending I didn't hear them.

Dr. Sharma, the treasurer of the Indo-Canada Society, pulls me into the hallway. He wants to know if I am worried about money. His wife, who has just come up from the basement with a tray of empty cups and glasses, scolds him. "Don't bother Mrs. Bhave with mundane details." She looks so monstrously pregnant her baby must be days overdue. I tell her she shouldn't be carrying heavy things. "Shaila," she says, smiling, "this is the fifth." Then she grabs a teenager by his shirttails. He slips his Walkman off his head. He has to be one of her four children, they have the same domed and dented foreheads. "What's the official word now?" she demands. The boy slips the headphones back on. "They're acting evasive, Ma. They're saying it could be an accident or a terrorist bomb."

All morning, the boys have been muttering, Sikh Bomb, Sikh Bomb. The men, not using the word, bow their heads in agreement. Mrs. Sharma touches her forehead at such a word. At least they've stopped talking about space debris and Russian lasers.

Two radios are going in the dining room. They are tuned to different stations. Someone must have brought the radios down from my boys' bedrooms. I haven't gone into their rooms since Kusum came running across the front lawn in her bathrobe. She looked so funny, I was laughing when I opened the door.

The big TV in the den is being whizzed through American networks and cable channels.

"Damn!" some man swears bitterly. "How can these preachers carry on like nothing's happened?" I want to tell him we're not that important. You look at the audience, and at the preacher in his blue robe with his beautiful white hair, the potted palm trees under a blue sky, and you know they care about nothing.

The phone rings and rings. Dr. Sharma's taken charge. "We're with her," he keeps saying. "Yes, yes, the doctor has given calming pills. Yes, yes, pills are having necessary effect." I wonder if pills alone explain this calm. Not peace, just a deadening quiet. I was always controlled, but never repressed. Sound can reach me, but my body is tensed, ready to scream. I hear their voices all around me. I hear my boys and Vikram cry, "Mommy, Shaila!" and their screams insulate me, like headphones.

The woman boiling water tells her story again and again. "I got the news first. My cousin called from Halifax before six A.M., can you imagine? He'd gotten up for prayers and his son was studying for medical exams and he heard on a rock channel that something had happened to a plane. They said first it had disappeared from the radar, like a giant eraser just reached out. His father called me, so I said to him, what do you mean, 'something bad'? You mean a hijacking? And he said, *behn*, there is no confirmation of anything yet, but check with your neighbors because a lot of them must be on that plane. So I called poor Kusum straightaway. I knew Kusum's husband and daughter were booked to go yesterday."

Kusum lives across the street from me. She and Satish had moved in less than a month ago. They said they needed a bigger place. All these people, the Sharmas and friends from the Indo-Canada Society had been there for the housewarming. Satish and Kusum made homemade tandoori on their big gas grill and even the white neighbors piled their plates high with that luridly red, charred, juicy chicken. Their younger daughter had danced, and even our boys had broken away from the Stanley Cup telecast to put in a reluctant appearance. Everyone took pictures for their albums and for the community newspapers—another of our families had made it big in Toronto—and now I wonder how many of those happy faces are gone. "Why does God give us so much if all along He intends to take it away?" Kusum asks me.

I nod. We sit on carpeted stairs, holding hands like children. "I never once told him that I loved him," I say. I was too much the well brought up woman. I was so well brought up I never felt comfortable calling my husband by his first name.

"It's all right," Kusum says. "He knew. My husband knew. They felt it. Modern young girls have to say it because what they feel is fake."

Kusum's daughter, Pam, runs in with an overnight case. Pam's in her McDonald's uniform. "Mummy! You have to get dressed!" Panic makes her cranky. "A reporter's on his way here."

"Why?"

"You want to talk to him in your bathrobe?" She starts to brush her mother's long hair. She's the daughter who's always in trouble. She dates Canadian boys and hangs out in the mall, shopping for tight sweaters. The younger one, the goody-goody one according to Pam, the one with a voice so sweet that when she sang *bhajans* for Ethiopian relief even a frugal man like my husband wrote out a hundred dollar check, *she* was on that plane. *She* was going to spend July and August with grandparents because Pam wouldn't go. Pam said she'd rather waitress at McDonald's. "If it's a choice between Bombay and Wonderland, I'm picking Wonderland," she'd said.

"Leave me alone," Kusum yells. "You know what I want to do? If I didn't have to look after you now, I'd hang myself."

Pam's young face goes blotchy with pain. "Thanks," she says, "don't let me stop you."

"Hush," pregnant Mrs. Sharma scolds Pam. "Leave your mother alone. Mr. Sharma will tackle the reporters and fill out the forms. He'll say what has to be said."

Pam stands her ground. "You think I don't know what Mummy's thinking? *Why her?* that's what. That's sick! Mummy wishes my little sister were alive and I were dead."

Kusum's hand in mine is trembly hot. We continue to sit on the stairs.

She calls before she arrives, wondering if there's anything I need. Her name is Judith Templeton and she's an appointee of the provincial government. "Multiculturalism?" I ask, and she says, "partially," but that her mandate is bigger. "I've been told you knew many of the people on the flight," she says. "Perhaps if you'd agree to help us reach the others . . . ?"

She gives me time at least to put on tea water and pick up the mess in the front room. I have a few *samosas* from Kusum's housewarming that I could fry up, but then I think, why prolong this visit?

Judith Templeton is much younger than she sounded. She wears a blue suit with a white blouse and a polka dot tie. Her blond hair is cut short, her only jewelry is pearl drop earrings. Her briefcase is new and expensive looking, a gleaming cordovan leather. She sits with it across her lap. When she looks out the front windows onto the street, her contact lenses seem to float in front of her light blue eyes.

"What sort of help do you want from me?" I ask. She has refused the tea, out of politeness, but I insist, along with some slightly stale biscuits.

"I have no experience," she admits. "That is, I have an MSW and I've worked in liaison with accident victims, but I mean I have no experience with a tragedy of this scale—"

"Who could?" I ask.

"—and with the complications of culture, language, and customs. Someone mentioned that Mrs. Bhave is a pillar—because you've taken it more calmly."

At this, perhaps, I frown, for she reaches forward, almost to take my hand. "I hope you understand my meaning, Mrs. Bhave. There are hundreds of people in Metro directly affected, like you, and some of them speak no English. There are some widows who've never handled money or gone on a bus, and there are old parents who still haven't eaten or gone outside their bedrooms. Some houses and apartments have been looted. Some wives are still hysterical. Some husbands are in shock and profound depression. We want to help, but our hands are tied in so many ways. We have to distribute money to some people, and there are legal documents—these things can be done. We have interpreters, but we don't always have the human touch, or maybe the right human touch. We don't want to make mistakes, Mrs. Bhave, and that's why we'd like to ask you to help us."

"More mistakes, you mean," I say.

"Police matters are not in my hands," she answers.

"Nothing I can do will make any difference," I say. "We must all grieve in our own way."

"But you are coping very well. All the people said, Mrs. Bhave is the strongest person of all. Perhaps if the others could see you, talk with you, it would help them."

"By the standards of the people you call hysterical, I am behaving very oddly and very badly, Miss Templeton." I want to say to her, *I wish I could scream, starve, walk into Lake Ontario, jump from a bridge.* "They would not see me as a model. I do not see myself as a model."

I am a freak. No one who has ever known me would think of me reacting this way. This terrible calm will not go away.

She asks me if she may call again, after I get back from a long trip that we all must make. "Of course," I say. "Feel free to call, anytime."

Four days later, I find Kusum squatting on a rock overlooking a bay in Ireland. It isn't a big rock, but it juts sharply out over water. This is as close as we'll ever get to them. June breezes balloon out her sari and unpin her knee-length hair. She has the bewildered look of a sea creature whom the tides have stranded.

It's been one hundred hours since Kusum came stumbling and screaming across my lawn. Waiting around the hospital, we've heard many stories. The police, the diplomats, they tell us things thinking that we're strong, that knowledge is helpful to the grieving, and maybe it is. Some, I know, prefer ignorance, or their own versions. The plane broke into two, they say. Unconsciousness was instantaneous. No one suffered. My boys must have just finished their breakfasts. They loved eating on planes, they loved the smallness of plates, knives, and forks. Last year they saved the airline salt and pepper shakers. Half an hour more and they would have made it to Heathrow.

Kusum says that we can't escape our fate. She says that all those people—our husbands, my boys, her girl with the nightingale voice, all those Hindus, Christians, Sikhs, Muslims, Parsis, and atheists on that plane—were fated to die together off this beautiful bay. She learned this from a swami in Toronto.

I have my Valium.

Six of us "relatives"—two widows and four widowers—choose to spend the day today by the waters instead of sitting in a hospital room and scanning photographs of the dead. That's what they call us now: relatives. I've looked through twenty-seven photos in two days. They're very kind to us, the Irish are very understanding. Sometimes understanding means freeing a tourist bus for this trip to the bay, so we can pretend to spy our loved ones through the glassiness of waves or in sun-speckled cloud shapes.

I could die here, too, and be content.

"What is that, out there?" She's standing and flapping her hands and for a moment I see a head shape bobbing in the waves. She's standing in the water, I, on the boulder. The tide is low, and a round, black, head-sized rock has just risen from the waves. She returns, her sari end dripping and ruined and her face is a twisted remnant of hope, the way mine was a hundred hours ago, still laughing but inwardly knowing that nothing but the ultimate tragedy could bring two women together at six o'clock on a Sunday morning. I watch her face sag into blankness.

"That water felt warm, Shaila," she says at length.

"You can't," I say. "We have to wait for our turn to come."

I haven't eaten in four days, haven't brushed my teeth.

"I know," she says. "I tell myself I have no right to grieve. They are in a better place than we are. My swami says I should be thrilled for them. My swami says depression is a sign of our selfishness."

Maybe I'm selfish. Selfishly I break away from Kusum and run, sandals slapping against stones, to the water's edge. What if my boys aren't lying pinned under the debris? What if they aren't stuck a mile below that innocent blue chop? What if, given the strong currents . . .

Now I've ruined my sari, one of my best. Kusum has joined me, knee-deep in water that feels to me like a swimming pool. I could settle in the water, and my husband would take my hand and the boys would slap water in my face just to see me scream.

"Do you remember what good swimmers my boys were, Kusum?"

"I saw the medals," she says.

One of the widowers, Dr. Ranganathan from Montreal, walks out to us, carrying his shoes in one hand. He's an electrical engineer. Someone at the hotel mentioned his work is famous around the world, something about the place where physics and electricity come together. He has lost a huge family, something indescribable. "With some luck," Dr. Ranganathan suggests to me, "a good swimmer could make it safely to some island. It is quite possible that there may be many, many microscopic islets scattered around."

"You're not just saying that?" I tell Dr. Ranganathan about Vinod, my elder son. Last year he took diving as well.

"It's a parent's duty to hope," he says. "It is foolish to rule out possibilities that have not been tested. I myself have not surrendered hope."

Kusum is sobbing once again. "Dear lady," he says, laying his free hand on her arm, and she calms down.

"Vinod is how old?" he asks me. He's very careful, as we all are. *Is*, not was.

"Fourteen. Yesterday he was fourteen. His father and uncle were going to take him down to the Taj and give him a big birthday party. I couldn't go with them because I couldn't get two weeks off from my stupid job in June." I process bills for a travel agent. June is a big travel month.

Dr. Ranganathan whips the pockets of his suit jacket inside out. Squashed roses, in darkening shades of pink, float on the water. He tore the roses off creepers in somebody's garden. He didn't ask anyone if he could pluck the roses, but now there's been an article about it in the local papers. When you see an Indian person, it says, please give him or her flowers.

"A strong youth of fourteen," he says, "can very likely pull to safety a younger one."

My sons, though four years apart, were very close. Vinod wouldn't let Mithun drown. *Electrical engineering*, I think, foolishly perhaps: this man knows important secrets of the universe, things closed to me. Relief spins me lightheaded. No wonder my boys' photographs haven't turned up in the gallery of photos of the recovered dead. "Such pretty roses," I say.

"My wife loved pink roses. Every Friday I had to bring a bunch home. I used to say, why? After twenty odd years of marriage you're still needing proof positive of my love?" He has identified his wife and three of his children. Then others from Montreal, the lucky ones, intact families with no survivors. He chuckles as he wades back to shore. Then he swings around to ask me a question. "Mrs. Bhave, you are wanting to throw in some roses for your loved ones? I have two big ones left."

But I have other things to float: Vinod's pocket calculator; a half-painted model B-52 for my Mithun. They'd want them on their island. And for my husband? For him I let fall into the calm, glass waters a poem I wrote in the hospital yesterday. Finally he'll know my feelings for him.

"Don't tumble, the rocks are slippery," Dr. Ranganathan cautions. He holds out a hand for me to grab.

Then it's time to get back on the bus, time to rush back to our waiting posts on hospital benches.

Kusum is one of the lucky ones. The lucky ones flew here, identified in multiplicate their loved ones, then will fly to India with the bodies for proper ceremonies. Satish is one of the few males who surfaced. The photos of faces we saw on the walls in an office at Heathrow and here in the hospital are mostly of women. Women have more body fat, a nun said to me matter-of-factly. They float better.

Today I was stopped by a young sailor on the street. He had loaded bodies, he'd gone into the water when—he checks my face for signs of strength—when the sharks were first spotted. I don't blush, and he breaks down. "It's all right," I say. "Thank you." I had heard about the sharks from Dr. Ranganathan. In his orderly mind, science brings understanding, it holds no terror. It is the shark's duty. For every deer there is a hunter, for every fish a fisherman.

The Irish are not shy; they rush to me and give me hugs and some are crying. I cannot imagine reactions like that on the streets of Toronto. Just strangers, and I am touched. Some carry flowers with them and give them to any Indian they see.

After lunch, a policeman I have gotten to know quite well catches hold of me. He says he thinks he has a match for Vinod. I explain what a good swimmer Vinod is.

"You want me with you when you look at photos?" Dr. Ranganathan walks ahead of me into the picture gallery. In these matters, he is a scientist, and I am grateful. It is a new perspective. "They have performed miracles," he says. "We are indebted to them."

The first day or two the policemen showed us relatives only one picture at a time; now they're in a hurry, they're eager to lay out the possibles, and even the probables.

The face on the photo is of a boy much like Vinod; the same intelligent eyes, the same thick brows dipping into a V. But this boy's features, even his cheeks, are puffier, wider, mushier.

"No." My gaze is pulled by other pictures. There are five other boys who look like Vinod.

The nun assigned to console me rubs the first picture with a fingertip. "When they've been in the water for a while, love, they look a little heavier." The bones under the skin are broken, they said on the first day—try to adjust your memories. It's important.

"It's not him. I'm his mother. I'd know."

"I know this one!" Dr. Ranganathan cries out suddenly from the back of the gallery. "And this one!" I think he senses that I don't want to find my boys. "They are the Kutty brothers. They were also from Montreal." I don't mean to be crying. On the contrary, I am ecstatic. My suitcase in the hotel is packed heavy with dry clothes for my boys.

The policeman starts to cry. "I am so sorry, I am so sorry, ma'am. I really thought we had a match."

With the nun ahead of us and the policeman behind, we, the unlucky ones without our children's bodies, file out of the makeshift gallery.

From Ireland most of us go on to India. Kusum and I take the same direct flight to Bombay, so I can help her clear customs quickly. But we have to argue with a man in uniform. He has large boils on his face. The boils swell and glow with sweat as we argue with him. He wants Kusum to wait in line and he refuses to take authority because his boss is on a tea break. But Kusum won't let her coffins out of sight, and I shan't desert her though I know that my parents, elderly and diabetic, must be waiting in a stuffy car in a scorching lot.

"You bastard!" I scream at the man with the popping boils. Other passengers press closer. "You think we're smuggling contraband in those coffins!"

Once upon a time we were well brought up women; we were dutiful wives who kept our heads veiled, our voices shy and sweet.

In India, I become, once again, an only child of rich, ailing parents. Old friends of the family come to pay their respects. Some are Sikh, and inwardly, involuntarily, I cringe. My parents are progressive people; they do not blame communities for a few individuals.

In Canada it is a different story now.

"Stay longer," my mother pleads. "Canada is a cold place. Why would you want to be all by yourself?" I stay.

Three months pass. Then another.

"Vikram wouldn't have wanted you to give up things!" they protest. They call my husband by the name he was born with. In Toronto he'd changed to Vik so the men he worked with at his office would find his name as easy as Rod or Chris. "You know, the dead aren't cut off from us!"

My grandmother, the spoiled daughter of a rich *zamindar*, shaved her head with rusty razor blades when she was widowed at sixteen. My grandfather died of childhood diabetes when he was nineteen, and she saw herself as the harbinger of bad luck. My mother grew up without parents, raised indifferently by an uncle, while her true mother slept in a hut behind the main estate house and took her food with the servants. She grew up a rationalist. My parents abhor mindless mortification.

The zamindar's daughter kept stubborn faith in Vedic rituals; my parents rebelled. I am trapped between two modes of knowledge. At thirty-six, I am too old to start over and too young to give up. Like my husband's spirit, I flutter between worlds.

Courting aphasia, we travel. We travel with our phalanx of servants and poor relatives. To hill stations and to beach resorts. We play contract bridge in dusty gymkhana clubs. We ride stubby ponies up crumbly mountain trails. At tea dances, we let ourselves be twirled twice round the ballroom. We hit the holy spots we hadn't made time for before. In Varanasi, Kalighat, Rishikesh, Hardwar, astrologers and palmists seek me out and for a fee offer me cosmic consolations.

Already the widowers among us are being shown new bride candidates. They cannot resist the call of custom, the authority of their parents and older brothers. They must marry; it is the duty of a man to look after a wife. The new wives will be young widows with children, destitute but of good family. They will make loving wives, but the men will shun them. I've had calls from the men over crackling Indian telephone lines. "Save me," they say, these substantial, educated, successful men of forty. "My parents are arranging a marriage for me." In a month they will have buried one family and returned to Canada with a new bride and partial family.

I am comparatively lucky. No one here thinks of arranging a husband for an unlucky widow.

Then, on the third day of the sixth month into this odyssey, in an abandoned temple in a tiny Himalayan village, as I make my offering of flowers and sweetmeats to the god of a tribe of animists, my husband descends to me. He is squatting next to a scrawny *sadhu* in moth-eaten robes. Vikram wears the vanilla suit he wore the last time I hugged him. The *sadhu* tosses petals on a better-fed flame, reciting Sanskrit mantras and sweeps his face of flies. My husband takes my hands in his.

You're beautiful, he starts. Then, *What are you doing here?*

Shall I stay? I ask. He only smiles, but already the image is fading. *You must finish alone what we started together.* No seaweed wreathes his mouth. He speaks too fast just as he used to when we were an envied family in our pink split-level. He is gone.

In the windowless altar room, smoky with joss sticks and clarified butter lamps, a sweaty hand gropes for my blouse. I do not shriek. The *sadhu* arranges his robe. The lamps hiss and sputter out.

When we come out of the temple, my mother says, "Did you feel something weird in there?"

My mother has no patience with ghosts, prophetic dreams, holy men, and cults.

"No," I lie. "Nothing."

But she knows that she's lost me. She knows that in days I shall be leaving.

Kusum's put her house up for sale. She wants to live in an ashram in Hardwar. Moving to Hardwar was her swami's idea. Her swami runs two ashrams, the one in Hardwar and another here in Toronto.

"Don't run away," I tell her.

"I'm not running away," she says. "I'm pursuing inner peace. You think you or that Ranganathan fellow are better off?"

Pam's left for California. She wants to do some modelling, she says. She says when she comes into her share of the insurance money she'll open a yoga-cum-aerobics studio in Hollywood. She sends me postcards so naughty I daren't leave them on the coffee table. Her mother has withdrawn from her and the world.

The rest of us don't lose touch, that's the point. Talk is all we have, says Dr. Ranganathan, who has also resisted his relatives and returned to Montreal and to his job, alone. He says, whom better to talk with than other relatives? We've been melted down and recast as a new tribe.

He calls me twice a week from Montreal. Every Wednesday night and every Saturday afternoon. He is changing jobs, going to Ottawa. But Ottawa is over a hundred miles away, and he is forced to drive two hundred and twenty miles a day. He can't bring himself to sell his house. The house is a temple, he says; the king-sized bed in the master bedroom is a shrine. He sleeps on a folding cot. A devotee.

There are still some hysterical relatives. Judith Templeton's list of those needing help and those who've "accepted" is in nearly perfect balance. Acceptance means you speak of your family in the past tense and you make active plans for moving ahead with your life. There are courses at Seneca and Ryerson we could be taking. Her gleaming leather briefcase is full of college catalogues and lists of cultural societies that need our help. She has done impressive work, I tell her.

"In the textbooks on grief management," she replies—I am her confidante, I realize, one of the few whose grief has not sprung bizarre obsessions— "there are stages to pass through: rejection, depression, acceptance, reconstruction." She has compiled a chart and finds that six months after the tragedy, none of us still reject reality, but only a handful are reconstructing. "Depressed Acceptance" is the plateau we've reached. Remarriage is a major step in reconstruction (though she's a little surprised, even shocked, over *how* quickly some of the men have taken on new families). Selling one's house and changing jobs and cities is healthy.

How do I tell Judith Templeton that my family surrounds me, and that like creatures in epics, they've changed shapes? She sees me as calm and accepting but worries that I have no job, no career. My closest friends are worse off than I. I cannot tell her my days, even my nights, are thrilling.

She asks me to help with families she can't reach at all. An elderly couple in Agincourt whose sons were killed just weeks after they had brought their parents over from a village in Punjab. From their names, I know they are Sikh. Judith Templeton and a translator have visited them twice with offers of money for air fare to Ireland, with bank forms, power-of-attorney forms, but they have refused to sign, or to leave their tiny apartment. Their sons' money is frozen in the bank. Their sons' investment apartments have been trashed by tenants, the furnishings sold off. The parents fear that anything they sign or any money they receive will end the company's or the country's obligations to them. They fear they are selling their sons for two airline tickets to a place they've never seen.

The high-rise apartment is a tower of Indians and West Indians, with a sprinkling of Orientals. The nearest bus stop kiosk is lined with women in saris. Boys practice cricket in the parking lot. Inside the building, even I wince a bit from the ferocity of onion fumes, the distinctive and immediate Indianness of frying *ghee,* but Judith Templeton maintains a steady flow of information. These poor old people are in imminent danger of losing their place and all their services.

I say to her, "They are Sikh. They will not open up to a Hindu woman." And what I want to add is, as much as I try not to, I stiffen now at the sight of beards and turbans. I remember a time when we all trusted each other in this new country, it was only the new country we worried about.

The two rooms are dark and stuffy. The lights are off, and an oil lamp sputters on the coffee table. The bent old lady has let us in, and her husband is wrapping a white turban over his oiled, hip-length hair. She immediately goes to the kitchen, and I hear the most familiar sound of an Indian home, tap water hitting and filling a teapot.

They have not paid their utility bills, out of fear and the inability to write a check. The telephone is gone; electricity and gas and water are soon to follow. They have told Judith their sons will provide. They are good boys, and they have always earned and looked after their parents.

We converse a bit in Hindi. They do not ask about the crash and I wonder if I should bring it up. If they think I am here merely as a translator, then they may feel insulted. There are thousands of Punjabi-speakers, Sikhs, in Toronto to do a better job. And so I say to the old lady, "I too have lost my sons, and my husband, in the crash."

Her eyes immediately fill with tears. The man mutters a few words which sound like a blessing. "God provides and God takes away," he says.

I want to say, but only men destroy and give back nothing. "My boys and my husband are not coming back," I say. "We have to understand that."

Now the old woman responds. "But who is to say? Man alone does not decide these things." To this her husband adds his agreement.

Judith asks about the bank papers, the release forms. With a stroke of the pen, they will have a provincial trustee to pay their bills, invest their money, send them a monthly pension.

"Do you know this woman?" I ask them.

The man raises his hand from the table, turns it over and seems to regard each finger separately before he answers. "This young lady is always coming here, we make tea for her and she leaves papers for us to sign." His eyes scan a pile of papers in the corner of the room. "Soon we will be out of tea, then will she go away?"

The old lady adds, "I have asked my neighbors and no one else gets *angrezi* visitors. What have we done?"

"It's her job," I try to explain. "The government is worried. Soon you will have no place to stay, no lights, no gas, no water."

"Government will get its money. Tell her not to worry, we are honorable people."

I try to explain the government wishes to give money, not take. He raises his hand. "Let them take," he says. "We are accustomed to that. That is no problem."

"We are strong people," says the wife. "Tell her that."

"Who needs all this machinery?" demands the husband. "It is unhealthy, the bright lights, the cold air on a hot day, the cold food, the four gas rings. God will provide, not government."

"When our boys return," the mother says. Her husband sucks his teeth. "Enough talk," he says.

Judith breaks in. "Have you convinced them?" The snaps on her cordovan briefcase go off like firecrackers in that quiet apartment. She lays the sheaf of legal papers on the coffee table. "If they can't write their names, an X will do— I've told them that."

Now the old lady has shuffled to the kitchen and soon emerges with a pot of tea and two cups. "I think my bladder will go first on a job like this," Judith says to me, smiling. "If only there was some way of reaching them. Please thank her for the tea. Tell her she's very kind."

I nod in Judith's direction and tell them in Hindi, "She thanks you for the tea. She thinks you are being very hospitable but she doesn't have the slightest idea what it means."

I want to say, humor her. I want to say, my boys and my husband are with me too, more than ever. I look in the old man's eyes and I can read his stubborn, peasant's message: *I have protected this woman as best I can. She is the only person I have left. Give to me or take from me what you will, but I will not sign for it. I will not pretend that I accept.*

In the car, Judith says, "You see what I'm up against? I'm sure they're lovely people, but their stubbornness and ignorance are driving me crazy. They think signing a paper is signing their sons' death warrants, don't they?"

I am looking out the window. I want to say, *In our culture, it is a parent's duty to hope.*

"Now Shaila, this next woman is a real mess. She cries day and night, and she refuses all medical help. We may have to—"

"—Let me out at the subway," I say.

"I beg your pardon?" I can feel those blue eyes staring at me.

It would not be like her to disobey. She merely disapproves, and slows at a corner to let me out. Her voice is plaintive. "Is there anything I said? Anything I did?"

I could answer her suddenly in a dozen ways, but I choose not to. "Shaila? Let's talk about it," I hear, then slam the door.

A wife and mother begins her new life in a new country, and that life is cut short. Yet her husband tells her: Complete what we have started. We, who stayed out of politics and came halfway around the world to avoid religious and political feuding have been the first in the New World to die from it. I no longer know what we started, nor how to complete it. I write letters to the editors of local papers and to members of Parliament. Now at least they admit it was a bomb. One MP answers back, with sympathy, but with a challenge. You want to make a difference? Work on a campaign. Work on mine. Politicize the Indian voter.

My husband's old lawyer helps me set up a trust. Vikram was a saver and a careful investor. He had saved the boys' boarding school and college fees. I sell the pink house at four times what we paid for it and take a small apartment downtown. I am looking for a charity to support.

We are deep in the Toronto winter, gray skies, icy pavements. I stay indoors, watching television. I have tried to assess my situation, how best to live my life, to complete what we began so many years ago. Kusum has written me from Hardwar that her life is now serene. She has seen Satish and has heard her daughter sing again. Kusum was on a pilgrimage, passing through a village when she heard a young girl's voice, singing one of her daughter's favorite *bhajans*. She followed the music through the squalor of a Himalayan village, to a hut where a young girl, an exact replica of her daughter, was fanning coals under the kitchen fire. When she appeared, the girl cried out, "Ma!" and ran away. What did I think of that?

I think I can only envy her.

Pam didn't make it to California, but writes me from Vancouver. She works in a department store, giving make-up hints to Indian and Oriental girls. Dr. Ranganathan has given up his commute, given up his house and job, and accepted an academic position in Texas where no one knows his story and he has vowed not to tell it. He calls me now once a week.

I wait, I listen, and I pray, but Vikram has not returned to me. The voices and the shapes and the nights filled with visions ended abruptly several weeks ago.

I take it as a sign.

One rare, beautiful, sunny day last week, returning from a small errand on Yonge Street, I was walking through the park from the subway to my apartment. I live equidistant from the Ontario Houses of Parliament and the University of Toronto. The day was not cold, but something in the bare trees caught my attention. I looked up from the gravel, into the branches and the clear blue sky beyond. I thought I heard the rustling of larger forms, and I waited a moment for voices. Nothing.

"What?" I asked.

Then as I stood in the path looking north to Queen's Park and west to the university, I heard the voices of my family one last time. *Your time has come,* they said. *Go, be brave.*

I do not know where this voyage I have begun will end. I do not know which direction I will take. I dropped the package on a park bench and started walking.

▪ Notes on Craft and Context

On Setting: Empathy and the Unfamiliar

One of the things fine writing can do is bridge the gap of cultures and bring what's distant near. Empathy—the ability to comprehend and sympathize with what another person feels—is central to the act of writing and, thereafter, reading; we enter the world of a book in much the way we enter a new relationship or town. What we understood to start with is not what we afterwards know.

Sometimes this exploration can feel like outward adventure—an armchair traveler discovering the South Seas or the North Pole with a reading lamp, then signing onto a whaling ship's crew without getting up from the couch. Sometimes the journey is inward, so the reader can experience a character's depression or delight. We extend our knowledge of the world by absorbing those who earlier reported on or persuasively imagined it; it's a pleasure every reader shares with every turning page.

Often, however, that empathetic exposure provides increased knowledge of pain. Not all information is pleasant—as, for example, the description of the Canadian bureaucracy in "The Management of Grief." And not all perception gives comfort; some truths—as, for example, our powerlessness in the face of terror—are hard to accept. If empathy consists of bringing what was distant near, then all of us are necessarily more vulnerable now. For one of the meanings of "novel" is "new," and one of the tasks of the writer has always been to dramatize news—in this case, an airliner's crash.

The Facts: Setting the Scene

It was a specific crash, a terrorist-engineered explosion, on June 22, 1985. Here are the facts: At 08:13 hours London time, Air India flight 182, which had left Toronto earlier—having taken on luggage and passengers from a flight originating in Vancouver—was about to start its descent into London's Heathrow Airport. The captain radioed that all was normal. Moments later, at 31,000 feet, the plane exploded and crashed into the Atlantic Ocean off the coast of Ireland. Three hundred and twenty-nine people died on board or in the water; some of the bodies were never recovered and were declared lost at sea.

A bearded Indian male wearing a mustard-colored turban had arrived at the ticket office in Vancouver and paid cash and checked luggage for two flights, but neither flight was boarded by the passenger in question. He was a Sikh; his name was Inderit Singh Reyat, and after the action these pages describe he and two confederates were arrested; Inderit Singh Reyat was convicted after a legal process that took years. (Although this is irrelevant to "The Management of Grief" itself, that day there was a second flight—Canadian Airlines 003, where the checked suitcase exploded in Narita Airport, killing two baggage handlers and injuring others.) This bare-bones outline is filled in and made vivid by Mukherjee's imagination.

On Collective Catastrophes and Shared Grief

In recent years the image of collective catastrophe has entered America's consciousness in a way that makes this time-bound story relevant again. It never did lose relevance, of course, but headlines have a way of fading and being—if not forgotten—superceded; the crash of American Airlines Flight 587 (en route from New York City to the Dominican Republic) in November 2001 makes the crash of which Bharati Mukherjee writes seem like ancient history. The terrorist assaults on the World Trade Center and the Pentagon on September 11, 2001, instruct us all in mortality and loss. There are many ways to write about catastrophe—detailing the specifics of an attack or the ways that we retaliate or mourn. And "The Management of Grief" takes as its principle subject the aftermath of horror, the condition of those who survive.

On Place and Displacement

This condition is all the more wrenching in the case of those who find themselves deracinated—rootless, far from home. The plight of this particular subset of society is made to seem even more poignant because of an inability to deal with it in standard "Western" terms. As Mukherjee and Blaise observe in *The Sorrow and the Terror:* "Fatalism was a temporary boon to government and insurance companies." Further, " . . . in the photo gallery some relatives had trouble recognizing the marked faces and bloated bodies . . . They had an easier time recognizing the photographs of friends and neighbours." Both of these assertions have the force of truthful summary, but both are more effective when dramatized as scenes.

American literature has, of late, come to mirror more entirely the polyglot and multicultural nature of our country; it's much less limited, much wider in scope than was the case a hundred years ago. Fewer strands in the complex fabric of our nation are today being ignored. (Mukherjee writes about Canada here, so we should enlarge the landscape of America to mean "North America," but the cultural context remains the same.) To give voice to the voiceless and display the barely visible—these are among the moral imperatives of the contemporary writer. If "escapist" entertainment deals with the rich and well established, "The Management of Grief" deals with the displaced and the dispossessed. A very private woman takes stage center to tell her community's story; the narrator, Mrs. Shaila Bhave, speaks of what she would far rather refuse to accept—the death of her husband and sons.

On Fate

A long-standing tenet of Western literature—going back at least as far as Aristotle—is that *character is fate.* Our destinies are linked to our behavior; virtue is rewarded, evil punished—or so the stories go. But it's impossible to claim that those who died inside the World Trade Center were in any personal sense responsible for their own fates; death came to them regardless of their private morality or behavior the evening before. We can admire the novels of Jane Austen without any serious awareness of the Napoleonic Wars her well-dressed soldiers fight in; the women and men of Mukherjee's tales are—no matter how much they might wish to avoid it—changed by what happens in a far-distant place. In some sense the characters of "The Management of Grief" can recognize the impersonal nature of the accident befalling them with greater ease than might their Western counterparts; "What have I done to deserve this?" we ask or, simply, "Why, why *me?*" In the wake of 9/11 such questions seem almost irrelevant, and the whole notion of life lived in a private context seems outdated if not quaint.

On Displaced Characters

The first sentence shows us that the narrator's routine has been disrupted. "A woman I don't know is boiling tea the Indian way in my kitchen." To have a stranger enter your kitchen to make tea is to suffer a sort of invasion ("There are a lot of women I don't know in my kitchen . . .") but it also suggests a gathering arrived to offer comfort; they are "whispering, and moving tactfully," and they prepare "tea the Indian way." Already we can assume the narrator is female and, quite likely, Indian; by the time we learn her husband's name is Vikram and she's being visited by "Dr. Sharma, the treasurer of the Indo-Canada Society," we have acquired a good deal of information about what's going on. And by the end of the second paragraph, when the "Westernized" boy with a Walkman who calls his mother "Ma," says, "They're saying it could be an accident or a terrorist bomb," we know that the precipitating action is a catastrophe and that we're in its immediate aftermath: "Sikh bomb."

Later, in a wrenching phrase, Mrs. Bhave says she envies "the lucky ones, intact families with no survivors"—by which she means those families who died together so that none are left to grieve. All her attention is focused on how to bring her loved ones back or, failing that, how to preserve them in memory so they remain—to her, at least—alive. She seems self-possessed, even unmoved by her loss, but this—as Judith Templeton fails to understand—is because she holds herself so severely in check: "I am a freak . . . This terrible calm will not go away."

On the Unreliable Narrator

Here is one of the technical challenges of this mode of storytelling: if the first-person narrator is in denial, what may we as readers understand that she herself refuses to? When "the nun assigned to console me rubs the first picture with a fingertip," for example, are we expected to deduce that this is a photo of Vinod dead and waterlogged, or is Shaila's maternal instinct sound and is this in fact a photo of some other mother's son? Later, when Vikram visits her "on the third day of the sixth month into this odyssey, in an abandoned temple in a tiny Himalayan village," does she hallucinate his presence or are we expected to believe that "My husband takes my hands in his"?

What's clear is Shaila Bhave's confusion, her increasing withdrawal from "proper" behavior. The story's title may well seem ironic; grief is scarcely something to be "managed" or dealt with in corporate fashion. Yet Mrs. Bhave is nonetheless a textbook case and she represents the textbook's "stages to pass through: rejection, depression, acceptance, reconstruction." She does so, however, in a manner that confounds her social worker; what Mrs. Bhave constructs is not Western "acceptance" but a form of "reconstruction" that has no established direction.

On Perception and Displacement

Consider these examples of the gulf between the women. "'Depressed Acceptance' is the plateau we've reached. Remarriage is a major step in reconstruction (though she's a little surprised over *how* quickly some of the men have taken on new families.)" Shaila's line is steeped in **irony**, an acid-tongued description of what Ms. Templeton can't appreciate about her clients' behavior. On the other hand, "I am comparatively lucky. No one here thinks of arranging a husband for an unlucky widow."

The narrator's self-described odyssey takes her from Canada to Ireland to India and back once more to Toronto—where, at story's end, a new journey will begin. "I dropped the package on a park bench and started walking." Off at the edge of the action we watch other modes of coping with mortality and loss. "Kusum has written me from Hardwar that her life is now serene. She has seen Satish and has heard her daughter sing again." The surviving daughter, Pam, is more realistic and less serene; her dreams of successful assimilation have been put on hold. "She works in a department store, giving make-up hints to Indian and Oriental girls." And Dr. Ranganathan has "accepted an academic position in Texas where no one knows his story and he has vowed not to tell it."

On Displacement as Bond and Conflict

The relationship of Dr. Ranganathan and Mrs. Bhave is another cultural marker here; their courtship—if that's the appropriate word—is circumspect and formal, an intimacy based on shared sorrow. As the widow reports, "I am trapped between two modes of knowledge. At thirty-six, I am too old to start over and too young to give up. Like my husband's spirit, I flutter between worlds." And when we watch her trapped between the two worlds of the government worker and the old Indian couple refusing all aid, we come to see how hard is the task of translation, how the "two modes of knowledge" can't meet. When Judith Templeton praises her for "coping very well," the widow wishes she " . . . *could scream, starve, walk into Lake Ontario, jump from a bridge.*" The well-intentioned bureaucrat shows, in effect, the futility of good intentions, and when Shaila Bhave gets out of her car, she rejects the bureaucratic mode; "I hear, then slam the door."

If only via rejection, therefore, we come to understand more clearly what these contradictory systems of belief and behavior entail. There's no doubt, for example, of the widow's devotion to her husband's memory but, as she tells her friend Kusum, "'I never once told him that I loved him . . . I was so well brought up I never felt comfortable calling my husband by his first name.'" Then, when she returns to India, she screams at the customs official: "You bastard . . . You think we're smuggling contraband in those coffins!" and is shocked by how much she has changed. "Once upon a time we were well brought up women; we were dutiful wives who kept our heads veiled, our voices shy and sweet."

On Time and Place in Displacement

Notice how each of the first two sentences in "The Management of Grief" contains the phrase, "I don't know." Mrs. Bhave's confession of ignorance is echoed in the final paragraph: "I do not know where this voyage I have begun will end. I do not know which direction I will take . . ." But her lack of information at tale's start transmutes into a willed uncertainty; the instruction "*Go, be brave*" suggests that this new pilgrimage may bring her out of darkness into light. Notice also how, to begin with, the narrator keeps track of the number of hours and days elapsed since the crash—then how time telescopes into seasons, a rapid succession of travels where "news" seems unimportant or at least beside the point.

Begun in shock and horror, the story ends in acquiescence—a pilgrim setting out. That voyager who drops her "package on a park bench" unburdens herself of possessions and embraces a new fate. The whole is present-tense reality-based fiction, but the alchemy of art here makes the strange familiar and what's familiar seem strange. We all have been touched by September 11, and this subset of society now stands for the country in general; we all can be instructed in "The Management of Grief."

▨ Applications and Connections

- Why do Mrs. Bhave and the Sikh couple choose to stay in Toronto without their loved ones? Why do Pam, Kusum, and Dr. Ranganathan move elsewhere? How do their destinations define their character? Consider how setting transcends the merely physical space where characters live. How is time a part of place? Does culture depend on place also, or is it portable? Does Judith Templeton too feel a sense of displacement?
- How are the grieving people treated differently in India, in Canada, and in Ireland? Compare and contrast the sense of shared displacement these characters feel with that of the soldiers in "The Things They Carried" and "In Another Country."
- How does the formality of diction in "The Management of Grief" mask the strange and even otherworldly nature of the experience described? Compare this approach to Carver's in "A Small, Good Thing."

▨ Exercises

1. Rewrite the first three pages in the third person, then the omniscient authorial voice.

2. Give a newspaper account of the accident, then the TV and CBC report.

3. Have Judith Templeton tell her coworker about her first meeting with Mrs. Bhave; then have her tell her lover about their last encounter in the car.

4. Write two more pages of "this voyage I have begun." Although Shaila declares "I do not know which direction I will take," conclude the story and provide her a direction.

5. Write a letter from Dr. Ranganathan to Mrs. Bhave; transcribe the telephone conversation when "He calls me now once a week."

6. Make the speaker a Russian émigré; make the accident transpire in a nuclear submarine.

7. Make the speaker an Irish policeman who conducts the grieving relatives to and from the bay.

8. "Kusum has written me from Hardwar that her life is now serene." Describe Kusum's serenity and her life in that newfound place.

9. In what ways, if any, would this story be altered if the "host" city were not Toronto but Detroit? New York? Tallahassee? Los Angeles? Your response can be in essay form or a short story or play.

10. Take a line from "Fenstad's Mother" and transpose it to this context. "To express grief on skates seemed almost impossible, and Shaila liked that." Have her learn to skate.

CHAPTER 8

POINT OF VIEW AND COMIC TIMING:
You and I

LORRIE MOORE, "How to Become a Writer"

■ **WRITER'S VIEW:** *Some of the lines in my story make me cringe with embarrassment (I was twenty-five years old when I wrote the thing; might this be offered up as a Forgiving Fact?)—would you consider my taking them out. That would be my only comment/query/contribution. (Letter to Nicholas Delbanco, 22 May 2001)*

Lorrie Moore was born in Glens Falls, New York, in 1957 and lives in Madison, Wisconsin, where she is a professor of English at the University of Wisconsin. She is the author of two novels, *Anagrams* (1986) and *Who Will Run the Frog Hospital?* (1994), and three collections of short stories. "How to Become a Writer" appeared in Moore's first collection, *Self-Help*, which was published in 1984. Her use of the second-person point of view and witty application of self-help manual rhetoric in that debut collection earned her immediate critical praise as an author capable of walking the fine line between humor and heartache. Although she deprecates her own achievement here and, in the letter cited above, refers to this as "a slight story," the piece is enduringly popular and has spawned a whole series of imitations. Moore's other collections *Like Life* (1990) and *Birds of America* (1998) solidified her position as a major voice in contemporary American fiction. Her stories have regularly appeared in *The Best American Short Stories* and *Prize Stories: The O. Henry Awards.*

In the collection *Self-Help*, there are two other stories explicitly titled in the same vein: "How to Be an Other Woman" and "How to Talk to Your Mother (Notes)." In these stories Lorrie Moore again employs the strategy of direct second-person address; both are structured as a series of **imperatives** and fragments. In "How to Be an Other Woman" there's a more or less sequential accounting of a love affair foredoomed to failure. It begins with the following paragraph:

> Meet in expensive beige raincoats, on a pea-soupy night. Like a detective movie. First, stand in front of Florsheim's Fifty-seventh Street window, press your face close to the glass, watch the fake velvet Hummels inside revolving around the wing tips; some white shoes, like your father wears, are propped up with garlands on a small mound of chemical snow. All the stores have closed. You can see your breath on the glass. Draw a peace sign. You are waiting for a bus.

Then "He emerges from nowhere, looks like Robert Culp . . ." (a dark-haired, conventionally handsome movie star of the period) and the attraction is immediate and, in a cinematic sense, predictable. By story's end the fog has dissipated and the romance is done. Here's the closure of the piece, its flat finality:

> He calls you occasionally at the office to ask how you are. You doodle numbers and curlicues on the corners of the Rolodex cards. Fiddle with your Phi Beta Kappa key. Stare out the window. You always, always, say: "Fine."

The notes in "How to Talk to Your Mother (Notes)" reverse chronology; the narrator relates the first fragment of the story when fully grown and motherless in 1982: "Without her, for years now . . ." Almost as though this were a movie in rewind, its sequencing reversed, the notes end more than forty years previously with such entries as:

> 1943. Ask your mother about babies. Have her read to you only the stories about babies. Ask her if she is going to have a baby. Ask her about the baby that died. Cry into her arm.
> 1940. Clutch her hair in your fist. Rub it against your cheek.

What seems important here, and importantly original, is the way the author manages—via period detail and offhand rhetoric—to establish context; there's an immediacy to this form of address that implicates the reader from the start. It's as though a stranger on a bus or in a coffee shop begins to talk to "you"; hard to turn away . . .

Moore's characters hail from towns like Oblong, Illinois, or Fitchville, U.S.A. They are ordinary hapless folk in bleak places, armed with sharp tongues and a keen sense of life's minor absurdities. Often, this has to do with language and the way we understand—or misunderstand—things through the half-heard sound of them; word play and punning abounds. One of her recent stories ("Community Life" from *Birds of America*, 1998) begins like this:

When Olena was a little girl, she had called them lie-berries—a fibbing fruit, a story store—and now she had a job in one. She had originally wanted to teach English literature, but when she failed to warm to the graduate study of it, its French-fried theories—a vocabulary of arson!— she'd transferred to library school, where everyone was taught to take care of books, tenderly, as if they were dishes or dolls.

Usually self-conscious and always self-aware, her characters are passive more often than active in the external or physical sense of the word; the *action* in and of "How to Become a Writer" is *interior*. These entries in a notebook may seem like casual snippets of speech, a monologue the reader manages to overhear, but they are artfully composed and hide what they reveal. Look, for example, for buried stories of family life within the family story here told.

How to Become a Writer

First, try to be something, anything, else. A movie star/astronaut. A movie star/missionary. A movie star/kindergarten teacher. President of the World. Fail miserably. It is best if you fail at an early age—say, fourteen. Early, critical disillusionment is necessary so that at fifteen you can write long haiku sequences about thwarted desire. It is a pond, a cherry blossom, a wind brushing against sparrow wing leaving for mountain. Count the syllables. Show it to your mom. She is tough and practical. She has a son in Vietnam and a husband who may be having an affair. She believes in wearing brown because it hides spots. She'll look briefly at your writing, then back up at you with a face blank as a donut. She'll say: "How about emptying the dishwasher?" Look away. Shove the forks in the fork drawer. Accidentally break one of the freebie gas station glasses. This is the required pain and suffering. This is only for starters.

In your high school English class look at Mr. Killian's face. Decide faces are important. Write a villanelle about pores. Struggle. Write a sonnet. Count the syllables: nine, ten, eleven, thirteen. Decide to experiment with fiction. Here you don't have to count syllables. Write a short story about an elderly man and woman who accidentally shoot each other in the head, the result of an inexplicable malfunction of a shotgun which appears mysteriously in their living room one night. Give it to Mr. Killian as your final project. When you get it back, he has written on it: "Some of your images are quite nice, but you have no sense of plot." When you are home, in the privacy of your own room, faintly scrawl in pencil beneath his black-inked comments: "Plots are for dead people, pore-face."

Take all the babysitting jobs you can get. You are great with kids. They love you. You tell them stories about old people who die idiot deaths. You sing them songs like "Blue Bells of Scotland," which is their favorite. And when they are in their pajamas and have finally stopped pinching each other, when they are fast asleep, you read every sex manual in the house, and wonder how on earth any-one could ever do those things with someone they truly loved. Fall asleep in a chair reading Mr. McMurphy's *Playboy*. When the McMurphys come home, they will tap you on the shoulder, look at the magazine in your lap, and grin. You will want to die. They will ask you if Tracey took her medicine all right. Explain, yes, she did, that you promised her a story if she would take it like a big girl and that seemed to work out just fine. "Oh, marvelous," they will exclaim.

Try to smile proudly.

Apply to college as a child psychology major.

As a child psychology major, you have some electives. You've always liked kids. Sign up for something called "The Ornithological Field Trip." It meets Tuesdays and Thursdays at two. When you arrive at Room 134 on the first day of class, everyone is sitting around a seminar table talking about metaphors. You've heard of these. After a short, excruciating while, raise your hand and say diffidently, "Excuse me, isn't this Birdwatching One-oh-one?" The class stops and turns to look at you. They seem to all have one face—giant and blank as a vandalized clock. Someone with a beard booms out, "No, this is Creative Writ-ing." Say: "Oh—right," as if perhaps you knew all along. Look down at your schedule. Wonder how the hell you ended up here. The computer, apparently, has made an error. You start to get up to leave and then don't. The lines at the registrar this week are huge. Perhaps you should stick with this mistake. Per-haps your creative writing isn't all that bad. Perhaps it is fate. Perhaps this is what your dad meant when he said, "It's the age of computers, Francie, it's the age of computers."

Decide that you like college life. In your dorm you meet many nice people. Some are smarter than you. And some, you notice, are dumber than you. You will continue, unfortunately, to view the world in exactly these terms for the rest of your life.

The assignment this week in creative writing is to narrate a violent hap-pening. Turn in a story about driving with your Uncle Gordon and another one about two old people who are accidentally electrocuted when they go to turn on a badly wired desk lamp. The teacher will hand them back to you with comments: "Much of your writing is smooth and energetic. You have, however, a ludicrous notion of plot." Write another story about a man and a woman who, in the very first paragraph, have their lower torsos accidentally blitzed away by dynamite. In the second paragraph, with the insurance money, they buy a frozen yogurt stand together. There are six more paragraphs. You read the whole thing out loud in class. No one likes it. They say your sense of plot is outrageous and incompetent. After class someone asks you if you are crazy.

Decide that perhaps you should stick to comedies. Start dating someone who is funny, someone who has what in high school you called a "really great sense of humor" and what now your creative writing class calls "self-contempt giving rise to comic form." Write down all of his jokes, but don't tell him you are doing this. Make up anagrams of his old girlfriend's name and name all of your socially handicapped characters with them. Tell him his old girlfriend is in all of your stories and then watch how funny he can be, see what a really great sense of humor he can have.

Your child psychology advisor tells you you are neglecting courses in your major. What you spend the most time on should be what you're majoring in. Say yes, you understand.

In creative writing seminars over the next two years, everyone continues to smoke cigarettes and ask the same things: "But does it work?" "Why should we care about this character?" "Have you earned this cliché?" These seem like important questions.

On days when it is your turn, you look at the class hopefully as they scour your mimeographs for a plot. They look back up at you, drag deeply, and then smile in a sweet sort of way.

You spend too much time slouched and demoralized. Your boyfriend suggests bicycling. Your roommate suggests a new boyfriend. You are said to be self-mutilating and losing weight, but you continue writing. The only happiness you have is writing something new, in the middle of the night, armpits damp, heart pounding, something no one has yet seen. You have only those brief, fragile, untested moments of exhilaration when you know: you are a genius. Understand what you must do. Switch majors. The kids in your nursery project will be disappointed, but you have a calling, an urge, a delusion, an unfortunate habit. You have, as your mother would say, fallen in with a bad crowd.

Why write? Where does writing come from? These are questions to ask yourself. They are like: Where does dust come from? Or: Why is there war? Or: If there's a God, then why is my brother now a cripple?

These are questions that you keep in your wallet, like calling cards. These are questions, your creative writing teacher says, that are good to address in your journals but rarely in your fiction.

The writing professor this fall is stressing the Power of the Imagination. Which means he doesn't want long descriptive stories about your camping trip last July. He wants you to start in a realistic context but then to alter it. Like recombinant DNA. He wants you to let your imagination sail, to let it grow big-bellied in the wind. This is a quote from Shakespeare.

Tell your roommate your great idea, your great exercise of imaginative power: a transformation of Melville to contemporary life. It will be about monomania and the fish-eat-fish world of life insurance in Rochester, New York. The first line will be "Call me Fishmeal," and it will feature a menopausal suburban husband named Richard, who because he is so depressed all the time is called "Mopey Dick" by his witty wife Elaine. Say to your roommate: "Mopey Dick, get it?" Your roommate looks at you, her face blank as a large Kleenex. She comes up to you, like a buddy, and puts an arm around your burdened shoulders. "Listen, Francie," she says, slow as speech therapy. "Let's go out and get a big beer."

The seminar doesn't like this one either. You suspect they are beginning to feel sorry for you. They say: "You have to think about what is happening. Where is the story here?"

The next semester the writing professor is obsessed with writing from personal experience. You must write from what you know, from what has happened to you. He wants deaths, he wants camping trips. Think about what has happened to you. In three years there have been three things: you lost your virginity; your parents got divorced; and your brother came home from a forest ten miles from the Cambodian border with only half a thigh, a permanent smirk nestled into one corner of his mouth.

About the first you write: "It created a new space, which hurt and cried in a voice that wasn't mine, 'I'm not the same anymore, but I'll be okay.'"

About the second you write an elaborate story of an old married couple who stumble upon an unknown land mine in their kitchen and accidentally blow themselves up. You call it: "For Better or for Liverwurst."

About the last you write nothing. There are no words for this. Your typewriter hums. You can find no words.

At undergraduate cocktail parties, people say, "Oh, you write? What do you write about?" Your roommate, who has consumed too much wine, too little cheese, and no crackers at all, blurts: "Oh, my god, she always writes about her dumb boyfriend."

Later on in life you will learn that writers are merely open, helpless texts with no real understanding of what they have written and therefore must half-believe anything and everything that is said of them. You, however, have not yet reached this stage of literary criticism. You stiffen and say, "I do not," the same way you said it when someone in the fourth grade accused you of really liking oboe lessons and your parents really weren't just making you take them.

Insist you are not very interested in any one subject at all, that you are interested in the music of language, that you are interested in—in—syllables, because they are the atoms of poetry, the cells of the mind, the breath of the soul. Begin to feel woozy. Stare into your plastic wine cup.

"Syllables?" you will hear someone ask, voice trailing off, as they glide slowly toward the reassuring white of the dip.

Begin to wonder what you do write about. Or if you have anything to say. Or if there even is such a thing as a thing to say. Limit these thoughts to no more than ten minutes a day; like sit-ups, they can make you thin.

You will read somewhere that all writing has to do with one's genitals. Don't dwell on this. It will make you nervous.

Your mother will come visit you. She will look at the circles under your eyes and hand you a brown book with a brown briefcase on the cover. It is entitled: *How to Become a Business Executive*. She has also brought the *Names for Baby* encyclopedia you asked for; one of your characters, the aging clown-school teacher, needs a new name. Your mother will shake her head and say: "Francie, Francie, remember when you were going to be a child psychology major?"

Say: "Mom, I like to write."

She'll say: "Sure you like to write. Of course. Sure you like to write."

Write a story about a confused music student and title it: "Schubert Was the One with the Glasses, Right?" It's not a big hit, although your roommate likes the part where the two violinists accidentally blow themselves up in a recital room. "I went out with a violinist once," she says, snapping her gum.

Thank god you are taking other courses. You can find sanctuary in nineteenth-century ontological snags and invertebrate courting rituals. Certain globular mollusks have what is called "Sex by the Arm." The male octopus, for instance, loses the end of one arm when placing it inside the female body during intercourse. Marine biologists call it "Seven Heaven." Be glad you know these things. Be glad you are not just a writer. Apply to law school.

From here on in, many things can happen. But the main one will be this: you decide not to go to law school after all, and, instead, you spend a good, big chunk of your adult life telling people how you decided not to go to law school after all. Somehow you end up writing again. Perhaps you go to graduate school. Perhaps you work odd jobs and take writing courses at night. Perhaps you are working on a novel and writing down all the clever remarks and intimate personal confessions you hear during the day. Perhaps you are losing your pals, your acquaintances, your balance.

You have broken up with your boyfriend. You now go out with men who, instead of whispering "I love you," shout: "Do it to me, baby." This is good for your writing.

Sooner or later you have a finished manuscript more or less. People look at it in a vaguely troubled sort of way and say, "I'll bet becoming a writer was always a fantasy of yours, wasn't it?" Your lips dry to salt. Say that of all the fantasies possible in the world, you can't imagine being a writer even making the top twenty. Tell them you were going to be a child psychology major. "I bet," they always sigh, "you'd be great with kids." Scowl fiercely. Tell them you're a walking blade.

Quit classes. Quit jobs. Cash in old savings bonds. Now you have time like warts on your hands. Slowly copy all of your friends' addresses into a new address book.

Vacuum. Chew cough drops. Keep a folder full of fragments.

An eyelid darkening sideways.

World as conspiracy.

Possible plot? A woman gets on a bus.

Suppose you threw a love affair and nobody came.

At home drink a lot of coffee. At Howard Johnson's order the cole slaw. Consider how it looks like the soggy confetti of a map: where you've been, where you're going—"You Are Here," says the red star on the back of the menu.

Occasionally a date with a face blank as a sheet of paper asks you whether writers often become discouraged. Say that sometimes they do and sometimes they do. Say it's a lot like having polio.

"Interesting," smiles your date, and then he looks down at his arm hairs and starts to smooth them, all, always, in the same direction.

◼ Notes on Craft and Context

On Second-Person Point of View

Lorrie Moore is neither the first nor last author to use a second-person narrator, but the "you" of her early stories is so appealing and vivid that in the years following her debut one could hardly imagine any other second-person narrator without thinking: *Lorrie Moore.* Her style is infectious, almost literally so; though the "you" in this story is a young woman called Francie who talks to herself, by implication and extension the "you" addresses each member of her readership and audience as well.

With this second-person narrator and the imperative forms engendered by the "how-to" approach, Moore turns the narrator's identity inside out. The reader settles easily into that familiar, conversational use of "you." The first few sentences, at least, seem geared to reflect the listener more than the speaker, and for a while the reader may even feel poised to become the protagonist of the story. This has to do with the imperative mood: "you" are taking orders at tale's start.

You as You and I

Yet by the time we learn "we" have a "tough and practical mother" whose son is in Vietnam and whose husband may be having an affair, we know that the "you" in this particular story probably won't refer to *us*—that it has a particular referent in the Francie whom Moore creates. Although the second-person perspective seems designed to bring us closer to the narrator, the narrator co-opts the reader's pronoun and reverses roles. "You," in this case, means "I," but it also means "you and I." The immediate result is an unsettling but wonderfully funny familiarity. We have "fallen in with a bad crowd," but it's amusing to find ourselves associated with Francie's embarrassing foibles: "When the McMurphys come home, they will tap you on the shoulder, look at the magazine in your lap, and grin. You will want to die."

In a story which repeatedly stresses the inability of all those blank faces to understand Francie's "thwarted desire" to be a writer, this use of the second-person narrator to unite Francie and the reader in a common plight seems particularly compelling. Sure, everyone wants to be a writer; we can almost hear Francie's mother telling us this. But Francie's tragedies—divorce, Vietnam—are also our nation's, and with each of her bumbling, thwarted attempts comes an increasing sense that this character's modest failures also represent our own. Success, in Moore's world, just doesn't seem a possibility.

On Parody

This "how-to" approach has, of course, parody at its core. The title itself pokes fun at "self-help" texts that fueled the personal improvement craze, and much of what follows is a record of embarrassment and loss. Moore overturns the notion that if we simply try hard and follow twelve easy steps we will succeed —or even, a little, improve.

Although Moore herself succeeded in becoming a writer, Francie never does attain this cherished-seeming goal. This story announces itself as a guide toward literary success, but Moore refuses to follow what would be the obvious plot line: from humble beginnings toward some tangible achievement. Francie ends with a manuscript that people look at "in a vaguely troubled sort of way," and the final encounter involves a companion who doesn't seem to understand her at all. We never know, of course, if Francie *does* become a writer or if her tongue stays firmly lodged in cheek; at the end she remains a beginner . . .

On Nontraditional Plot

By extension therefore also, the writer establishes a distance between herself and her character-speaker; this is an invented autobiography, even if the character aspires to the profession of the author. If Francie were to succeed as a writer the story would fail as a parody of the self-improvement model. "Plots are for dead people," and this story can have no traditional plot.

What Moore offers instead is a chain of episodes linked by chronology and theme but never quite building toward a narrative climax. The final episodes register the same sense of isolation and thwarted expectation as do the early ones: "Perhaps you are losing your pals, your acquaintances, your balance." What matters most is pattern. Each episode functions not so much as an integral link in a chain of events but as a reiteration, a variation on the central theme.

The following passage serves as an example:

The assignment this week in creative writing is to narrate a violent happening. Turn in a story about driving with your Uncle Gordon and another one about two old people who are accidentally electrocuted when they go to turn on a badly wired desk lamp. The teacher will hand them back to you with comments: "Much of your writing is smooth and energetic. You have, however, a ludicrous notion of plot." Write another story about a man and a woman who, in the very first paragraph, have their lower torsos accidentally blitzed away by dynamite. In the second paragraph, with the insurance money, they buy a frozen yogurt stand together. There are six more paragraphs. You read the whole thing out loud in class. No one likes it. They say your sense of plot is outrageous and incompetent. After class someone asks you if you are crazy.

Not One Climax, but Many: Episodic Plot

Francie begins with a mundane challenge: narrate a violent happening for creative writing class. But this simple assignment immediately takes on ridiculous proportions. Moore begins in deadpan fashion by going against our expectations—driving with Uncle Gordon shouldn't, in a more perfect world, be a violent happening—then builds toward greater silliness by going to extremes (electrocution by badly wired desk lamp). This is the first small climax of the passage, and it is immediately resolved by the teacher's disappointing—if appropriate—response. A ludicrous notion of plot, indeed. Francie's next story builds toward an explosion which serves as this passage's other rising point. Yet that climax, too, resolves itself in characteristically banal ways: the victims buy a frozen yogurt stand with their insurance money. Francie's imagination sails "big-bellied in the wind" only for a moment before dropping back to earth. No one likes her stories. Someone asks her if she's crazy.

Moore's story thus rises and falls not in a single climax at the two-thirds point but again and again, in every episode, within the span of a few phrases. This pattern is visible even on the level of sentence structure. Notice the growing exhilaration inherent in the longer sentences of this passage, and the way in which syntax and word choice (the colloquial "blitzed") create their own drama (ending with "dynamite"): "Write another story about a man and a woman who, in the very first paragraph, have their lower torsos accidentally blitzed away by dynamite."

Humor: Rhythm and Diction

Since the story so resolutely depends on simple, clipped sentences ("Your typewriter hums."), when Moore's sentences stretch for more than one line we sit up and take notice. She creates a kind of syncopation from line to line, so that the complex formal phraseology is followed by the flat declarative, "There are six more paragraphs." The episode winds down after this, registering disappointment in one truncated phrase after the next.

This is a skill any good comic understands: the humor of a story depends on the rhythms of diction as much as on anything else. Moore's choice of words contributes to the effect. Her vocabulary is so casual and low-key in this story that phrases like "self-contempt giving rise to comic form" or "the Power of the Imagination" are immediately recognized as inflated by comparison. Moore plays with this **juxtaposition** of high and low styles to comic effect, placing "monomania" next to "fish-eat-fish world" and a "menopausal suburban husband named Richard" next to the words "Mopey Dick."

Point of View: Sharing the Joke and the Darkness

Part of this has to do with the nature of humor: laughter depends on an audience. It's easier to find things funny and to laugh out loud when others are laughing beside you; a comic doesn't want to play to or practice his or her routines in an empty room. This too depends on second-person address; the writer and the speaker—who are not, of course, identical—and the reader-listener all share in the same joke.

The darker undercurrents of this story function similarly. "The writing professor is obsessed with writing from personal experience":

> He wants deaths, he wants camping trips. Think about what has happened to you. In three years there have been three things: you lost your virginity; your parents got divorced; and your brother came home from a forest ten miles from the Cambodian border with only half a thigh, a permanent smirk nestled into one corner of his mouth.

The first two events are handled in Francie's fiction with increasing silliness, building toward yet another explosion and the title, "For Better or for Liverwurst," with its embittered play on words. For the third there are no words, no comedy, but that "permanent smirk" and the exploding landmines bursting through ludicrous plot lines now have their context. We understand what humor can do to distract us from the dark absurdities of fate. It is Lorrie Moore's achievement that her readers can be, at one and the same time, amused and aghast; in this very early story of this very gifted writer the singular style is already established and the signature in place.

▌ Applications and Connections

- When in the story—at which sentence or phrase—do you relax into the second-person narrative? The first exercise below prompts you to rewrite "How to Become a Writer" from different points of view. When you transpose the point of view, what else will change, in terms of narrative distance but also in characterization? Is this second-person narrator a full-fledged character, someone "real"? Does she stand alone or do you, as reader, feel like a necessary part of her?
- Although this story parodies the self-help genre, featuring a central character who fails to succeed, how could the story be of help to aspiring writers? What

would the story lose if Francie became a famous writer by its last paragraph? Compare Moore's approach to writing about writing to Barth's in "Lost in the Funhouse."

- If someone at a party asked you what you write about, what would you say? What would your friends, classmates, professors, or parents say? Why is it so hard for a writer—supposedly a master of description—to describe this, and do you agree with Moore's narrator that a writer will half believe anything people tell her about her writing?

Exercises

1. Transpose this story into first-person narration. Then into third-person narration. Then omniscient. (I, She, They.)

2. Write one of Francie's short stories with the mayhem and the accidents fleshed out.

3. Compose her **villanelle.** (A nineteen-line poem with elaborate rhyme schemes and stanzaic repetition.)

4. Write a short story on one of the following: (a) how to become a painter, (b) how to become a jazz drummer, or (c) how to become a jockey or disc jockey or dancer, a bowling or chess champion, etc.

5. Rewrite any page of Lorrie Moore's story with the utmost seriousness, tongue dislodged from cheek.

6. Write a parent-teacher conference in which Mr. Killian discusses Francie's work.

7. Keep a folder full of fragments (*"An eyelid darkening sideways. / World as conspiracy. / Possible plot? A woman gets on a bus. / Suppose you threw a love affair and nobody came."*) Write forty more.

8. Write a story about a confused music student and title it: "Beethoven was the one with the hearing aid, right?"

9. Find words—perhaps Tim O'Brien's—for the third of the stories of "personal experience" ("... your brother came home from a forest ten miles from the Cambodian border with only half a thigh ...") Describe how "Your typewriter hums."

10. "Why write? Where does writing come from?" Answer in the voice of Barrett or Ford or Kincaid.

Examples of Student Work

(*Editor's Note:* In many bookstores nowadays, the "Self-Help" section takes up as much space as do the "Literature" shelves. It's not perhaps surprising that the short story collection by Lorrie Moore—and this story in particular—have spawned a host of admiring imitations; the idea touches a nerve. Short stories by Peter Ho Davies and Junot Diaz—to name only two of the authors included in our anthology—have borrowed this style and approach; "How to Be an Expatriate" and "How to Date a Browngirl, Blackgirl, Whitegirl, or Halfie" are published examples, by Davies and Diaz respectively, of that sincerest form of flattery in which writers so often engage.

In the fall semester of 2000, I taught a course of "Imitations" to eighteen undergraduates at the University of Michigan. No single story on the syllabus inspired more, and more sympathetic, attempts at imitation than "How to Become a Writer." Some of the substitute activities that engaged my students' tongue-in-cheek attention were, in alphabetical order: "How to Become a Beatnik," "How to Become a Bowler," "How to Become a Cellist," "How to Eat with Chopsticks," "How to Get over Puppy Love," "How to Become a Jock," "How to Become a Lap Dancer," "How to Be a Swimmer," and "How to Become a Waitress."

Excerpts from two of those exercises follow. The exercises each are too lengthy to reproduce in their entirety, but here are some sample paragraphs that establish tone.)

Stephanie Anderson, EXERCISE 4: "How to Become a Beatnik"

```
First, try to be something, anything else. A brain
surgeon/car mechanic. A brain surgeon/lawyer. A brain
surgeon/high school drama teacher. The Chairman of the
European Union. Fail miserably. It is best if you fail at
an early age—say, 16. Early, critical disillusionment is
necessary so that at twenty you are forced to deal with
your shortcomings. You start buying used purple corduroys
and work-shirts. Show them to your mom. She is pragmatic
and firm. She has a juvenile delinquent as a son and an
alcoholic husband. She believes in wearing tan panty hose
only in the summer. She'll look at your clothes in
horror. Her face pinches up at you and she'll yell:
"Do you want to look like a bum? We buy you nice things
and . . ." She walks away. You stomp downstairs to your
room. Slam your door loudly. Cry. This is the required
pain and suffering. Pick up a book. This is where it
starts.
      . . . You now walk more leisurely through the
halls. You're beat. You carry The Dharma Bums with you
everywhere. As a senior, you have more freedom and you
feel independent. You sit in the corners around the
outside of the building and "smoke." At lunch, you play
Grateful Dead tapes on an old tape deck. You and your
closest friends carry around MEAD journals to record your
random thoughts. To intimidate the freshmen you rant
lines from Shakespeare or Poe as you and your friends
dance down their hallway. You "hang" with your friends.
You "dig" coffeehouse jams. You "catch" Blue Fuzz every
```

weekend at Café V. Rhythm and blues is your new passion.
You identify with Jack Kerouac, Mike is Neal Cassady,
Mark is Gary Snyder. You are inseparable. You dream of
starting the next social revolution.

      . . . Decide that you need to find a used clothing
store. Go exploring. You're in a new city. You're gonna
like being in a city. You and your roommate wander
through town. Find a store. You buy new pants and two new
rough looking shirts. She asks if you are a lesbian. You
say no, you are on a path toward enlightenment, you don't
believe in materialism as an important aspect of life.
Your new roommate asks if you are a hippie. You say,
"No, not really." She says she likes the hippie
lifestyle. You both smile in agreement. You buy a pair of
old blue sneakers. She buys a sundress made out of a
sheet. You two are going to be able to live together.
You buy beads and a woven rug for your room. Your
roommate already has an electric teakettle. You buy cups
and saucers at a second hand shop. And a toaster. You buy
candles. Candles are a great addition to a dingy dorm
room, great for meditation. Your roommate knows yoga.

Zachary Bernstein, EXERCISE 4: "How to Become a Bowler"

First, try to be something, anything else. A rock
star/economist. A rock star/rabbi. A rock star/T-ball
coach. A writer. Fail miserably. It is best to fail at an
early age—say, fourteen. Early, critical disillusionment
is necessary so that at fifteen you can leave the five-pin
standing and not completely lose faith in yourself. Count
the pins lying down. Show them to your dad. He is stern
and cynical. He has a daughter at the bar and a wife who
is definitely having an affair. He believes in wearing
tinted glasses because they hide the eyes. He'll glance
at your spare pin, then back at you with a face blank as
beer foam. He'll say, "How about mowing the lawn later?"
Look away. Hurl your ball down the lane. Accidentally aim
for the gutter. This is the required pain and suffering.
This is only for starters.

      In your high school English class look at Mr. Brando's
hands. Decide hands are important. Write a villanelle
about fingers. Suffer. Write a sonnet. Count the
syllables: ten, ten, ten, ten. In every line, you knock
down ten syllables. Relish sonnets. Decide to experiment
with fiction. Write a short story about an elderly woman
who accidentally smashes her elderly husband's head with
a bowling ball, the result of developing her new spin
technique in their living room. Give it to Mr. Brando as

your final project. When you get it back, he has written on it: "Your images are quite imaginative, your plot needs to be torqued just a little, but your release and follow-through are all wrong to get the kind of spin to which your refer." When you are home, in the privacy of the basement, boldly trace your middle finger with a red magic marker.

    . . . Decide you like college life, In your dorm, you meet a lot of friendly people. Some bowl better than you. And some, you sense, bowl worse than you. You will continue, unfortunately, to view the world in exactly these terms for the rest of your life.

CHAPTER 9

DRAMATIC ENCOUNTER:
Mixing the Accidental and the Foreordained

FLANNERY O'CONNOR, "A Good Man Is Hard to Find"

■ **WRITER'S VIEW:** *This story has been called grotesque, but I prefer to call it literal. A good story is literal in the same sense that a child's drawing is literal. When a child draws, he doesn't intend to distort but to set down exactly what he sees, and as his gaze is direct, he sees the lines that create motion. Now the lines of motion that interest the writer are usually invisible. They are lines of spiritual motion. And in this story you should be on the lookout for such things as the action of grace in the Grandmother's soul, and not for the dead bodies.* ("The Element of Suspense in 'A Good Man Is Hard to Find,'" from Mystery and Manners, *1969*)

Flannery O'Connor was born in Savannah, Georgia, in 1925, the only child of Catholic parents. When she was thirteen, her family moved to the small town of Milledgeville, Georgia. Soon afterwards, her father contracted lupus, a disease that would take his life in 1941 and, eventually, O'Connor's own life in 1964. She graduated from the Georgia State College for Women in 1945, then received a master's degree at the Iowa Writer's Workshop in Iowa City. Her teacher there, Paul Engle, described O'Connor's Georgia accent as so strong when they first met that, after several attempts to comprehend her speech, he finally had to ask her to write down what she wanted to say.

O'Connor became a shy, silent fixture in the back of the classroom, working hard at stories rooted in Southern culture and Catholic sensibility. The **cadences** of Southern speech course through her fiction, and she urged other writers, too, to "(take) advantage of what's yours." As she explained, "We in the South live in a society that is rich in contradiction, rich in irony, rich in contrast, and particularly rich in its speech" ("Writing Short Stories," in *Mystery and Manners*). O'Connor did take advantage of that tradition and richness, though her characters by and large exist on poverty's edge; her stories and novels are known for their dark humor, a view of human nature that at times may seem **grotesque.** There are traces of the influence of other Southern writers in her work—most notably the gothic strain of her great predecessor, William Faulkner—but much of her work defies comparison as well as easy imitation; it is, to use a much-overused word, *original.*

O'Connor published her first story, "The Geranium," in 1946, and soon placed other early stories with *Mademoiselle* and *Sewanee Review*. In 1947 she won a contest which offered her a contract for her first novel, *Wise Blood*, and thereafter moved to Yaddo, an artists' colony in upstate New York. O'Connor worked on this short novel for years, struggling to reconcile her editors' expectations with her own, and discarding, in the end, about two thousand pages. "Writing a novel is a terrible experience," she later said. "You never know if you will finish it or it will finish you" (*Athens Banner-Herald*, 10 Aug. 1961). Eventually, O'Connor obtained a release from her contract and sold the book to a different publisher, Harcourt, Brace, who published *Wise Blood* in 1952.

In the meantime, however, she had contracted lupus and moved back to Milledgeville, where she spent many months in and out of the hospital, in grave health. Unable to climb stairs, O'Connor moved with her mother to a family farm, "Andalusia," where she spent her time painting, raising swans and peacocks, and—often in great pain—writing.

In 1955 she published her first collection of short stories, *A Good Man Is Hard to Find*, and in 1957 received a first prize in the O. Henry Awards for her story "Greenleaf." She repeated this achievement in 1963 and 1965. Her second novel, *The Violent Bear It Away*, was published in 1960, and her last collection of stories, *Everything That Rises Must Converge*, was published in 1965, a year after O'Connor's death from complications of lupus.

In 1969 her occasional prose, speeches, and essays were collected in *Mystery and Manners*, and her complete stories were collected in a 1971 edition which earned her a posthumous National Book Award. O'Connor is remembered not just as a modern master of the short story form, but also—from interviews, letters, and speeches—for her wise and fiercely witty voice. When asked whether writing programs stifle writers, O'Connor famously replied, "My opinion is that they don't stifle enough of them."

A Good Man Is Hard to Find

The Grandmother didn't want to go to Florida. She wanted to visit some of her connections in east Tennessee and she was seizing at every chance to change Bailey's mind. Bailey was the son she lived with, her only boy. He was sitting on the edge of his chair at the table, bent over the orange sports section of the *Journal.* "Now look here, Bailey," she said, "see here, read this," and she stood with one hand on her thin hip and the other rattling the newspaper at his bald head. "Here this fellow that calls himself The Misfit is aloose from the Federal Pen and headed toward Florida and you read here what it says he did to these people. Just you read it. I wouldn't take my children in any direction with a criminal like that aloose in it. I couldn't answer to my conscience if I did."

Bailey didn't look up from his reading so she wheeled around then and faced the children's mother, a young woman in slacks, whose face was as broad and innocent as a cabbage and was tied around with a green head-kerchief that had two points on the top like a rabbit's ears. She was sitting on the sofa, feeding the baby his apricots out of a jar. "The children have been to Florida before," the old lady said. "You all ought to take them somewhere else for a change so they would see different parts of the world and be broad. They never have been to east Tennessee."

The children's mother didn't seem to hear her but the eight-year-old boy, John Wesley, a stocky child with glasses, said, "If you don't want to go to Florida, why dontcha stay at home?" He and the little girl, June Star, were reading the funny papers on the floor.

"She wouldn't stay at home to be queen for a day," June Star said without raising her yellow head.

"Yes, and what would you do if this fellow, The Misfit, caught you?" the grandmother asked.

"I'd smack his face," John Wesley said.

"She wouldn't stay at home for a million bucks," June Star said. "Afraid she'd miss something. She has to go everywhere we go."

"All right, Miss," the grandmother said. "Just remember that the next time you want me to curl your hair."

June Star said her hair was naturally curly.

The next morning the grandmother was the first one in the car, ready to go. She had her big black valise that looked like the head of a hippopotamus in one corner, and underneath it she was hiding a basket with Pitty Sing, the cat, in it. She didn't intend for the cat to be left alone in the house for three days because he would miss her too much and she was afraid he might brush against one of the gas burners and accidentally asphyxiate himself. Her son, Bailey, didn't like to arrive at a motel with a cat.

She sat in the middle of the back seat with John Wesley and June Star on either side of her. Bailey and the children's mother and the baby sat in front and they left Atlanta at eight forty-five with the mileage on the car at 55890. The grandmother wrote this down because she thought it would be interesting to say how many miles they had been when they got back. It took them twenty minutes to reach the outskirts of the city.

The old lady settled herself comfortably, removing her white cotton gloves and putting them up with her purse on the shelf in front of the back window. The children's mother still had on slacks and still had her head tied up in a green kerchief, but the grandmother had on a navy blue straw sailor hat with a bunch of white violets on the brim and a navy blue dress with a small white dot in the print. Her collar and cuffs were white organdy trimmed with lace and at her neckline she had pinned a purple spray of cloth violets containing a sachet. In case of an accident, anyone seeing her dead on the highway would know at once that she was a lady.

She said she thought it was going to be a good day for driving, neither too hot nor too cold, and she cautioned Bailey that the speed limit was fifty-five miles an hour and that the patrolmen hid themselves behind billboards and small clumps of trees and sped out after you before you had a chance to slow down. She pointed out interesting details of the scenery: Stone Mountain; the blue granite that in some places came up to both sides of the highway; the brilliant red clay banks slightly streaked with purple; and the various crops that made rows of green lace-work on the ground. The trees were full of silver-white sunlight and the meanest of them sparkled. The children were reading comic magazines and their mother had gone back to sleep.

"Let's go through Georgia fast so we won't have to look at it much," John Wesley said.

"If I were a little boy," said the grandmother, "I wouldn't talk about my native state that way. Tennessee has the mountains and Georgia has the hills."

"Tennessee is just a hillbilly dumping ground," John Wesley said, "and Georgia is a lousy state too."

"You said it," June Star said.

"In my time," said the grandmother, folding her thin veined fingers, "children were more respectful of their native states and their parents and everything else. People did right then. Oh look at the cute little pickaninny!" she said and pointed to a Negro child standing in the door of a shack. "Wouldn't that make a picture, now?" she asked and they all turned and looked at the little Negro out of the back window. He waved.

"He didn't have any britches on," June Star said.

"He probably didn't have any," the grandmother explained. "Little niggers in the country don't have things like we do. If I could paint, I'd paint that picture," she said.

The children exchanged comic books.

The grandmother offered to hold the baby and the children's mother passed him over the front seat to her. She set him on her knee and bounced him and told him about the things they were passing. She rolled her eyes and screwed up her mouth and stuck her leathery thin face into his smooth bland one. Occasionally he gave her a faraway smile. They passed a large cotton field with five or six graves fenced in the middle of it, like a small island. "Look at the graveyard!" the grandmother said, pointing it out. "That was the old family burying ground. That belonged to the plantation."

"Where's the plantation?" John Wesley asked.

"Gone with the Wind," said the grandmother. "Ha. Ha."

When the children finished all the comic books they had brought, they opened the lunch and ate it. The grandmother ate a peanut butter sandwich and an olive and would not let the children throw the box and the paper napkins out the window. When there was nothing else to do they played a game by choosing a cloud and making the other two guess what shape it suggested. John Wesley took one the shape of a cow and June Star guessed a cow and John Wesley said, no, an automobile, and June Star said he didn't play fair, and they began to slap each other over the grandmother.

The grandmother said she would tell them a story if they would keep quiet. When she told a story, she rolled her eyes and waved her head and was very dramatic. She said once when she was a maiden lady she had been courted by a Mr. Edgar Atkins Teagarden from Jasper, Georgia. She said he was a very good-looking man and a gentleman and that he brought her a watermelon every Saturday afternoon with his initials cut in it, E. A. T. Well, one Saturday, she said, Mr. Teagarden brought the watermelon and there was nobody at home and he left it on the front porch and returned in his buggy to Jasper, but she never got the watermelon, she said, because a nigger boy ate it when he saw the initials, E. A. T.! This story tickled John Wesley's funny bone and he giggled and giggled but June Star didn't think it was any good. She said she wouldn't marry a man that just brought her a watermelon on Saturday. The grandmother said she would have done well to marry Mr. Teagarden because he was a gentleman and had bought Coca-Cola stock when it first came out and that he had died only a few years ago, a very wealthy man.

They stopped at The Tower for barbecued sandwiches. The Tower was a part stucco and part wood filling station and dance hall set in a clearing outside of Timothy. A fat man named Red Sammy Butts ran it and there were signs stuck here and there on the building and for miles up and down the highway saying, TRY RED SAMMY'S FAMOUS BARBECUE. NONE LIKE FAMOUS RED SAMMY'S! RED SAM! THE FAT BOY WITH THE HAPPY LAUGH! A VETERAN! RED SAMMY'S YOUR MAN!

Red Sammy was lying on the bare ground outside The Tower with his head under a truck while a gray monkey about a foot high, chained to a small chinaberry tree, chattered nearby. The monkey sprang back into the tree and got on the highest limb as soon as he saw the children jump out of the car and run toward him.

Inside, The Tower was a long dark room with a counter at one end and tables at the other and dancing space in the middle. They all sat down at a board table next to the nickelodeon and Red Sam's wife, a tall burnt-brown woman with hair and eyes lighter than her skin, came and took their order. The children's mother put a dime in the machine and played "The Tennessee Waltz," and the grandmother said that tune always made her want to dance. She asked Bailey if he would like to dance but he only glared at her. He didn't have a naturally sunny disposition like she did and trips made him nervous. The grandmother's brown eyes were very bright. She swayed her head from side to side and pretended she was dancing in her chair. June Star said play something she could tap to so the children's mother put in another dime and played a fast number and June Star stepped out onto the dance floor and did her tap routine.

"Ain't she cute?" Red Sam's wife said, leaning over the counter. "Would you like to come be my little girl?"

"No, I certainly wouldn't," June Star said. "I wouldn't live in a broken-down place like this for a million bucks!" and she ran back to the table.

"Ain't she cute?" the woman repeated, stretching her mouth politely.

"Aren't you ashamed?" hissed the grandmother.

Red Sam came in and told his wife to quit lounging on the counter and hurry up with these people's order. His khaki trousers reached just to his hip bones and his stomach hung over them like a sack of meal swaying under his shirt. He came over and sat down at a table nearby and let out a combination sigh and yodel. "You can't win," he said. "You can't win," and he wiped his sweating red face off with a gray handkerchief. "These days you don't know who to trust," he said. "Ain't that the truth?"

"People are certainly not nice like they used to be," said the grandmother.

"Two fellers came in here last week," Red Sammy said, "driving a Chrysler. It was a old beat-up car but it was a good one and these boys looked all right to me. Said they worked at the mill and you know I let them fellers charge the gas they bought? Now why did I do that?"

"Because you're a good man!" the grandmother said at once.

"Yes'm, I suppose so," Red Sam said as if he were struck with this answer.

His wife brought the orders, carrying the five plates all at once without a tray, two in each hand and one balanced on her arm. "It isn't a soul in this green world of God's that you can trust," she said. "And I don't count nobody out of that, not nobody," she repeated, looking at Red Sammy.

"Did you read about that criminal, The Misfit, that's escaped?" asked the grandmother.

"I wouldn't be a bit surprised if he didn't attact this place right here," said the woman. "If he hears about it being here, I wouldn't be none surprised to see him. If he hears it's two cent in the cash register, I wouldn't be a tall surprised if he . . ."

"That'll do," Red Sam said. "Go bring these people their Co' Colas," and the woman went off to get the rest of the order.

"A good man is hard to find," Red Sammy said. "Everything is getting terrible. I remember the day you could go off and leave your screen door unlatched. Not no more."

He and the grandmother discussed better times. The old lady said that in her opinion Europe was entirely to blame for the way things were now. She said the way Europe acted you would think we were made of money and Red Sam said it was no use talking about it, she was exactly right. The children ran outside into the white sunlight and looked at the monkey in the lacy chinaberry tree. He was busy catching fleas on himself and biting each one carefully between his teeth as if it were a delicacy.

They drove off again into the hot afternoon. The grandmother took cat naps and woke up every few minutes with her own snoring. Outside of Toombsboro she woke up and recalled an old plantation that she had visited in this neighborhood once when she was a young lady. She said the house had six white columns across the front and that there was an avenue of oaks leading up to it and two little wooden trellis arbors on either side in front where you sat down with your suitor after a stroll in the garden. She recalled exactly which road to turn off to get to it. She knew that Bailey would not be willing to lose any time looking at an old house, but the more she talked about it, the more she wanted to see it once again and find out if the little twin arbors were still standing. "There was a secret panel in this house," she said craftily, not telling the truth but wishing that she were, "and the story went that all the family silver was hidden in it when Sherman came through but it was never found . . ."

"Hey!" John Wesley said. "Let's go see it! We'll find it! We'll poke all the woodwork and find it! Who lives there? Where do you turn off at? Hey Pop, can't we turn off there?"

"We never have seen a house with a secret panel!" June Star shrieked. "Let's go to the house with the secret panel! Hey Pop, can't we go see the house with the secret panel!"

"It's not far from here, I know," the grandmother said. "It wouldn't take over twenty minutes."

Bailey was looking straight ahead. His jaw was as rigid as a horseshoe. "No," he said.

The children began to yell and scream that they wanted to see the house with the secret panel. John Wesley kicked the back of the front seat and June Star hung over her mother's shoulder and whined desperately into her ear that they never had any fun even on their vacation, that they could never do what THEY wanted to do. The baby began to scream and John Wesley kicked the back of the seat so hard that his father could feel the blows in his kidney.

"All right!" he shouted and drew the car to a stop at the side of the road. "Will you all shut up? Will you all just shut up for one second? If you don't shut up, we won't go anywhere."

"It would be very educational for them," the grandmother murmured.

"All right," Bailey said, "but get this: this is the only time we're going to stop for anything like this. This is the one and only time."

"The dirt road that you have to turn down is about a mile back," the grandmother directed. "I marked it when we passed."

"A dirt road," Bailey groaned.

After they had turned around and were headed toward the dirt road, the grandmother recalled other points about the house, the beautiful glass over the front doorway and the candle-lamp in the hall. John Wesley said that the secret panel was probably in the fireplace.

"You can't go inside this house," Bailey said. "You don't know who lives there."

"While you all talk to the people in front, I'll run around behind and get in a window," John Wesley suggested.

"We'll all stay in the car," his mother said.

They turned onto the dirt road and the car raced roughly along in a swirl of pink dust. The grandmother recalled the times when there were no paved roads and thirty miles was a day's journey. The dirt road was hilly and there were sudden washes in it and sharp curves on dangerous embankments. All at once they would be on a hill, looking down over the blue tops of trees for miles around, then the next minute, they would be in a red depression with the dust-coated trees looking down on them.

"This place had better turn up in a minute," Bailey said, "or I'm going to turn around."

The road looked as if no one had traveled on it in months.

"It's not much farther," the grandmother said and just as she said it, a horrible thought came to her. The thought was so embarrassing that she turned red in the face and her eyes dilated and her feet jumped up, upsetting her valise in the corner. The instant the valise moved, the newspaper top she had over the basket under it rose with a snarl and Pitty Sing, the cat, sprang onto Bailey's shoulder.

The children were thrown to the floor and their mother, clutching the baby, was thrown out the door onto the ground; the old lady was thrown into the front seat. The car turned over once and landed right-side-up in a gulch off the side of the road. Bailey remained in the driver's seat with the cat—gray-striped with a broad white face and an orange nose—clinging to his neck like a caterpillar.

As soon as the children saw they could move their arms and legs, they scrambled out of the car, shouting, "We've had an ACCIDENT!" The grandmother was curled up under the dashboard, hoping she was injured so that Bailey's wrath would not come down on her all at once. The horrible thought she had had before the accident was that the house she had remembered so vividly was not in Georgia but in Tennessee.

Bailey removed the cat from his neck with both hands and flung it out the window against the side of a pine tree. Then he got out of the car and started looking for the children's mother. She was sitting against the side of the red gutted ditch, holding the screaming baby, but she only had a cut down her face and a broken shoulder. "We've had an ACCIDENT!" the children screamed in a frenzy of delight.

"But nobody's killed," June Star said with disappointment as the grandmother limped out of the car, her hat still pinned to her head but the broken front brim standing up at a jaunty angle and the violet spray hanging off the side. They all sat down in the ditch, except the children, to recover from the shock. They were all shaking.

"Maybe a car will come along," said the children's mother hoarsely.

"I believe I have injured an organ," said the grandmother, pressing her side, but no one answered her. Bailey's teeth were clattering. He had on a yellow sport shirt with bright blue parrots designed in it and his face was as yellow as the shirt. The grandmother decided that she would not mention that the house was in Tennessee.

The road was about ten feet above and they could see only the tops of the trees on the other side of it. Behind the ditch they were sitting in there were more woods, tall and dark and deep. In a few minutes they saw a car some distance away on top of a hill, coming slowly as if the occupants were watching them. The grandmother stood up and waved both arms dramatically to attract their attention. The car continued to come on slowly, disappeared around a bend and appeared again, moving even slower, on top of the hill they had gone over. It was a big black battered hearse-like automobile. There were three men in it.

It came to a stop just over them and for some minutes, the driver looked down with a steady expressionless gaze to where they were sitting, and didn't speak. Then he turned his head and muttered something to the other two and they got out. One was a fat boy in black trousers and a red sweat shirt with a silver stallion embossed on the front of it. He moved around on the right side of them and stood staring, his mouth partly open in a kind of loose grin. The other had on khaki pants and a blue striped coat and a gray hat pulled down very low, hiding most of his face. He came around slowly on the left side. Neither spoke.

The driver got out of the car and stood by the side of it, looking down at them. He was an older man than the other two. His hair was just beginning to gray and he wore silver-rimmed spectacles that gave him a scholarly look. He had a long creased face and didn't have on any shirt or undershirt. He had on blue jeans that were too tight for him and was holding a black hat and a gun. The two boys also had guns.

"We've had an ACCIDENT!" the children screamed.

The grandmother had the peculiar feeling that the bespectacled man was someone she knew. His face was as familiar to her as if she had known him all her life but she could not recall who he was. He moved away from the car and began to come down the embankment, placing his feet carefully so that he wouldn't slip. He had on tan and white shoes and no socks, and his ankles were red and thin. "Good afternoon," he said. "I see you all had you a little spill."

"We turned over twice!" said the grandmother.

"Oncet," he corrected. "We seen it happen. Try their car and see will it run, Hiram," he said quietly to the boy with the gray hat.

"What you got that gun for?" John Wesley asked. "Whatcha gonna do with that gun?"

"Lady," the man said to the children's mother, "would you mind calling them children to sit down by you? Children make me nervous. I want all you all to sit down right together there where you're at."

"What are you telling US what to do for?" June Star asked.

Behind them the line of woods gaped like a dark open mouth. "Come here," said their mother.

"Look here now," Bailey began suddenly, "we're in a predicament! We're in . . ."

The grandmother shrieked. She scrambled to her feet and stood staring. "You're The Misfit!" she said. "I recognized you at once!"

"Yes'm," the man said, smiling slightly as if he were pleased in spite of himself to be known, "but it would have been better for all of you, lady, if you hadn't of reckernized me."

Bailey turned his head sharply and said something to his mother that shocked even the children. The old lady began to cry and The Misfit reddened.

"Lady," he said, "don't you get upset. Sometimes a man says things he don't mean. I don't reckon he meant to talk to you thataway."

"You wouldn't shoot a lady, would you?" the grandmother said and removed a clean handkerchief from her cuff and began to slap at her eyes with it.

The Misfit pointed the toe of his shoe into the ground and made a little hole and then covered it up again. "I would hate to have to," he said.

"Listen," the grandmother almost screamed, "I know you're a good man. You don't look a bit like you have common blood. I know you must come from nice people!"

"Yes mam," he said, "finest people in the world." When he smiled he showed a row of strong white teeth. "God never made a finer woman than my mother and my daddy's heart was pure gold," he said. The boy with the red sweat shirt had come around behind them and was standing with his gun at his hip. The Misfit squatted down on the ground. "Watch them children, Bobby Lee," he said. "You know they make me nervous." He looked at the six of them huddled together in front of him and he seemed to be embarrassed as if he couldn't think of anything to say. "Ain't a cloud in the sky," he remarked, looking up at it. "Don't see no sun but don't see no cloud neither."

"Yes, it's a beautiful day," said the grandmother. "Listen," she said, "you shouldn't call yourself The Misfit because I know you're a good man at heart. I can just look at you and tell."

"Hush!" Bailey yelled. "Hush! Everybody shut up and let me handle this!" He was squatting in the position of a runner about to sprint forward but he didn't move.

"I pre-chate that, lady," The Misfit said and drew a little circle in the ground with the butt of his gun.

"It'll take a half a hour to fix this here car," Hiram called, looking over the raised hood of it.

"Well, first you and Bobby Lee get him and that little boy to step over yonder with you," The Misfit said, pointing to Bailey and John Wesley. "The boys want to ast you something," he said to Bailey. "Would you mind stepping back in them woods there with them?"

"Listen," Bailey began, "we're in a terrible predicament! Nobody realizes what this is," and his voice cracked. His eyes were as blue and intense as the parrots in his shirt and he remained perfectly still.

The grandmother reached up to adjust her hat brim as if she were going to the woods with him but it came off in her hand. She stood staring at it and after a second she let it fall on the ground. Hiram pulled Bailey up by the arm as if he were assisting an old man. John Wesley caught hold of his father's hand and Bobby Lee followed. They went off toward the woods and just as they reached the dark edge, Bailey turned and supporting himself against a gray naked pine trunk, he shouted, "I'll be back in a minute, Mamma, wait on me!"

"Come back this instant!" the mother shrilled but they all disappeared into the woods.

"Bailey Boy!" the grandmother called in a tragic voice but she found she was looking at The Misfit squatting on the ground in front of her. "I just know you're a good man," she said desperately. "You're not a bit common!"

"Nome, I ain't a good man," The Misfit said after a second as if he had considered her statement carefully, "but I ain't the worst in the world neither. My daddy said I was a different breed of dog from my brothers and sisters. 'You know,' Daddy said, 'it's some that can live their whole life out without asking about it and it's others has to know why it is, and this boy is one of the latters. He's going to be into everything!'" He put on his black hat and looked up suddenly and then away deep into the woods as if he were embarrassed again. "I'm sorry I don't have on a shirt before you ladies," he said, hunching his shoulders slightly. "We buried our clothes that we had on when we escaped and we're just making do until we can get better. We borrowed these from some folks we met," he explained.

"That's perfectly all right," the grandmother said. "Maybe Bailey has an extra shirt in his suitcase."

"I'll look and see terreckly," The Misfit said.

"Where are they taking him?" the children's mother screamed.

"Daddy was a card himself," The Misfit said. "You couldn't put anything over on him. He never got in trouble with the Authorities though. Just had the knack of handling them."

"You could be honest too if you'd only try," said the grandmother. "Think how wonderful it would be to settle down and live a comfortable life and not have to think about somebody chasing you all the time."

The Misfit kept scratching in the ground with the butt of his gun as if he were thinking about it. "Yes'm, somebody is always after you," he murmured.

The grandmother noticed how thin his shoulder blades were just behind his hat because she was standing up looking down on him. "Do you ever pray?" she asked.

He shook his head. All she saw was the black hat wiggle between his shoulder blades. "Nome," he said.

There was a pistol shot from the woods, followed closely by another. Then silence. The old lady's head jerked around. She could hear the wind move through the tree tops like a long satisfied insuck of breath. "Bailey Boy!" she called.

"I was a gospel singer for a while," The Misfit said. "I been most everything. Been in the arm service, both land and sea, at home and abroad, been twict married, been an undertaker, been with the railroads, plowed Mother Earth, been in a tornado, seen a man burnt alive oncet," and looked up at the children's mother and the little girl who were sitting close together, their faces white and their eyes glassy; "I even seen a woman flogged," he said.

"Pray, pray," the grandmother began, "pray, pray . . ."

"I never was a bad boy that I remember of," The Misfit said in an almost dreamy voice, "but somewheres along the line I done something wrong and got sent to the penitentiary. I was buried alive," and he looked up and held her attention to him by a steady stare.

"That's when you should have started to pray," she said. "What did you do to get sent to the penitentiary that first time?"

"Turn to the right, it was a wall," The Misfit said, looking up again at the cloudless sky. "Turn to the left, it was a wall. Look up it was a ceiling, look down it was a floor. I forget what I done, lady. I set there and set there, trying to remember what it was I done and I ain't recalled it to this day. Oncet in a while, I would think it was coming to me, but it never come."

"Maybe they put you in by mistake," the old lady said vaguely.

"Nome," he said. "It wasn't no mistake. They had the papers on me."

"You must have stolen something," she said.

The Misfit sneered slightly. "Nobody had nothing I wanted," he said. "It was a head-doctor at the penitentiary said what I had done was kill my daddy but I known that for a lie. My daddy died in nineteen ought nineteen of the epidemic flu and I never had a thing to do with it. He was buried in the Mount Hopewell Baptist churchyard and you can go there and see for yourself."

"If you would pray," the old lady said, "Jesus would help you."

"That's right," The Misfit said.

"Well then, why don't you pray?" she asked trembling with delight suddenly.

"I don't want no help," he said. "I'm doing all right by myself."

Bobby Lee and Hiram came ambling back from the woods. Bobby Lee was dragging a yellow shirt with bright blue parrots in it.

"Throw me that shirt, Bobby Lee," The Misfit said. The shirt came flying at him and landed on his shoulder and he put it on. The grandmother couldn't name what the shirt reminded her of. "No, lady," The Misfit said while he was buttoning it up, "I found out the crime don't matter. You can do one thing or you can do another, kill a man or take a tire off a car, because sooner or later you're going to forget what it was you done and just be punished for it."

The children's mother had begun to make heaving noises as if she couldn't get her breath. "Lady," he asked, "would you and that little girl like to step off yonder with Bobby Lee and Hiram and join your husband?"

"Yes, thank you," the mother said faintly. Her left arm dangled helplessly and she was holding the baby, who had gone to sleep, in the other. "Hep that lady up, Hiram," The Misfit said as she struggled to climb out of the ditch, "and Bobby Lee, you hold onto that little girl's hand."

"I don't want to hold hands with him," June Star said. "He reminds me of a pig."

The fat boy blushed and laughed and caught her by the arm and pulled her off into the woods after Hiram and her mother.

Alone with The Misfit, the grandmother found that she had lost her voice. There was not a cloud in the sky nor any sun. There was nothing around her but woods. She wanted to tell him that he must pray. She opened and closed her mouth several times before anything came out. Finally she found herself saying, "Jesus, Jesus," meaning, Jesus will help you, but the way she was saying it, it sounded as if she might be cursing.

"Yes'm," The Misfit said as if he agreed. "Jesus thown everything off balance. It was the same case with Him as with me except He hadn't committed any crime and they could prove I had committed one because they had the papers on me. Of course," he said, "they never shown me my papers. That's why I sign myself now. I said long ago, you get you a signature and sign everything you do and keep a copy of it. Then you'll know what you done and you can hold up the crime to the punishment and see do they match and in the end you'll have something to prove you ain't been treated right. I call myself The Misfit," he said, "because I can't make what all I done wrong fit what all I gone through in punishment."

There was a piercing scream from the woods, followed closely by a pistol report. "Does it seem right to you, lady, that one is punished a heap and another ain't punished at all?"

"Jesus!" the old lady cried. "You've got good blood! I know you wouldn't shoot a lady! I know you come from nice people! Pray! Jesus, you ought not to shoot a lady. I'll give you all the money I've got!"

"Lady," The Misfit said, looking beyond her far into the woods, "there never was a body that give the undertaker a tip."

There were two more pistol reports and the grandmother raised her head like a parched old turkey hen crying for water and called, "Bailey Boy, Bailey Boy!" as if her heart would break.

"Jesus was the only One that ever raised the dead," The Misfit continued, "and He shouldn't have done it. He thrown everything off balance. If He did what He said, then it's nothing for you to do but throw away everything and follow Him, and if He didn't, then it's nothing for you to do but enjoy the few minutes you got left the best way you can—by killing somebody or burning down his house or doing some other meanness to him. No pleasure but meanness," he said and his voice had become almost a snarl.

"Maybe He didn't raise the dead," the old lady mumbled, not knowing what she was saying and feeling so dizzy that she sank down in the ditch with her legs twisted under her.

"I wasn't there so I can't say He didn't," The Misfit said. "I wisht I had of been there," he said, hitting the ground with his fist. "It ain't right I wasn't there because if I had of been there I would of known. Listen lady," he said in a high voice, "if I had of been there I would of known and I wouldn't be like I am now." His voice seemed about to crack and the grandmother's head cleared for an instant. She saw the man's face twisted close to her own as if he were going to cry and she murmured, "Why you're one of my babies. You're one of my own children!" She reached out and touched him on the shoulder. The Misfit sprang back as if a snake had bitten him and shot her three times through the chest. Then he put his gun down on the ground and took off his glasses and began to clean them.

Hiram and Bobby Lee returned from the woods and stood over the ditch, looking down at the grandmother who half sat and half lay in a puddle of blood with her legs crossed under her like a child's and her face smiling up at the cloudless sky.

Without his glasses, The Misfit's eyes were red-rimmed and pale and defenseless-looking. "Take her off and throw her where you thrown the others," he said, picking up the cat that was rubbing itself against his leg.

"She was a talker, wasn't she?" Bobby Lee said, sliding down the ditch with a yodel.

"She would of been a good woman," The Misfit said, "if it had been somebody there to shoot her every minute of her life."

"Some fun!" Bobby Lee said.

"Shut up, Bobby Lee," The Misfit said. "It's no real pleasure in life."

▪ Notes on Craft and Context

On the Plot

Imagine a good friend comes to you, flush with her latest idea for a short story. "It'll be an American classic," she says. "A family of six travels to Florida by car while a dangerous convict is on the loose. In the car sits the quiet, stiff-lipped father, his silent wife, their infant, and two badly behaved, sassy children, as well as a grandmother who irritates all of them and passes her Old Southern judgment on everything she sees. She brings along her cat. On a deserted road, the cat jumps out of her bag, shocking the father, who flips the car into a ditch. The family is, for the most part, uninjured—the mother only breaks her shoulder—but as luck would have it, they have stumbled upon the dangerous convict and his friends. They spend some time talking together, and then the Misfit—that's his name—commences to kill the family members one by one."

She flashes you a malicious grin. "And it will have religion too."

An American classic it is, though Flannery O'Connor would have been, of course, too hard on herself to make such a boastful prediction. O'Connor's accomplishments in this story are many: the eerie humor, the economical rendering of each character's personality, the **inflected dialogue** and subtle inclusion of Southern and Christian concerns. But perhaps most remarkable in terms of craft is her innovative plotting of those events which lead to the final and fatal encounter.

On the Foreordained

In retrospect, it's clear the first paragraph announces the conclusion of the story. "The Grandmother didn't want to go to Florida," we read. "'I wouldn't take my children in any direction with a criminal like that aloose in it.'" O'Connor inserts these ominous lines into an otherwise casual conversation, masking or even mocking the possibility that this family could ever encounter The Misfit. The children read their funny papers calmly, oblivious to the danger the Grandmother points out. Bailey, like his cabbage-faced wife, pays no heed—and we think, perhaps, neither should we. She's a talker, we gather, this Grandmother, and after all, her real motivation lies elsewhere. She is not so much concerned for her family's safety as eager to visit her connections in east Tennessee.

This mixture of the comic and the terrifying renders the story unsettling and its tone hard to define. (In part perhaps this has to do with the author's use of dialect; words like "aloose," "terrectly," and "Nome" evoke a world where speech veers away from the norm.) Although the plot when summarized appears "sensational" and depends upon coincidence, at each stage of the action O'Connor disrupts expectation and prepares the reader for her lethal closing scenes. "In case of an accident," we learn early on, "anyone seeing her dead on the highway would know at once that she was a lady." When The Misfit drives up to the family in the ditch, what we see is "a big black battered hearse-like automobile," and we assume death has arrived.

On Humor and Horror

At the same time O'Connor leavens the story's darkest moments with humor. "We've had an ACCIDENT!" the children scream with delight when The Misfit and his men appear. The Misfit cracks jokes and apologizes for his attire, and everyone chitchats about the weather as they proceed to their deaths. Call it grotesque or **surreal,** it is certainly disturbing, and this mixture of darkness and light pervades the story from start to finish. By juxtaposing disparate elements—a beautiful bright yellow and blue parrot shirt stolen from a corpse—O'Connor paves the way for the surreal, mysterious experience at story's end. The first killings take place "offstage" and are reported to us via screams and gunshots; the final murder takes place "stage center"; we watch the Misfit fire his gun and the grandmother bleed and fall.

Plot: Escalating Danger

What begins as a casual road trip, complicated only by small family conflicts, turns into a journey through a wasteland of the South; this is a landscape complete with poverty, the specter of gutted plantations, killers and thieves on the loose and, let's not forget, a monkey chained to a tree. Scene by scene, the potential for disaster escalates. O'Connor develops each ominous hint, making more real the possibility of catastrophe until her characters come face to face with evil and, in that confrontation, achieve a brief moment of grace.

On Character Driving Plot

Consider the roles of the hidden cat, the family members, Red Sammy. How would this narrative proceed without them? A skilled storyteller, O'Connor understands that a difficult, pushy character can instigate an action as no passive soul could do. Time and again it is the Grandmother's unflinching will that drives the plot. She *must* bring and hide Pitty-sing (a cat named for a character in Gilbert and Sullivan's "The Mikado" but with a darker secondary meaning to the name). She *must* recollect this phantom house—forgetting its actual location—and manipulate her son into driving a dangerous road. It's in the nature of her chatty, know-it-all character to admit recognizing The Misfit. And she must, when faced with death, struggle to save herself by saving a murderer's soul.

All this flows quite naturally from the Grandmother's personality as we come to understand it. If she were an amicable, undemanding sort riding quietly in the back seat, this family would proceed to Florida, and it is hard to imagine how they could encounter The Misfit except by improbable or overplotted coincidence. The personality of the Grandmother, however—her will, her mischief and mistakes—renders this story's action both possible and plausible. And O'Connor prepares for the ending in other ways as well.

On Hints from Minor Characters

Take, as an example, the role Red Sammy plays. In one sense the episode at this roadside dance hall seems merely a casual diversion on the family's journey. Yet the "two fellers" who charged their gas last week and failed to pay for it contribute to an atmosphere of criminality and ill-will in the region. When talk turns to The Misfit, we see that the Grandmother's fear of him, so disregarded by her family, is in fact echoed and amplified by others in the community. "'I wouldn't be a bit surprised if he didn't attact this place right here,'" Red Sammy's wife warns, and her husband's response, "That'll do," sends contradictory signals. Either he thinks she's being needlessly melodramatic, or Red Sammy considers the threat of The Misfit so real it's liable to frighten their customers away.

On Free Will and Predestination

O'Connor leaves both possibilities open. She makes tangible the potential for danger, then allows her characters to ramble along on their chosen path, veering sometimes towards journey's end, sometimes away. This is the essence of high drama. The killer on the loose, the cat sleeping on the floorboards, the dangerous embankments on a deserted dirt road: all are potential threats from which we hope against hope this family will escape.

Of course, they don't and can't. If character is fate, as Aristotle maintains, then these characters and their story are fated to reach this particular conclusion. The Grandmother remembers the true location of the old house, upsetting the cat in the bag, who leaps onto Bailey's shoulder, causing him to swerve off the road. It all happens terribly quickly; it's over in the span of a single paragraph. And then slowly, dipping in and out of sight, the hearse-like car of The Misfit comes on the scene . . .

On Pace and the Dramatic Encounter: Sustaining Hope

A student once asked, in a discussion of this story, why the men didn't just shoot everyone at once, right there in the ditch. This is an excellent question. The answer may lie more in O'Connor's aims for the story and her gift for dramatic dialogue than in any criminal strategy or personal motivation we may ascribe to the killers.

For openers, the story would be half as long.

The arrival of The Misfit and his men occurs almost precisely at the midpoint of the narrative, yet within moments of their arrival it becomes obvious that none of the main characters will survive. Why should we read on, knowing the conclusion?

Brilliantly, O'Connor retards the **pace** here and complicates the action. While she is content to confine the car accident to one brief paragraph, the family's gruesome final moments on earth take up half the span of the tale. The division of these murders into separate episodes does more than prolong the drama at a critical moment; it opens up further possibilities. After Bailey and the boy are taken away, will the women be raped or in some other manner mistreated? Will the killers refrain from shooting a lady? Can the Grandmother talk them out of it? The reader, like the Grandmother, is reduced to desperation, hoping against hope until the last terrible moment. The readerly conviction that the main character, the point-of-view character, couldn't possibly be destroyed—otherwise what would happen to the story?—mirrors perfectly the Grandmother's denial of the imminence of her own death.

On Character and Grace

Bailey's wife sees things quite differently. She makes a few heaving noises on hearing the gunshots, then accepts The Misfit's offer of a trip to the woods with a peaceful, polite, "Yes, thank you." In this way she accepts her own murder—and that of her children—as foregone; when asked to "join your husband" she goes meekly, willingly.

The Grandmother, ill-suited for such sacrifice, grasps at straws. "Jesus!" she cries. "You've got good blood! I know you wouldn't shoot a lady! I know you come from nice people! Pray!" The nearer she comes to her death, the more fiercely she clings to her moral imperatives and code of social behavior. There is good blood and bad blood, there is Jesus, there is the power of prayer to transform and redeem. The Misfit may be correct in the end when he says, "She would of been a good woman, if it had been somebody there to shoot her every minute of her life," because in the author's eyes this scene tests the Grandmother's faith. O'Connor explained, "the man in the violent situation reveals those qualities least dispensable in his personality, those qualities which are all he will have to take into eternity with him" (*Mystery and Manners*, 114).

What the Grandmother reveals of herself in this moment, and how she reveals it, is something of a mystery. On the most concrete level, we can say that the woman is in shock, incoherent, and when The Misfit comes rushing toward her wearing Bailey's colorful parrot shirt, she simply and plainly mistakes him for her son. *"Why you're one of my babies. You're one of my own children!"* All her babbling in that moment may seem no more significant or lucid than The Misfit's confused meditations on Jesus.

On Symbolic and Thematic Implications

"We live in an unbelieving age," O'Connor wrote (*Mystery and Manners*, 159). For the unbelieving, this concrete reading of the scene may suffice. But O'Connor herself saw the Grandmother's gesture as nothing short of a moment of grace. She explained, "Her head clears for an instant and she realizes, even in her limited way, that she is responsible for the man before her and joined to him by ties of kinship which have their roots deep in the mystery she has been prattling about so far. And at this point, she does the right thing, she makes the right gesture" (*Mystery and Manners*, 112).

Once again, however, O'Connor leaves open multiple possibilities, perhaps not so much to appease the unbelieving as to preserve the *mystery* of the Grandmother's gesture. Faith, after all, does not rest on definite facts. That "A Good Man Is Hard to Find" appears self-evident in the world here described, but "hard" is not "impossible"; goodness exists on this earth. And there's an implicit parallel drawn to the Savior's sacrificial gesture in which He too claims "ties of kinship" with humanity and gives up the ghost.

After the Dramatic Encounter

At what would otherwise be the end of the line, the bleak termination of the story, O'Connor manages to fashion a kind of escape; her characters—and, by extension, her readers—rise to yet another dramatic and religious plane. By reaching out to The Misfit and claiming him as her own, the Grandmother transcends death. It ceases to matter whether or not she can convert The Misfit and save her own life. In her attempt to save The Misfit she has—even if inadvertently—saved her immortal soul.

The Misfit's response is cool: he cleans his glasses, presumably of blood. He picks up the cat "that was rubbing itself against his leg." He is, in other words, going about his business, as are the cat and the men and the rest of the world. "A Good Man Is Hard to Find" would be an entirely different—perhaps unbearably sentimental—story if The Misfit repented at this moment. Yet O'Connor leaves open a sliver of possibility for redemption even here, and in the story's final line. When Bobby Lee begins wisecracking, The Misfit suddenly sobers: "Shut up, Bobby Lee. It's no real pleasure in life."

> ▓ **WRITER'S VIEW:** *I prefer to think that, however unlikely this may seem, the old lady's gesture, like the mustard-seed, will grow to be a great crow-filled tree in the Misfit's heart, and will be enough of a pain to him there to turn him into the prophet he was meant to become. But that's another story.* (Mystery and Manners)

How appropriate that this moment of grace and salvation would emerge in O'Connor's imagination as a vision so dark and haunting as a "great crow-filled tree." (Note also that a mustard seed wouldn't plausibly become a great crow-filled tree; here too the transformation would be magical.) For the dark and the comic commingle in O'Connor's universe; the real and surreal buttress one another; faith and transcendence touch down in the midst of the basest unbelievers.

"In any case," she wrote, "I hope that if you consider these points in connection with the story, you will come to see it as something more than an account of a family murdered on the way to Florida" (*Mystery and Manners*, 114).

▓ Applications and Connections

- Although the story isn't told from the grandmother's point of view or in her voice, the third-person narrator stays close to her and lets the reader know her perception of the characters and plot. The grandmother's unspoken thoughts are the only ones revealed to us: the house is in Tennessee, not Georgia, the cat shouldn't be left alone for three days, and although Bailey and his children have names, "the children's mother" isn't worthy of one—or even the reference "Bailey's wife." How, if the story is the grandmother's, does she still come across, like the rest of her family, as slightly ridiculous? How does the narrator's story judge the grandmother as she judges those around her? Is the point of view affected when she dies?
- What is important to keep in mind when writing a story where the plot is preordained? How does O'Connor drive the characters to a destiny we come to expect through a series of self-made choices and accidents? Read Sophocles' *Oedipus*, where a man accidentally fulfills his destiny—to kill his father and marry his mother—by relentlessly seeking to avoid it. How is the grandmother both like and unlike Oedipus? How is The Misfit like both of them?
- When writing a **dramatic encounter,** ask yourself: What are the stakes? What can be lost by the end of the scene, and how much will that loss matter to the

characters and to the reader? How do you feel when each of the family members in "A Good Man Is Hard to Find" is shot, and why? Where are your sympathies, and what in the story influences them?

Exercises

1. Re-create the newspaper article the Grandmother is reading in the first scene, describing The Misfit and his misdeeds.

2. The children's mother is remarkably quiet in this story and seems to play a very small role. Yet O'Connor still manages to reveal a great deal about her. Fill a page with a description of the mother's character, based on what you can discover by reading carefully.

3. Alter several scenes of the story to make each family member more likeable. Make the children sweet and well-behaved, the Grandmother quiet and considerate, etc. In what ways would such changes cripple this story?

4. Pinpoint all the small, ominous details (e.g., "In case of an accident, anyone seeing her dead on the highway would know at once that she was a lady"). Retype the text, deleting all such lines, and reread the story. What is the effect?

5. Notice the strange, almost grotesque **similes** that O'Connor uses throughout the story: "[the mother's] face was as broad and innocent as a cabbage" or "her big black valise that looked like the head of a hippopotamus." Write similes like these for ten other objects or characters appearing in the story. Insert them into the text.

6. Read the story to a friend who has never read it. At the end of every page, ask your friend what he or she thinks will happen next. Jot down the answers and chart O'Connor's plot twists.

7. Identify the ways in which this story is "time-bound." The mention of "Queen for a day"—a television show in the 1950's—for example, or the use of words like "pickaninny" or the notion that Atlanta is a city small enough to cross in three-quarters of an hour. Then update; point to what if anything would change if this story took place in 2003.

8. Insert a scene in the early pages in which Bailey and his wife, before leaving for Florida, discuss the Grandmother and how they feel about her. Do so in dialect.

9. Write five variations on the ending, beginning each variation with the Grandmother's final exclamation, "Why you're one of my babies. You're one of my own children!"

10. Write a letter from Flannery O'Connor's editor urging her to delete, change, or clarify The Misfit's comments about Jesus in the final scene. Write a response from O'Connor, explaining and justifying those lines.

CHAPTER 10

LANGUAGE AND FORM:
The Power of Data and Lists

TIM O'BRIEN, "The Things They Carried"

WRITER'S VIEW: *In any war story, but especially a true one, it's difficult to separate what happened from what seemed to happen. What seems to happen becomes its own happening and has to be told that way. The angles of vision are skewed . . . The pictures get jumbled; you tend to miss a lot. And then afterward, when you go to tell about it, there is always that surreal seemingness, which makes the story seem untrue, but which in fact represents the hard and exact truth as it seemed. ("How to Tell a True War Story,"* The Things They Carried *[New York: Houghton Mifflin, 1990])*

Tim O'Brien was born in 1946 and raised in the small town of Worthington, Minnesota. His father was an insurance salesman; his mother taught in elementary school. In the mid to late 1960's, while the United States grew more deeply engaged in the war in Vietnam, O'Brien was majoring in political science at Macalester College. Like many other students of his generation, he opposed the war—but his political efforts were, by his own account, modest. He participated in a few peace vigils, wrote antiwar editorials for the school paper, and rang doorbells for presidential candidate and activist Eugene McCarthy. O'Brien explains, "I had kind of a smug attitude about it all, thinking, 'well, I'm a good student, and smart, and they won't take me as a soldier'" ("Writing Vietnam," Brown University President's Lecture, 21 Apr. 1999).

Just after graduation in the early summer of 1968, however, O'Brien came back from an afternoon on the golf course to find a draft notice waiting. He passed the rest of the summer in a daze of disbelief, contemplating whether or not to report for service. "I thought about Canada. I thought about jail," he later wrote. "But in the end I could not bear the prospect of rejection: by my family, my country, my friends, my hometown . . . I was a coward. I went to Vietnam" ("The Vietnam in Me," *New York Times Magazine,* 2 Oct. 1994).

Those last two sentences pose a frequent seeming paradox in O'Brien's fiction and nonfiction. Again and again, his work probes the nature of courage and overturns our conventional assumptions about soldiering and fear. In O'Brien's world the soldier's greatest terror is not death but "the fear of blushing. Men killed, and died, because they were embarrassed not to" (*The Things They Carried,* 21).

This particular "grunt" served as an infantryman in Alpha Company in the Quang Nai province of Vietnam in 1969–70 and was stationed in My Lai a year after the massacre there. He received several medals for wartime service, including the Purple Heart. After finishing his tour of duty, O'Brien entered graduate school at Harvard to study government, but an internship at the *Washington Post* led him away from Harvard and into a career as journalist and, finally, as a fiction writer.

In 1973 O'Brien published his first book, the memoir, *If I Die in a Combat Zone: Box Me Up and Ship Me Home,* and in 1975 he published his first novel, *Northern Lights.* His second novel, *Going After Cacciato* (1978), won the National Book Award, and his collection of short stories, *The Things They Carried* (1990), was a finalist for the Pulitzer Prize and the National Book Critics Circle Award. His other works include *The Nuclear Age* (1985), *In the Lake of the Woods* (1994), *Tomcat in Love* (1998), and *July, July* (2002).

Like many of the characters in his fiction, O'Brien seems haunted by the experience of combat, unable to relegate it comfortably to the past. Although he has written on other topics, the majority of his books deal in some way with Vietnam and the transforming effects of battle—a battle from which (though the deserter in *Going After Cacciato* literally walks out of Southeast Asia) there's no true escape. Continually, even obsessively, O'Brien describes the condition of life as a soldier and war's aftermath. It is his great subject and recurrent theme.

The psychoanalyst Sigmund Freud, in *Beyond the Pleasure Principle,* wrote of **thanatos** as opposed to *eros*—how his patients keep returning to the memory of pain. The death wish, Freud deduced, has as powerful a claim on our attention as does the erotic component of life, and though O'Brien would not see the opposition of these two desires in psychoanalytic terms, he writes of their compelling and complex interaction. Time after time in his stories and novels, his characters are forced to deal with what they can't forget. Decades after the war's end, O'Brien remains one of America's foremost and most accomplished writers of the Vietnam experience.

The Things They Carried

First Lieutenant Jimmy Cross carried letters from a girl named Martha, a junior at Mount Sebastian College in New Jersey. They were not love letters, but Lieutenant Cross was hoping, so he kept them folded in plastic at the bottom of his rucksack. In the late afternoon, after a day's march, he would dig his foxhole, wash his hands under a canteen, unwrap the letters, hold them with the tips of his fingers, and spend the last hour of light pretending. He would imagine romantic camping trips into the White Mountains in New Hampshire. He would sometimes taste the envelope flaps, knowing her tongue had been there. More than anything, he wanted Martha to love him as he loved her, but the letters were mostly chatty, elusive on the matter of love. She was a virgin, he was almost sure. She was an English major at Mount Sebastian, and she wrote beautifully about her professors and roommates and midterm exams, about her respect for Chaucer and her great affection for Virginia Woolf. She often quoted lines of poetry; she never mentioned the war, except to say, Jimmy, take care of yourself. The letters weighed 10 ounces. They were signed Love, Martha, but Lieutenant Cross understood that Love was only a way of signing and did not mean what he sometimes pretended it meant. At dusk, he would carefully return the letters to his rucksack. Slowly, a bit distracted, he would get up and move among his men, checking the perimeter, then at full dark he would return to his hole and watch the night and wonder if Martha was a virgin.

The things they carried were largely determined by necessity. Among the necessities or near-necessities were P-38 can openers, pocket knives, heat tabs, wristwatches, dog tags, mosquito repellent, chewing gum, candy, cigarettes, salt tablets, packets of Kool-Aid, lighters, matches, sewing kits, Military Payment Certificates, C rations, and two or three canteens of water. Together, these items weighed between 15 and 20 pounds, depending upon a man's habits or rate of metabolism. Henry Dobbins, who was a big man, carried extra rations; he was especially fond of canned peaches in heavy syrup over pound cake. Dave Jensen, who practiced field hygiene, carried a toothbrush, dental floss, and several hotel-sized bars of soap he'd stolen on R&R in Sydney, Australia. Ted Lavender, who was scared, carried tranquilizers until he was shot in the head outside the village of Than Khe in mid-April. By necessity, and because it was SOP, they all carried steel helmets that weighed 5 pounds including the liner and camouflage cover. They carried the standard fatigue jackets and trousers. Very few carried underwear. On their feet they carried jungle boots—2.1

pounds—and Dave Jensen carried three pairs of socks and a can of Dr. Scholl's foot powder as a precaution against trench foot. Until he was shot, Ted Lavender carried six or seven ounces of premium dope, which for him was a necessity. Mitchell Sanders, the RTO, carried condoms. Norman Bowker carried a diary. Rat Kiley carried comic books. Kiowa, a devout Baptist, carried an illustrated New Testament that had been presented to him by his father, who taught Sunday school in Oklahoma City, Oklahoma. As a hedge against bad times, however, Kiowa also carried his grandmother's distrust of the white man, his grandfather's old hunting hatchet. Necessity dictated. Because the land was mined and booby-trapped, it was SOP for each man to carry a steel-centered, nylon-covered flak jacket, which weighed 6.7 pounds, but which on hot days seemed much heavier. Because you could die so quickly, each man carried at least one large compress bandage, usually in the helmet band for easy access. Because the nights were cold, and because the monsoons were wet, each carried a green plastic poncho that could be used as a raincoat or groundsheet or makeshift tent. With its quilted liner, the poncho weighed almost two pounds, but it was worth every ounce. In April, for instance, when Ted Lavender was shot, they used his poncho to wrap him up, then to carry him across the paddy, then to lift him into the chopper that took him away.

They were called legs or grunts.

To carry something was to hump it, as when Lieutenant Jimmy Cross humped his love for Martha up the hills and through the swamps. In its intransitive form, to hump meant to walk, or to march, but it implied burdens far beyond the transitive.

Almost everyone humped photographs. In his wallet, Lieutenant Cross carried two photographs of Martha. The first was a Kodacolor snapshot signed Love, though he knew better. She stood against a brick wall. Her eyes were gray and neutral, her lips slightly open as she stared straight-on at the camera. At night, sometimes, Lieutenant Cross wondered who had taken the picture, because he knew she had boyfriends, because he loved her so much, and because he could see the shadow of the picture-taker spreading out against the brick wall. The second photograph had been clipped from the 1968 Mount Sebastian yearbook. It was an action shot—women's volleyball—and Martha was bent horizontal to the floor, reaching, the palms of her hands in sharp focus, the tongue taut, the expression frank and competitive. There was no visible sweat. She wore white gym shorts. Her legs, he thought, were almost certainly the legs of a virgin, dry and without hair, the left knee cocked and carrying her entire weight, which was just over one hundred pounds.

Lieutenant Cross remembered touching that left knee. A dark theater, he remembered, and the movie was *Bonnie and Clyde,* and Martha wore a tweed skirt, and during the final scene, when he touched her knee, she turned and looked at him in a sad, sober way that made him pull his hand back, but he would always remember the feel of the tweed skirt and the knee beneath it and the sound of the gunfire that killed Bonnie and Clyde, how embarrassing it was, how slow and oppressive. He remembered kissing her good night at the dorm door. Right then, he thought, he should've done something brave. He should've carried her up the stairs to her room and tied her to the bed and touched that left knee all night long. He should've risked it. Whenever he looked at the photographs, he thought of new things he should've done.

What they carried was partly a function of rank, partly of field specialty.

As a first lieutenant and platoon leader, Jimmy Cross carried a compass, maps, code books, binoculars, and a .45-caliber pistol that weighed 2.9 pounds fully loaded. He carried a strobe light and the responsibility for the lives of his men.

As an RTO, Mitchell Sanders carried the PRC-25 radio, a killer, 26 pounds with its battery.

As a medic, Rat Kiley carried a canvas satchel filled with morphine and plasma and malaria tablets and surgical tape and comic books and all the things a medic must carry, including M&M's for especially bad wounds, for a total weight of nearly 20 pounds.

As a big man, therefore a machine gunner, Henry Dobbins carried the M-60, which weighed 23 pounds unloaded, but which was almost always loaded. In addition, Dobbins carried between 10 and 15 pounds of ammunition draped in belts across his chest and shoulders.

As PFCs or Spec 4s, most of them were common grunts and carried the standard M-16 gas-operated assault rifle. The weapon weighed 7.5 pounds unloaded, 8.2 pounds with its full 20-round magazine. Depending on numerous factors, such as topography and psychology, the riflemen carried anywhere from 12 to 20 magazines, usually in cloth bandoliers, adding on another 8.4 pounds at minimum, 14 pounds at maximum. When it was available, they also carried M-16 maintenance gear—rods and steel brushes and swabs and tubes of LSA oil—all of which weighed about a pound. Among the grunts, some carried the M-79 grenade launcher, 5.9 pounds unloaded, a reasonably light weapon except for the ammunition, which was heavy. A single round weighed 10 ounces. The typical load was 25 rounds. But Ted Lavender, who was scared, carried 34 rounds when he was shot and killed outside Than Khe, and he went down under an exceptional burden, more than 20 pounds of ammunition, plus the flak jacket and helmet and rations and water and toilet paper and tranquilizers and all the rest, plus the unweighed fear. He was dead weight. There was no twitching or flopping. Kiowa, who saw it happen, said it was like watching a rock fall, or a big sandbag or something—just boom, then down— not like the movies where the dead guy rolls around and does fancy spins and goes ass over teakettle—not like that, Kiowa said, the poor bastard just flat-fuck fell. Boom. Down. Nothing else. It was a bright morning in mid-April. Lieutenant Cross felt the pain. He blamed himself. They stripped off Lavender's canteens and ammo, all the heavy things, and Rat Kiley said the obvious, the guy's dead, and Mitchell Sanders used his radio to report one U.S. KIA and to request a chopper. Then they wrapped Lavender in his poncho. They carried him out to a dry paddy, established security, and sat smoking the dead man's dope until the chopper came. Lieutenant Cross kept to himself. He pictured Martha's smooth young face, thinking he loved her more than anything, more than his men, and now Ted Lavender was dead because he loved her so much and could not stop thinking about her. When the dustoff arrived, they carried Lavender aboard. Afterward they burned Than Khe. They marched until dusk, then dug their holes, and that night Kiowa kept explaining how you had to be there, how fast it was, how the poor guy just dropped like so much concrete. Boom-down, he said. Like cement.

In addition to the three standard weapons—the M-60, M-16, and M-79— they carried whatever presented itself, or whatever seemed appropriate as a means of killing or staying alive. They carried catch-as-catch-can. At various times, in various situations, they carried M-14s and CAR-15s and Swedish Ks and grease guns and captured AK-47s and Chi-Coms and RPGs and Simonov carbines and black market Uzis and .38-caliber Smith & Wesson handguns and 66 mm LAWs and shotguns and silencers and blackjacks and bayonets and C-4 plastic explosives. Lee Strunk carried a slingshot; a weapon of last resort, he called it. Mitchell Sanders carried brass knuckles. Kiowa carried his grand-father's feathered hatchet. Every third or fourth man carried a Claymore anti-personnel mine—3.5 pounds with its firing device. They all carried fragmentation grenades—14 ounces each. They all carried at least one M-18 colored smoke grenade—24 ounces. Some carried CS or tear gas grenades. Some carried white phosphorus grenades. They carried all they could bear, and then some, including a silent awe for the terrible power of the things they carried.

In the first week of April, before Lavender died, Lieutenant Jimmy Cross received a good-luck charm from Martha. It was a simple pebble, an ounce at most. Smooth to the touch, it was a milky white color with flecks of orange and violet, oval-shaped, like a miniature egg. In the accompanying letter, Martha wrote that she had found the pebble on the Jersey shoreline, precisely where the land touched water at high tide, where things came together but also separated. It was this separate-but-together quality, she wrote, that had inspired her to pick up the pebble and to carry it in her breast pocket for several days, where it seemed weightless, and then to send it through the mail, by air, as a token of her truest feelings for him. Lieutenant Cross found this romantic. But he wondered what her truest feelings were, exactly, and what she meant by separate-but-together. He wondered how the tides and waves had come into play on that afternoon along the Jersey shoreline when Martha saw the pebble and bent down to rescue it from geology. He imagined bare feet. Martha was a poet, with the poet's sensibilities, and her feet would be brown and bare, the toenails unpainted, the eyes chilly and somber like the ocean in March, and though it was painful, he wondered who had been with her that afternoon. He imagined a pair of shadows moving along the strip of sand where things came together but also separated. It was phantom jealousy, he knew, but he couldn't help himself. He loved her so much. On the march, through the hot days of early April, he carried the pebble in his mouth, turning it with his tongue, tasting sea salt and moisture. His mind wandered. He had difficulty keeping his attention on the war. On occasion he would yell at his men to spread out the column, to keep their eyes open, but then he would slip away into daydreams, just pretending, walking barefoot along the Jersey shore, with Martha, carrying nothing. He would feel himself rising. Sun and waves and gentle winds, all love and lightness.

What they carried varied by mission.

When a mission took them to the mountains, they carried mosquito netting, machetes, canvas tarps, and extra bug juice.

If a mission seemed especially hazardous, or if it involved a place they knew to be bad, they carried everything they could. In certain heavily mined AOs, where the land was dense with Toe Poppers and Bouncing Betties, they took turns humping a 28-pound mine detector. With its headphones and big sensing plate, the equipment was a stress on the lower back and shoulders, awkward to handle, often useless because of the shrapnel in the earth, but they carried it anyway, partly for safety, partly for the illusion of safety.

On ambush, or other night missions, they carried peculiar little odds and ends. Kiowa always took along his New Testament and a pair of moccasins for silence. Dave Jensen carried night-sight vitamins high in carotene. Lee Strunk carried his slingshot; ammo, he claimed, would never be a problem. Rat Kiley carried brandy and M&M's candy. Until he was shot, Ted Lavender carried the starlight scope, which weighed 6.3 pounds with its aluminum carrying case. Henry Dobbins carried his girlfriend's pantyhose wrapped around his neck as a comforter. They all carried ghosts. When dark came, they would move out single file across the meadows and paddies to their ambush coordinates, where they would quietly set up the Claymores and lie down and spend the night waiting.

Other missions were more complicated and required special equipment. In mid-April, it was their mission to search out and destroy the elaborate tunnel complexes in the Than Khe area south of Chu Lai. To blow the tunnels, they carried one-pound blocks of pentrite high explosives, four blocks to a man, 68 pounds in all. They carried wiring, detonators, and battery-powered clackers. Dave Jensen carried earplugs. Most often, before blowing the tunnels, they were ordered by higher command to search them, which was considered bad news, but by and large they just shrugged and carried out orders. Because he was a big man, Henry Dobbins was excused from tunnel duty. The others would draw numbers. Before Lavender died there were 17 men in the platoon, and whoever drew the number 17 would strip off his gear and crawl in head-first with a flashlight and Lieutenant Cross's .45-caliber pistol. The rest of them would fan out as security. They would sit down or kneel, not facing the hole, listening to the ground beneath them, imagining cobwebs and ghosts, whatever was down there—the tunnel walls squeezing in—how the flashlight seemed impossibly heavy in the hand and how it was tunnel vision in the very strictest sense, compression in all ways, even time, and how you had to wiggle in—ass and elbows—a swallowed-up feeling—and how you found yourself worrying about odd things: Will your flashlight go dead? Do rats carry rabies? If you screamed, how far would the sound carry? Would your buddies hear it? Would they have the courage to drag you out? In some respects, though not many, the waiting was worse than the tunnel itself. Imagination was a killer.

On April 16, when Lee Strunk drew the number 17, he laughed and muttered something and went down quickly. The morning was hot and very still. Not good, Kiowa said. He looked at the tunnel opening, then out across a dry paddy toward the village of Than Khe. Nothing moved. No clouds or birds or people. As they waited, the men smoked and drank Kool-Aid, not talking much, feeling sympathy for Lee Strunk but also feeling the luck of the draw. You win some, you lose some, said Mitchell Sanders, and sometimes you settle for a rain check. It was a tired line and no one laughed.

Henry Dobbins ate a tropical chocolate bar. Ted Lavender popped a tranquilizer and went off to pee.

After five minutes, Lieutenant Jimmy Cross moved to the tunnel, leaned down, and examined the darkness. Trouble, he thought—a cave-in maybe. And then suddenly, without willing it, he was thinking about Martha. The stresses and fractures, the quick collapse, the two of them buried alive under all that weight. Dense, crushing love. Kneeling, watching the hole, he tried to concentrate on Lee Strunk and the war, all the dangers, but his love was too much for him, he felt paralyzed, he wanted to sleep inside her lungs and breathe her blood and be smothered. He wanted her to be a virgin and not a virgin, all at once. He wanted to know her. Intimate secrets: Why poetry? Why so sad? Why that grayness in her eyes? Why so alone? Not lonely, just alone— riding her bike across campus or sitting off by herself in the cafeteria—even dancing, she danced alone—and it was the aloneness that filled him with love. He remembered telling her that one evening. How she nodded and looked away. And how, later, when he kissed her, she received the kiss without returning it, her eyes wide open, not afraid, not a virgin's eyes, just flat and uninvolved.

Lieutenant Cross gazed at the tunnel. But he was not there. He was buried with Martha under the white sand at the Jersey shore. They were pressed together, and the pebble in his mouth was her tongue. He was smiling. Vaguely, he was aware of how quiet the day was, the sullen paddies, yet he could not bring himself to worry about matters of security. He was beyond that. He was just a kid at war, in love. He was twenty-four years old. He couldn't help it.

A few moments later Lee Strunk crawled out of the tunnel. He came up grinning, filthy but alive. Lieutenant Cross nodded and closed his eyes while the others clapped Strunk on the back and made jokes about rising from the dead.

Worms, Rat Kiley said. Right out of the grave. Fuckin' zombie.

The men laughed. They all felt great relief.

Spook city, said Mitchell Sanders.

Lee Strunk made a funny ghost sound, a kind of moaning, yet very happy, and right then, when Strunk made that high happy moaning sound, when he went *Ahhooooo,* right then Ted Lavender was shot in the head on his way back from peeing. He lay with his mouth open. The teeth were broken. There was a swollen black bruise under his left eye. The cheekbone was gone. Oh shit, Rat

Kiley said, the guy's dead. The guy's dead, he kept saying, which seemed pro-found—the guy's dead. I mean really.

The things they carried were determined to some extent by superstition. Lieutenant Cross carried his good-luck pebble. Dave Jensen carried a rabbit's foot. Norman Bowker, otherwise a very gentle person, carried a thumb that had been presented to him as a gift by Mitchell Sanders. The thumb was dark brown, rubbery to the touch, and weighed four ounces at most. It had been cut from a VC corpse, a boy of fifteen or sixteen. They'd found him at the bottom of an irrigation ditch, badly burned, flies in his mouth and eyes. The boy wore black shorts and sandals. At the time of his death he had been carrying a pouch of rice, a rifle, and three magazines of ammunition.

You want my opinion, Mitchell Sanders said, there's a definite moral here.

He put his hand on the dead boy's wrist. He was quiet for a time, as if counting a pulse, then he patted the stomach, almost affectionately, and used Kiowa's hunting hatchet to remove the thumb.

Henry Dobbins asked what the moral was.

Moral?

You know. *Moral.*

Sanders wrapped the thumb in toilet paper and handed it across to Nor-man Bowker. There was no blood. Smiling, he kicked the boy's head, watched the flies scatter, and said, It's like with that old TV show—Paladin. Have gun, will travel.

Henry Dobbins thought about it.

Yea, well, he finally said. I don't see no moral.

There it *is,* man.

Fuck off.

They carried USO stationery and pencils and pens. They carried Sterno, safety pins, trip flares, signal flares, spools of wire, razor blades, chewing tobacco, liberated joss sticks and statuettes of the smiling Buddha, candles, grease pencils, *The Stars and Stripes,* fingernail clippers, Psy Ops leaflets, bush hats, bolos, and much more. Twice a week, when the resupply choppers came in, they carried hot chow in green mermite cans and large canvas bags filled with iced beer and soda pop. They carried plastic water containers, each with a two-gallon capacity. Mitchell Sanders carried a set of starched tiger fatigues for special occasions. Henry Dobbins carried Black Flag insecticide. Dave

Jensen carried empty sandbags that could be filled at night for added protection. Lee Strunk carried tanning lotion. Some things they carried in common. Taking turns, they carried the big PRC-77 scrambler radio, which weighed 30 pounds with its battery. They shared the weight of memory. They took up what others could no longer bear. Often, they carried each other, the wounded or weak. They carried infections. They carried chess sets, basketballs, Vietnamese-English dictionaries, insignia of rank, Bronze Stars and Purple Hearts, plastic cards imprinted with the Code of Conduct. They carried diseases, among them malaria and dysentery. They carried lice and ringworm and leeches and paddy algae and various rots and molds. They carried the land itself—Vietnam, the place, the soil—a powdery orange-red dust that covered their boots and fatigues and faces. They carried the sky. The whole atmosphere, they carried it, the humidity, the monsoons, the stink of fungus and decay, all of it, they carried gravity. They moved like mules. By daylight they took sniper fire, at night they were mortared, but it was not battle, it was just the endless march, village to village, without purpose, nothing won or lost. They marched for the sake of the march. They plodded along slowly, dumbly, leaning forward against the heat, unthinking, all blood and bone, simple grunts, soldiering with their legs, toiling up the hills and down into the paddies and across the rivers and up again and down, just humping, one step and then the next and then another, but no volition, no will, because it was automatic, it was anatomy, and the war was entirely a matter of posture and carriage, the hump was everything, a kind of inertia, a kind of emptiness, a dullness of desire and intellect and conscience and hope and human sensibility. Their principles were in their feet. Their calculations were biological. They had no sense of strategy or mission. They searched the villages without knowing what to look for, not caring, kicking over jars of rice, frisking children and old men, blowing tunnels, sometimes setting fires and sometimes not, then forming up and moving on to the next village, then other villages, where it would always be the same. They carried their own lives. The pressures were enormous. In the heat of early afternoon, they would remove their helmets and flak jackets, walking bare, which was dangerous but which helped ease the strain. They would often discard things along the route of march. Purely for comfort, they would throw away rations, blow their Claymores and grenades, no matter, because by nightfall the resupply choppers would arrive with more of the same, then a day or two later still more, fresh watermelons and crates of ammunition and sunglasses and woolen sweaters —the resources were stunning—sparklers for the Fourth of July, colored eggs for Easter—it was the great American war chest—the fruits of science, the smokestacks, the canneries, the arsenals at Hartford, the Minnesota forests, the machine shops, the vast fields of corn and wheat—they carried like freight trains; they carried it on their backs and shoulders—and for all the ambiguities of Vietnam, all the mysteries and unknowns, there was at least the single abiding certainty that they would never be at a loss for things to carry.

After the chopper took Lavender away, Lieutenant Jimmy Cross led his men into the village of Than Khe. They burned everything. They shot chickens and dogs, they trashed the village well, they called in artillery and watched the wreckage, then they marched for several hours through the hot afternoon, and then at dusk, while Kiowa explained how Lavender died, Lieutenant Cross found himself trembling.

He tried not to cry. With his entrenching tool, which weighed five pounds, he began digging a hole in the earth.

He felt shame. He hated himself. He had loved Martha more than his men, and as a consequence Lavender was now dead, and this was something he would have to carry like a stone in his stomach for the rest of the war.

All he could do was dig. He used his entrenching tool like an ax, slashing, feeling both love and hate, and then later, when it was full dark, he sat at the bottom of his foxhole and wept. It went on for a long while. In part, he was grieving for Ted Lavender, but mostly it was for Martha, and for himself, because she belonged to another world, which was not quite real, and because she was a junior at Mount Sebastian College in New Jersey, a poet and a virgin and uninvolved, and because he realized she did not love him and never would.

Like cement, Kiowa whispered in the dark. I swear to God—boom, down. Not a word.

I've heard this, said Norman Bowker.

A pisser, you know? Still zipping himself up. Zapped while zipping.

All right, fine. That's enough.

Yeah, but you had to see it, the guy just—

I *heard,* man. Cement. So why not shut the fuck *up*?

Kiowa shook his head sadly and glanced over at the hole where Lieutenant Jimmy Cross sat watching the night. The air was thick and wet. A warm dense fog had settled over the paddies and there was the stillness that precedes rain.

After a time Kiowa sighed.

One thing for sure, he said. The lieutenant's in some deep hurt. I mean that crying jag—the way he was carrying on—it wasn't fake or anything, it was real heavy-duty hurt. The man cares.

Sure, Norman Bowker said.

Say what you want, the man does care.

We all got problems.

Not Lavender.

No, I guess not, Bowker said. Do me a favor, though.

Shut up?

That's a smart Indian. Shut up.

Shrugging, Kiowa pulled off his boots. He wanted to say more, just to lighten up his sleep, but instead he opened his New Testament and arranged it beneath his head as a pillow. The fog made things seem hollow and unattached. He tried not to think about Ted Lavender, but then he was thinking how fast it was, no drama, down and dead, and how it was hard to feel anything except surprise. It seemed unchristian. He wished he could find some great sadness, or even anger, but the emotion wasn't there and he couldn't make it happen. Mostly he felt pleased to be alive. He liked the smell of the New Testament under his cheek, the leather and ink and paper and glue, whatever the chemicals were. He liked hearing the sounds of night. Even his fatigue, it felt fine, the stiff muscles and the prickly awareness of his own body, a floating feeling. He enjoyed not being dead. Lying there, Kiowa admired Lieutenant Jimmy Cross's capacity for grief. He wanted to share the man's pain, he wanted to care as Jimmy Cross cared. And yet when he closed his eyes, all he could think was Boom-down, and all he could feel was the pleasure of having his boots off and the fog curling in around him and the damp soil and the Bible smells and the plush comfort of night.

After a moment Norman Bowker sat up in the dark.

What the hell, he said. You want to talk, *talk*. Tell it to me.

Forget it.

No, man, go on. One thing I hate, it's a silent Indian.

For the most part they carried themselves with poise, a kind of dignity. Now and then, however, there were times of panic, when they squealed or wanted to squeal but couldn't, when they twitched and made moaning sounds and covered their heads and said Dear Jesus and flopped around on the earth and fired their weapons blindly and cringed and sobbed and begged for the noise to stop and went wild and made stupid promises to themselves and to

God and to their mothers and fathers, hoping not to die. In different ways, it happened to all of them. Afterward, when the firing ended, they would blink and peek up. They would touch their bodies, feeling shame, then quickly hiding it. They would force themselves to stand. As if in slow motion, frame by frame, the world would take on the old logic—absolute silence, then the wind, then sunlight, then voices. It was the burden of being alive. Awkwardly, the men would reassemble themselves, first in private, then in groups, becoming soldiers again. They would repair the leaks in their eyes. They would check for casualties, call in dustoffs, light cigarettes, try to smile, clear their throats and spit and begin cleaning their weapons. After a time someone would shake his head and say, No lie, I almost shit my pants, and someone else would laugh, which meant it was bad, yes, but the guy had obviously not shit his pants, it wasn't that bad, and in any case nobody would ever do such a thing and then go ahead and talk about it. They would squint into the dense, oppressive sunlight. For a few moments, perhaps, they would fall silent, lighting a joint and tracking its passage from man to man, inhaling, holding in the humiliation. Scary stuff, one of them might say. But then someone else would grin or flick his eyebrows and say, Roger-dodger, almost cut me a new asshole, *almost.*

There were numerous such poses. Some carried themselves with a sort of wistful resignation, others with pride or stiff soldierly discipline or good humor or macho zeal. They were afraid of dying but they were even more afraid to show it.

They found jokes to tell.

They used a hard vocabulary to contain the terrible softness. *Greased* they'd say. *Offed, lit up, zapped while zipping.* It wasn't cruelty, just stage presence. They were actors. When someone died, it wasn't quite dying, because in a curious way it seemed scripted, and because they had their lines mostly memorized, irony mixed with tragedy, and because they called it by other names, as if to encyst and destroy the reality of death itself. They kicked corpses. They cut off thumbs. They talked grunt lingo. They told stories about Ted Lavender's supply of tranquilizers, how the poor guy didn't feel a thing, how incredibly tranquil he was.

There's a moral here, said Mitchell Sanders.

They were waiting for Lavender's chopper, smoking the dead man's dope.

The moral's pretty obvious, Sanders said, and winked. Stay away from drugs. No joke, they'll ruin your day every time

Cute, said Henry Dobbins.

Mind blower, get it? Talk about wiggy. Nothing left, just blood and brains.

They made themselves laugh.

There it is, they'd say. Over and over—there it is, my friend, there it is—as if the repetition itself were an act of poise, a balance between crazy and almost crazy, knowing without going, there it is, which meant be cool, let it ride, because Oh yeah, man, you can't change what can't be changed, there it is, there it absolutely and positively and fucking well *is*.

They were tough.

They carried all the emotional baggage of men who might die. Grief, terror, love, longing—these were intangibles, but the intangibles had their own mass and specific gravity, they had tangible weight. They carried shameful memories. They carried the common secret of cowardice barely restrained, the instinct to run or freeze or hide, and in many respects this was the heaviest burden of all, for it could never be put down, it required perfect balance and perfect posture. They carried their reputations. They carried the soldier's greatest fear, which was the fear of blushing. Men killed, and died, because they were embarrassed not to. It was what had brought them to the war in the first place, nothing positive, no dreams of glory or honor, just to avoid the blush of dishonor. They died so as not to die of embarrassment. They crawled into tunnels and walked point and advanced under fire. Each morning, despite the unknowns, they made their legs move. They endured. They kept humping. They did not submit to the obvious alternative, which was simply to close the eyes and fall. So easy, really. Go limp and tumble to the ground and let the muscles unwind and not speak and not budge until your buddies picked you up and lifted you into the chopper that would roar and dip its nose and carry you off to the world. A mere matter of falling, yet no one ever fell. It was not courage, exactly; the object was not valor. Rather, they were too frightened to be cowards.

By and large they carried these things inside, maintaining the masks of composure. They sneered at sick call. They spoke bitterly about guys who had found release by shooting off their own toes or fingers. Pussies, they'd say. Candyasses. It was fierce, mocking talk, with only a trace of envy or awe, but even so the image played itself out behind their eyes.

They imagined the muzzle against flesh. So easy: squeeze the trigger and blow away a toe. They imagined it. They imagined the quick, sweet pain, then the evacuation to Japan, then a hospital with warm beds and cute geisha nurses.

And they dreamed of freedom birds.

At night, on guard, staring into the dark, they were carried away by jumbo jets. They felt the rush of takeoff. *Gone!* they yelled. And then velocity—wings and engines—a smiling stewardess—but it was more than a plane, it was a real bird, a big sleek silver bird with feathers and talons and high screeching. They were flying. The weights fell off; there was nothing to bear. They laughed and held on tight, feeling the cold slap of wind and altitude, soaring, thinking *It's over, I'm gone!*—they were naked, they were light and free—it was all lightness, bright and fast and buoyant, light as light, a helium buzz in the brain, a giddy bubbling in the lungs as they were taken up over the clouds and the war, beyond duty, beyond gravity and mortification and global entanglements— *Sin loi!* they yelled. *I'm sorry, motherfuckers, but I'm out of it, I'm goofed, I'm on a space cruise, I'm gone!*—and it was a restful, unencumbered sensation, just riding the light waves, sailing that big silver freedom bird over the mountains and oceans, over America, over the farms and great sleeping cities and cemeteries and highways and the golden arches of McDonald's, it was flight, a kind of fleeing, a kind of falling, falling higher and higher, spinning off the vast, silent vacuum where there were no burdens and where everything weighed exactly nothing—*Gone!* they screamed. *I'm sorry but I'm gone!*—and so at night, not quite dreaming, they gave themselves over to lightness, they were carried, they were purely borne.

On the morning after Ted Lavender died, First Lieutenant Jimmy Cross crouched at the bottom of his foxhole and burned Martha's letters. Then he burned the two photographs. There was a steady rain falling, which made it difficult, but he used heat tabs and Sterno to build a small fire, screening it with his body, holding the photographs over the tight blue flame with the tips of his fingers.

He realized it was only a gesture. Stupid, he thought. Sentimental, too, but mostly just stupid.

Lavender was dead. You couldn't burn the blame.

Besides, the letters were in his head. And even now, without photographs, Lieutenant Cross could see Martha playing volleyball in her white gym shorts and yellow T-shirt. He could see her moving in the rain.

When the fire died out, Lieutenant Cross pulled his poncho over his shoulders and ate breakfast from a can.

There was no great mystery, he decided.

In those burned letters Martha had never mentioned the war, except to say, Jimmy, take care of yourself. She wasn't involved. She signed the letters Love, but it wasn't love, and all the fine lines and technicalities did not matter.

Virginity was no longer an issue. He hated her. Yes, he did. He hated her. Love, too, but it was a hard, hating kind of love.

The morning came up wet and blurry. Everything seemed part of everything else, the fog and Martha and the deepening rain.

He was a soldier, after all.

Half smiling, Lieutenant Jimmy Cross took out his maps. He shook his head hard, as if to clear it, then bent forward and began planning the day's march. In ten minutes, or maybe twenty, he would rouse the men and they would pack up and head west, where the maps showed the country to be green and inviting. They would do what they had always done. The rain might add some weight, but otherwise it would be one more day layered upon all the other days.

He was realistic about it. There was that new hardness in his stomach. He loved her but he hated her.

No more fantasies, he told himself.

Henceforth, when he thought about Martha, it would be only to think that she belonged elsewhere. He would shut down the daydreams. This was not Mount Sebastian, it was another world, where there were no pretty poems or midterm exams, a place where men died because of carelessness and gross stupidity. Kiowa was right. Boom-down, and you were dead, never partly dead.

Briefly, in the rain, Lieutenant Cross saw Martha's gray eyes gazing back at him.

He understood.

It was very sad, he thought. The things men carried inside. The things men did or felt they had to do.

He almost nodded at her, but didn't.

Instead he went back to his maps. He was now determined to perform his duties firmly and without negligence. It wouldn't help Lavender, he knew that, but from this point on he would comport himself as an officer. He would dispose of his good-luck pebble. Swallow it, maybe, or use Lee Strunk's slingshot, or just drop it along the trail. On the march he would impose strict field discipline. He would be careful to send out flank security, to prevent straggling or bunching up, to keep his troops moving at the proper pace and at the proper interval. He would insist on clean weapons. He would confiscate the remainder of Lavender's dope. Later in the day, perhaps, he would call the men together and speak to them plainly. He would accept the blame for what had happened to Ted Lavender. He would be a man about it. He would look them in the eyes, keeping his chin level, and he would issue the new SOPs in a calm, impersonal tone of voice, a lieutenant's voice, leaving no room for argument or discussion. Commencing immediately, he'd tell them, they would no longer abandon equipment along the route of march. They would police up their acts. They would get their shit together, and keep it together, and maintain it neatly and in good working order.

He would not tolerate laxity. He would show strength, distancing himself.

Among the men there would be grumbling, of course, and maybe worse, because their days would seem longer and their loads heavier, but Lieutenant Jimmy Cross reminded himself that his obligation was not to be loved but to lead. He would dispense with love; it was not now a factor. And if anyone quarreled or complained, he would simply tighten his lips and arrange his shoulders in the correct command posture. He might give a curt little nod. Or he might not. He might just shrug and say, Carry on, then they would saddle up and form into a column and move out toward the villages west of Than Khe.

Notes on Craft and Context

The Challenges of "True" Narrative

"The Things They Carried" is the first story in Tim O'Brien's 1990 collection of the same name, and it provides us with an introduction to the cast of characters who populate the pages of the book. All of the stories are interrelated, involving a man named Tim (sometimes "Timmy") O'Brien and the other infantrymen in his platoon. O'Brien follows these soldiers through Vietnam and the years following the war, focusing not just on military engagement and those who survive, but also on the challenge posed by narrative itself. His characters struggle repeatedly to communicate their Vietnam experiences to one another and to loved ones who never witnessed the conflict firsthand. At the same time, in several stories "Tim O'Brien" (the author's namesake and literary double or *doppelgänger)* addresses the difficulties inherent in trying to tell/write a true account of having fought in Vietnam.

On Form: The List Story

In terms of **form** "The Things They Carried" is what some critics define as a "list story." Rather than organizing his narrative in a sequence of dramatic scenes building toward climax and resolution, O'Brien makes a list and then weaves his tale through and around it. The list, in other words, provides the backbone for as well as the shape of the action reported—both skeleton and skin. It provides no simple beginning, middle, and end, with, as in a conventional **Aristotelian narrative,** a crisis arriving at the two-thirds point. *This* crisis is everywhere, the danger so constant that a man's death can be announced almost as an afterthought or narrative aside. The central events of the action—Lee Strunk's trip into the tunnel, Ted Lavender's death, Jimmy Cross's enchantment and disenchantment with Martha—occur and recur in the beginning, middle, *and* end. For this reason the story may seem merely an odd jumble of episodes inserted haphazardly into the long litany of "the things they carried." But the list format—with its predictable recurrence and nearly musical opposition of segments—determines the story's structure.

It may be that O'Brien employed the list to evoke the repetitive actions of the experience of combat itself. O'Brien's list marches on and on as do the grunts, "like mules . . . just humping, one step and then the next and then another." The episodes interrupting that march emerge like fragments of memories: jumbled and out of order, with the details growing clear at one point, hazy the next, then altering altogether.

On the Tonality and Weight of Lists

In the second section of this story we find the first full-fledged catalogue of "the things they carried": "pocket knives, heat tabs, wristwatches, dog tags, mosquito repellent, chewing gum, candy . . ." O'Brien itemizes the field possessions of these grunts right down to the precise weight of each "necessity." As he proceeds, however, the inventory starts to include not just the objects but men:

> Henry Dobbins, who was a big man, carried extra rations; he was especially fond of canned peaches in heavy syrup over pound cake. Dave Jensen, who practiced field hygiene, carried a toothbrush, dental floss, and several hotel-sized bars of soap he'd stolen on R&R in Sydney, Australia. Ted Lavender, who was scared, carried tranquilizers until he was shot in the head outside the village of Than Khe in mid-April.

Notice O'Brien's technique here: the most revealing and devastating information is routinely slipped into the back corners of sentences, in modifying phrases and subordinate clauses like "until he was shot in the head." When a writer positions the words "until he was shot" as a grammatical equivalent of the preceding phrase "he was especially fond of canned peaches in heavy syrup," the reader may assume that the author/narrator has grown numb to the horrors of war. There's objectification here, as well as a kind of parataxis in the nonhierarchical listing of details: syrup and bullets grow indistinguishable on the shared space of the page. This is precisely the mindset—the listmaker's automatic sequencing—into which O'Brien invites us.

At the same time this inventory conveys a terrible sense of abundance. When men become "grunts" or "legs," distinguished from one another only by what they carry, they lose their value; they are reduced to objectified items which can be replaced by the next shipments from home. Too, the list conveys a sense of order, of a systematic military regimen. The fourth section, with its series of sentences beginning, "As a first lieutenant and platoon leader, Jimmy

Cross carried" or "As an RTO, Mitchell Sanders carried" transforms the men, at least temporarily, into nothing but ranks and gear. Near the end of this long recital, filled with the jargon and details of war paraphernalia, O'Brien slips Ted Lavender's death into the inventory. And he concludes with a pun:

> A single round weighed 10 ounces. The typical load was 25 rounds. But Ted Lavender, who was scared, carried 34 rounds when he was shot and killed outside Than Khe, and he went down under an exceptional burden, more than 20 pounds of ammunition, plus the flak jacket and helmet and rations and water and toilet paper and tranquilizers and all the rest, plus the unweighed fear. He was dead weight.

On Style and Rhythm

Stylistically, O'Brien relies on the standard listing devices of **litany**: repetition, parallel sentence structure, and consistent rhythm. Consider how often Ted Lavender's name is tagged with the follow-up line, "who was scared" or how many times Kiowa repeats the words, "boom-down," to describe the dead man's fall. Notice the long passages comprised of parallel sentences, all beginning with the same phrase:

> They carried diseases, among them malaria and dysentery. They carried lice and ringworm and leeches and paddy algae and various rots and molds. They carried the land itself—Vietnam, the place, the soil—a powdery orange-red dust that covered their boots and fatigues and faces. They carried the sky.

The effect is mind-numbing; we sense a narrator either deadened to these horrors or trying desperately, through a basic repetition of facts, to restore for himself and others "conscience and hope and human sensibility." To carry "diseases . . . lice and ringworm and leeches" is not to do so willingly, and by the time "They carried the sky" the burden has grown superhuman and, as a consequence, abstract.

Notice, too, the rhythm of these passages. When O'Brien presents the basic details of a real-time scene his sentences are simple and brief: "A few moments later Lee Strunk crawled out of the tunnel. He came up grinning, filthy but alive." In the lists, on the other hand, O'Brien's phrases pile up relentlessly, creating a sort of rhetorical excess: "They plodded along slowly, dumbly, leaning forward against the heat, unthinking, all blood and bone, simple grunts, soldiering with their legs, toiling up the hills and down into the paddies and across the rivers and up again and down . . ." Here O'Brien allows himself, as stylist, to replicate the slow, strained progress of the soldiers in their weary forward march, and the result is a stirring, poetic litany that courses through this narrative with a momentum of its own.

On Dialogue and Specific Language

It's not an accident, either, that the spoken utterance of this story—its dialogue —is by and large monosyllabic, colloquial, and more often than not profane. Compare the language of these Vietnam "grunts" to the characters in Mukherjee, Moore, or O'Connor, and you'll see how liberal is the use of four-letter words—how closely O'Brien matches the rhythms of plain speech. And where not profane he's casual: *"Greased . . . Offed, lit up, zapped while zipping"* comes as a kind of counterpoint to the bureaucratic rhetoric of propaganda. When Jimmy Cross tells himself "No more fantasies" he's giving up on more than the romantic notion of Martha; he rids himself of verbal illusions as well. *"I'm sorry, motherfuckers, but I'm out of it, I'm goofed, I'm on a space cruise, I'm gone!"* entails a kind of poetry that's not so much high-flown as matter-of-fact, down to earth.

On the Individual and Universal Character

The men in "The Things They Carried" are burdened not just by the gear they carry but by their own "grief, terror, love, longing." The sad message of the book is that these burdens are never lifted. The veterans in O'Brien's stories carry their memories, their shame and secret history for years. Just as Jimmy Cross blames himself for Ted Lavender's death, in a later story Norman Bowker will blame himself for the death of Kiowa, and the narrator "Tim O'Brien" will assume guilt for the death of a slender young VC soldier. O'Brien dedicates his book to these men, "the men of Alpha Company," listing the names Jimmy Cross, Norman Bowker, Rat Kiley, Mitchell Sanders, Henry Dobbins, and Kiowa. The uninitiated might therefore assume that the book is a memoir, not a work of fiction. O'Brien seems not so much to be "making up stories" as recording history, revealing the truth about these men's past and that of our country.

Yet the names in the dedication are invented. These men are not old friends from the war but characters O'Brien imagines, right down to his own namesake. The author explains his approach in a short story near the end of *The Things They Carried:*

Good Form

It's time to be blunt.

I'm forty-three years old, true, and I'm a writer now, and a long time ago I walked through Quang Nai Province as a foot soldier.

Almost everything else is invented.

But it's not a game. It's a form. Right here, now, as I invent myself, I'm thinking of all I want to tell you about why this book is written as it is. For instance, I want to tell you this: twenty years ago I watched a man die on a trail near the village of My Khe. I did not kill him. But I was present, you see, and my presence was guilt enough. I remember his face, which was not a pretty face, because his jaw was in his throat, and I remember feeling the burden of responsibility and grief. I blamed myself. And rightly so, because I was present.

But listen. Even *that* story is made up.

I want you to feel what I felt. I want you to know why story-truth is truer sometimes than happening-truth.

Here is the happening-truth. I was once a soldier. There were many bodies, real bodies with real faces, but I was young then and I was afraid to look. And now, twenty years later, I'm left with faceless responsibility and faceless grief.

Here is the story-truth. He was a slim, dead, almost dainty young man of about twenty. He lay in the center of a red clay trail near the village of My Khe. His jaw was in his throat. His one eye was shut, the other eye was a star-shaped hole. I killed him.

What stories can do, I guess, is make things present.

I can look at things I never looked at. I can attach faces to grief and love and pity and God. I can be brave. I can make myself feel again.

"Daddy, tell the truth," Kathleen can say, "did you ever kill anybody?" And I can say, honestly, "Of course not."

Or I can say, honestly, "Yes."

On Invention as Truth Seeking and Narrative Posturing

Perhaps it won't overly complicate matters to mention that O'Brien does not have a daughter named Kathleen. (This strategy is tipped off in the very first sentence of "The Things They Carried"; the college which Martha attends— "Mount Sebastian College in New Jersey"—doesn't exist. Nor, we may presume, does she.) In such a system the first-person point of view seems no more and no less trustworthy than the third person or the omniscient authorial; the line between the "Tim O'Brien" of *The Things They Carried* and the "I" of "Good Form" is a difficult one to draw.

Rather than ponder the endless "lying" ramifications of the narrative posture O'Brien assumes even as he's "coming clean," however, let's concede it all to be beside the point. His approach is not new, after all. Surely this is something most writers do: combine the raw **material** of personal experience with details invented or culled from elsewhere to create a story that represents reality. Indeed, the whole purpose of witness-bearing fiction is to capture—in a word web of imagined event—what the writer believes to be truth.

In an essay describing his early fondness for magic tricks, O'Brien compares the challenge of creating a successful illusion to the task of composition:

▨ **WRITER'S VIEW:** *Writing fiction is a solitary endeavor. You shape your own universe. You practice all the time, then practice some more. You pay* *attention to craft. You aim for tension and suspense, a sense of drama, displaying in concrete terms the actions and reactions of human beings contesting problems of the heart. You try to make art. You strike for wholeness, seeking continuity and flow, each element performing both as cause and effect, always hoping to create, or to re-create, the great illusions of life.* ("The Magic Show," Writers on Writing, *eds. Pack and Parini, 1985.*)

Drawing Connections: Hemingway and Barth

Two of our previous authors are importantly relevant here. The first, of course, is Hemingway—whose mantle as a "war correspondent" O'Brien would seem to have inherited, and whose stories of the First World War form an indispensable part of the cultural backdrop to those of Vietnam. The soldier's prayer in the foxhole from *In Our Time* could—with almost no updating or alteration—be spoken instead by Rat Kiley or Jimmy Cross.

Less obvious but just as relevant is the postmodern mode of John Barth; there's the same technical virtuosity in "The Things They Carried" as that which was deployed in "Lost in the Funhouse." Clearly, the subject's a good deal less innocent and the characters have a good deal less fun; the humor of O'Brien's soldiers is sardonic and even despairing throughout. But the same authorial obtrusiveness and fascination with tale telling—a self-reflexive commentary on the nature of the story told—figures importantly in each of these fictions. If John Barth were to write of armed conflict, he might well have chosen to do so in Tim O'Brien's terms.

From Imitation to Original Creation

In an essay titled "Tradition and the Individual Talent," T. S. Eliot suggests that every new work of genuine art alters those that went before, just as it derives from them—and "The Things They Carried" seems an apt demonstration of the poet's theory. By borrowing from Hemingway this contemporary author has renewed him, and those who write of future wars will necessarily have to deal with the example of O'Brien. It's one way an act of "imitation" can fire the imagination and become, instead, "original"; it's how to strip those words of quotes and make them seem no longer opposite but linked.

▓ Applications and Connections

- Consider how O'Brien uses lists to both individually characterize and universalize these soldiers. What do certain men carry that makes them unique, that sets them apart? What do they carry in common? Focus specifically on Lieutenant Cross—what he carries and how he changes; do you identify with him more as an individual or as a soldier, and why?

- Why does O'Brien choose to repeat certain details—certain things that are carried—and what does this accomplish? Also, what things do the soldiers abandon or destroy along the way—what they cease to carry—and what are the thematic implications? What is the significance of Lieutenant Cross's order to no longer leave anything behind?
- The verb "carried" is used many times in the story, and within a number of sentences it serves as a **zeugma**, changing its definition midsentence as it modifies both the concrete and abstract: "He carried a strobe light and the responsibility for the lives of his men" or "They carried all they could bear, and then some, including a silent awe for the terrible power of the things they carried." Consider the implications of moving from the tangible and physical to the metaphorical or less tangible with the same word. What does the word "carry" and its repetition suggest? When O'Brien introduces the word "hump," does it carry the same kind of resonance? Look at places in the story where "hump" is used rather than "carry" and see if there is a common reason for the shift in vocabulary.

Exercises

1. Write a short story consisting of one extended scene—with dialogue and consecutive progression of events—presenting the day Lee Strunk went down in the tunnel and Ted Lavender was shot in the head.

2. Write a series of letters between Martha and Jimmy Cross. Write some of Martha's poems, and give Jimmy's thoughts on them.

3. Write letters to and from any of the other men in this story.

4. Write Martha's story at Mount Sebastian College in New Jersey. Why poetry? Why so sad? Why so alone? Who else does she know in Vietnam? Is she seeing anyone at home? What does she think of Jimmy? How much do his letters mean to her? If you like, use O'Brien's style of listing things for Martha's story too.

5. Weigh everything in your backpack; make a list. Fill your bag with your daily necessities—canned goods, shampoo, toothpaste, books—until it weighs at least 20 pounds. Carry it around campus for a day or a week. Report on the experience.

6. Alter the group presented in this story. Make it a group of climbers on Mt. Everest; boy/girl scouts hiking in the Porcupine Mountains; door-to-door canvassers for the Sierra Club; homeless people; college kids moving into the dorms freshman year.

7. Write a story about Lieutenant Cross, and perhaps the other men, when they first return to the states and re-enter American society. Use the same listing techniques that O'Brien uses here.

8. Make a list poem based on items found in this story, but write it in your own words. For example, write a list poem about the choppers arriving with fresh supplies, or one on the weapons they carried.

9. Reconstruct the author's outline for this story.

10. Write a scene in which the men unpack Ted Lavender's bag, distributing and discarding what they find.

Examples of Student Work

(*Editor's Note:* Here are examples of student responses to Exercise 6. Though both of these transpositions—from battlefield to nursing home and outward-bound excursion —are inventive and amusing, they serve to remind us of the essential seriousness of O'Brien's listing; this strategy makes most sense when the "things" listed entail life and death. O'Brien tells us just enough; to elaborate—as do these students—is to diffuse the effect.)

Benjamin Zick, EXERCISE 6

Jimmy Cross carried letters from a girl named Martha, a senior at Cedar Knoll Retirement Center in Jackson. She gave him a new letter every Wednesday night at bingo. Sometimes, if he was lucky, they included poetry. They were not love letters, but Jimmy Cross liked to imagine. Due to a stroke, Martha lost the ability to speak and communicated by letter. Since his wife had died and he entered the nursing home he had become quite fond of Martha. He yearned for female companionship and found it in her.

Everyone in the nursing home carried something. The things they carried were largely determined by necessity and superstition. Jimmy Cross had his letters. Martha had her crochet hooks. Lee Strunk, one of the nurses at the home, carried a stethoscope and a small pebble given to him by his youngest daughter. Kiowa, one of the stranger fellas in the home, always carried in one hand a white cane, although everyone knew he wasn't blind. He carried aspirin, ibuprofen, cough suppressants and every other over-the-counter drug available. He also carried 6 or 7 ounces of premium dope, which for him was a necessity. Together it all weighed 3 pounds, but Kiowa was young, only in his sixties, he had good legs. Henry Dobbins was diabetic and always carried a 3 ounce chocolate bar, in case his blood sugar was low. Ted Lavender carried his oxygen task; he couldn't breathe without it. It weighed

35 pounds, but had its own cart. He also carried a gold cross. To help me bear the weight, he said. Mitchell Sanders carried his inhaler, which weighed about 3 ounces. They shared the weight of memory. They took up what others could no longer bear. Often, they carried each other, the wounded or weak. They carried infections. They carried terminal illness. They carried their own lives. The pressures were enormous.

On April 16, when Lee Strunk drew the number 17, Jimmy Cross laughed and muttered something and glanced down at his card quickly. The bingo hall was hot and stirring. I-23, I-19, I-27, I-21, no I-17. Jimmy Cross couldn't buy a bingo, it wasn't his night.

Emily Neenan, EXERCISE 6

Outward Bound leader Rob Semen carried letters from a little girl named Alexis, his daughter from Newport, Rhode Island. They had never met, but Rob was hoping, so he kept them in the envelope from the first letter she wrote at the bottom of his backpack. In the late afternoon, after the day's hike, he would set up his tarp, light the fire, take out the letters, hold them next to his heart, and spend the last hour of light pretending. He would imagine taking her hiking and mountain biking into the Cascade Mountains of Northern California. He would sometimes smell the letters, knowing they smelled like her mother. More than anything he wanted to hear her call him "daddy," but the letters always started off, "Dear Rob." She didn't know he was her dad, he was almost sure. She was in third grade, and wrote about learning the times tables and playing left wing for the local youth soccer team; she rarely asked about his hiking excursions, except to say, Rob, don't fall off a mountain. The letters weighed 10 ounces. They were signed, Love, Alexis, but Outward Bound Leader Rob understood that Love was only a way of signing and did not mean what he sometimes pretended it meant. At dusk, he would gently return the letters to his backpack. Slowly, a bit distracted, he would get up and move among his Outward Bound hikers, checking that the food bag was secure in the trees, then at full dark he would return to his tarp and stare at the stars and wonder if Alexis ever scored a goal for her soccer team . . .

What they carried was partly a function of their role in the group, partly representative of their attitude about being on Outward Bound.

As a 10-year Outward Bound leader, Rob Semen carried sparks, a hunting knife, a first aid kit and extra rappelling equipment.

As a joker, Aaron Koskinaris carried playing cards, UNO, gummy bears, and markers so he could write on people after they went to bed at night.

CHAPTER 11

THE PROCESS OF REVISION:
Inflected English

BERNARD MALAMUD, "The Magic Barrel"

> ▦ **WRITER'S VIEW:** *Working alone to create stories, despite serious inconveniences, is not a bad way to live our human loneliness. (Author's introduction to* The Stories of Bernard Malamud *[New York: Farrar, Straus & Giroux, 1983])*

 Bernard Malamud was born in New York City in 1914; he died there in 1986. Much of his professional life, however, was spent as a teacher outside of that city—first at Oregon State College, then at Bennington College in Vermont. In *The Natural* (1952) he wrote about baseball, in *The Fixer* (1966) of anti-Semitism in Russia. In *A New Life* (1961) his protagonist is a teacher newly arrived in the Pacific Northwest, and in *Dubin's Lives* (1979) the title figure has been long-established in the rural Northeast. Malamud is nonetheless best known as a writer of immigrant experience and the urban poor; his characters are city dwellers, often—though not exclusively—Jewish and adrift. In many of his short stories—as in his second novel, *The Assistant* (1957), and *The Tenants* (1971)—the world of the New York City tenement frames, as he put it, "my sad and comic tales."

The Magic Barrel (1958), a collection of short stories of which we'll read the title piece, won the National Book Award for fiction. He also received the National Book Award in 1967, and was much celebrated in his lifetime, both in this country and abroad. Among his honors were the Rosenthal Foundation Award of the National Institute of Arts and Letters, the Pulitzer Prize, and the American Academy-Institute Gold Medal for Fiction. Additional books by this writer include the story collections *Idiots First* (1963), *Pictures of*

Fidelman (1969), *Rembrandt's Hat* (1973), and *The Stories of Bernard Mala-mud* (1983). His novel *God's Grace* appeared in 1982 and *The People and Uncollected Stories* was published posthumously in 1989. *Talking Horse: Bernard Malamud on Life and Work,* a collection of his unpublished essays and speeches, appeared in 1996.

Critics have called him—together with such authors as Saul Bellow and Philip Roth—a leader of a flourishing movement of "Jewish-American" fiction in the latter half of the twentieth century. But Malamud repudiated the notion that he was only or entirely a Jewish writer, preferring to be known as a Jew who resided in America and wrote his fictions here. (Bharati Mukherjee has written that she was greatly influenced by Malamud, and this is one of the ways in which his attitude about identity came to shape her own.) More to the artistic point was his interest in **fable** and allegory—the way a figure could be both particular and representative, both specific and abstract.

The label "magic realist" has been affixed to Malamud also, and with some justification; only a little offstage from his stories lies a world of wonders —populated by talking horses and intelligent apes and baseball heroes imported from King Arthur's Court. This author's sensibility is less like Hemingway's or Ford's than that of O'Connor or our next author, Jamaica Kincaid. Malamud accepts both the mundane presence of the supernatural and the redemptive power of belief.

This, from a later short story in his collection, *Pictures of Fidelman: An Exhibition.* A failed yet aspiring painter, Arthur Fidelman, goes to Italy to study the visual arts, and his apprenticeship could serve as a model for *The Sincerest Form:*

> The copyist throws himself into his work with passion. He has swallowed lightning and hopes it will strike wherever he touches. Yet he has nagging doubts he can do the job right and fears he will never escape alive from the Hotel du Ville. He tries at once to paint the Titian directly on canvas but hurriedly scrapes it clean when he sees what a garish mess he has made. The Venus is insanely disproportionate and the maids in the background foreshortened into dwarfs. He then takes Angel's advice and makes several drawings on paper to master the composition before committing it again to canvas.
>
> Angelo and Scarpio come up every night and shake their heads over the drawings.
>
> "Not even close," says the padrone.
>
> "Far from it," says Scarpio.
>
> "I'm trying," Fidelman says, anguished.
>
> "Try harder," Angelo answers grimly.

Were there a motto for Malamud's performance as writer, it resides in the exchange above: *"I'm trying,"* says the anguished apprentice. *"Try harder,"* the master insists. From the "passion" of one who "has swallowed lightning" to the artist plagued by "nagging doubts . . . and fears" we can map this writer's terrain. There's an insistent linkage of morality and art.

The Magic Barrel

Not long ago there lived in uptown New York, in a small, almost meager room, though crowded with books, Leo Finkle, a rabbinical student at the Yeshiva University. Finkle, after six years of study, was to be ordained in June and had been advised by an acquaintance that he might find it easier to win himself a congregation if he were married. Since he had no present prospects of marriage, after two tormented days of turning it over in his mind he called in Pinye Salzman, a marriage broker whose two-line advertisement he had read in *The Forward.*

The matchmaker appeared one night out of the dark fourth-floor hallway of the graystone rooming house where Finkle lived, grasping a black, strapped portfolio that had been worn thin with use. Salzman, who had been long in the business, was of slight but dignified build, wearing an old hat, and an overcoat too short and tight for him. He smelled frankly of fish, which he loved to eat, and although he was missing a few teeth, his presence was not displeasing, because of an amiable manner curiously contrasted with mournful eyes. His voice, his lips, his wisp of beard, his bony fingers were animated, but give him a moment of repose and his mild blue eyes revealed a depth of sadness, a characteristic that put Leo a little at ease although the situation, for him, was inherently tense.

He at once informed Salzman why he had asked him to come, explaining that but for his parents, who had married comparatively late in life, he was alone in the world. He had for six years devoted himself almost entirely to his studies, as a result of which, understandably, he had found himself without time for social life and the company of young women. Therefore he thought it the better part of trial and error—of embarrassing fumbling—to call in an experienced person to advise him on these matters. He remarked in passing that the function of the marriage broker was ancient and honorable, highly approved in the Jewish community, because it made practical the necessary without hindering joy. Moreover, his own parents had been brought together by a matchmaker. They had made, if not a financially profitable marriage—

since neither had possessed any worldly goods to speak of—at least a successful one in the sense of their everlasting devotion to each other. Salzman listened in embarrassed surprise, sensing a sort of apology. Later, however, he experienced a glow of pride in his work, an emotion that had left him years ago, and he heartily approved of Finkle.

The two went to their business. Leo had led Salzman to the only clear place in the room, a table near a window that overlooked the lamp-lit city. He seated himself at the matchmaker's side but facing him, attempting by an act of will to suppress the unpleasant tickle in his throat. Salzman eagerly unwrapped his portfolio and removed a loose rubber band from a thin packet of much-handled cards. As he flipped through them, a gesture and sound that physically hurt Leo, the student pretended not to see and gazed steadfastly out the window. Although it was still February, winter was on its last legs, a sign of which he had for the first time in years begun to notice. He now observed the round white moon, moving high in the sky through a cloud menagerie, and watched with half-open mouth as it penetrated a huge hen, and dropped out of her like an egg laying itself. Salzman, though pretending through eyeglasses he had just slipped on to be engaged in scanning the writing on the cards, stole occasional glances at the young man's distinguished face, noting with pleasure the long, severe scholar's nose, brown eyes heavy with learning, sensitive yet ascetic lips, and a certain almost hollow quality of the dark cheeks. He gazed around at shelves upon shelves of books and let out a soft, contented sigh.

When Leo's eyes fell upon the cards, he counted six spread out in Salzman's hand.

"So few?" he asked in disappointment.

"You wouldn't believe me how much cards I got in my office," Salzman replied. "The drawers are already filled to the top, so I keep them now in a barrel, but is every girl good for a new rabbi?"

Leo blushed at this, regretting all he had revealed of himself in a curriculum vitae he had sent to Salzman. He had thought it best to acquaint him with his strict standards and specifications, but in having done so, felt he had told the marriage broker more than was absolutely necessary.

He hesitantly inquired, "Do you keep photographs of your clients on file?"

"First comes family, amount of dowry, also what kind promises," Salzman replied, unbuttoning the tight coat and settling himself in the chair. "After comes pictures, rabbi."

"Call me Mr. Finkle. I'm not yet a rabbi."

Salzman said he would, but instead called him doctor, which he changed to rabbi when Leo was not listening too attentively.

Salzman adjusted his horn-rimmed spectacles, gently cleared his throat, and read in an eager voice the contents of the top card:

"Sophie P. Twenty-four years. Widow one year. No children. Educated high school and two years college. Father promises eight thousand dollars. Has wonderful wholesale business. Also real estate. On the mother's side comes teachers, also one actor. Well known on Second Avenue."

Leo gazed up in surprise. "Did you say a widow?"

"A widow don't mean spoiled, rabbi. She lived with her husband maybe four months. He was a sick boy she made a mistake to marry him."

"Marrying a widow has never entered my mind."

"This is because you have no experience. A widow, especially if she is young and healthy like this girl, is a wonderful person to marry. She will be thankful to you the rest of her life. Believe me, if I was looking now for a bride, I would marry a widow."

Leo reflected, then shook his head.

Salzman hunched his shoulders in an almost imperceptible gesture of disappointment. He placed the card down on the wooden table and began to read another:

"Lily H. High school teacher. Regular. Not a substitute. Has savings and new Dodge Car. Lived in Paris one year. Father is successful dentist thirty-five years. Interested in professional man. Well-Americanized family. Wonderful opportunity.

"I know her personally," said Salzman. "I wish you could see this girl. She is a doll. Also very intelligent. All day you could talk to her about books and theyater and what not. She also knows current events."

"I don't believe you mentioned her age?"

"Her age?" Salzman said, raising his brows. "Her age is thirty-two years."

Leo said after a while, "I'm afraid that seems a little too old."

Salzman let out a laugh. "So how old are you, rabbi?"

"Twenty-seven."

"So what is the difference, tell me, between twenty-seven and thirty-two? My own wife is seven years older than me. So what did I suffer?—Nothing. If Rothschild's daughter wants to marry you, would you say on account her age, no?"

"Yes," Leo said dryly.

Salzman shook off the no in the yes. "Five years don't mean a thing. I give you my word that when you will live with her for one week you will forget her age. What does it mean five years—that she lived more and knows more than somebody who is younger? On this girl, God bless her, years are not wasted. Each one that it comes makes better the bargain."

"What subject does she teach in high school?"

"Languages. If you heard the way she speaks French, you will think it is music. I am in the business twenty-five years, and I recommend her with my whole heart. Believe me, I know what I'm talking, rabbi."

"What's on the next card?" Leo said abruptly.

Salzman reluctantly turned up the third card:

"Ruth K. Nineteen years. Honor student. Father offers thirteen thousand cash to the right bridegroom. He is a medical doctor. Stomach specialist with marvelous practice. Brother-in-law owns own garment business. Particular people."

Salzman looked as if he had read his trump card.

"Did you say nineteen?" Leo asked with interest.

"On the dot."

"Is she attractive?" He blushed. "Pretty?"

Salzman kissed his fingertips. "A little doll. On this I give you my word. Let me call the father tonight and you will see what means pretty."

But Leo was troubled. "You're sure she's that young?"

"This I am positive. The father will show you the birth certificate."

"Are you positive there isn't something wrong with her?" Leo insisted.

"Who says there is wrong?"

"I don't understand why an American girl her age should go to a marriage-broker."

A smile spread over Salzman's face.

"So for the same reason you went, she comes."

Leo flushed. "I am pressed for time."

Salzman, realizing he had been tactless, quickly explained. "The father came, not her. He wants she should have the best, so he looks around himself. When we will locate the right boy he will introduce him and encourage. This makes a better marriage than if a young girl without experience takes for herself. I don't have to tell you this."

"But don't you think this young girl believes in love?" Leo spoke uneasily.

Salzman was about to guffaw but caught himself and said soberly, "Love comes with the right person, not before."

Leo parted dry lips but did not speak. Noticing that Salzman had snatched a glance at the next card, he cleverly asked, "How is her health?"

"Perfect," Salzman said, breathing with difficulty. "Of course, she is a little lame on her right foot from an auto accident that it happened to her when she was twelve years, but nobody notices on account she is so brilliant and also beautiful."

Leo got up heavily and went to the window. He felt curiously bitter and upbraided himself for having called in the marriage broker. Finally, he shook his head.

"Why not?" Salzman persisted, the pitch of his voice rising.

"Because I detest stomach specialists."

"So what do you care what is his business? After you marry her do you need him? Who says he must come every Friday night in your house?"

Ashamed of the way the talk was going, Leo dismissed Salzman, who went home with heavy, melancholy eyes.

Though he had felt only relief at the marriage broker's departure, Leo was in low spirits the next day. He explained it as arising from Salzman's failure to produce a suitable bride for him. He did not care for his type of clientele. But when Leo found himself hesitating whether to seek out another matchmaker, one more polished than Pinye, he wondered if it could be—his protestations to the contrary, and although he honored his father and mother—that he did not, in essence, care for the matchmaking institution? This thought he quickly put out of mind and yet found himself still upset. All day he ran around in the woods—missed an important appointment, forgot to give out his laundry, walked out of a Broadway cafeteria without paying and had to run back with his ticket in his hand; had even not recognized his landlady in the street when she passed with a friend and courteously called over, "A good evening to you, Doctor Finkle." By nightfall, however, he had regained sufficient calm to sink his nose into a book and there found peace from his thoughts.

Almost at once there came a knock on the door. Before Leo could say enter, Salzman, commercial cupid, was standing in the room. His face was gray and meager, his expression hungry, and he looked as if he would expire on his feet. Yet the marriage broker managed, by some trick of the muscles, to display a broad smile.

"So, good evening. I am invited?"

Leo nodded, disturbed to see him again, yet unwilling to ask the man to leave.

Beaming still, Salzman laid his portfolio on the table. "Rabbi, I got for you tonight good news."

"I've asked you not to call me rabbi. I'm still a student."

"Your worries are finished. I have for you a first-class bride."

"Leave me in peace concerning this subject." Leo pretended lack of interest.

"The world will dance at your wedding."

"Please, Mr. Salzman, no more."

"But first must come back my strength," Salzman said weakly. He fumbled with the portfolio straps and took out of the leather case an oily paper bag, from which he extracted a hard, seeded roll and a small smoked whitefish. With a quick motion of his hand he stripped the fish out of its skin and began ravenously to chew. "All day in a rush," he muttered.

Leo watched him eat.

"A sliced tomato you have maybe?" Salzman hesitantly inquired.

"No."

The marriage broker shut his eyes and ate. When he had finished he carefully cleaned up the crumbs and rolled up the remains of the fish, in the paper bag. His spectacled eyes roamed the room until he discovered, amid some piles of books, a one-burner gas stove. Lifting his hat he humbly asked, "A glass tea you got, rabbi?"

Conscience-stricken, Leo rose and brewed the tea. He served it with a chunk of lemon and two cubes of lump sugar, delighting Salzman.

After he had drunk his tea, Salzman's strength and good spirits were restored.

"So tell me, rabbi," he said amiably, "you considered some more the three clients I mentioned yesterday?"

"There was no need to consider."

"Why not?"

"None of them suits me."

"What then suits you?"

Leo let it pass because he could give only a confused answer.

Without waiting for a reply, Salzman asked, "You remember this girl I talked to you—the high-school teacher?"

"Age thirty-two?"

But, surprisingly, Salzman's face lit in a smile. "Age twenty-nine."

Leo shot him a look. "Reduced from thirty-two?"

"A mistake," Salzman avowed. "I talked today with the dentist. He took me to his safety-deposit box and showed me the birth certificate. She was twenty-nine years last August. They made her a party in the mountains where she went for her vacation. When her father spoke to me the first time I forgot to write the age and I told you thirty-two, but now I remember this was a different client, a widow."

"The same one you told me about, I thought she was twenty-four?"

"A different. Am I responsible that the world is filled with widows?"

"No, but I'm not interested in them, nor, for that matter, in schoolteachers."

Salzman pulled his clasped hands to his breast. Looking at the ceiling he devoutly exclaimed, "Yiddishe kinder, what can I say to somebody that he is not interested in high school teachers? So what then are you interested?"

Leo flushed but controlled himself.

"In what else will you be interested," Salzman went on, "if you not interested in this fine girl that she speaks four languages and has personally in the bank ten thousand dollars? Also her father guarantees further twelve thousand. Also she has a new car, wonderful clothes, talks on all subjects, and she will give you a first-class home and children. How near do we come in our life to paradise?"

"If she's so wonderful, why wasn't she married ten years ago?"

"Why?" said Salzman with a heavy laugh. "—Why? Because she is *partikiler.* This is why. She wants the *best.*"

Leo was silent, amused at how he had entangled himself. But Salzman had aroused his interest in Lily H., and he began seriously to consider calling on her. When the marriage broker observed how intently Leo's mind was at work on the facts he had supplied, he felt certain they would soon come to an agreement.

Late Saturday afternoon, conscious of Salzman, Leo Finkle walked with Lily Hirschorn along Riverside Drive. He walked briskly and erectly, wearing with distinction the black fedora he had that morning taken with trepidation out of the dusty hat box on his closet shelf, and the heavy black Saturday coat he had thoroughly whisked clean. Leo also owned a walking stick, a present from a distant relative, but quickly put temptation aside and did not use it. Lily, petite and not unpretty, had on something signifying the approach of spring. She was au courant, animatedly, with all sorts of subjects, and he weighed her words and found her surprisingly sound—score another for Salzman, whom he uneasily sensed to be somewhere around, hiding perhaps in a tree along the street, flashing the lady signals with a pocket mirror; or perhaps a cloven-hoofed Pan, piping nuptial ditties as he danced his invisible way before them, strewing wild buds on the walk and purple grapes in their path, symbolizing fruit of a union, though there was of course still none.

Lily startled Leo by remarking, "I was thinking of Mr. Salzman, a curious figure, wouldn't you say?"

Not certain what to answer, he nodded.

She bravely went on, blushing. "I for one am grateful for his introducing us. Aren't you?"

He courteously replied, "I am."

"I mean," she said with a little laugh—and it was all in good taste, or at least gave the effect of being not in bad—"do you mind that we came together so?"

He was not displeased with her honesty, recognizing that she meant to set the relationship aright, and understanding that it took a certain amount of experience in life, and courage, to want to do it quite that way. One had to have some sort of past to make that kind of beginning.

He said that he did not mind. Salzman's function was traditional and honorable—valuable for what it might achieve, which, he pointed out, was frequently nothing.

Lily agreed with a sigh. They walked on for a while and she said after a long silence, again with a nervous laugh, "Would you mind if I asked you something a little bit personal? Frankly, I find the subject fascinating." Although Leo shrugged, she went on half embarrassedly, "How was it that you came to your calling? I mean, was it a sudden passionate inspiration?"

Leo, after a time, slowly replied, "I was always interested in the Law."

"You saw revealed in it the presence of the Highest?"

He nodded and changed the subject. "I understand that you spent a little time in Paris, Miss Hirschorn?"

"Oh, did Mr. Salzman tell you, Rabbi Finkle?" Leo winced but she went on. "It was ages ago and almost forgotten. I remember I had to return for my sister's wedding."

And Lily would not be put off. "When," she asked in a slightly trembly voice, "did you become enamored of God?"

He stared at her. Then it came to him that she was talking not about Leo Finkle but a total stranger, some mystical figure, perhaps even passionate prophet that Salzman had dreamed up for her—no relation to the living or dead. Leo trembled with rage and weakness. The trickster had obviously sold her a bill of goods, just as he had him, who'd expected to become acquainted with a young lady of twenty-nine, only to behold, the moment he had laid eyes upon her strained and anxious face, a woman past thirty-five and aging rapidly. Only his self-control had kept him this long in her presence.

"I am not," he said gravely, "a talented religious person," and in seeking words to go on, found himself possessed by shame and fear. "I think," he said in a strained manner, "that I came to God not because I loved him but because I did not."

This confession he spoke harshly because its unexpectedness shook him.

Lily wilted. Leo saw a profusion of loaves of bread go flying like ducks high over his head, not unlike the winged loaves by which he had counted himself to sleep last night. Mercifully, then, it snowed, which he would not put past Salzman's machinations.

He was infuriated with the marriage broker and swore he would throw him out of the room the moment he reappeared. But Salzman did not come that night, and when Leo's anger had subsided, an unaccountable despair grew in its place. At first he thought this was caused by his disappointment in Lily, but before long it became evident that he had involved himself with Salzman without a true knowledge of his own intent. He gradually realized—with an emptiness that seized him with six hands—that he had called in the broker to find him a bride because he was incapable of doing it himself. This terrifying insight he had derived as a result of his meeting and conversation with Lily Hirschorn. Her probing questions had somehow irritated him into revealing—to himself more than her—the true nature of his relationship to God, and from that it had come upon him, with shocking force, that apart from his parents, he had never loved anyone. Or perhaps it went the other way, that he did not love God so well as he might, because he had not loved man. It seemed to Leo that his whole life stood starkly revealed and he saw himself for the first time as he truly was—unloved and loveless. This bitter but somehow not fully unexpected revelation brought him to a point of panic, controlled only by extraordinary effort. He covered his face with his hands and cried.

The week that followed was the worst of his life. He did not eat and lost weight. His beard darkened and grew ragged. He stopped attending seminars and almost never opened a book. He seriously considered leaving the Yeshiva, although he was deeply troubled at the thought of the loss of all his years of study—saw them like pages torn from a book, strewn over the city—and at the devastating effect of this decision upon his parents. But he had lived without knowledge of himself, and never in the Five Books and all the Commentaries —mea culpa—had the truth been revealed to him. He did not know where to turn, and in all this desolating loneliness there was no *to whom*, although he often thought of Lily but not once could bring himself to go downstairs and make the call. He became touchy and irritable, especially with his landlady, who asked him all manner of personal questions; on the other hand, sensing his own disagreeableness, he waylaid her on the stairs and apologized abjectly,

until, mortified, she ran from him. Out of this, however, he drew the consolation that he was a Jew and that a Jew suffered. But gradually, as the long and
terrible week drew to a close, he regained his composure and some idea of purpose in life: to go on as planned. Although he was imperfect, the ideal was not.
As for his quest of a bride, the thought of continuing afflicted him with anxiety
and heartburn, yet perhaps with this new knowledge of himself he would be
more successful than in the past. Perhaps love would now come to him and a
bride to that love. And for this sanctified seeking who needed a Salzman?

The marriage broker, a skeleton with haunted eyes, returned that very
night. He looked, withal, the picture of frustrated expectancy—as if he had
steadfastly waited the week at Miss Lily Hirschorn's side for a telephone call
that never came.

Casually coughing, Salzman came immediately to the point. "So how did
you like her?"

Leo's anger rose and he could not refrain from chiding the matchmaker:
"Why did you lie to me, Salzman?"

Salzman's pale face went dead white, the world had snowed on him.

"Did you not state that she was twenty-nine?" Leo insisted.

"I give you my word—"

"She was thirty-five, if a day. *At least* thirty-five."

"Of this don't be too sure. Her father told me—"

"Never mind. The worst of it is that you lied to her."

"How did I lie to her, tell me?"

"You told her things about me that weren't true. You made me out to be
more, consequently less than I am. She had in mind a totally different person, a
sort of semi-mystical Wonder Rabbi."

"All I said, you was a religious man."

"I can imagine."

Salzman sighed. "This is my weakness that I have," he confessed. "My wife
says to me I shouldn't be a salesman, but when I have two fine people that they
would be wonderful to be married, I am so happy that I talk too much." He
smiled wanly. "This is why Salzman is a poor man."

Leo's anger left him. "Well, Salzman, I'm afraid that's all."

The marriage broker fastened hungry eyes on him.

"You don't want anymore a bride?"

"I do," said Leo, "but I have decided to seek her in another way. I am no
longer interested in an arranged marriage. To be frank, I now admit the necessity of premarital love. That is, I want to be in love with the one I marry."

"Love?" said Salzman, astounded. After a moment he remarked, "For us, our love is our life, not for the ladies. In the ghetto they—"

"I know, I know," said Leo. "I've thought of it often. Love, I have said to myself, should be a product of living and worship rather than its own end. Yet for myself I find it necessary to establish the level of my need and fulfill it."

Salzman shrugged but answered, "Listen, rabbi, if you want love, this I can find for you also. I have such beautiful clients that you will love them the minute your eyes will see them."

Leo smiled unhappily. "I'm afraid you don't understand."

But Salzman hastily unstrapped his portfolio and withdrew a manila packet from it.

"Pictures," he said, quickly laying the envelope on the table.

Leo called after him to take the pictures away, but as if on the wings of the wind, Salzman had disappeared.

March came. Leo returned to his regular routine. Although he felt not quite himself yet—lacked energy—he was making plans for a more active social life. Of course it would cost something, but he was an expert in cutting corners; and when there were no corners left he would make circles rounder. All the while Salzman's pictures had lain on the table, gathering dust. Occasionally as Leo sat studying, or enjoying a cup of tea, his eyes fell on the manila envelope, but he never opened it.

The days went by and no social life to speak of developed with a member of the opposite sex—it was difficult, given the circumstances of his situation. One morning Leo toiled up the stairs to his room and stared out the window at the city. Although the day was bright his view of it was dark. For some time he watched the people in the street below hurrying along and then turned with a heavy heart to his little room. On the table was the packet. With a sudden relentless gesture he tore it open. For a half hour he stood by the table in a state of excitement, examining the photographs of the ladies Salzman had included. Finally, with a deep sigh he put them down. There were six, of varying degrees of attractiveness, but look at them long enough and they all became Lily Hirschorn: all past their prime, all starved behind bright smiles, not a true personality in the lot. Life, despite their frantic yoohooings, had passed them by; they were pictures in a briefcase that stank of fish. After a while, however, as Leo attempted to return the photographs into the envelope, he found in it another, a snapshot of the type taken by a machine for a quarter. He gazed at it a moment and let out a low cry.

Her face deeply moved him. Why, he could at first not say. It gave him the impression of youth—spring flowers, yet age—a sense of having been used to the bone, wasted; this came from the eyes, which were hauntingly familiar, yet absolutely strange. He had a vivid impression that he had met her before, but try as he might he could not place her, although he could almost recall her name, as if he had read it in her own handwriting. No, this couldn't be; he would have remembered her. It was not, he affirmed, that she had an extraordinary beauty—no, though her face was attractive enough; it was that *something* about her moved him. Feature for feature, even some of the ladies of the photographs could do better, but she leaped forth to his heart—had *lived,* or wanted to—more than just wanted, perhaps regretted how she had lived—had somehow deeply suffered: it could be seen in the depths of those reluctant eyes, and from the way the light enclosed and shone from her, and within her, opening realms of possibility: this was her own. Her he desired. His head ached and eyes narrowed with the intensity of his gazing, then as if an obscure fog had blown up in the mind, he experienced fear of her and was aware that he had received an impression, somehow, of evil. He shuddered, saying softly, it is thus with us all. Leo brewed some tea in a small pot and sat sipping it without sugar, to calm himself. But before he had finished drinking, again with excitement he examined the face and found it good: good for Leo Finkle. Only such a one could understand him and help him seek whatever he was seeking. She might, perhaps, love him. How she had happened to be among the discards in Salzman's barrel he could never guess, but he knew he must urgently go find her.

Leo rushed downstairs, grabbed up the Bronx telephone book, and searched for Salzman's home address. He was not listed, nor was his office. Neither was he in the Manhattan book. But Leo remembered having written down the address on a slip of paper after he had read Salzman's advertisement in the "personals" column of the *Forward.* He ran up to his room and tore through his papers, without luck. It was exasperating. Just when he needed the matchmaker he was nowhere to be found. Fortunately Leo remembered to look in his wallet. There on a card he found his name written and a Bronx address. No phone number was listed, the reason—Leo now recalled—he had originally communicated with Salzman by letter. He got on his coat, put a hat on over his skullcap and hurried to the subway station. All the way to the far end of the Bronx he sat on the edge of his seat. He was more than once tempted to take out the picture and see if the girl's face was as he remembered, but he refrained, allowing the snapshot to remain in his inside coat pocket, content to have her so close. When the train pulled into the station he was waiting at the door and bolted out. He quickly located the street Salzman had advertised.

The building he sought was less than a block from the subway, but it was not an office building, nor even a loft, nor a store in which one could rent office space. It was a very old tenement house. Leo found Salzman's name in pencil on a soiled tag under the bell and climbed three dark flights to his apartment. When he knocked, the door was opened by a thin, asthmatic, gray-haired woman in felt slippers.

"Yes?" she said, expecting nothing. She listened without listening. He could have sworn he had seen her, too, before but knew it was an illusion.

"Salzman—does he live here? Pinye Salzman," he said, "the matchmaker?"

She stared at him for a long minute. "Of course."

He felt embarrassed. "Is he in?"

"No." Her mouth, though left open, offered nothing more.

"The matter is urgent. Can you tell me where his office is?"

"In the air." She pointed upward.

"You mean he has no office?" Leo asked.

"In his socks."

He peered into the apartment. It was sunless and dingy, one large room divided by a half-open curtain, beyond which he could see a sagging metal bed. The near side of the room was crowded with rickety chairs, old bureaus, a three-legged table, racks of cooking utensils, and all the apparatus of a kitchen. But there was no sign of Salzman or his magic barrel, probably also a figment of his imagination. An odor of frying fish made Leo weak to the knees.

"Where is he?" he insisted. "I've got to see your husband."

At length she answered, "So who knows where he is? Every time he thinks a new thought he runs to a different place. Go home, he will find you."

"Tell him Leo Finkle."

She gave no sign she had heard.

He walked downstairs, depressed.

But Salzman, breathless, stood waiting at his door.

Leo was astounded and overjoyed. "How did you get here before me?"

"I rushed."

"Come inside."

They entered. Leo fixed tea, and a sardine sandwich for Salzman. As they were drinking he reached behind him for the packet of pictures and handed them to the marriage broker.

Salzman put down his glass and said expectantly, "You found somebody you like?"

"Not among these."

The marriage broker turned away.

"Here is the one I want." Leo held forth the snapshot.

Salzman slipped on his glasses and took the picture into his trembling hand. He turned ghastly and let out a groan.

"What's the matter?" cried Leo.

"Excuse me. Was an accident this picture. She isn't for you."

Salzman frantically shoved the manila packet into his portfolio. He thrust the snapshot into his pocket and fled down the stairs.

Leo, after momentary paralysis, gave chase and cornered the marriage broker in the vestibule. The landlady made hysterical outcries but neither of them listened.

"Give me back the picture, Salzman."

"No." The pain in his eyes was terrible.

"Tell me who she is then."

"This I can't tell you. Excuse me."

He made to depart, but Leo, forgetting himself, seized the matchmaker by his tight coat and shook him frenziedly.

"Please," said Salzman. *"Please."*

Leo ashamedly let him go. "Tell me who she is," he begged. "It is very important for me to know."

"She is not for you. She is a wild one—wild, without shame. This is not a bride for a rabbi."

"What do you mean, wild?"

"Like an animal. Like a dog. For her to be poor was a sin. This is why to me she is dead now."

"In God's name, what do you mean?"

"Her I can't introduce to you," Salzman cried.

"Why are you so excited?"

"Why, he asks," Salzman said, bursting into tears. "This is my baby, my Stella, she should burn in hell."

Leo hurried up to bed and hid under the covers. Under the covers he thought his life through. Although he soon fell asleep he could not sleep her out of his mind. He woke, beating his breast. Though he prayed to be rid of her, his prayers went unanswered. Through days of torment he endlessly struggled not to love her; fearing success, he escaped it. He then concluded to convert her to goodness, himself to God. The idea alternately nauseated and exalted him.

He perhaps did not know that he had come to a final decision until he encountered Salzman in a Broadway cafeteria. He was sitting alone at a rear table, sucking the bony remains of a fish. The marriage broker appeared haggard, and transparent to the point of vanishing.

Salzman looked up at first without recognizing him. Leo had grown a pointed beard and his eyes were weighted with wisdom.

"Salzman," he said, "love has at last come to my heart."

"Who can love from a picture?" mocked the marriage broker.

"It is not impossible."

"If you can love her, then you can love anybody. Let me show you some new clients that they just sent me their photographs. One is a little doll."

"Just her I want," Leo murmured.

"Don't be a fool, doctor. Don't bother with her."

"Put me in touch with her, Salzman," Leo said humbly. "Perhaps I can be of service."

Salzman had stopped eating and Leo understood with emotion that it was now arranged.

Leaving the cafeteria, he was, however, afflicted by a tormenting suspicion that Salzman had planned it all to happen this way.

Leo was informed by letter that she would meet him on a certain corner, and she was there one spring night, waiting under a street lamp. He appeared, carrying a small bouquet of violets and rosebuds. Stella stood by the lamppost, smoking. She wore white with red shoes, which fitted his expectations, although in a troubled moment he had imagined the dress red, and only the shoes white. She waited uneasily and shyly. From afar he saw that her eyes— clearly her father's—were filled with desperate innocence. He pictured, in her, his own redemption. Violins and lit candles revolved in the sky. Leo ran forward with flowers outthrust.

Around the corner, Salzman, leaning against a wall, chanted prayers for the dead.

▨ Notes on Craft and Context

At Bennington College, in 1984, Malamud delivered a lecture titled "Long Work, Short Life" (an allusion to the Latin tag-phrase, *Ars Longa, Vita Brevis Est*). Its closing assertions are characteristic in diction and stance—self-assured yet modest, a high priest of aesthetics who's wearing a business suit:

▨ **WRITER'S VIEW:** *I have written almost all my life. My writing has drawn, out of a reluctant soul, a measure of astonishment at the nature of life. And the more I wrote well, the better I felt I had to write.*

In writing I had to say what had happened to me, yet present it as though it had been magically revealed. I began to write seriously when I had taught myself the discipline necessary to achieve what I wanted. When I touched that time, my words announced themselves to me. I have given my life to writing without regret, except when I consider what in my work I might have done better. I wanted my writing to be as good as it must be, and on the whole I think it is. I would write a book, or a short story, at least three times—once to understand it, the second time to improve the prose, and a third to compel it to say what it still must say.

Somewhere I put it this way: first drafts are for learning what one's fiction wants him to say. Revision works with that knowledge to enlarge and enhance an idea, to reform it. Revision is one of the exquisite pleasures of writing: "The men and things of today are wont to lie fairer and truer in tomorrow's meadow," Henry Thoreau said.

I don't regret the years I put into my work. Perhaps I regret the fact that I was not two men, one who could live a full life apart from writing: and one who lived in art, exploring all he had to experience and know how to make his work right: yet not regretting that he had put his life into the art of perfecting the work. ("Long Work, Short Life," lecture, Bennington College, 1984)

Revision as Creation

Malamud was a careful, even a compulsive, writer; he revised continually—sometimes as many as eighteen drafts and never less than three. Story after story and chapter after chapter represent this process of revision; his work did not spring full-blown out of the surrounding air. In contrast to Roy Hobbs—the "natural" home-run hitter in his novel about baseball—he always worked hard at his fiction; he practiced hours each day on his swing. Malamud hand-wrote the *third* draft of *The Assistant*, for example, after his wife had typed a second draft from the handwritten first. Outline after outline and query after query provide a kind of "lesson plan," as though the habits of the high school teacher stayed deeply ingrained in the professional author; he became his own instructor in the discipline of art.

On the Process of Revision

Malamud kept a record of his journal entries for "The Magic Barrel," and we can therefore analyze the text—its "visions and revisions"—with reference to authorial intention. So let's look at "The Magic Barrel" in light of its author's journal notes. Malamud himself described the genesis of this story, as well as some of the difficulties he had in working it up, working it out. It's an important act of auto-analysis, a way of charting the tracks of the imagination and the process of composition.

Here are some pertinent remarks:

First there is a note in my journal, dated March 8, 1954. It reads: "Go back to the poetic, evocative, singing—often symbolic short story. Use all you've got. Go for more than one story—but make story good."

This was a reaction against the short, realistic pieces that I had been writing for a while. In other words, I had the basic feeling for the story, you might call it, long before I got the idea for the story. And I might say that it is that kind of feeling that still conditions some of my most recent stories, though not all.

His first note for the story as such came on August 21, 1954.

"The Marriage Broker's Daughter." A m.b. tries to interest a young man in a bride. The young man won't hear of it; he wants marriage for love. The m.b. then attempts to dig up a girl he thinks the young man will fall in love with. No go. By accident the young man sees the m.b.'s daughter and goes mad over her. He tries to get her father's permission to court her. The m.b. refuses a) because the daughter is the apple of his eye, b) because he will not be done out of a commission. The young man somehow gets the girl. Not sure what the miracle is but he's got to do something that satisfies everyone but the m.b. He (the m.b.) has to be disappointed yet resigned. Once I work out the meaning of the piece I'll have the ending. Season with Chagall?

Then Malamud makes several more notes; he has been translating Yiddish short stories about marriage brokers, though he never met one . . .

I was having trouble with the story; it was not developing into the sort of thing I wanted.

Then one day my wife and I were having a discussion, in the course of which she said, 'You talk a good deal about love, but you don't always love.'

Later on I admitted to myself that what she had said was true, and thinking about it I concluded that the problem of not loving, or of not being able to love, was one of the central problems of our existence; so I immediately tied it up with the idea for my story. Here was a man who wanted to marry for love; would it not be dramatic if he wanted to do so to prove that he could love?

September 14, 1954.

The Marriage Broker's Daughter—further development.

The main character is a rabbinical student. He is close to God— weeps for him at night—but he has difficulty loving his fellow men, hence he is a sad person. To him comes a m.b. offering a bride. This will help him when he is looking for a congregation. The student turns down the m.b. on grounds that he wants to marry for love. The m.b. shrugs. Perhaps the young man tells his need to love. He believes or has been told this will lead him to love of others. But the m.b. prevails and the student goes out with two of his clients: a Miss Hirschorn who has money and even soul but is without beauty; then there is a beautiful girl who is rather empty. Neither of them suits the student. The m.b., unwilling to give up, hands him some pictures of girls and tells him to make a choice. None interest the student. (On the back of each picture is a legend describing the attributes of the girl in round figures—also "well-Americanized") until he comes to the one who makes him glow. He calls the m.b. and he comes a'running. When he sees the picture he pooh-poohs—it was included by mistake. The girl is married. The student, after a time, suspects something and demands more information about the girl. Finally the m.b. confesses the girl is his daughter—a *vilder*. She is a bad girl—the bane of his life. The student thinks it over and sees a way of life with her. He can help her to goodness, she can help him to love. Despite the denials of the m.b. the student insists on meeting the girl. He will come that night. He does with a wild song in his heart. Behind the door the m.b. chants a prayer for the dead.

This is pretty much the story; the changes that were made were made in the writing.

The title of the story came from a phrase in the marriage broker's speech. I had at one point listed about a dozen names and then the idea that the barrel was magic came into my head. I did not have that in mind until the story was half written.

Some other autobiographical elements are:

1. the rooming house.
2. in a sense, the time of year: between end of winter and spring is to me a very dramatic time.
3. the tomato, a detail from childhood.

The story has been interpreted in two ways, as realism and as fantasy. I had meant it to be realistic, but two things conditioned some people's reading of it. In the original version Salzman says somewhere, referring to his daughter, "For her to be poor was a sin. This is why she is dead now." And the Chagallean **imagery** of the ending convinces some that it was meant to be fantasy. Either interpretation suits me, I thought, then in the ms I sent to the publisher I altered Salzman's speech so that it now reads, "This is why to me she is dead now."

(*Editor's Note:* Note how the addition of those two words—"to me"—changes the entire interpretation, making it a personal reaction on Salzman's part rather than a statement of fact.)

The daughter of the marriage broker came into my head full grown;
I can't account for her; and I've forgotten some other details of source,
but there is quite a good deal of invention in the story.

The one other lesson from experience I would like to leave with
young short story writers was that the story was almost all thought out
before it was written, usual with me. ("The Magic Barrel," *Talking Horse,
Bernard Malamud on Life and Work,* Alan Cheuse and Nicholas Delbanco,
eds. [New York: Columbia University Press, 1996])

On Creating and Revising Characters

Leo Finkle the rabbinical student and Pinye Salzman, who "smelled frankly of
fish," manage somehow to be at one and the same time **stock characters** and, in
their behavior, original. The *luftmensch* Salzman is a familiar type from Yiddish theatre and short stories, a weightless man who lives on air—though in
his notes the author admits "I had never met a marriage broker." Leo Finkle, by
contrast, carries somewhere about him a whiff of personal history; his creator
too was once a lonely and studious person in a rooming house.

On Magical Realism

What matters here, however, is invention. One hallmark of the work is its
seeming-seamless blend of fact and fantasy—a **"magic realism."** Consider how
the loaves of bread fly past the character's head, almost as though in a painting
by Marc Chagall—in his journal Malamud reminded himself to "Season with
Chagall," as though his story was a stew requiring spice—or the image of the
moon creating itself like an egg in a cloud hen. Salzman manages to appear on
Finkle's doorstep almost by the sheer act of wishing, and the photograph
proves talismanic. For both rabbinical student and marriage broker, the snapshot of the "fallen woman" Stella (Latin for "star") conjures actual blood and
flesh.

In some ways, however, this story offers an old-fashioned and traditional
version of "love at first sight." Literally, love enters through the eyes. When
Finkle first sees Stella's photograph he's behaving like a creature in a fairytale;
the fatal die has been cast. It's not unlike the poet Dante falling under the spell
of Beatrice in *La Vita Nuova,* or Petrarch enamored of Laura in his lifelong
sonnet sequence: one glance is all it takes. And there's a whiff too of the pagan
tradition that love is a condition—often dangerous, oppressive—over which
the lover has no control; for better or for worse, this form of romance proves
irresistible.

On Style and Dialogue

Diction—the characters' spoken utterance—is **idiomatic** throughout. Salzman
and his wife appear almost to be speaking in translation; their English is
recently acquired and poor. Finkle and Lily Hirschorn are better assimilated,

more fluent in English and therefore "Americanized." Also, it's worth noticing who does and doesn't talk. The landlady calls out a greeting, Lily is enthusiastic in conversation, Salzman unstoppably so. Devotion is wordless, however; the girl in the red dress says nothing we can hear.

On Style and Description

Malamud's descriptive prose is equally inflected. Look at such idiomatic usage as "an emptiness that seized him with six hands" or "the world had snowed on him." Look at the descriptions of the girls in Salzman's album: "Life, despite their frantic yoohooings, had passed them by; they were pictures in a briefcase that stank of fish." Or, "Her he desired." Or an oppositional pairing such as "Salzman, commercial cupid," where *cupidity* suggests both the fact of commerce and romantic love.

On Plot and Point of View

The authorial point of view is omniscient; the narrator goes in and out of character at will. Consider the progression of Salzman's meager meals: from his smoked fish to his request for a tomato and tea, from the encounter in the diner to his living room. When Finkle forgets and then remembers to provide food and drink for his guest, the wheels of the story revolve as well; when he decides that love of God must be earned via the love of a "sinful" woman, the narrative marries, as it were, spiritual and bodily yearnings; it's the soul made flesh. The fierce and vivid circumstance, the colloquial austerity of language, the unexpected plot twists that, in retrospect, feel foreordained: all these signal mastery.

Getting the Ending Right

As does the wit. Much of "The Magic Barrel" is humorous—the reeking Salzman, the **vaudeville** series of slammed doors, appearances and disappearances, the comic disjunction between the advertised and actual truth about the hopeful ladies in the marriage broker's file. There's a series of missed signals that verge on the burlesque. But, as is always the case with this author, the laughter shades to grief; when a figure in Malamud's fiction weeps, the tears are real, not feigned.

Which brings us to the story's close, its problematic final line: "Around the corner, Salzman, leaning against a wall, chanted prayers for the dead." Is Salzman's daughter dead to him, or has he somehow also died, or is the mourning general and Kaddish all-inclusive? Is Salzman deluded; is Leo; is the girl irredeemably whorish or about to be redeemed? For there's salvation in the lovers' story, surely: "Violins and lit candles revolved in the sky. Leo ran forward with flowers outthrust." Here we see a painting by Chagall translated from canvas to page, and to the young couple at least the story's end appears happy.

Malamud himself announced, "Don't worry about the ending. If you think about it it will come to you," but the "desperate innocence" of Salzman's daughter is at least in part offset by her corrupted worldliness. That star-struck creature, Leo, may be embracing ruination when he offers the cigarette-smoking Stella a bouquet. When Leo "pictured, in her, his own redemption" is that picture accurate or wishful merely; is their happiness provisional or lasting; what wall does Pinye lean against, and why?

On Theme without Reduction

Nothing in the scene is simple; nothing means only one thing. For there's a grace note, too, of the possibility that the marriage broker has orchestrated all of this, even at the risk of his own forfeited commission; "Leaving the cafeteria, (Finkle) was, however, afflicted by a tormenting suspicion that Salzman had planned it all to happen this way." Perhaps Salzman sees in Finkle his daughter's last best hope and his prayer for the girl who had been "to me . . . dead" results in her new life.

Great art is irreducible; it cannot be summarized in a single, simple phrase. Each and all of the interpretations suggested above belong to the **tableau**: a girl smoking in the lamplight, a young man running toward her with flowers, a father around the corner weeping, chanting prayers for the dead. The scene as set by Malamud permits no final analysis, no resolution that's a solution; what happens next is not for us to know.

▮ Applications and Connections

- How do creation and revision overlap in the writing process? When—if ever —are they distinct acts? Malamud says: "First drafts are for learning what one's fiction wants him to say. Revision works with that knowledge to enlarge and enhance an idea, to reform it." Because Malamud charts the theme/plot of his stories before writing them, is even his first draft a form of revision? Malamud's method—to keep a journal, to plot out and change events away from the actual story—can be a successful way to both plan and revise. Even if you are the kind of writer who revises while immersed, give this method a try; it could grant you distance and a fresh perspective.
- How is "The Magic Barrel" itself about that process of reinvention and clarification? In what ways is writing fiction inescapably an act of revision?
- The inflected English of "The Magic Barrel" extends beyond its characters' dialogue. Why is the descriptive prose also inflected, and why inconsistently? What kind of atmosphere does this give the story? How does this stylistic choice affect other elements of craft: point of view, characterization, plot, theme(s)? When in a story would you use inflected or altered English in dialogue? In description?

▨ Exercises

1. Write the history of "the magic barrel" itself; was it a pork barrel earlier, a barrel for pickles; is it made out of wood or metal, a basket or a pail? Describe.

2. Write the scene in which Lily H. goes home and tells her parents about the young rabbinical student she's met.

3. Have Finkle go home to *his* parents and describe his doubts about the Yeshiva and his religious calling. Then have him tell them he plans to marry a "fallen woman" and believes he can save Stella because of the depth of his love.

4. "Her he desired." Describe the courtship of Leo and Stella, their first conversation, their first kiss, their first night of sex.

5. Rewrite the ending so that Finkle does not get the girl. Have him marry the dentist's daughter instead; what kind of car does he drive; what business does he go into; what's his handicap at golf?

6. Update this story, but still using Malamud's diction and tone; have a PhD candidate in English or film studies, etc., fall in love with this year's supermodel or rock star on the basis of a photograph. Use the first person, not third.

7. As is often the case with fairy tales, there are three chances and choices provided; Salzman shows Finkle three candidates out of six in the first visit. Describe the other three.

8. Take a painting by Chagall and write a story about it.

9. Write the last scene twenty times, starting with the opening phrase "Leo was informed by letter . . ." and ending with the final " . . . prayers for the dead." Start with whatever language and phrasing you choose, but make your changes in each of the next nineteen versions so that we end up reading precisely what Malamud wrote.

10. Write your own story called "The Magic Barrel"—keeping only Malamud's title and changing everything else; take a detail from your own childhood—as Malamud took the tomato—and introduce it into this story: a baseball glove, a ballet slipper, a Pokemon, a pony . . . Keep journal entries on the process of revision.

CHAPTER 12

AUTOBIOGRAPHY VS. INVENTION:
Blending Fantasy and Reality

JAMAICA KINCAID, "My Mother"

▓ **WRITER'S VIEW:** *It was an Eden I loved so much, one from which I could not wait to escape . . . Eden is like that, so rich in comfort, it tempts me to cause discomfort; I am in a state of constant discomfort and I like this state so much I would like to share it.* (My Garden Book *[New York: Farrar, Straus & Giroux, 1999])*

© 2003 by Jill Krementz

Jamaica Kincaid was born Elaine Potter Richardson in 1949 in St. Johns, Antigua, a small Caribbean island in the British West Indies. Although her mother later married a cabinet-maker and had three other children, all boys, Kincaid was raised at first by her mother alone, and images of her mother and the close bond they shared run through much of her writing. Kincaid was a precocious child educated in the government school system, which was largely shaped by British influence and which fostered in this particular student a growing disdain for England. At the age of seventeen Kincaid went to the U.S. to work as an *au pair*—an experience reported on in her novel *Lucy.* Before long she found her way to New York City, changed her name, and began writing for magazines such as *Ms., Ingenue,* and the *Village Voice.* She became a regular writer for the *New Yorker,* which published her first short stories as well as brief prose pieces in its "Talk of the Town" page; these have been collected in *Talk Stories* (2001).

Kincaid is perhaps best known for turning the facts of her personal history into fictions that blend fantasy and reality, the imagined and the actual. Her books defy easy classification, falling in the gray area between story and novel, autobiography and fiction; the incantatory rhythms of her first-person narrator have the quality of song. "Whatever a novel is," Kincaid has said, "I'm not it, and whatever a short story is, I'm not it" (Interview with Kay Bonetti, *Conversations with American Novelists* [Columbia: University of Missouri Press, 1997]). Notice the perhaps intentional confusion here: Of course an author is neither "a novel" nor "a short story," and what she truly means is "I don't write a standard sort of prose." But to say, in effect, "I'm not a novel or short story" is to blur the distinction and blot the line between the artist and her art—as this particular writer has been doing all along.

At the Bottom of the River (1983), which includes the short story "My Mother," explores the Antigua of her childhood; it does so with a characteristic blend of nostalgia and bitterness. Kincaid revisited the topic of childhood and family life in her novels *Annie John* (1985), *Lucy* (1991), *The Autobiography of My Mother* (1996), and *Mr. Potter* (2002). She has also written works of nonfiction, including two books about Antigua: *A Small Place* (2000) and *My Brother* (1998). In 1999 she published a set of essays on her current passion, gardening: *My Garden (Book)* and in 2001 a collection of the work that first appeared in the *New Yorker,* titled *Talk Stories.* Kincaid now lives in Bennington, Vermont, with her two children, Annie and Harold; she teaches at Harvard University.

In the pages that follow watch for those moments when memory becomes imagination, fact shifts into fantasy. There's a seamless merging here of the real and the surreal, and its effect is both childlike and hallucinatory, as if a gifted young person were making up stories to frighten her friends. Indeed, the British urge their children not to "tell a story" when they warn them not to lie—and Elaine Richardson/Jamaica Kincaid has been making things up ever since.

My Mother

Immediately on wishing my mother dead and seeing the pain it caused her, I was sorry and cried so many tears that all the earth around me was drenched. Standing before my mother, I begged her forgiveness, and I begged so earnestly that she took pity on me, kissing my face and placing my head on her bosom to rest. Placing her arms around me, she drew my head closer and closer to her bosom, until finally I suffocated. I lay on her bosom, breathless, for a time uncountable, until one day, for a reason she has kept to herself, she took me out and stood me under a tree and I started to breathe again. I cast a sharp glance at her and said to myself, "So." Instantly I grew my own bosoms, small mounds at first, leaving a small, soft place between them, where, if ever necessary, I could rest my own head. Between my mother and me now were the tears I had cried, and I gathered up some stones and banked them in so that they formed a small pond. The water in the pond was thick and black and poisonous, so that only unnamable invertebrates could live in it. My mother and I now watched each other carefully, always making sure to shower the other with words and deeds of love and affection.

I was sitting on my mother's bed trying to get a good look at myself. It was a large bed and it stood in the middle of a large, completely dark room. The room was completely dark because all the windows had been boarded up and all the crevices stuffed with black cloth. My mother lit some candles and the room burst into a pink-like, yellow-like glow. Looming over us, much larger than ourselves, were our shadows. We sat mesmerized because our shadows had made a place between themselves, as if they were making room for someone else. Nothing filled up the space between them, and the shadow of my mother sighed. The shadow of my mother danced around the room to a tune that my own shadow sang, and then they stopped. All along, our shadows had grown thick and thin, long and short, had fallen at every angle, as if they were controlled by the light of day. Suddenly my mother got up and blew out the candles and our shadows vanished. I continued to sit on the bed, trying to get a good look at myself.

My mother removed her clothes and covered thoroughly her skin with a thick gold-colored oil, which had recently been rendered in a hot pan from the livers of reptiles with pouched throats. She grew plates of metal-colored scales on her back, and light, when it collided with this surface, would shatter and collapse into tiny points. Her teeth now arranged themselves into rows that reached all the way back to her long white throat. She uncoiled her hair from her head and then removed her hair altogether. Taking her head into her large palms, she flattened it so that her eyes, which were by now ablaze, sat on top of her head and spun like two revolving balls. Then, making two lines on the soles of each foot, she divided her feet into crossroads. Silently, she had instructed me to follow her example, and now I too traveled along on my white underbelly, my tongue darting and flickering in the hot air. "Look," said my mother.

My mother and I were standing on the seabed side by side, my arms laced loosely around her waist, my head resting securely on her shoulder, as if I needed the support. To make sure she believed in my frailness, I sighed occasionally—long soft sighs, the kind of sigh she had long ago taught me could evoke sympathy. In fact, how I really felt was invincible. I was no longer a child but I was not yet a woman. My skin had just blackened and cracked and fallen away and my new impregnable carapace had taken full hold. My nose had flattened; my hair curled in and stood out straight from my head simultaneously;

my many rows of teeth in their retractable trays were in place. My mother and I wordlessly made an arrangement—I sent out my beautiful sighs, she received them; I leaned ever more heavily on her for support, she offered her shoulder, which shortly grew to the size of a thick plank. A long time passed, at the end of which I had hoped to see my mother permanently cemented to the seabed. My mother reached out to pass a hand over my head, a pacifying gesture, but I laughed and, with great agility, stepped aside. I let out a horrible roar, then a self-pitying whine. I had grown big, but my mother was bigger, and that would always be so. We walked to the Garden of Fruits and there ate to our hearts' satisfaction. We departed through the southwesterly gate, leaving as always, in our trail, small colonies of worms.

With my mother, I crossed, unwillingly, the valley. We saw a lamb grazing and when it heard our footsteps it paused and looked up at us. The lamb looked cross and miserable. I said to my mother, "The lamb is cross and miserable. So would I be, too, if I had to live in a climate not suited to my nature." My mother and I now entered the cave. It was the dark and cold cave. I felt something growing under my feet and I bent down to eat it. I stayed that way for years, bent over eating whatever I found growing under my feet. Eventually, I grew a special lens that would allow me to see in the darkest of darkness; eventually, I grew a special coat that kept me warm in the coldest of coldness. One day I saw my mother sitting on a rock. She said, "What a strange expression you have on your face. So cross, so miserable, as if you were living in a climate not suited to your nature." Laughing, she vanished. I dug a deep, deep hole. I built a beautiful house, a floorless house, over the deep, deep hole. I put in lattice windows, most favored of windows by my mother, so perfect for looking out at people passing by without her being observed. I painted the house itself yellow, the windows green, colors I knew would please her. Standing just outside the door, I asked her to inspect the house. I said, "Take a look. Tell me if it's to your satisfaction." Laughing out of the corner of a mouth I could not see, she stepped inside. I stood just outside the door, listening carefully, hoping to hear her land with a thud at the bottom of the deep, deep hole. Instead, she walked up and down in every direction, even pounding her heel on the air. Coming outside to greet me, she said, "It is an excellent house. I would be honored to live in it," and then vanished. I filled up the hole and burnt the house to the ground.

My mother has grown to an enormous height. I have grown to an enormous height also, but my mother's height is three times mine. Sometimes I cannot see from her breasts on up, so lost is she in the atmosphere. One day, seeing her sitting on the seashore, her hand reaching out in the deep to caress the belly of a striped fish as he swam through a place where two seas met, I glowed red with anger. For a while then I lived alone on the island where there were eight full moons and I adorned the face of each moon with expressions I had seen on my mother's face. All the expressions favored me. I soon grew tired of living in this way and returned to my mother's side. I remained, though glowing red with anger, and my mother and I built houses on opposite banks of the dead pond. The dead pond lay between us; in it, only small invertebrates with poisonous lances lived. My mother behaved toward them as if she had suddenly found herself in the same room with relatives we had long since risen above. I cherished their presence and gave them names. Still I missed my mother's close company and cried constantly for her, but at the end of each day when I saw her return to her house, incredible and great deeds in her wake, each of them singing loudly her praises, I glowed and glowed again, red with anger. Eventually, I wore myself out and sank into a deep, deep sleep, the only dreamless sleep I have ever had.

One day my mother packed my things in a grip and, taking me by the hand, walked me to the jetty, placed me on board a boat, in care of the captain. My mother, while caressing my chin and cheeks, said some words of comfort to me because we had never been apart before. She kissed me on the forehead and turned and walked away. I cried so much my chest heaved up and down, my whole body shook at the sight of her back turned toward me, as if I had never seen her back turned toward me before. I started to make plans to get off the boat, but when I saw that the boat was encased in a large green bottle, as if it were about to decorate a mantelpiece, I fell asleep, until I reached my destination, the new island. When the boat stopped, I got off and I saw a woman with feet exactly like mine, especially around the arch of the instep. Even though the face was completely different from what I was used to, I recognized this woman as my mother. We greeted each other at first with great caution and politeness, but as we walked along, our steps became one, and as we talked, our voices became one voice, and we were in complete union in every other way. What peace came over me then, for I could not see where she left off and I began, or where I left off and she began.

My mother and I walk through the rooms of her house. Every crack in the floor holds a significant event: here, an apparently healthy young man suddenly dropped dead; here a young woman defied her father and, while riding her bicycle to the forbidden lovers' meeting place, fell down a precipice, remaining a cripple for the rest of a very long life. My mother and I find this a beautiful house. The rooms are large and empty, opening on to each other, waiting for people and things to fill them up. Our white muslin skirts billow up around our ankles, our hair hangs straight down our backs as our arms hang straight at our sides. I fit perfectly in the crook of my mother's arm, on the curve of her back, in the hollow of her stomach. We eat from the same bowl, drink from the same cup; when we sleep, our heads rest on the same pillow. As we walk through the rooms, we merge and separate, merge and separate; soon we shall enter the final stage of our evolution.

The fishermen are coming in from sea; their catch is bountiful, my mother has seen to that. As the waves plop, plop against each other, the fishermen are happy that the sea is calm. My mother points out the fishermen to me, their contentment is a source of my contentment. I am sitting in my mother's enormous lap. Sometimes I sit on a mat she has made for me from her hair. The lime trees are weighed down with limes—I have already perfumed myself with their blossoms. A hummingbird has nested on my stomach, a sign of my fertileness. My mother and I live in a bower made from flowers whose petals are imperishable. There is the silvery blue of the sea, crisscrossed with sharp darts of light, there is the warm rain falling on the clumps of castor bush, there is the small lamb bounding across the pasture, there is the soft ground welcoming the soles of my pink feet. It is in this way my mother and I have lived for a long time now.

■ Notes on Craft and Context

Reading Genre: Fantasy or Reality?

This story challenges many narrative conventions and may, at times, leave us wondering how best to read it. In what way do these separate episodes fit together? Where is the plot line? How are we to deal with the magical, surreal elements? Do we take them at face value and let the language transport us into a dreamlike, spell-bound, otherworldly place, or read them instead as metaphors for the ways in which a real mother and daughter interact?

Kincaid makes possible both readings, but leaves no question that the kind of story she wants to tell here, the kind of mother and daughter she wishes to portray, could not be confined to or conveyed by means of a conventional narrative. This mother is *godlike*. Like a creature in fable or **myth**, she is tall as the sky; she can walk on air; she transforms herself into animal shapes. She functions simultaneously as the narrator's closest ally or model, and as the narrator's oppressive, invincible foe. The daughter may grow big, but the mother is bigger, "and that would always be so."

On Autobiography in Fiction

This figure of a grand and powerful mother pervades Kincaid's fiction, and Kincaid has often noted the autobiographical underpinnings of the intense and conflicted mother-daughter relationships at the heart of her stories and novels. In much of her work, the mother and daughter are uncommonly close and affectionate until the daughter's early adolescence, at which point their bond breaks. It's not far-fetched to draw analogies to the author's experience as an only child until her mother married and began to have additional children when Kincaid was nine. To the no-longer solitary child, this felt like a fall from grace and even expulsion from Eden. "I thought I was the only thing my mother truly loved in the world," Kincaid has said, "and when it dawned on me that it wasn't so, I was devastated" ("Straight from the Heart" by Emily Listfield; *Harper's Bazaar* [Oct. 1990]).

Kincaid's mother, Annie Richardson Drew, was raised in a Methodist family on the island of Dominica. Despite their religious affiliation, the family was still in some ways affected by the local religion, Obeah, which involves elements of the supernatural: witchcraft, magic, and spells. As a child in Antigua, Kincaid believed in *jablesses,* creatures who could transform themselves into animals. Kincaid's mother, fearing that a spell had been put on her daughter, once sent the girl to visit her grandmother in Dominica, because it was believed that evil spirits could not cross water. Kincaid later recalled that when, on arrival, she saw her grandmother for the first time, she recognized her relative immediately.

It's possible to see in these facts the origins of several of this story's episodes. Certainly an awareness of Kincaid's own nostalgia for a childhood and an Antigua that she later lost will inform our reading of this story, and a grasp of the Obeah beliefs in *jablesses* and magic helps provide a context for the characters' physical transformations. Some critics have gone further, reading the second section of the story as a depiction of an Obeah ritual designed to remove this spell, and the journey by boat as a possible analogue to that trip to Dominica.

On Culture: Reinventing Narrative

Yet if we attempt merely to connect the dots between the fantastic episodes in this story and the analogous facts of Kincaid's own biography, we run the risk of reducing this story unnecessarily and forcing it by such reduction into the Western model of narrative which Kincaid resists. Her decision to write her story this way is not simply informed by her personal or cultural world views, but by political convictions as well—namely, her reaction against the cultural domination of England in colonial Antigua.

■ **WRITER'S VIEW:** *I was brought up to understand that English traditions were right and mine were wrong. Within the life of an English person* *there was always clarity, and within an English culture there was always clarity, but within my life and culture was ambiguity. A person who is dead in England is dead. A person where I come from who is dead might not be dead. I was taught to think of ambiguity as magic, a shadiness and an illegitimacy, not the real thing of Western civilization. (Interview with Kay Bonetti,* Conversations with American Novelists *[Columbia: University of Missouri Press, 1997])*

In an important essay, "On Seeing England for the First Time," Kincaid describes the omnipresence of English influence in her schools and upbringing, from the "Made in England" labels on her food and clothing to the table manners and grooming habits her mother encouraged. In school she read English authors, learned English history, and was required, again and again on tests, to "Draw a map of England." She writes, "I did not know then that this statement was meant to make me feel in awe and small whenever I heard the word 'England': awe at its existence, small because I was not from it."

On Autobiography and Symbol

From that recollected sense of awe and smallness before the map of England it is simple enough to trace a parallel to the feelings of the daughter and mother in this story. The mother seems satisfied only when the daughter remains in a position of weakness. In Kincaid's world, the mother, much like mother England, "colonizes" her subject so completely and fosters such a sense of longing for unattainable power that even acts of nurturing bear elements of destruction and degradation. When the mother takes pity on the daughter in the first section of this story, her kisses and comforting embrace suffocate the narrator. The mother's control over her offspring is limitless and—or so it would seem—capricious: "I lay on her bosom, breathless, for a time uncountable, until one day, for a reason she has kept to herself, she shook me out and stood me under a tree and I started to breathe again."

Representative Character and Conflict

The daughter's **conflict** between her desire to attain the mother's power by destroying her and her remorse over this desire is introduced in the very first lines of this story, and it remains the story's central—even its sole—conflict. Subsequent sections of the story reiterate this point. The daughter wishes her mother dead, wishes her mother "permanently cemented to the seabed," and attempts to trick her into falling into a great pit by building a beautiful house over it. The mother, however, remains indestructible. The final scene, rife with images of tranquility and contentment, shows the narrator contemplating her own fertility—her capacity to become a parent herself—yet she is all the while seated in her mother's "enormous" lap. Although the first-person narrator grows bigger and more powerful and develops her own skills of manipulation and magic, the mother stays invincible.

Note also the resolute refusal to give these characters names. They are "mother" and "daughter"—generic folk, representative figures, as in another famous story by Kincaid, a monologue called "Girl." Imagine how differently the whole would read if, say, this were the story of Jane and Jean, or Tabitha and Queen Latifah. These generations are abstract as well as specific; they're not people we would recognize in the grocery store checkout line or trying on shoes in the mall.

Episodic Plot: Transformation and Flux

It is difficult to say whether the parent-child relation of "My Mother," in the end, has truly evolved into something more peaceful and mutually satisfying, or whether this is just another calm, perhaps illusory moment in the unbreakable cycle of their struggle for power. By creating a world in which nothing remains the way it initially seemed—characters change shapes, die, come back to life— Kincaid in effect makes permanent resolution of their conflict inconceivable. The world described here exists only in a state of transformation and flux.

Indeed, these acts of alteration shape each episode and are one of the story's recurring motifs. Most of the sections begin in a state of relative normalcy, then advance toward a magical transformation. The third section, for example, begins, "My mother removed her clothes and covered thoroughly her skin with a thick gold-colored oil . . ." This seems entirely possible in the real world, until we learn that the oil "had recently been rendered in a hot pan from the livers of reptiles with pouched throats." At this point we are at least in a relatively exotic world, though it may still be to some degree realistic. Kincaid's next sentence, however, thrusts us firmly into an *other*world: "She grew plates of metal-colored scales on her back, and light, when it collided with this surface, would shatter and collapse into tiny points."

Concrete Detail in Invention

Notice, throughout, Kincaid's intense attention to concrete detail even as she moves into a realm that is increasingly abstract and difficult to imagine. The mother doesn't simply grow reptilian teeth and an elongated jaw; "Her teeth now arranged themselves into rows that reached all the way back to her long white throat." The daughter doesn't simply follow suit, becoming serpentine herself; she imitates her role-model and travels along on her "white underbelly," with her tongue "darting and flickering in the hot air." Kincaid provides just enough detail on a small scale to make these transformations palpable, even as uncertainties about the bigger picture remain: what kind of reptiles have they become, exactly? How? Why? And is this a subjective or objective account of metamorphosis; do they *actually* change shape?

By offering particular small details, Kincaid satisfies the reader's need to see and smell *something*, while retaining a great deal of mystery in the presentation of her images. Cumulatively, the details surrounding these transformations flood the imagination, creating, in Kincaid's Antigua, a landscape of vibrant flora and fauna in which anything can happen.

On Imitation and Autobiography

A writer this writer has studied closely and admires is the American expatriate Gertrude Stein (1874–1946). An experimental author who spent much of her productive life in France, Stein too wrote about her family and the country she had left behind, as in *The Making of Americans* (a long book written in 1906–08 and published in 1925.) In *Lectures in America* (1935), she described her own intentions and idiosyncratic use of language: "I struggled with the ridding myself of nouns. I knew that nouns must go in poetry as they had gone in prose if anything that is everything was to go on meaning something."

One of Stein's most attractive and accessible books is a memoir she ascribed to her companion, Alice B. Toklas (1877–1967). The ostensible author of *The Autobiography of Alice B. Toklas* (1933) in fact writes mostly about Gertrude Stein —and she does so in flowing, unpunctuated prose filled with repetition. In musical terms the "reprise" of such a phrase as "anything that is everything was to go on meaning something" has to do with variations on a theme.

On Interchangeable Identity and Language

Jamaica Kincaid's *The Autobiography of My Mother* (1996) is in that sense also a variation on a theme and cap tip to a much-admired predecessor; it's an excellent example of that "sincerest form" this book has been organized by—the flattery of imitation.

Here too the author enters a consciousness not her own and titles her book an "autobiography" as opposed to a biography, then categorizes it as "a novel." This suggests the kind of interchangeable identity described in "My Mother," and it's useful to compare that short story with the later, longer work. Here, for example, is the opening beat of the novel, in which "my mother" talks about "my mother."

> My mother died at the moment I was born, and so for my whole life there was nothing standing between myself and eternity; at my back was always a bleak, black wind. I could not have known at the beginning of my life that this would be so; I only came to know this in the middle of my life, just at the time when I was no longer young and realized that I had less of some of the things I used to have in abundance and more of some of the things I had scarcely had at all. And this realization of loss and gain made me look backward and forward: at my beginning was this woman whose face I had never seen, but at my end was nothing, no one between me and

the black room of the world. (*The Autobiography of My Mother* [New York: Farrar, Straus & Giroux, 1996])

Note the sonorous abstraction of such a phrase as "between myself and eternity," as well as the phrase, "the black room of the world." Or the romantic opening assertion with its single syllables and rhyme: "at my back was always a bleak, black wind." Further, the book's last paragraph begins as follows and could almost have been written by Stein; it's incantatory and even biblical in its use of words such as "harken" and "vanity." And the brave assertion, "all that is impersonal I have made personal" is a kind of reversal of the writer's habitual challenge—how to make of her own and private experience a word world the reader can enter and thereafter share:

> The days are long, the days are short. The nights are a blank; they harken to something, but I refuse to become familiar with it. To that period of time called day I profess an indifference; such a thing is a vanity but known only to me; all that is impersonal I have made personal. Since I do not matter, I do not long to matter, but I matter anyway. (*Autobiography of My Mother*)

The Concrete in the Abstract

In place of the clarity she associates with Western civilization, Kincaid offers a story ruled by a shifting, dreamlike logic. Nothing is what it seems; every shape can alter. Time both expands and contracts. Repetition is a characteristic rhetorical device; words and whole phrases are repeated—almost as though the generations copy and echo each other. Chronological order is not a given; indeed, it seems entirely beside the point. Yet in the face of this ambiguity Kincaid anchors "My Mother" with lush, precise detail, patterns of conflict and relief, and two monumental characters whose desire and struggle would stretch the bounds of any narrative.

▨ Applications and Connections

- How do we distinguish metaphor from the fantastic? Does Kincaid do so, and does she have to? What is fantastic in real relationships between characters? About place and time—here consider the line: "Instantly I grew my own bosoms"? And conversely, what do you think is "real" about stories that would be classified as science fiction or fantasy? Can a story be purely invention and still resonate?
- The language in "My Mother" is lush and ripe with description. So why is there so little dialogue, and what is its purpose when it does appear? Why is the dialogue so scripted and formal? On the first page why do we only hear that the narrator wished her mother dead, and not the words themselves?

- Kincaid pursues similar themes and explores a semiautobiographical mother-daughter relationship in a number of her works. She approaches the relationship from different angles, asks different questions, and shifts the focus. Although these works are, in a way, revisions of one another, they can and should coexist. The truth is that some themes are so large and so important to a writer that they themselves are a driving force for creation, and they are complex enough that they can be revisited time and time again, always yielding something new. What questions continue to surface in your work? What themes obsess you and which relationships drive you to distraction?

Exercises

1. Create the outline from which Kincaid wrote this story: *Author's Notes.*

2. Rewrite two sections of this story from the mother's perspective and in her voice.

3. Write the script for a stage or screen adaptation of all or part of this tale.

4. Turn this story, using only Kincaid's language, into a series of poems—with at least two poetic forms (a **ballad**, a **sonnet**, a **dramatic monologue, free verse,** etc.)

5. Rewrite this story, conveying all the complexities of the relationship between mother and daughter, but do so in a strictly realist style; in the third person.

6. Compose the diary of a neighbor/community member/social worker who has been observing this mother and daughter.

7. Write a letter from Kincaid's editor to the author, explaining in detail why one section of this story is unnecessary.

8. Rewrite this story as a children's book (illustrations optional).

9. Have the estranged father telling his son (the narrator's elder brother) why he had to leave the house and island; do this as dialogue only.

10. Write, as a unit in "The Autobiography of My Mother," the scene where the mother takes her daughter to the dock and sends her away in the boat: have this happen in 1850, 1900, 1950, 2000. What, if anything, changes?

Examples of Student Work

(*Editor's Note:* These seemed like particularly challenging exercises—or, perhaps, the voice was and is a particularly hard one to imitate. Nonetheless, the student samples that follow are inventive and ambitious, experimental in their several ways of dealing with "My Mother." Often they take the precise language of the original but change the format of presentation, and the way the words *look* change the way that they *sound*. It seems appropriate, given Kincaid's own refusal to abide by labels such as "novel" and "short story," that what we have here are poems and a screenplay. It's worth repeating at this chapter's end that these exercises are signposts, not the road itself—and that a copy need not be exact. To transpose the prose fiction of our twelve authors into verse or movie script is to recognize that imitation can release and not confine your writing; do with it what you will.)

Michael K. Hung, EXERCISE 4: "My Mother: A Series of Poems"

TRANSFORMATION

My mother removed her clothes
And covered thoroughly her skin
With a thick, gold-colored oil,
Which had recently been rendered
From the livers of reptiles
    With pouched throats.
    She grew plates,
Metal-colored scales on her
Back, and light, when it collided
With this surface, would shatter
And collapse into tiny points,
Her teeth now arranged themselves
    Far down her
    Long white throat.
She uncoiled her hair, then
Removed it altogether, took
Her head in her large palms and
Flattened it. Eyes, now ablaze, sat
Atop her head and spun like
    Revolving
    Balls. Two lines
On the soles of each foot divided her
Feet into crossroads, and she silently
    Instructed me
    To follow her.
Now I too traveled along on my white
Underbelly with my tongue flickering.
    "Look," said my mother.

ONE TO LOOK UP TO

My mother
has grown
  to an
enormous

                    h
                    e
                    I
                    g
                    h
                    t.
                 I have
                 grown
                 to an   But my
               enormous   mother's height
                 height   is three
                 also.   times mine.

Ray Howell, EXERCISE 3

FADE IN:

EXT. MOTHER'S HOUSE FRONT—EARLY EVENING
A WIDE SHOT encompasses the entire front
yard of the KINCAID HOUSE. It is a
tropical island setting and quite
beautiful. PALM TREES and other FLORA
flourish in the yard and around the house.
The ground is golden sand. We get a
feeling of privacy within the TREES, their
wide leaves protecting us from outside
observation. This is a surreal bubble
in which the laws of nature do not
necessarily apply. The HOUSE is a small,
one-level dwelling, shack-like, brown and
neat but very plain. The sky above and
behind the HOUSE is colored with sunset.
The scene is dominated by earthy colors:
browns, muted oranges, reds, and yellows.
We hear a girl SOBBING.

We slowly FOCUS on two FIGURES standing
in front of the HOUSE. They are JAMAICA
and her MOTHER. MOTHER is in her
mid-thirties, with sharp features. She
stands at least two feet taller than
JAMAICA. They stand facing each other,
just over an arm's length away. MOTHER'S
stance is authoritarian and powerful,
but as we get closer we can see that her
face is contorted in pain and grief. We
realize that the SOBBING sounds are coming

from JAMAICA< WEEPING pitifully and
uncontrollably.

                    JAMAICA
   . . .I'm sorry . . . I'm so sorry . . .
Oh, my God, please,
I'm sorry . . .

JAMAICA'S head is down, her body bent. The
ground here is dark and wet with TEARS.
She is about twelve years old, but not
showing any signs of puberty yet. Her features are very similar to her MOTHER'S,
but younger and softer. As she continues
to WEEP, her MOTHER'S face becomes more
gentle and caring.

                    JAMAICA (cont'd)
   . . .I'm sorry . . . I don't wish you
were dead . . . I don't . . .
I'm sorry. . . . Sorry . . . Please . . .
forgive me . . .

MOTHER steps closer to JAMAICA, wraps her
arms around her, and KISSES her on the
head.

CLOSE on JAMAICA'S face as MOTHER gently
presses it into her large bosom.

                    MOTHER
Shhhhhh. . . . Shhhhhh.

Slow FADE to WHITE as we hear JAMAICA'S
WEEPING and BREATHING slow, then stop
entirely. WHITE SILENCE.

FADE IN to JAMAICA'S FACE, still on her
MOTHER'S chest. MOTHER takes JAMAICA by
the shoulders and gently shakes her.
JAMAICA opens her eyes and takes a large
breath, as if she has not drawn breath in
years. We PULL BACK to see:

EXT. MOTHER'S HOUSE FRONT—EARLY MORNING

We are in the same place, but the scene
is now dominated by pastels and bright
colors. TROPICAL BUSHES show their
FLOWERS. The sun has just risen and the
sky is glowing with a soft blue light.

JAMAICA appears slightly older, and now
has noticeable BREASTS. Her MOTHER looks
at her kindly and knowingly. She too has
aged, and new WRINKLES show on her face.
She releases JAMAICA'S shoulders and steps
back. JAMAICA looks at herself and her
surroundings quickly, then back at her
mother with a sharp questioning gaze.

                    JAMAICA
So.

PART II

An Anthology

Editor's Note: Here are a dozen additional short stories, each with ten exercises in "imitation" attached. The arrangement is alphabetical, not chronological; again the emphasis is on contemporary American authors. But fiction thrives on variety, and exceptions prove the rule. The first and final of these writers—John Cheever and Eudora Welty—died in the previous century; their work remains "contemporary" nonetheless. Further, the concept of "American" has been much expanded. Peter Ho Davies, Jamaica Kincaid, and Bharati Mukherjee were not born in this country, and authors such as Junot Diaz, Gish Jen, and Jhumpa Lahiri write of the immigrant experience. Individually and collectively, they describe our nation's component parts in ways that enlarge the whole.

The purpose of these additional examples is twofold. First, the techniques of reading and writing discussed more fully in the text of *The Sincerest Form* would be of little value if not applicable elsewhere. What we propose is an *approach* to prose, a way of entering a particular mind-and-language set; if this strategy is to succeed, it must work for other authors equally. And, second, the teacher and student can here pick and choose, substituting Story A for Story B or deciding to continue at semester's end. We have dispensed with the apparatus of discussion—biographical notes and critical analysis—but each of these stories deserves close attention and can be studied with profit. They represent but a small sampling of the world of words.

REUNION
by John Cheever

The last time I saw my father was in Grand Central Station. I was going from my grandmother's in the Adirondacks to a cottage on the Cape that my mother had rented, and I wrote my father that I would be in New York between trains for an hour and a half, and asked if we could have lunch together. His secretary wrote to say that he would meet me at the information booth at noon, and at twelve o'clock sharp I saw him coming through the crowd. He was a stranger to me—my mother divorced him three years ago and I hadn't been with him since—but as soon as I saw him I felt that he was my father, my flesh and blood, my future and my doom. I knew that when I was grown I would be something like him; I would have to plan my campaigns within his limitations. He was a big, good-looking man, and I was terribly happy to see him again. He struck me on the back and shook my hand. "Hi, Charlie," he said. "Hi, boy. I'd like to take you up to my club, but it's in the Sixties, and if you have to catch an early train I guess we'd better get something to eat around here." He put his arm around me, and I smelled my father the way my mother sniffs a rose. It was a rich compound of whiskey, after-shave lotion, shoe polish, woolens, and the rankness of a mature male. I hoped that someone would see us together. I wished that we could be photographed. I wanted some record of our having been together.

We went out of the station and up a side street to a restaurant. It was still early, and the place was empty. The bartender was quarreling with a delivery boy, and there was one very old waiter in a red coat down by the kitchen door. We sat down, and my father hailed the waiter in a loud voice. "*Kellner!*" he shouted. "*Garçon! Cameriere! You!*" His boisterousness in the empty restaurant seemed out of place. "Could we have a little service here!" he shouted. "Chop-chop." Then he clapped his hands. This caught the waiter's attention, and he shuffled over to our table.

"Were you clapping your hands at me?" he asked.

"Calm down, calm down, *sommelier*," my father said. "If it isn't too much to ask of you—if it wouldn't be too much above and beyond the call of duty, we would like a couple of Beefeater Gibsons."

"I don't like to be clapped at," the waiter said.

"I should have brought my whistle," my father said. "I have a whistle that is audible only to the ears of old waiters. Now, take out your little pad and your little pencil and see if you can get this straight: two Beefeater Gibsons. Repeat after me: two Beefeater Gibsons."

"I think you'd better go somewhere else," the waiter said quietly.

"That," said my father, "is one of the most brilliant suggestions I have ever heard. Come on, Charlie, let's get the hell out of here."

I followed my father out of that restaurant into another. He was not so boisterous this time. Our drinks came, and he cross-questioned me about the baseball season. He then struck the edge of his empty glass with his knife and began shouting again. "*Garçon! Kellner! Cameriere! You!* Could we trouble you to bring us two more of the same."

"How old is the boy?" the waiter asked.

"That," my father said, "is none of your God-damned business."

"I'm sorry, sir," the waiter said, "but I won't serve the boy another drink."

"Well, I have some news for you," my father said. "I have some very interesting news for you. This doesn't happen to be the only restaurant in New York. They've opened another on the corner. Come on, Charlie."

He paid the bill, and I followed him out of that restaurant into another. Here the waiters wore pink jackets like hunting coats, and there was a lot of horse tack on the walls. We sat down, and my father began to shout again. "Master of the hounds! Tallyhoo and all that sort of thing. We'd like a little something in the way of a stirrup cup. Namely, two Bibson Geefeaters."

"Two Bibson Geefeaters?" the waiter asked, smiling.

"You know damned well what I want," my father said angrily. "I want two Beefeater Gibsons, and make it snappy. Things have changed in jolly old England. So my friend the duke tells me. Let's see what England can produce in the way of a cocktail."

"This isn't England," the waiter said.

"Don't argue with me," my father said. "Just do as you're told."

"I just thought you might like to know where you are," the waiter said.

"If there is one thing I cannot tolerate," my father said, "it is an impudent domestic. Come on, Charlie."

The fourth place we went to was Italian. "*Buon giorno,*" my father said. "*Per favore, possiamo avere due cocktail americani, forti, forti. Molto gin, poco vermut.*"

"I don't understand Italian," the waiter said.

"Oh, come off it," my father said. "You understand Italian, and you know damned well you do. *Vogliamo due cocktail americani. Subito.*"

The waiter left us and spoke with the captain, who came over to our table and said, "I'm sorry, sir, but this table is reserved."

"All right," my father said. "Get us another table."

"All the tables are reserved," the captain said.

"I get it," my father said. "You don't desire our patronage. Is that it? Well, the hell with you. *Vada all' inferno.* Let's go, Charlie."

"I have to get my train," I said.

"I'm sorry, sonny," my father said. "I'm terribly sorry." He put his arm around me and pressed me against him. "I'll walk you back to the station. If there had only been time to go up to my club."

"That's all right, Daddy," I said.

"I'll get you a paper," he said. "I'll get you a paper to read on the train."

Then he went up to a newsstand and said, "Kind sir, will you be good enough to favor me with one of your God-damned, no-good, ten-cent afternoon papers?" The clerk turned away from him and stared at a magazine cover. "Is it asking too much, kind sir," my father said, "is it asking too much for you to sell me one of your disgusting specimens of yellow journalism?"

"I have to go, Daddy," I said. "It's late."

"Now, just wait a second, sonny," he said. "Just wait a second. I want to get a rise out of this chap."

"Goodbye, Daddy," I said, and I went down the stairs and got my train, and that was the last time I saw my father.

Exercises for John Cheever's "Reunion."

1. Write a letter from Richard Ford to the literate ghost of John Cheever ("Dear Mr. Cheever . . ."), explaining why you titled your own recent short story "Reunion" and set it in Grand Central Station. Explain why you wanted to pay **homage** in this fashion: what is constant in the situation, what has changed.

2. Write a letter from the literary executor of John Cheever's estate ("Dear Mr. Ford . . ."), suggesting that there may be grounds for legal action unless the title "Reunion" is changed. Copyright law does not govern the use of titles, but there are issues of intellectual property rights infringement here.

3. Rewrite "Reunion" from the father's point of view: "The last time I saw my son was in Grand Central Station . . ."

4. Rewrite "Reunion" as a third-person story; then have two of the waiters talking that afternoon about the drunken customer who tried to order lunch.

5. Write a story about what happens when Charlie gets off the train in Cape Cod and his mother meets him and asks, "How was lunch with Daddy?"

6. Write an essay on the distinction between embarrassment and shame. Use "Reunion" as an example of how the former shifts into the latter—and how "Bibson Geefeaters" marks the transition here.

7. "I wished that we could be photographed. I wanted some record of our having been together," says the narrator at the end of the first paragraph. What sort of record is this?

8. ". . . my future and my doom. I knew that when I was grown I would be something like him . . ." Write a description of Charlie at forty; what sort of life does he live?

9. Clearly the father in this story is an educated man as well as a privileged one. Rewrite the story in a lower-class vein—no foreign languages or references to "my club" etc.; turn these mid-town restaurants into small-town bars.

10. "'I'm sorry, sonny,' my father said. 'I'm terribly sorry.'" Does he mean this? Why? Rewrite a page of "Reunion" *without* dialogue as descriptive prose.

RELIEF
by Peter Ho Davies

Sometime between the cheese and the fruit, while the port was still being passed, Lieutenant Wilby allowed a sweet but rather too boisterous fart to slip between his buttocks. The company around the mess table was talking quietly, listening to the sound of the liquor filling the glasses, holding it up in the lamplight to relish its color against the white canvas of the tent. It was, Lieutenant Bromhead had just explained, a bottle from General Chelmsford's own stock, and not the regulation port issued to officers. A hush of appreciation had fallen over the table.

Of course, Wilby had known the fart was coming, but it was much louder and more prolonged than he had anticipated, and the look of surprise on his face would have given him away even if Major Black, to his left, the port already extended, had not said, "Wilby!" in a sharp, shocked bellow.

"Sorry, sir," Wilby said. His face burned as if he'd been sitting in front of the hearth at home, reading by the firelight. He risked one quick glance up and around the table. "Sorry, sirs." Chaplain Pierce was looking down into his lap, exactly as he did when saying grace, and Captain Ferguson's mustache was jumping slightly at the corners, like the whiskers of a cat that had just scented a bowl of cream. Lieutenant Chard, however, sat just as he appeared in his photographs, his huge pale face tipped back like a great slab rising above his thick dark beard.

As for Bromhead, he looked only slightly puzzled. "What?" he said. "What is it?"

Wilby, staring down at the crumbs of Stilton on his plate, groaned inwardly. Bromhead's famed deafness was going to be the end of him.

He looked up under his brow as Bromhead's batman, who had just placed the fruit on the table, leaned forward and whispered all too audibly in his ear, "The lieutenant farted, sir."

"Chard?" Bromhead asked. Behind his beard, the older lieutenant turned the color of claret. Bromhead himself wore only a thin mustache and sideburns, and Wilby thought he saw a flicker of a smile cross his face.

The batman leaned in to him again. "Wilby," he whispered.

"Ah," Bromhead said sadly. He stared at his glass. An uncomfortable silence fell over the mess table. Wilby's mortification was complete. And, perhaps because he wished himself dead, a small portion of his recent life flashed before his eyes.

The lieutenant had been suffering from terrible flatulence all the way from Helpmakaar. At first he had thought it was something to do with his last meal (a deer shot, several times, by Major Black, which he could hardly have refused in any case), but as the column approached Rourke's Drift, his bowels seemed in as great an uproar as ever. Fortunately, the ride had been made at a canter and he'd been able to clench his mount between his legs and smother the worst farts against his saddle—although the horse had tossed her head at some of the more drawn-out ones—but as they came in sight of the mission station, the major spurred them into a trot and then a gallop so that their pennant snapped overhead like a whip. Legs braced in the stirrups, knees bent, his body canted forward over his mount's neck, the lieutenant had had no choice but to release a crackling stream of utterance.

At first there was some undeniable relief in this, but as each dip and rise and tussock jarred loose further bursts, he was obliged to cry "Ya" and "Ho," as if encouraging his horse, to mask the worst outbreaks. He was grateful that over the drumming of hooves and the blare of the bugler who had hastily run out to welcome them to camp, no one seemed to notice, but the severity of the attack made him doubt that he had not soiled his breeches, and at the first opportunity he sought out the latrine to reassure himself.

Having put his mind at rest, seen to his tentage, and placed his horse in the care of the groom he shared with the other junior officers, Wilby had taken himself off to the perimeter of the camp. Despite the newly built walls and the freshly dug graves—they were overgrown already, but their silhouettes clearly visible in the long pale grass—it was all familiar to him from the articles in the *Army Gazette,* and in his mind he traced the events of the famous defense that had been fought there not three months before.

Fewer than a hundred able-bodied men, a single company plus those left behind at the mission hospital, had fought off a force of some five thousand Zulus—part of the same *impi* that had wiped out fifteen hundred men at Isandhlwana the previous day. They had held out for upwards of ten hours of continuous close fighting and inflicted almost five hundred casualties on the enemy. It was a glorious tale, and Wilby didn't need to look at the page from the *Gazette* that he kept in his tunic pocket to recall all the details. He had read and reread it so often on the ride out from Durban that it felt as fragile as an illuminated manuscript. "You'd think it was a love letter," the major had scoffed.

He should be rejoicing to be here, standing on the ground of the most famous battle in the world, and yet he felt only the churning of his wretched stomach. Tomorrow they would ride out, the first patrol to visit the site of Isandhlwana since the massacre.

He stared off in the direction they would take in the morning. The ferry across the drift was moored about two hundred yards away, and on the far bank the track ran beside the river for a half-mile or so and then cut away over a low rise and out of sight. Wilby found himself thinking of the Derbyshire countryside near his home . . . and fishing—up to his thighs in the dark cool water, feeling the pull of the current but dry inside his thick leather waders. He supposed the sight of the river must have brought it to mind.

It was Ferguson who found him out there. He saw the captain running toward him, his red tunic among the waving grass, shouting his news.

"Wils, we are invited to dine with Bromhead and Chard. You, myself, the major, and Pierce."

"Truly?" Wilby caught his friend's arm, and Ferguson stooped for a moment to catch his breath. Then he shook himself free and took a step back, squared his shoulders and held up his hand as if reading from a card.

"Lieutenants Bromhead and Chard request the pleasure of Major Black and his staff's company for dinner in their mess at eight o'clock."

Of course, it was a little unusual for two lieutenants to invite a major to dinner, but by then Bromhead and Chard were expected to be made majors themselves—not to mention the Victoria Crosses everyone was predicting—and the breach of etiquette seemed altogether forgivable to Wilby. A dinner with Gonville Bromhead and Merriot Chard was simply the most sought-after invitation in the whole of Natal in the spring of 1889.

"Good Lord, Fergie," he said. "Why, I must change."

He had spent the next hour in his suspenders and undershirt, polishing the buttons of his tunic, slipping a small brass plate behind them to protect the fabric and then working the polish into the raised regimental crests and burnishing them to a glow. Next he worked on his boots, smearing long streaks of bootblack up and down, working them into the hide with a swift circular motion and then bringing the leather to a shine with a stiff brush. He thought hard about the thin beard and mustache he had begun to grow three weeks before and with a sigh pulled out his razor. Ferguson, waxing his own mustache, paused and watched him in silence, but Wilby refused to meet his eye. His mustache would never be as good as the captain's anyway. Fergie's handlebar was justly famous in the regiment, said to be wide enough for troopers riding behind him to see both ends. Wilby knew that wasn't quite true. The captain had made him check, with Wilby standing behind him trying to make out both waxed tips. In the end they had had to call in the chaplain, and standing shoulder to shoulder, about five feet behind Ferguson, Wilby and Pierce had each been able to see a tip of mustache on either side.

Wilby lathered the soap in his shaving mug and applied it with the badger-hair brush his father had given him before he'd come out on campaign. The razor was dull and he had to pause to strop it, but he managed to shave without drawing blood.

Finally, he extracted his second set of epaulets and his best collar from the tissue paper he kept them in and had Ferguson fix them in place. The fragrant smell of hair oil filled their tent as they each in turn vigorously applied a brush to the other's tunic. Without a decent mirror, they paused and scrutinized each other carefully, then bowed deeply—Wilby from the waist, Ferguson taking a step back and dropping his arm in a flourish.

The meal had gone well at first. The major had introduced him to first Chard and then Bromhead and he'd looked them both in the eyes (Chard's gray, Bromhead's brown) and shaken hands firmly. In between, he had made to clasp his hands behind his back and been sure to rub them on his tunic to ensure they were dry. "How do you do, sir?" he had said to each in turn.

"Very well," Chard had said in his gruff way.

"Splendid," Bromhead had told him a little too loudly. The story of Bromhead's deafness—that he would almost certainly have been pensioned off if his older brother had not been on Chelmsford's staff—was well known among the junior officers. It was said that he had only been given B company of the 2nd/24th because it was composed almost entirely of Welshmen and it was thought that his deafness wouldn't be so noticeable or important to men who spoke English with such an impenetrable accent. There was even a joke that Bromhead's company had only received its posting at Rourke's Drift because the lieutenant thought the general had been offering him more *pork rib* at the mess table. "Rather," he was reputed to have said. "Very tasty."

Some of the officers still made fun of Bromhead, but Wilby put it down to simple jealousy. For his own part, he thought it more, not less, heroic that Bromhead had overcome his disability. He had a theory that amid all the noise of battle a deaf man might have an advantage, might come to win the respect of men hoarse from shouting and deafened by the report of their arms.

At dinner, Wilby had waited until the major and Ferguson had each made some remark or other, nodded at each response, and echoed the chaplain's compliments on the food. Only then, as the batman passed the gravy boat among them, did he ask a question of his own.

"How does it feel?" he said. "I mean, how does it feel to be heroes?"

Bromhead looked at him closely for a moment, but it was Chard who answered.

"Well," he began. He stroked his beard, and it made an audible rasping sound. "I would have to say, principally, the sensation is one of relief. Relief to be alive after all—not like the poor devils you'll see tomorrow—but also relief to have learned some truth about myself. To have found I am possessed of—for want of a better word—courage."

"I say," murmured Ferguson. He grinned at Wilby.

What a blowhard, Bromhead thought. It pained him that Chard's name and his own should be so inextricably linked. Bromhead and Chard. Chard and Bromhead. He felt like a blasted vaudevillian.

"It's an ambition fulfilled," Chard went on, ignoring the interruption. "Since I was a little chap I remember wondering—as who has not?—if I were a brave fellow. Cowardice, funk—more than any imagined beast or goblin, that was my great terror. And now I have my answer." He paused and looked around the table slowly, and this time it was harder for Wilby to hold his gaze. "If the chaplain will be so good as to forgive me, I rather fancy it is as if I have stood before Saint Peter himself, not knowing if I were a bally sinner or no, and dashed me if he hasn't found my name there among the elect."

The chaplain smiled and bobbed his head complacently. Wilby and Ferguson glanced at each other again, their eyes bright but not quite meeting in their excitement.

"Heavens!" said Bromhead, clearing his throat. "For my part, being a hero is nothing so like how I fancy a beautiful young debutante must feel." There was a puzzled round of laughter, but Wilby saw Chard press his lips together—a white line behind his dark beard—and kept his own features still. "You've seen them at balls, gentlemen, there are one or two each season, those girls who aren't quite sure but then discover all of a sudden quite how delightful they are. Oh, I don't know. Perhaps their mamas had told them so, but they'd not believed them. After all, that's what mamas are for. They'd not known whether to listen to their doting fathers and all those old loyal servants, surely too ugly to know what was beautiful or not anymore. And then, in one evening, confound it, they know. And all around them, suddenly, why who but our own good selves, gentlemen—suitors all."

Wilby could see Ferguson smile, and he knew he was thinking of Ethel, his betrothed. He had seen such women as Bromhead described, but his own smile was more rueful. (He remembered one long conversation with a certain Miss Fanshaw, who had cheerfully told him that she had sent no less than five white feathers to men she knew at the time of the Crimea—"And you know," she had told him earnestly, "not one of them returned home alive.") The major he knew would be thinking of his wife, home in Bath, and the chaplain, he supposed, of God. He saw Chard, bored, study his reflection in the silverware.

"Anyway," the major said. "Put us out of our misery. Let's hear the details of this famous defense of yours, eh? Give us the story from the horse's mouth, so to speak."

"Oh, well." Bromhead opened his hands. "It was fairly fierce, I suppose. The outcome was in doubt for some hours." He faltered, and Wilby, who had been leaning forward eagerly, sat back and saw the others look disappointed. This was, after all, what they had come for.

Chard, however, stepped in. He was an officer of engineers and he believed in telling a tale correctly.

He told them about the hours of hand-to-hand combat, of the bayonets that the men called lungers, and of the assegais of the Zulus. How the men's guns had become so hot from firing that they cooked off rounds as soon as they were loaded, causing the men to miss; so hot that the soft brass shell casings melted in the breeches and had to be dug out with a knife before the whole futile process could begin again. He told them about men climbing up on the wall they'd built of biscuit boxes and mealie bags and lunging down into the darkness; of the black hands reaching up to grab the barrels and the shrieks of pain when they touched the hot glowing metal—shrieks that were oddly louder than the soft grunts men gave as a bayonet or assegai found its mark. He told them about the sound of bullets clattering into the biscuit boxes at the base of the wall and rustling in the mealie bags nearer the top, so that you knew the Zulus were getting their range. He described men overpowered, dragged from the walls, surrounded by warriors. How the Zulus knocked them down and ripped open their tunics, and the popping sound of buttons flying loose. "That would be the last sound a lot of our chaps heard," he said. With their tunics open, the Zulus would disembowel them, opening men from balls to breastbone with one swift strike.

"I swear I'll never be able to see another button pop loose from a shirt without thinking of it," Chard said. He took a sip of wine. "Of course, you'll see a good deal of that handiwork tomorrow, I'll warrant."

That was when Wilby began to feel his flatulence return, and his discomfort grew even when Bromhead broke in and explained that the Zulus believed that opening a man's chest was the only way to set his spirit free from his dead body.

"Really, it's an act of mercy as they see it," he said. "I hope so, at least. There was one poor chap of mine, a Private Williams. Bit of a no-account, but a decent sort. I saw him get fairly dragged over the wall before I caught hold his leg. This was quite in the thick of it. There were so many Zulus trying to rush us from all sides, they were like water swirling round a rock in a stream. Quite a ghastly tug of war I had for him with them. Every time they had him to their side he'd give one of those little grunts Chard was talking about, but then I'd pull like mad, and when I had him more to me he'd look up and say in a cheery way, 'Much obliged, sir.' In the end, they began to swarm over the walls all about us and I had to let him go to draw my pistol. I told him I was sorry—I fancied he'd be in a bad panic, you know—but he just said, 'Not at all, sir,' and 'Thank you kindly, sir.'"

Bromhead paused.

"I was going to write to his people. Say how sorry I was I couldn't save him. But dashed if he didn't join up under a false name. A lot of the Welshmen do, it seems. For a long time I thought they were all just called Evans and Williams and Jones and what-have-you, but it turns out that those are just the most obvious false names for them to choose. His blamed leg—you know, I can't get it out of my mind, how remarkably warm it was."

He sat back, and the batman took the opportunity to step forward with the port. Bromhead watched in silence as the glasses filled with redness.

Wilby had managed a few quiet expulsions, but then came the surprising and ruinous fart.

The silence around the table seemed to go on for hours—Wilby could hear the pickets calling out their challenge to the final patrols of the evening. Finally Bromhead looked over and said genially, "Preserved potatoes." He shook his head. "Make you fart like a confounded horse."

He waved his man forward with the cigars, and as they passed around he leaned in toward the table and looked around at them all.

"Reminds me of a story," he said, cutting the end of his cigar. "I haven't thought of it in years, mind you—about a bally Latin class, of all things." He ran the end of the cigar around his tongue and raised his chin for the batman to light him. "Hardly the story you expected to hear, but I'll beg your indulgence." He took a mighty puff and began.

"Well, we had this old tyrant of a master—Marlow, his name was—of the habit of making us work at our books in silence every other afternoon. Any noise and he would beat you with a steel ruler that he carried from his days in the navy. Now that was fear. I swear it was rumored among us—a rumor spread no doubt by older lads to put a fright on us—that boys had lost fingers, chopped clean off at the knuckle by that ruler.

"I must have been upwards of twelve or so. I can't recall quite the circumstances, but I'd bent over from my desk to retrieve a pen I'd dropped—or more likely some blighter had thrown—on the floor. We were always trying to get some other poor bugger to make a sound and bring down the tyrant's wrath upon his head, but anyhow, as I say, I'd bent over to pick up my pen—I was in the middle of translating 'Horatio on the Bridge' or some such rot—and what do you know but I farted. Quite surprised myself. Quite taken aback, I was. Not that it was an especially, you know, loud one. More of a pop really. Or a squeak. Hang me if that's not it either. Let's just say somewhere between a pop and a squeak. Hardly a decent fart at all—if the truth be told, it's rather astonishing I can remember it so well. No matter. Whatever the precise sound of the expulsion, in that room with everyone trying to be still it was like a bally pistol shot, like the crack of a whip.

"Well, the fellows behind me, of course, went off into absolute fits and gales. Up jumps the tyrant, brandishing his ruler, and I fancy I'm for the high jump now. The whole room falls silent as the grave as the old man stalks up the aisle between our desks, looking hard all about him.

"'John Beddows,' he says to one of the chaps behind me, and his voice is veritable steel, 'would you mind telling me what is the source of this hilarity?'

"'Nothing, sir,' says John—a decent enough sort, loafer that he was—and I begin to think I might be spared, but dash me if the old man doesn't persist.

"'Nothing,' he says. 'You had to be laughing at something, boy. Only idiots laugh at nothing. Are you an idiot, Mister Beddows?' And he bent that ruler in his hands.

"'No, sir,' says John, pulling a long face. 'Please, sir. Gonville Bromhead farted, sir.'"

Wilby glanced around the table and saw that Ferguson was grinning broadly, his teeth showing around his cigar. The chaplain, too, was struggling to keep a straight face, and even Major Black had a curious look in his eye. Only Chard showed no glimmer of humor. He had stubbed out his cigar and taken an apple, which he was chewing steadily.

"Of course," Bromhead went on, "you can imagine the pandemonium. You'd have thought there was a murder in progress, and to be honest I could have cheerfully strangled Beddows. I let out a swear or two under my breath, but the tyrant himself was at a loss for a moment. All I could do was snatch my hands up from where they'd been lying on the desk and press them into my pockets.

"'Silence!' the tyrant finally bellowed, and then, with me cringing, 'That's quite enough drollery, gentlemen. Back to work. All of you.'

"Of course, it was only a reprieve of sorts. The worst was still to come. By and by we came out for our break and the other chaps started up a game of tag. I was too angry or ashamed to join them. I took myself off to a corner of the yard and watched. One person would be on, his tie would be undone, and he'd tag another, who'd also pull his tie open, and they'd keep tagging until they all had their ties hanging loose. Only when some of them ran closer to me did I catch the name of the game. 'Funky Farters.'" Bromhead looked around him, his face a mask of tragedy.

"That dashed game became the craze at school for months, although I can tell you I never played it. I had dreams, nightmares really, of boys going home at the holidays and teaching it to their friends and in this way the detestable game—and my disgrace—spreading to every durned school in England. Can you imagine? I couldn't shake the notion. I thought with certitude that affair would be the only thing I'd be known for in my whole life. I thought, *I'll die and my only lasting contribution to this life will be a fart in a confounded Latin class.*"

The table was roaring with laughter by now, the chaplain dabbing at his eyes with his napkin, Ferguson clutching his sides, and the major positively braying. Ash from the almost extinguished cigar in his hand peppered the table as he shook. Wilby found himself laughing too, uncontrollably relieved. He caught Bromhead's eye and the older lieutenant nodded.

The meal broke up shortly after—the major's patrol would have to leave camp at first light—and the men went out into the night to find their own tents. Bromhead leaned back in his chair and watched the major sidle up to Wilby and Ferguson and say, "I remember once letting loose a mighty one on parade in India," and the two young officers staggered with laughter. The chaplain was the last to leave. He smiled at Bromhead and shook his head. "An edifying tale." Then he hurried after the other three, and Bromhead saw him put an arm around Wilby's shoulder.

Only Chard stalked off alone, his back straight and his chin held high. "Now that man," Bromhead said to his batman, "mark my words, has never farted in his life. It'd break his back to let rip now." He lit another cigar and smoked it thoughtfully while the batman cleared the plates from the table.

"It's a terrible thing being afraid, Watkins, do you not think?"

The batman said he thought it was.

"Join me," Bromhead said, and he poured out two glasses of the celebrated port and they sat and drank in silence for a moment.

"Bloody rum thing. Zulus thinking to find a fellow's soul in his entrails, eh?"

The batman nodded. The port tasted like syrup to him, and later he would need a swig of his squareface—the army-issue gin in its square bottle—to take the taste away.

It was late, and the light breeze through the tent felt cold to Bromhead. He always took more of a chill when he'd been drinking. He pulled a blanket off the cot behind him and draped it around his shoulders. "Like an old woman," he said. He wrapped his arms around himself under the blanket, clutching his shoulders, and thought again how really remarkably *warm* Private Williams's leg had felt.

"Wake me," he said to the batman, "before the major's patrol leaves in the morning. I think I should like to see them off."

Exercises for Peter Ho Davies's "Relief."

1. Set an incident of this tale in (a) the Civil War, (b) the Wild West, or (c) Vietnam.

2. Change the affliction to (a) hiccoughs, (b) Tourette's syndrome, or (c) bulimia.

3. Continue Chard's speech on bravery for two additional paragraphs. Have Ferguson respond.

4. Let Bromhead write a letter home, describing the dawn sortie and the need for additional port.

5. Wilby, at sixty, remembers his own flatulence and tries to console a young soldier who has just befouled his pants. Write the scene.

6. Tell the final sequence from the "batman's" point of view.

7. Have Wilby attend the dinner unshaven; provide a discussion of beard growth and how Ferguson waxes his moustache points and what the half-deaf Bromhead hears. Look at the movie *Zulu* and include this as a scene.

8. Have the officers make fun of Bromhead; look at Joseph Conrad's "Heart of Darkness" and have the character of Marlow remember this story too.

9. Be an outraged conservative parent who writes the local school board that this story is immoral and writes the local library that it should be banned.

10. Pitch an ad campaign for bladder and bowel control; use images from "Relief."

HOW TO DATE A BROWNGIRL, BLACKGIRL, WHITEGIRL, OR HALFIE
by Junot Diaz

Wait for your brother and your mother to leave the apartment. You've already told them that you're feeling too sick to go to Union City to visit that tía who likes to squeeze your nuts. (He's gotten big, she'll say.) And even though your moms knows you ain't sick you stuck to your story until finally she said, Go ahead and stay, malcriado.

Clear the government cheese from the refrigerator. If the girl's from the Terrace stack the boxes behind the milk. If she's from the Park or Society Hill hide the cheese in the cabinet above the oven, way up where she'll never see. Leave yourself a reminder to get it out before morning or your moms will kick your ass. Take down any embarrassing photos of your family in the campo, especially the one with the half-naked kids dragging a goat on a rope leash. The kids are your cousins and by now they're old enough to understand why you're doing what you're doing. Hide the pictures of yourself with an Afro. Make sure the bathroom is presentable. Put the basket with all the crapped-on toilet paper under the sink. Spray the bucket with Lysol, then close the cabinet.

Shower, comb, dress. Sit on the couch and watch TV. If she's an outsider her father will be bringing her, maybe her mother. Neither of them want her seeing any boys from the Terrace—people get stabbed in the Terrace—but she's strong-headed and this time will get her way. If she's a whitegirl you know you'll at least get a hand job.

The directions were in your best handwriting, so her parents won't think you're an idiot. Get up from the couch and check the parking lot. Nothing. If the girl's local, don't sweat it. She'll flow over when she's good and ready. Sometimes she'll run into her other friends and a whole crowd will show up at your apartment and even though that means you ain't getting shit it will be fun anyway and you'll wish these people would come over more often. Sometimes the girl won't flow over at all and the next day in school she'll say sorry, smile and you'll be stupid enough to believe her and ask her out again.

Wait and after an hour go out to your corner. The neighborhood is full of traffic. Give one of your boys a shout and when he says, Are you still waiting on that bitch? say, Hell yeah.

Get back inside. Call her house and when her father picks up ask if she's there. He'll ask, Who is this? Hang up. He sounds like a principal or a police chief, the sort of dude with a big neck, who never has to watch his back. Sit and wait. By the time your stomach's ready to give out on you, a Honda or maybe a Jeep pulls in and out she comes.

Hey, you'll say.

Look, she'll say. My mom wants to meet you. She's got herself all worried about nothing.

Don't panic. Say, Hey, no problem. Run a hand through your hair like the whiteboys do even though the only thing that runs easily through your hair is Africa. She will look good. The white ones are the ones you want the most, aren't they, but usually the out-of-towners are black, blackgirls who grew up with ballet and Girl Scouts, who have three cars in their driveways. If she's a halfie don't be surprised that her mother is white. Say, Hi. Her moms will say hi and you'll see that you don't scare her, not really. She will say that she needs easier directions to get out and even though she has the best directions in her lap give her new ones. Make her happy.

You have choices. If the girl's from around the way, take her to El Cibao for dinner. Order everything in your busted-up Spanish. Let her correct you if she's Latina and amaze her if she's black. If she's not from around the way, Wendy's will do. As you walk to the restaurant talk about school. A local girl won't need stories about the neighborhood but the other ones might. Supply the story about the loco who'd been storing canisters of tear gas in his basement for years, how one day the canisters cracked and the whole neighborhood got a dose of the military-strength stuff. Don't tell her that your moms knew right away what it was, that she recognized its smell from the year the United States invaded your island.

Hope that you don't run into your nemesis, Howie, the Puerto Rican kid with the two killer mutts. He walks them all over the neighborhood and every now and then the mutts corner themselves a cat and tear it to shreds, Howie laughing as the cat flips up in the air, its neck twisted around like an owl, red meat showing through the soft fur. If his dogs haven't cornered a cat, he will walk behind you and ask, Hey, Yunior, is that your new fuckbuddy?

Let him talk. Howie weighs about two hundred pounds and could eat you if he wanted. At the field he will turn away. He has new sneakers, and doesn't want them muddy. If the girl's an outsider she will hiss now and say, What a fucking asshole. A homegirl would have been yelling back at him the whole time, unless she was shy. Either way don't feel bad that you didn't do anything. Never lose a fight on a first date or that will be the end of it.

Dinner will be tense. You are not good at talking to people you don't know. A halfie will tell you that her parents met in the Movement, will say, Back then people thought it a radical thing to do. It will sound like something her parents made her memorize. Your brother once heard that one and said, Man, that sounds like a whole lot of Uncle Tomming to me. Don't repeat this.

Put down your hamburger and say, It must have been hard.

She will appreciate your interest. She will tell you more. Black people, she will say, treat me real bad. That's why I don't like them. You'll wonder how she feels about Dominicans. Don't ask. Let her speak on it and when you're both finished eating walk back into the neighborhood. The skies will be magnificent. Pollutants have made Jersey sunsets one of the wonders of the world. Point it out. Touch her shoulder and say, That's nice, right?

Get serious. Watch TV but stay alert. Sip some of the Bermúdez your father left in the cabinet, which nobody touches. A local girl may have hips and a thick ass but she won't be quick about letting you touch. She has to live in the same neighborhood you do, has to deal with you being all up in her business. She might just chill with you and then go home. She might kiss you and then go, or she might, if she's reckless, give it up, but that's rare. Kissing will suffice. A whitegirl might just give it up right then. Don't stop her. She'll take her gum out of her mouth, stick it to the plastic sofa covers and then will move close to you. You have nice eyes, she might say.

Tell her that you love her hair, that you love her skin, her lips, because, in truth, you love them more than you love your own.

She'll say, I like Spanish guys, and even though you've never been to Spain, say, I like you. You'll sound smooth.

You'll be with her until about eight-thirty and then she will want to wash up. In the bathroom she will hum a song from the radio and her waist will keep the beat against the lip of the sink. Imagine her old lady coming to get her, what she would say if she knew her daughter had just lain under you and blown your name, pronounced with her eighth-grade Spanish, into your ear. While she's in the bathroom call one of your boys and say, Lo hice, loco. Or just sit back on the couch and smile.

But usually it won't work this way. Be prepared. She will not want to kiss you. Just cool it, she'll say. The halfie might lean back, breaking away from you. She will cross her arms, say, I hate my tits. Stroke her hair but she will pull away. I don't like anybody touching my hair, she will say. She will act like somebody you don't know. In school she is known for her attention-grabbing laugh, as high and far-ranging as a gull, but here she will worry you. You will not know what to say.

You're the only kind of guy who asks me out, she will say. Your neighbors will start their hyena calls, now that the alcohol is in them. You and the blackboys.

Say nothing. Let her button her shirt, let her comb her hair, the sound of it stretching like a sheet of fire between you. When her father pulls in and beeps, let her go without too much of a good-bye. She won't want it. During the next hour the phone will ring. You will be tempted to pick it up. Don't. Watch the shows you want to watch, without a family around to debate you. Don't go downstairs. Don't fall asleep. It won't help. Put the government cheese back in its place before your moms kills you.

▨ Exercises for Junot Diaz's, "How to Date a Browngirl, Blackgirl, Whitegirl, or Halfie."

1. Imagine that you're Lorrie Moore reading this imitation of your work and try to decide if you're pleased or displeased. Write Junot Diaz a letter, as Moore ("Dear Junot . . ."), and make it a critical letter, or a fan's.

2. Write Lorrie Moore a letter ("Dear Lorrie . . .") from Junot Diaz's point of view, explaining why you borrowed her formula and in what spirit you copied her title. Tell her, for instance, that Peter Ho Davies did the same in "How to Be an Expatriate" and then explain how far, here, your tongue was in cheek.

3. Rewrite this story as "How to Date a Widow, a Divorcee, Your Best Friend's Girlfriend, Your Business Partner's Fiancée."

4. Describe the attempted seduction from the girls' point of view. In the voice of (a) a browngirl, (b) a blackgirl, (c) a whitegirl, or (d) a halfie. Then have the four of them meet in the locker room and discuss the "date" together.

5. Transpose the first two pages of this story from the second-person point of view to the first.

6. Transpose the last two pages of this story from the second-person point of view to the third.

7. Describe the neighborhood—its sociology, economy, ethnic mix, crime rate, etc.—in the omniscient authorial mode.

8. Have "your" brother and mother talk about what you're up to while they go to Union City and visit your aunt. Do this scene entirely in dialogue.

9. Have the narrator of this story, a father now, talk to his own son or daughter about the parties/escapades/temptations of youth. Do so as a warning or, alternatively, as a boast.

10. Write about the truths of self-loathing and desire buried in a sentence such as: "Tell her that you love her hair, that you love her skin, her lips, because, in truth, you love them more than you love your own." Does he mean this and what does it mean?

WE DIDN'T

by Stuart Dybek

> We did it in front of the mirror
> And in the light. We did it in darkness,
> In water, and in the high grass.
> — *"We Did It," Yehuda Amichai*

We didn't in the light; we didn't in darkness. We didn't in the fresh-cut summer grass or in the mounds of autumn leaves or on the snow where moonlight threw down our shadows. We didn't in your room on the canopy bed you slept in, the bed you'd slept in as a child, or in the back seat of my father's rusted Rambler which smelled of the smoked chubs and kielbasa that he delivered on weekends from my Uncle Vincent's meat market. We didn't in your mother's Buick Eight where a rosary twined the rearview mirror like a beaded black snake with silver, cruciform fangs.

At the dead end of our lovers' lane—a side street of abandoned factories—where I perfected the pinch that springs open a bra; behind the lilac bushes in Marquette Park where you first touched me through my jeans and your nipples, swollen against transparent cotton, seemed the shade of lilacs; in the balcony of the now defunct Clark Theater where I wiped popcorn salt from my palms and slid them up your thighs and you whispered, "I feel like Doris Day is watching us," we didn't.

How adept we were at fumbling, how perfectly mistimed our timing, how utterly we confused energy with ecstasy.

Remember that night becalmed by heat, and the two of us, fused by sweat, trembling as if a wind from outer space that only we could feel was gusting across Oak Street Beach? Wound in your faded Navajo blanket, we lay soul kissing until you wept with wanting.

We'd been kissing all day—all summer—kisses tasting of different shades of lip gloss and too many Cokes. The lake had turned hot pink, rose rapture, pearl amethyst with dusk, then washed in night black with a ruff of silver foam.

Beyond a momentary horizon, silent bolts of heat lightning throbbed, perhaps setting barns on fire somewhere in Indiana. The beach that had been so crowded was deserted as if there was a curfew. Only the bodies of lovers remained behind, visible in lightning flashes, scattered like the fallen on a battlefield, a few of them moaning, waiting for the gulls to pick them clean.

On my fingers your slick scent mixed with the coconut musk of the suntan lotion we'd repeatedly smeared over one another's bodies. When your bikini top fell away, my hands caught your breasts, memorizing their delicate weight, my palms cupped as if bringing water to parched lips.

Along the Gold Coast, high-rises began to glow, window added to window, against the dark. In every lighted bedroom, couples home from work were stripping off their business suits, falling to the bed, and doing it. They did it before mirrors and pressed against the glass in streaming shower stalls, they did it against walls and on the furniture in ways that required previously unimagined gymnastics which they invented on the spot. They did it in honor of man and woman, in honor of beast, in honor of God. They did it because they'd been released, because they were home free, alive, and private, because they couldn't wait any longer, couldn't wait for the appointed hour, for the right time or temperature, couldn't wait for the future, for messiahs, for peace on earth and justice for all. They did it because of the Bomb, because of pollution, because of the Four Horsemen of the Apocalypse, because extinction might be just a blink away. They did it because it was Friday night. It was Friday night and somewhere delirious music was playing—flutter-tongued flutes, muted trumpets meowing like tomcats in heat, feverish plucking and twanging, tomtoms, congas, and gongs all pounding the same pulsebeat.

I stripped your bikini bottom down the skinny rails of your legs and you tugged my swimsuit past my tan. Swimsuits at our ankles, we kicked like swimmers to free our legs, almost expecting a tide to wash over us the way the tide rushes in on Burt Lancaster and Deborah Kerr in their famous love scene on the beach in *From Here to Eternity*—a scene so famous that although neither of us had seen the movie, our bodies assumed the exact position of movie stars on the sand and you whispered to me softly, "I'm afraid of getting pregnant," and I whispered back, "Don't worry, I have protection," then, still kissing you, felt for my discarded cutoffs and the wallet in which for the last several months I had carried a Trojan as if it was a talisman. Still kissing, I tore its flattened, dried-out wrapper and it sprang through my fingers like a spring from a clock and dropped to the sand between our legs. My hands were shaking. In a panic, I groped for it, found it, tried to dust it off, tried, as Burt Lancaster never had to, to slip it on without breaking the mood, felt the grains of sand inside it, a throb of lightning, and the Great Lake behind us became, for all practical purposes, the Pacific and your skin tasted of salt and to the insistent question that my hips were asking, your body answered yes, your thighs opened like wings from my waist as we surfaced panting from a kiss that left you pleading *oh Christ yes,* a yes gasped sharply as a cry of pain so that for a moment I thought that we *were* already doing it and that somehow I had missed the instant when I entered you, entered you in the bloodless way in which a young man discards his own virginity, entered you as if passing through a gateway into the rest of my life, into a life as I wanted it to be lived *yes* but O then I realized that we were still floundering unconnected in the slick between us and there was sand in the Trojan as we slammed together still feeling for that perfect fit, still in the *Here* groping for an *Eternity* that was only a fine adjustment away, just a millimeter to the left or a fraction of an inch further south though with all the adjusting the sandy Trojan was slipping off and then it was gone but yes you kept repeating although your head was shaking no-not-quite-almost and our hearts were going like mad and you said yes Yes wait . . . Stop!

"What?" I asked, still futilely thrusting as if I hadn't quite heard you.

"Oh, God!" you gasped, pushing yourself up. "What's coming?"

"Julie, what's the matter?" I asked, confused, and then the beam of a spotlight swept over us and I glanced into its blinding eye.

All around us lights were coming, speeding across the sand. Blinking blindness away, I rolled from your body to my knees, feeling utterly defenseless in the way that only nakedness can leave one feeling. Headlights bounded toward us, spotlights crisscrossing, blue dome lights revolving as squad cars converged. I could see other lovers, caught in the beams, fleeing bare-assed through the litter of garbage that daytime hordes had left behind and that night had deceptively concealed. You were crying, clutching the Navajo blanket to your breasts with one hand and clawing for your bikini with the other, and I was trying to calm your terror with reassuring phrases such as, "Holy shit! I don't fucking believe this!"

Swerving and fishtailing in the sand, police calls pouring from their radios, the squad cars were on us, and then they were by us while we sat struggling on our clothes.

They braked at the water's edge, and cops slammed out brandishing huge flashlights, their beams deflecting over the dark water. Beyond the darting of those beams, the far-off throbs of lightning seemed faint by comparison.

"Over there, goddamn it!" one of them hollered, and two cops sloshed out into the shallow water without even pausing to kick off their shoes, huffing aloud for breath, their leather cartridge belts creaking against their bellies.

"Grab the son of a bitch! It ain't gonna bite!" one of them yelled, then they came sloshing back to shore with a body slung between them.

It was a woman—young, naked, her body limp and bluish beneath the play of flashlight beams. They set her on the sand just past the ring of drying, washed-up alewives. Her face was almost totally concealed by her hair. Her hair was brown and tangled in a way that even wind or sleep can't tangle hair, tangled as if it had absorbed the ripples of water—thick strands, slimy-looking like dead seaweed.

"She's been in there a while, that's for sure," a cop with a beer belly said to a younger, crew-cut cop who had knelt beside the body and removed his hat as if he might be considering the kiss of life.

The crew-cut officer brushed the hair away from her face and the flashlight beams settled there. Her eyes were closed. A bruise or a birthmark stained the side of one eye. Her features appeared swollen—her lower lip protruding as if she was pouting.

An ambulance siren echoed across the sand, its revolving red light rapidly approaching.

"Might as well take their sweet-ass time," the beer-bellied cop said.

We had joined the circle of police surrounding the drowned woman almost without realizing that we had. You were back in your bikini, robed in the Navajo blanket, and I had slipped on my cutoffs, my underwear still dangling out of a back pocket.

Their flashlight beams explored her body, causing its whiteness to gleam. Her breasts were floppy; her nipples looked shriveled. Her belly appeared inflated by gallons of water. For a moment, a beam focused on her mound of pubic hair which was overlapped by the swell of her belly, and then moved almost shyly away down her legs, and the cops all glanced at us—at you, especially—above their lights, and you hugged your blanket closer as if they might confiscate it as evidence or to use as a shroud.

When the ambulance pulled up, one of the black attendants immediately put a stethoscope to the drowned woman's swollen belly and announced, "Drowned the baby, too."

Without saying anything, we turned from the group, as unconsciously as we'd joined them, and walked off across the sand, stopping only long enough at the spot where we had lain together like lovers in order to stuff the rest of our gear into a beach bag, to gather our shoes, and for me to find my wallet and kick sand over the forlorn, deflated-looking Trojan that you pretended not to notice. I was grateful for that.

Behind us, the police were snapping photos, flashbulbs throbbing like lightning flashes, and the lightning itself still distant but moving in closer, thunder rumbling audibly now, driving a lake wind before it so that gusts of sand tingled against the metal sides of the ambulance.

Squinting, we walked toward the lighted windows of the Gold Coast, while the shadows of gapers attracted by the whirling emergency lights hurried past up toward the shore.

"What happened? What's going on?" they asked us as they passed without waiting for an answer, and we didn't offer one, just continued walking silently in the dark.

It was only later that we talked about it, and once we began talking about the drowned woman it seemed we couldn't stop.

"She was pregnant," you said. "I mean I don't want to sound morbid, but I can't help thinking how the whole time we were, we almost—you know—there was this poor dead woman and her unborn child washing in and out behind us."

"It's not like we could have done anything for her even if we had known she was there."

"But what if we *had* found her? What if after we had—you know," you said, your eyes glancing away from mine and your voice tailing into a whisper, "what if after we did it, we went for a night swim and found her in the water?"

"But, Jules, we didn't," I tried to reason, though it was no more a matter of reason than anything else between us had ever been.

It began to seem as if each time we went somewhere to make out—on the back porch of your half-deaf, whiskery Italian grandmother who sat in the front of the apartment cackling before *I Love Lucy* reruns; or in your girlfriend Ginny's basement rec room when her parents were away on bowling league nights and Ginny was upstairs with her current crush, Brad; or way off in the burbs, at the Giant Twin Drive-In during the weekend they called Elvis Fest—the drowned woman was with us.

We would kiss, your mouth would open, and when your tongue flicked repeatedly after mine, I would unbutton the first button of your blouse, revealing the beauty spot at the base of your throat which matched a smaller spot I loved above a corner of your lips, and then the second button that opened on a delicate gold cross—that I had always tried to regard as merely a fashion statement—dangling above the cleft of your breasts. The third button exposed the lacy swell of your bra, and I would slide my hand over the patterned mesh, feeling for the firmness of your nipple rising to my fingertip, but you would pull slightly away, and behind your rapid breath your kiss would grow distant, and I would kiss harder trying to lure you back from wherever you had gone, and finally, holding you as if only consoling a friend, I'd ask, "What are you thinking?" although, of course, I knew.

"I don't want to think about her but I can't help it. I mean it seems like some kind of weird omen or something, you know?"

"No, I don't know," I said. "It was just a coincidence."

"Maybe if she'd been further away down the beach, but she was so close to us. A good wave could have washed her up right beside us."

"Great, then we could have had a *ménage à trois*."

"Gross! I don't believe you just said that! Just because you said it in French doesn't make it less disgusting."

"You're driving me to it. Come on, Jules, I'm sorry," I said, "I was just making a dumb joke to get a little different perspective on things."

"What's so goddamn funny about a woman who drowned herself and her baby?"

"We don't even know for sure she did."

"Yeah, right, it was just an accident. Like she just happened to be going for a walk pregnant and naked, and she fell in."

"She could have been on a sailboat or something. Accidents happen; so do murders."

"Oh, like murder makes it less horrible? Don't think that hasn't occurred to me. Maybe the bastard who knocked her up killed her, huh?"

"How should I know? You're the one who says you don't want to talk about it and then gets obsessed with all kinds of theories and scenarios. Why are we arguing about a woman we don't even know, who doesn't have the slightest thing to do with us?"

"I *do* know about her," you said. "I dream about her."

"You dream about her?" I repeated, surprised. "Dreams you remember?"

"Sometimes they wake me up. Like I dreamed I was at my nonna's cottage in Michigan. Off her beach they've got a raft for swimming and in my dream I'm swimming out to it, but it keeps drifting further away until it's way out on the water and I'm so tired that if I don't get to it I'm going to drown. Then, I notice there's a naked person sunning on it and I start yelling, 'Help!' and she looks up, brushes her hair out of her face, and offers me a hand, but I'm too afraid to take it even though I'm drowning because it's her."

"God! Jules, that's creepy."

"I dreamed you and I were at the beach and you bring us a couple hot dogs but forget the mustard, so you have to go all the way back to the stand for it."

"Hot dogs, no mustard—a little too Freudian, isn't it?"

"Honest to God, I dreamed it. You go off for mustard and I'm wondering why you're gone so long, then a woman screams a kid has drowned and immediately the entire crowd stampedes for the water and sweeps me along with it. It's like one time when I was little and got lost at the beach, wandering in a panic through this forest of hairy legs and pouchy crotches, crying for my mother. Anyway, I'm carried into the water by the mob and forced under, and I think, this is it, I'm going to drown, but I'm able to hold my breath longer than could ever be possible. It feels like a flying dream—flying under water—and then I see this baby down there flying, too, and realize it's the kid everyone thinks has drowned, but he's no more drowned than I am. He looks like Cupid or one of those baby angels that cluster around the face of God."

"Pretty weird. What do you think it means? Something to do with drowning maybe, or panic?"

"It means the baby who drowned inside her that night was a love child—a boy—and his soul was released there to wander through the water."

"You really believe that?"

We argued about the interpretation of dreams, about whether dreams were symbolic or psychic, prophetic or just plain nonsense, until you said, "Look, you can believe what you want about your dreams, but keep your nose out of mine, O.K.?"

We argued about the drowned woman, about whether her death was a suicide or a murder, about whether her appearance that night was an omen or a coincidence, which, you argued, is what an omen is anyway: a coincidence that means something. By the end of summer, even if we were no longer arguing about the woman, we had acquired the habit of arguing about everything else. What was better: dogs or cats, rock or jazz, Cubs or Sox, tacos or egg rolls, right or left, night or day—we could argue about anything.

It no longer required arguing or necking to summon the drowned woman; everywhere we went she surfaced by her own volition: at Rocky's Italian Beef, at Lindo Mexico, at the House of Dong, our favorite Chinese restaurant, a place we still frequented because they had let us sit and talk until late over tiny cups of jasmine tea and broken fortune cookies earlier in the year, when it was winter and we had first started going together. We would always kid about going there. "Are you in the mood for Dong tonight?" I'd ask. It was a dopey joke, and you'd break up at its repeated dopiness. Back then, in winter, if one of us ordered the garlic shrimp, we would both be sure to eat them so that later our mouths tasted the same when we kissed.

Even when she wasn't mentioned, she was there with her drowned body— so dumpy next to yours—and her sad breasts with their wrinkled nipples and sour milk—so saggy beside yours which were still budding—with her swollen belly and her pubic bush colorless in the glare of electric light, with her tangled, slimy hair and her pouting, placid face—so lifeless beside yours—and her skin a pallid white, lightning-flash white, flashbulb white, a whiteness that couldn't be duplicated in daylight—how I'd come to hate that pallor, so cold beside the flush of your skin.

There wasn't a particular night when we finally broke up, just as there wasn't a particular night when we began going together, but I do remember a night in fall when I guessed that it was over. We were parked in the Rambler at the dead end of the street of factories that had been our lovers' lane, listening to a drizzle of rain and dry leaves sprinkle the hood. As always, rain revitalized the smells of the smoked fish and kielbasa in the upholstery. The radio was on too low to hear, the windshield wipers swished at intervals as if we were driving, and the windows were steamed as if we'd been making out. But we'd been arguing as usual, this time about a woman poet who had committed suicide, whose work you were reading. We were sitting, no longer talking or touching, and I remember thinking that I didn't want to argue with you anymore. I didn't want to sit like this in silence; I wanted to talk excitedly all night as we once had, I wanted to find some way that wasn't corny-sounding to tell you how much fun I'd had in your company, how much knowing you had meant to me, and how I had suddenly realized that I'd been so intent on becoming lovers that I'd overlooked how close we'd been as friends. I wanted you to know that. I wanted you to like me again.

"It's sad," I started to say, meaning that I was sorry we had reached a point of sitting silently together, but before I could continue, you challenged the statement.

"What makes you so sure it's sad?"

"What do you mean, what makes me so sure?" I asked, confused by your question, and surprised there could be anything to argue over no matter what you thought I was talking about.

You looked at me as if what was sad was that I would never understand. "For all either one of us knows," you said, "she could have been triumphant!"

Maybe when it really ended was that night when I felt we had just reached the beginning, that one time on the beach in the summer between high school and college, when our bodies rammed together so desperately that for a moment I thought we did it, and maybe in our hearts we had, although for me, then, doing it in one's heart didn't quite count. If it did, I suppose we'd all be Casanovas.

I remember riding home together on the El that night, feeling sick and defeated in a way I was embarrassed to mention. Our mute reflections emerged like negative exposures on the dark, greasy window of the train. Lightning branched over the city and when the train entered the subway tunnel, the lights inside flickered as if the power was disrupted although the train continued rocketing beneath the Loop.

When the train emerged again we were on the South Side and it was pouring, a deluge as if the sky had opened to drown the innocent and guilty alike. We hurried from the El station to your house, holding the Navajo blanket over our heads until, soaked, it collapsed. In the dripping doorway of your apartment building, we said goodnight. You were shivering. Your bra showed through the thin blouse plastered to your skin. I swept the wet hair away from your face and kissed you lightly on the lips, then you turned and went inside. I stepped into the rain and you came back out calling after me.

"What?" I asked, feeling a surge of gladness to be summoned back into the doorway with you.

"Want an umbrella?"

I didn't. The downpour was letting up. It felt better to walk back to the El feeling the rain rinse the sand out of my hair, off my legs, until the only places where I could still feel its grit was the crotch of my cutoffs and in each squish of my shoes. A block down the street, I passed a pair of Jockey shorts lying in a puddle and realized they were mine, dropped from my back pocket as we ran to your house. I left them behind, wondering if you'd see them and recognize them the next day.

By the time I had climbed the stairs back to the El platform, the rain had stopped. Your scent still hadn't washed from my fingers. The station—the entire city, it seemed—dripped and steamed. The summer sound of crickets and nighthawks echoed from the drenched neighborhood. Alone, I could admit how sick I felt. For you, it was a night that would haunt your dreams. For me, it was another night when I waited, swollen and aching, for what I had secretly nicknamed the Blue Ball Express.

Literally lovesick, groaning inwardly with each lurch of the train and worried that I was damaged for good, I peered out at the passing yellow-lit stations where lonely men stood posted before giant advertisements, pictures of glamorous models defaced by graffiti—the same old scrawled insults and pleas: FUCK YOU, EAT ME. At this late hour the world seemed given over to men without women, men waiting in abject patience for something indeterminate, the way I waited for our next times. I avoided their eyes so that they wouldn't see the pity in mine, pity for them because I'd just been with you, your scent was still on my hands, and there seemed to be so much future ahead.

For me it was another night like that, and by the time I reached my stop I knew I would be feeling better, recovered enough to walk the dark street home making up poems of longing that I never wrote down. I was the D. H. Lawrence of not doing it, the voice of all the would-be lovers who ached and squirmed but still hadn't. From our contortions in doorways, on stairwells, and in the bucket seats of cars we could have composed a *Kama Sutra* of interrupted bliss. It must have been that night when I recalled all the other times of walking home after seeing you, so that it seemed as if I was falling into step behind a parade of my former selves—myself walking home on the night we first kissed, myself on the night when I unbuttoned your blouse and kissed your breasts, myself on the night that I lifted your skirt above your thighs and dropped to my knees—each succeeding self another step closer to that irrevocable moment for which our lives seemed poised.

But we didn't, not in the moonlight, or by the phosphorescent lanterns of lightning bugs in your backyard, not beneath the constellations that we couldn't see, let alone decipher, nor in the dark glow that had replaced the real darkness of night, a darkness already stolen from us; not with the skyline rising behind us while the city gradually decayed, not in the heat of summer while a Cold War raged; despite the freedom of youth and the license of first love—because of fate, karma, luck, what does it matter?—we made not doing it a wonder, and yet we didn't, we didn't, we never did.

▨ Exercises for Stuart Dybek's "We Didn't."

1. Notice the lyricism and rhythm of Dybek's prose, the almost incantatory effect of the refrain, "we didn't." Choose a few pages and rewrite them, breaking up sentences and rephrasing things to remove this fluidity and rhythm. What happens to the story?

2. Atmosphere. Change the time and setting of the story to Los Angeles, 1992, or Miami, 2000. Alter the cultural references—Elvis Fest, the Bomb, *From Here to Eternity*—accordingly. What follows?

3. Have something else wash up on shore, or have the washed up body be that of a woman who isn't pregnant. Re-create the ending from that point onward.

4. Change the refrain to "we did it . . ." and see what becomes of the story.

5. Locate Yehuda Amichai's "We Did It" and analyze the relationship between the two texts.

6. Change the "you" of the story to a third-person "her." Rewrite the story from Jules's perspective.

7. Rewrite the crucial scene on the beach, but without any cops, squad cars, or headlights. Have all the lovers on the beach discover the body in relative silence.

8. Write the story in the present tense.

9. Rewrite the story, having nothing wash up on the beach to interrupt them. What becomes of this couple?

10. Write the story of the narrator's eventual first sexual experience with someone else. Is the drowned girl on his mind? Write Jules's first experience, asking the same question.

IN THE CEMETERY WHERE
AL JOLSON IS BURIED
by Amy Hempel

for Jessica

"Tell me things I won't mind forgetting," she said. "Make it useless stuff or skip it."

I began. I told her insects fly through rain, missing every drop, never getting wet. I told her no one in America owned a tape recorder before Bing Crosby did. I told her the shape of the moon is like a banana—you see it looking full, you're seeing it end-on.

The camera made me self-conscious and I stopped. It was trained on us from a ceiling mount—the kind of camera banks use to photograph robbers. It played our image to the nurses down the hall in Intensive Care.

"Go on, girl," she said, "you get used to it."

I had my audience. I went on. Did she know that Tammy Wynette had changed her tune? Really. That now she sings "Stand By Your *Friends*"? Paul Anka did it too, I said. Does "You're Having *Our* Baby." He got sick of all that feminist bitching.

"What else?" she said. "Have you got something else?"

Oh yes. For her I would always have something else.

"Did you know when they taught the first chimp to talk, it lied? When they asked her who did it on the desk, she signed back Max, the janitor. And when they pressed her, she said she was sorry, that it was really the project director. But she was a mother, so I guess she had her reasons."

"Oh, that's good," she said. "A parable."

"There's more about the chimp," I said. "But it will break your heart."

"No thanks," she says, and scratches at her mask.

We look like good-guy outlaws. Good or bad, I am not used to the mask yet. I keep touching the warm spot where my breath, thank God, comes out. She is used to hers. She only ties the strings on top. The other ones—a pro by now—she lets hang loose.

We call this place the Marcus Welby Hospital. It's the white one with the palm trees under the opening credits of all those shows. A Hollywood hospital, though in fact it is several miles west. Off camera, there is a beach across the street.

She introduces me to a nurse as "the Best Friend." The impersonal article is more intimate. It tells me that *they* are intimate, my friend and her nurse.

"I was telling her we used to drink Canada Dry Ginger Ale and pretend we were in Canada."

"That's how dumb *we* were," I say.

"You could be sisters," the nurse says.

So how come, I'll bet they are wondering, it took me so long to get to such a glamorous place? But do they ask?

They do not ask.

Two months, and how long is the drive?

The best I can explain it is this—I have a friend who worked one summer in a mortuary. He used to tell me stories. The one that really got to me was not the grisliest, but it's the one that did. A man wrecked his car on 101 going south. He did not lose consciousness. But his arm was taken down to the wet bone—and when he looked at it—it scared him to death. I mean, he died.

So I didn't dare look any closer. But now I'm doing it—and hoping I won't be scared to death.

She shakes out a summer-weight blanket, showing a leg you did not want to see. Except for that, you look at her and understand the law that requires *two* people to be with the body at all times.

"I thought of something," she says. "I thought of it last night. I think there is a real and present need here. You know," she says, "like for someone to do it for you when you can't do it yourself. You call them up whenever you want—like when push comes to shove."

She grabs the bedside phone and loops the cord around her neck.

"Hey," she says, "the End o' the Line."

She keeps on, giddy with something. But I don't know with what.

"The giveaway was the solarium," she says. "That's where Marcus Welby broke the news to his patients. Then here's the real doctor suggesting we talk in the solarium. So I knew I was going to die.

"I can't remember," she says, "what does Kübler-Ross say comes after Denial?"

It seems to me Anger must be next. Then Bargaining, Depression, and so on and so forth. But I keep my guesses to myself.

"The only thing is," she says, "is where's Resurrection? God knows I want to do it by the book. But she left out Resurrection."

She laughs, and I cling to the sound the way someone dangling above a ravine holds fast to the thrown rope.

We could have cried then, but when we didn't, we couldn't.

"Tell me," she says, "about that chimp with the talking hands. What do they do when the thing ends and the chimp says, 'I don't want to go back to the zoo'?"

When I don't say anything, she says, "O.K.—then tell me another animal story. I like animal stories. But not a sick one—I don't want to know about all the Seeing Eye dogs going blind."

No, I would not tell her a sick one.

"How about the hearing-ear dogs?" I say. "They're not going deaf, but they are getting very judgmental. For instance, there's this golden retriever in Jersey, he wakes up the deaf mother and drags her into the daughter's room because the kid has got a flashlight and is reading under the covers."

"Oh, you're killing me," she says. "Yes, you're definitely killing me."

"They say the smart dog obeys, but the smarter dog knows when to *disobey*."

"Yes," she says, "the smarter *anything* knows when to disobey. Now, for example."

She is flirting with the Good Doctor, who has just appeared. Unlike the Bad Doctor, who checks the I.V. drip before saying good morning, the Good Doctor says things like "God didn't give epileptics a fair shake." He awards himself points for the cripples he could have hit in the parking lot. Because the Good Doctor is a little in love with her he says maybe a year. He pulls a chair up to her bed and suggests I might like to spend an hour on the beach.

"Bring me something back," she says. "Anything from the beach. Or the gift shop. Taste is no object."

The doctor slowly draws the curtain around her bed.

"Wait!" she cries.

I look in at her.

"Anything," she says, "except a magazine subscription."

The doctor turns away.

I watch her mouth laugh.

What seems dangerous often is not—black snakes, for example, or clear-air turbulence. While things that just lie there, like this beach, are loaded with jeopardy. A yellow dust rising from the ground, the heat that ripens melons overnight—this is earthquake weather. You can sit here braiding the fringe on your towel and the sand will all of a sudden suck down like an hourglass. The air roars. In the cheap apartments onshore, bathtubs fill themselves and gardens roll up and over like green waves. If nothing happens, the dust will drift and the heat deepen till fear turns to desire. Nerves like that are only bought off by catastrophe.

"It never happens when you're thinking about it," she observed once.

"Earthquake, earthquake, earthquake," she said.

"Earthquake, earthquake, earthquake," I said.

Like the aviaphobe who keeps the plane aloft with prayer, we kept it up till an aftershock cracked the ceiling.

That was after the big one in '72. We were in college; our dormitory was five miles from the epicenter. When the ride was over and my jabbering pulse began to slow, she served five parts champagne to one part orange juice and joked about living in Ocean View, Kansas. I offered to drive her to Hawaii on the new world psychics predicted would surface the next time, or the next.

I could not say that now—next. *Whose* next? she could ask.

Was I the only one who noticed that the experts had stopped saying *if* and now spoke of *when?* Of course not; the fearful ran to thousands. We watched the traffic of Japanese beetles for deviation. Deviation might mean more natural violence.

I wanted her to be afraid with me, but she said, "I don't know. I'm just not."

She was afraid of nothing, not even of flying.

I have this dream before a flight where we buckle in and the plane moves down the runway. It takes off at thirty-five miles an hour, and then we're airborne, skimming on tree tops. Still, we arrive in New York on time. It is so pleasant. One night I flew to Moscow this way.

She flew with me once. That time she flew with me she ate macadamia nuts while the wings bounced. She knows the wing tips can bend thirty feet up and thirty feet down without coming off. She believes it. She trusts the laws of aerodynamics. My mind stampedes. I can almost accept that a battleship floats, and everybody knows steel sinks.

I see fear in her now and am not going to try to talk her out of it. She is right to be afraid.

After a quake, the six o'clock news airs a film clip of first-graders yelling at the broken playground per their teacher's instructions.

"*Bad* earth!" they shout, because anger is stronger than fear.

But the beach is standing still today. Everyone on it is tranquilized, numb or asleep. Teenaged girls rub coconut oil on each other's hard-to-reach places. They smell like macaroons. They pry open compacts like clamshells; mirrors catch the sun and throw a spray of white rays across glazed shoulders. The girls arrange their wet hair with silk flowers the way they learned in *Seventeen*. They pose.

A formation of low-riders pulls over to watch with a six-pack. They get vocal when the girls check their tan lines. When the beer is gone, so are they—flexing their cars on up the boulevard.

Above this aggressive health are the twin wrought-iron terraces, painted flamingo pink, of the Palm Royale. Someone dies there every time the sheets are changed. There's an ambulance in the driveway, so the remaining residents line the balconies, rocking and not talking, one-upped.

The ocean they stare at is dangerous, and not just the undertow. You can almost see the slapping tails of sand sharks keeping cruising bodies alive.

If she looked, she could see this, some of it, from her window. She would be the first to say how little it takes to make a thing all wrong.

There was a second bed in the room when I returned. For two beats I didn't get it. Then it hit me like an open coffin.

She wants every minute, I thought. She wants my life.

"You missed Gussie," she said.

Gussie is her parents' 300-pound narcoleptic maid. Her attacks often come at the ironing board. The pillowcases in that family are all bordered with scorch.

"It's a hard trip for her," I said. "How is she?"

"Well, she didn't fall asleep, if that's what you mean. Gussie's great—you know what she said? She said, 'Darlin' just keep prayin', down on your knees.'"

She shrugged, "See anybody good?"

"No," I said, "just the new Charlie's Angel. And I saw Cher's car down near the Arcade."

"Cher's car is worth *three* Charlie's Angels," she said. "What else am I missing?"

"It's earthquake weather," I told her.

"The best thing to do about earthquakes," she said, "is not to live in California."

"That's useful," I said. "You sound like Reverend Ike: 'The best thing to do for the poor is not be one of them.'"

We're crazy about Reverend Ike.

I noticed her face was bloated.

"You know," she said, "I feel like hell. I'm about to stop having fun."

"The ancients have a saying," I said. "'There are times when the wolves are silent; there are times when the moon howls.'"

"What's that, Navajo?"

"Palm Royale lobby graffiti," I said. "I bought a paper there. I'll read to you."

"Even though I care about nothing?" she said.

I turned to page three, to a UPI filler datelined Mexico City. I read her "Man Robs Bank with Chicken," about a man who bought a barbecued chicken at a stand down the block from a bank. Passing the bank, he got the idea. He walked in and approached a teller. He pointed the brown paper bag at her and she handed over the day's receipts. It was the smell of barbecue sauce that eventually led to his capture.

The story made her hungry, she said, so I took the elevator down six floors to the cafeteria and brought back all the ice cream she wanted. We lay side by side, adjustable beds cranked up for optimal TV viewing, littering the sheets with Good Humor wrappers, picking toasted almonds out of the gauze. We were Lucy and Ethel, Mary and Rhoda in extremis. The blinds were closed to keep light off the screen.

We watched a movie starring men we used to think we wanted to sleep with. Hers was a tough cop out to stop mine, a vicious rapist who went after cocktail waitresses.

"This is a good movie," she said, when snipers felled them both.

I missed her already; my straight man, my diary.

A Filipino nurse tiptoed in and gave her an injection. She removed the pile of Popsicle sticks from the nightstand—enough to splint a small animal.

The injection made us sleepy—me in the way I picked up her inflection till her mother couldn't tell us apart on the phone. We slept.

I dreamed she was a decorator, come to furnish my house. She worked in secret, singing to herself. When she finished, she guided me proudly to the door. "How do you like it?" she asked, easing me inside.

Every beam and sill and shelf and knob was draped in black bunting, with streamers and black crepe looped around darkened mirrors.

"I have to go home," I said when she woke up.

She thought I meant home to her house in the Canyon, and I had to say, No, *home* home. I twisted my hands in the hackneyed fashion of people in pain. I was supposed to offer something. The Best Friend. I could not even offer to come back.

I felt weak and small and failed. Also exhilarated. I had a convertible in the parking lot. Once out of that room, I would drive it too fast down the coast highway through the crab-smelling air. A stop in Malibu for sangria. The music in the place would be sexy and loud. They would serve papaya and shrimp and watermelon ice. After dinner I would pick up beach boys. I would shimmer with life, buzz with heat, vibrate with health, stay up all night with one and then the other.

Without a word, she yanked off her mask and threw it on the floor. She kicked at the blankets and moved to the door. She must have hated having to pause for breath and balance before slamming out of Isolation, and out of the second room, the one where you scrub and tie on the white masks.

A voice shouted her name in alarm, and people ran down the corridor. The Good Doctor was paged over the intercom. I opened the door and the nurses at the station stared hard, as if this flight had been my idea.

"Where is she?" I asked, and they nodded to the supply closet.

I looked in. Two nurses were kneeling beside her on the floor, talking to her in low voices. One held a mask over her nose and mouth, the other rubbed her back in slow circles. The nurses glanced up to see if I was the doctor, and when they saw I wasn't, they went back to what they were doing.

"There, there, honey," they cooed.

On the morning she was moved to the cemetery, the one where Al Jolson is buried, I enrolled in a Fear of Flying class. "What is your worst fear?" the instructor asked, and I answered, "That I will finish this course and still be afraid."

I sleep with a glass of water on the nightstand so I can see by its level if the coastal earth is trembling or if the shaking is still me.

What do I remember? I remember only the useless things I hear—that Bob Dylan's mother invented Wite-out, that twenty-three people must be in a room before there is a fifty-fifty chance two will have the same birthdate. Who cares whether or not it's true? In my head there are bath towels swaddling this stuff. Nothing else seeps through.

I review those things that will figure in the retelling: a kiss through surgical gauze, the pale hand correcting the position of the wig. I noted these gestures as they happened, not in any retrospect. Though I don't know why looking *back* should show us more than looking *at*. It is just possible I will say I stayed the night. And who is there that can say I did not?

Nothing else gets through until I think of the chimp, the one with the talking hands.

In the course of the experiment, that chimp had a baby. Imagine how her trainers must have thrilled when the mother, without prompting, began to sign to the newborn. Baby, drink milk. Baby, play ball. And when the baby died, the mother stood over the body, her wrinkled hands moving with animal grace, forming again and again the words, Baby, come hug, Baby, come hug, fluent now in the language of grief.

▓ Exercises for Amy Hempel's "In the Cemetery Where Al Jolson Is Buried."

1. Write scenes preceding the narrator's arrival at her friend's bedside: from the two months before she came to visit, from her drive to Los Angeles, from her first moments walking into the hospital.

2. Create an extended flashback with dialogue from the two friends' good old healthy days. Insert it in the story.

3. Write a scene in which the nurses, or the patient, ask the narrator why she has taken so long to come and pay a visit.

4. Rewrite the story without any jokes, filling the gaps with serious dialogue. What happens to the story's tone?

5. Change the story to past tense. What happens?

6. What role do the Hollywood references—Marcus Welby, Al Jolson, Charlie's Angels—play in the story? Change the references, change the setting. Discuss the differences.

7. Write extensive character sketches of the two main characters, giving them names, occupations, families, more history. Slip this information into the story at various points. What is the effect?

8. Make a list of all the references to animals in this story. What is their function? Replace them with a different set of references.

9. "I see fear in her now and am not going to try to talk her out of it. She is right to be afraid." Draw this reflection out in an extended scene with dialogue.

10. Write a short story about a visit you paid to a friend or family member in a hospital—or one you received if you yourself have been hospitalized. Try this in the present tense, then past tense, and see which you prefer.

WHO'S IRISH?

by Gish Jen

In China, people say mixed children are supposed to be smart, and definitely my granddaughter Sophie is smart. But Sophie is wild, Sophie is not like my daughter Natalie, or like me. I am work hard my whole life, and fierce besides. My husband always used to say he is afraid of me, and in our restaurant, busboys and cooks all afraid of me too. Even the gang members come for protection money, they try to talk to my husband. When I am there, they stay away. If they come by mistake, they pretend they are come to eat. They hide behind the menu, they order a lot of food. They talk about their mothers. Oh, my mother have some arthritis, need to take herbal medicine, they say. Oh, my mother getting old, her hair all white now.

I say, Your mother's hair used to be white, but since she dye it, it become black again. Why don't you go home once in a while and take a look? I tell them, Confucius say a filial son knows what color his mother's hair is.

My daughter is fierce too, she is vice president in the bank now. Her new house is big enough for everybody to have their own room, including me. But Sophie take after Natalie's husband's family, their name is Shea. Irish. I always thought Irish people are like Chinese people, work so hard on the railroad, but now I know why the Chinese beat the Irish. Of course, not all Irish are like the Shea family, of course not. My daughter tell me I should not say Irish this, Irish that.

How do you like it when people say the Chinese this, the Chinese that, she say.

You know, the British call the Irish heathen, just like they call the Chinese, she say.

You think the Opium War was bad, how would you like to live right next door to the British, she say.

And that is that. My daughter have a funny habit when she win an argument, she take a sip of something and look away, so the other person is not embarrassed. So I am not embarrassed. I do not call anybody anything either.

I just happen to mention about the Shea family, an interesting fact: four brothers in the family, and not one of them work. The mother, Bess, have a job before she got sick, she was executive secretary in a big company. She is handle everything for a big shot, you would be surprised how complicated her job is, not just type this, type that. Now she is a nice woman with a clean house. But her boys, every one of them is on welfare, or so-called severance pay, or so-called disability pay. Something. They say they cannot find work, this is not the economy of the fifties, but I say, Even the black people doing better these days, some of them live so fancy, you'd be surprised. Why the Shea family have so much trouble? They are white people, they speak English. When I come to this country, I have no money and do not speak English. But my husband and I own our restaurant before he die. Free and clear, no mortgage. Of course, I understand I am just lucky, come from a country where the food is popular all over the world. I understand it is not the Shea family's fault they come from a country where everything is boiled. Still, I say.

She's right, we should broaden our horizons, say one brother Jim, at Thanksgiving. Forget about the car business. Think about egg rolls.

Pad thai, say another brother, Mike. I'm going to make my fortune in pad thai. It's going to be the new pizza.

I say, You people too picky about what you sell. Selling egg rolls not good enough for you, but at least my husband and I can say, We made it. What can you say? Tell me. What can you say?

Everybody chew their tough turkey.

I especially cannot understand my daughter's husband John, who has no job but cannot take care of Sophie either. Because he is a man, he say, and that's the end of the sentence.

Plain boiled food, plain boiled thinking. Even his name is plain boiled: John. Maybe because I grew up with black bean sauce and hoisin sauce and garlic sauce, I always feel something is missing when my son-in-law talk.

But, okay: so my son-in-law can be man, I am baby-sitter. Six hours a day, same as the old sitter, crazy Amy, who quit. This is not so easy, now that I am sixty-eight, Chinese age almost seventy. Still, I try. In China, daughter take care of mother. Here it is the other way around. Mother help daughter, mother ask, Anything else I can do? Otherwise daughter complain mother is not support-ive. I tell daughter, We do not have this word in Chinese, *supportive*. But my daughter too busy to listen, she has to go to meeting, she has to write memo while her husband go to the gym to be a man. My daughter say otherwise he will be depressed. Seems like all his life he has this trouble, depression.

No one wants to hire someone who is depressed, she say. It is important for him to keep his spirits up.

Beautiful wife, beautiful daughter, beautiful house, oven can clean itself automatically. No money left over, because only one income, but lucky enough, got the baby-sitter for free. If John lived in China, he would be very happy. But he is not happy. Even at the gym things go wrong. One day, he pull a muscle. Another day, weight room too crowded. Always something.

Until finally, hooray, he has a job. Then he feel pressure.

I need to concentrate, he say. I need to focus.

He is going to work for insurance company. Salesman job. A paycheck, he say, and at least he will wear clothes instead of gym shorts. My daughter buy him some special candy bars from the health-food store. They say THINK! on them, and are supposed to help John think.

John is a good-looking boy, you have to say that, especially now that he shave so you can see his face.

I am an old man in a young man's game, say John.

I will need a new suit, say John.

This time I am not going to shoot myself in the foot, say John.

Good, I say.

She means to be supportive, my daughter say. Don't start the send her back to China thing, because we can't.

Sophie is three years old American age, but already I see her nice Chinese side swallowed up by her wild Shea side. She looks like mostly Chinese. Beautiful black hair, beautiful black eyes. Nose perfect size, not so flat looks like something fell down, not so large looks like some big deal got stuck in wrong face. Everything just right, only her skin is a brown surprise to John's family. So brown, they say. Even John say it. She never goes in the sun, still she is that color, he say. Brown. They say, Nothing the matter with brown. They are just surprised. So brown. Nattie is not that brown, they say. They say, It seems like Sophie should be a color in between Nattie and John. Seems funny, a girl named Sophie Shea be brown. But she is brown, maybe her name should be Sophie Brown. She never go in the sun, still she is that color, they say. Nothing the matter with brown. They are just surprised.

The Shea family talk is like this sometimes, going around and around like a Christmas-tree train.

Maybe John is not her father, I say one day, to stop the train. And sure enough, train wreck. None of the brothers ever say the word *brown* to me again.

Instead, John's mother, Bess, say, I hope you are not offended.

She say, I did my best on those boys. But raising four boys with no father is no picnic.

You have a beautiful family, I say.

I'm getting old, she say.

You deserve a rest, I say. Too many boys make you old.

I never had a daughter, she say. You have a daughter.

I have a daughter, I say. Chinese people don't think a daughter is so great, but you're right. I have a daughter.

I was never against the marriage, you know, she say. I never thought John was marrying down. I always thought Nattie was just as good as white.

I was never against the marriage either, I say. I just wonder if they look at the whole problem.

Of course you pointed out the problem, you are a mother, she say. And now we both have a granddaughter. A little brown granddaughter, she is so precious to me.

I laugh. A little brown granddaughter, I say. To tell you the truth, I don't know how she came out so brown.

We laugh some more. These days Bess need a walker to walk. She take so many pills, she need two glasses of water to get them all down. Her favorite TV show is about bloopers, and she love her bird feeder. All day long, she can watch that bird feeder, like a cat.

I can't wait for her to grow up, Bess say. I could use some female company.

Too many boys, I say.

Boys are fine, she say. But they do surround you after a while.

You should take a break, come live with us, I say. Lots of girls at our house.

Be careful what you offer, say Bess with a wink. Where I come from, people mean for you to move in when they say a thing like that.

Nothing the matter with Sophie's outside, that's the truth. It is inside that she is like not any Chinese girl I ever see. We go to the park, and this is what she does. She stand up in the stroller. She take off all her clothes and throw them in the fountain.

Sophie! I say. Stop!

But she just laugh like a crazy person. Before I take over as baby-sitter, Sophie has that crazy-person sitter, Amy the guitar player. My daughter thought this Amy very creative—another word we do not talk about in China. In China, we talk about whether we have difficulty or no difficulty. We talk about whether life is bitter or not bitter. In America, all day long, people talk about creative. Never mind that I cannot even look at this Amy, with her shirt so short that her belly button showing. This Amy think Sophie should love her body. So when Sophie take off her diaper, Amy laugh. When Sophie run around naked, Amy say she wouldn't want to wear a diaper either. When Sophie go *shu-shu* in her lap, Amy laugh and say there are no germs in pee. When Sophie take off her shoes, Amy say bare feet is best, even the pediatrician say so. That is why Sophie now walk around with no shoes like a beggar child. Also why Sophie love to take off her clothes.

Turn around! say the boys in the park. Let's see that ass!

Of course, Sophie does not understand. Sophie clap her hands, I am the only one to say, No! This is not a game.

It has nothing to do with John's family, my daughter say. Amy was too permissive, that's all.

But I think if Sophie was not wild inside, she would not take off her shoes and clothes to begin with.

You never take off your clothes when you were little, I say. All my Chinese friends had babies, I never saw one of them act wild like that.

Look, my daughter say. I have a big presentation tomorrow.

John and my daughter agree Sophie is a problem, but they don't know what to do.

You spank her, she'll stop, I say another day.

But they say, Oh no.

In America, parents not supposed to spank the child.

It gives them low self-esteem, my daughter say. And that leads to problems later, as I happen to know.

My daughter never have big presentation the next day when the subject of spanking come up.

I don't want you to touch Sophie, she say. No spanking, period.

Don't tell me what to do, I say.

I'm not telling you what to do, say my daughter. I'm telling you how I feel.

I am not your servant, I say. Don't you dare talk to me like that.

My daughter have another funny habit when she lose an argument. She spread out all her fingers and look at them, as if she like to make sure they are still there.

My daughter is fierce like me, but she and John think it is better to explain to Sophie that clothes are a good idea. This is not so hard in the cold weather. In the warm weather, it is very hard.

Use your words, my daughter say. That's what we tell Sophie. How about if you set a good example.

As if good example mean anything to Sophie. I am so fierce, the gang members who used to come to the restaurant all afraid of me, but Sophie is not afraid.

I say, Sophie, if you take off your clothes, no snack.

I say, Sophie, if you take off your clothes, no lunch.

I say, Sophie, if you take off your clothes, no park.

Pretty soon we are stay home all day, and by the end of six hours she still did not have one thing to eat. You never saw a child stubborn like that.

I'm hungry! she cry when my daughter come home.

What's the matter, doesn't your grandmother feed you? My daughter laugh.

No! Sophie say. She doesn't feed me anything!

My daughter laugh again. Here you go, she say.

She say to John, Sophie must be growing.

Growing like a weed, I say.

Still Sophie take off her clothes, until one day I spank her. Not too hard, but she cry and cry, and when I tell her if she doesn't put her clothes back on I'll spank her again, she put her clothes back on. Then I tell her she is good girl, and give her some food to eat. The next day we go to the park and, like a nice Chinese girl, she does not take off her clothes.

She stop taking off her clothes, I report. Finally!

How did you do it? my daughter ask.

After twenty-eight years experience with you, I guess I learn something, I say.

It must have been a phase, John say, and his voice is suddenly like an expert.

His voice is like an expert about everything these days, now that he carry a leather briefcase, and wear shiny shoes, and can go shopping for a new car. On the company, he say. The company will pay for it, but he will be able to drive it whenever he want.

A free car, he say. How do you like that.

It's good to see you in the saddle again, my daughter say. Some of your family patterns are scary.

At least I don't drink, he say. He say, And I'm not the only one with scary family patterns.

That's for sure, say my daughter.

Everyone is happy. Even I am happy, because there is more trouble with Sophie, but now I think I can help her Chinese side fight against her wild side. I teach her to eat food with fork or spoon or chopsticks, she cannot just grab into the middle of a bowl of noodles. I teach her not to play with garbage cans. Sometimes I spank her, but not too often, and not too hard.

Still, there are problems. Sophie like to climb everything. If there is a railing, she is never next to it. Always she is on top of it. Also, Sophie like to hit the mommies of her friends. She learn this from her playground best friend, Sinbad, who is four. Sinbad wear army clothes every day and like to ambush his mommy. He is the one who dug a big hole under the play structure, a foxhole he call it, all by himself. Very hardworking. Now he wait in the foxhole with a shovel full of wet sand. When his mommy come, he throw it right at her.

Oh, it's all right, his mommy say. You can't get rid of war games, it's part of their imaginative play. All the boys go through it.

Also, he like to kick his mommy, and one day he tell Sophie to kick his mommy too.

I wish this story is not true.

Kick her, kick her! Sinbad say.

Sophie kick her. A little kick, as if she just so happened was swinging her little leg and didn't realize that big mommy leg was in the way. Still I spank Sophie and make Sophie say sorry, and what does the mommy say?

Really, it's all right, she say. It didn't hurt.

After that, Sophie learn she can attack mommies in the playground, and some will say, Stop, but others will say, Oh, she didn't mean it, especially if they realize Sophie will be punished.

This is how, one day, bigger trouble come. The bigger trouble start when Sophie hide in the foxhole with that shovel full of sand. She wait, and when I come look for her, she throw it at me. All over my nice clean clothes.

Did you ever see a Chinese girl act this way?

Sophie! I say. Come out of there, say you're sorry.

But she does not come out. Instead, she laugh. Naaah, naah-na, naaa-naaa, she say.

I am not exaggerate: millions of children in China, not one act like this.

Sophie! I say. Now! Come out now!

But she know she is in big trouble. She know if she come out, what will happen next. So she does not come out. I am sixty-eight, Chinese age almost seventy, how can I crawl under there to catch her? Impossible. So I yell, yell, yell, and what happen? Nothing. A Chinese mother would help, but American mothers, they look at you, they shake their head, they go home. And, of course, a Chinese child would give up, but not Sophie.

I hate you! she yell. I hate you, Meanie!

Meanie is my new name these days.

Long time this goes on, long long time. The foxhole is deep, you cannot see too much, you don't know where is the bottom. You cannot hear too much either. If she does not yell, you cannot even know she is still there or not. After a while, getting cold out, getting dark out. No one left in the playground, only us.

Sophie, I say. How did you become stubborn like this? I am go home without you now.

I try to use a stick, chase her out of there, and once or twice I hit her, but still she does not come out. So finally I leave. I go outside the gate.

Bye-bye! I say. I'm go home now.

But still she does not come out and does not come out. Now it is dinnertime, the sky is black. I think I should maybe go get help, but how can I leave a little girl by herself in the playground? A bad man could come. A rat could come. I go back in to see what is happen to Sophie. What if she have a shovel and is making a tunnel to escape?

Sophie! I say.

No answer.

Sophie!

I don't know if she is alive. I don't know if she is fall asleep down there. If she is crying, I cannot hear her.

So I take the stick and poke.

Sophie! I say. I promise I no hit you. If you come out, I give you a lollipop.

No answer. By now I worried. What to do, what to do, what to do? I poke some more, even harder, so that I am poking and poking when my daughter and John suddenly appear.

What are you doing? What is going on? say my daughter.

Put down that stick! say my daughter.

You are crazy! say my daughter.

John wiggle under the structure, into the foxhole, to rescue Sophie.

She fell asleep, say John the expert. She's okay. That is one big hole.

Now Sophie is crying and crying.

Sophia, my daughter say, hugging her. Are you okay, peanut? Are you okay?

She's just scared, say John.

Are you okay? I say too. I don't know what happen, I say.

She's okay, say John. He is not like my daughter, full of questions. He is full of answers until we get home and can see by the lamplight.

Will you look at her? he yell then. What the hell happened?

Bruises all over her brown skin, and a swollen-up eye.

You are crazy! say my daughter. Look at what you did! You are crazy!

I try very hard, I say.

How could you use a stick? I told you to use your words!

She is hard to handle, I say.

She's three years old! You cannot use a stick! say my daughter.

She is not like any Chinese girl I ever saw, I say.

I brush some sand off my clothes. Sophie's clothes are dirty too, but at least she has her clothes on.

Has she done this before? ask my daughter. Has she hit you before?

She hits me all the time, Sophie say, eating ice cream.

Your family, say John.

Believe me, say my daughter.

A daughter I have, a beautiful daughter. I took care of her when she could not hold her head up. I took care of her before she could argue with me, when she was a little girl with two pigtails, one of them always crooked. I took care of her when we have to escape from China, I took care of her when suddenly we live in a country with cars everywhere, if you are not careful your little girl get run over. When my husband die, I promise him I will keep the family together, even though it was just two of us, hardly a family at all.

But now my daughter take me around to look at apartments. After all, I can cook, I can clean, there's no reason I cannot live by myself, all I need is a telephone. Of course, she is sorry. Sometimes she cry, I am the one to say everything will be okay. She say she have no choice, she doesn't want to end up divorced. I say divorce is terrible, I don't know who invented this terrible idea. Instead of live with a telephone, though, surprise, I come to live with Bess. Imagine that. Bess make an offer and, sure enough, where she come from, people mean for you to move in when they say things like that. A crazy idea, go to live with someone else's family, but she like to have some female company, not like my daughter, who does not believe in company. These days when my daughter visit, she does not bring Sophie. Bess say we should give Nattie time, we will see Sophie again soon. But seems like my daughter have more presentation than ever before, every time she come she have to leave.

I have a family to support, she say, and her voice is heavy, as if soaking wet. I have a young daughter and a depressed husband and no one to turn to.

When she say no one to turn to, she mean me.

These days my beautiful daughter is so tired she can just sit there in a chair and fall asleep. John lost his job again, already, but still they rather hire a baby-sitter than ask me to help, even they can't afford it. Of course, the new baby-sitter is much younger, can run around. I don't know if Sophie these days is wild or not wild. She call me Meanie, but she like to kiss me too, sometimes. I remember that every time I see a child on TV. Sophie like to grab my hair, a fistful in each hand, and then kiss me smack on the nose. I never see any other child kiss that way.

The satellite TV has so many channels, more channels than I can count, including a Chinese channel from the Mainland and a Chinese channel from Taiwan, but most of the time I watch bloopers with Bess. Also, I watch the bird feeder—so many, many kinds of birds come. The Shea sons hang around all the time, asking when will I go home, but Bess tell them, Get lost.

She's a permanent resident, say Bess. She isn't going anywhere.

Then she wink at me, and switch the channel with the remote control.

Of course, I shouldn't say Irish this, Irish that, especially now I am become honorary Irish myself, according to Bess. Me! Who's Irish? I say, and she laugh. All the same, if I could mention one thing about some of the Irish, not all of them of course, I like to mention this: Their talk just stick. I don't know how Bess Shea learn to use her words, but sometimes I hear what she say a long time later. *Permanent resident. Not going anywhere.* Over and over I hear it, the voice of Bess.

Exercises for Gish Jen's "Who's Irish?"

1. Describe the speaker in third-person prose; provide a portrait of her—size, shape, dress, accent, etc.—and then do the same in the voice of Natalie, John, Sophie, and Bess.

2. Turn the spoken utterance into "standard" American English; rid the first page of inflection.

3. Have the Shea brothers go to a bar together and talk about what happened at the playground earlier that day.

4. Have John, at the insurance office, tell his coworkers and customers about his wife and mother-in-law.

5. Write the story of your own relative trying to adjust to the values and the systems of behavior in America. This person may have come across on the *Mayflower* or last year in the back of a pick-up truck; use his or her own voice.

6. "My husband always used to say he is afraid of me, and in our restaurant, busboys and cooks all afraid of me too." Write a scene in the restaurant before "her hair all white now."

7. "Everybody chew their tough turkey." Describe the preparations in the kitchen for this Thanksgiving meal.

8. Discuss the comedy here; find examples of misunderstanding and mala-propism. Try to bridge the "cultural divide" by having an Irish and Chinese couple discover that their ancestors worked on the same section of railroad track in Colorado a hundred years ago.

9. Have Bess and her "permanent resident" watch *All in the Family* on TV.

10. Have Sophie, at twenty, remember her dead grandmother while visiting the grave.

SEXY
by Jhumpa Lahiri

It was a wife's worst nightmare. After nine years of marriage, Laxmi told Miranda, her cousin's husband had fallen in love with another woman. He sat next to her on a plane, on a flight from Delhi to Montreal, and instead of flying home to his wife and son, he got off with the woman at Heathrow. He called his wife, and told her he'd had a conversation that had changed his life, and that he needed time to figure things out. Laxmi's cousin had taken to her bed.

"Not that I blame her," Laxmi said. She reached for the Hot Mix she munched throughout the day, which looked to Miranda like dusty orange cereal. "Imagine. An English girl, half his age." Laxmi was only a few years older than Miranda, but she was already married, and kept a photo of herself and her husband, seated on a white stone bench in front of the Taj Mahal, tacked to the inside of her cubicle, which was next to Miranda's. Laxmi had been on the phone for at least an hour, trying to calm her cousin down. No one noticed; they worked for a public radio station, in the fund-raising department, and were surrounded by people who spent all day on the phone, soliciting pledges.

"I feel worst for the boy," Laxmi added. "He's been at home for days. My cousin said she can't even take him to school."

"It sounds awful," Miranda said. Normally Laxmi's phone conversations—mainly to her husband, about what to cook for dinner—distracted Miranda as she typed letters, asking members of the radio station to increase their annual pledge in exchange for a tote bag or an umbrella. She could hear Laxmi clearly, her sentences peppered every now and then with an Indian word, through the laminated wall between their desks. But that afternoon Miranda hadn't been listening. She'd been on the phone herself, with Dev, deciding where to meet later that evening.

"Then again, a few days at home won't hurt him." Laxmi ate some more Hot Mix, then put it away in a drawer. "He's something of a genius. He has a Punjabi mother and a Bengali father, and because he learns French and English at school he already speaks four languages. I think he skipped two grades."

Dev was Bengali, too. At first Miranda thought it was a religion. But then he pointed it out to her, a place in India called Bengal, in a map printed in an issue of *The Economist*. He had brought the magazine specially to her apartment, for she did not own an atlas, or any other books with maps in them. He'd pointed to the city where he'd been born, and another city where his father had been born. One of the cities had a box around it, intended to attract the reader's eye. When Miranda asked what the box indicated, Dev rolled up the magazine, and said, "Nothing you'll ever need to worry about," and he tapped her playfully on the head.

Before leaving her apartment he'd tossed the magazine in the garbage, along with the ends of the three cigarettes he always smoked in the course of his visits. But after she watched his car disappear down Commonwealth Avenue, back to his house in the suburbs, where he lived with his wife, Miranda retrieved it, and brushed the ashes off the cover, and rolled it in the opposite direction to get it to lie flat. She got into bed, still rumpled from their lovemaking, and studied the borders of Bengal. There was a bay below and mountains above. The map was connected to an article about something called the Gramin Bank. She turned the page, hoping for a photograph of the city where Dev was born, but all she found were graphs and grids. Still, she stared at them, thinking the whole while about Dev, about how only fifteen minutes ago he'd propped her feet on top of his shoulders, and pressed her knees to her chest, and told her that he couldn't get enough of her.

She'd met him a week ago, at Filene's. She was there on her lunch break, buying discounted pantyhose in the Basement. Afterward she took the escalator to the main part of the store, to the cosmetics department, where soaps and creams were displayed like jewels, and eye shadows and powders shimmered like butterflies pinned behind protective glass. Though Miranda had never bought anything other than a lipstick, she liked walking through the cramped, confined maze, which was familiar to her in a way the rest of Boston still was not. She liked negotiating her way past the women planted at every turn, who sprayed cards with perfume and waved them in the air; sometimes she would find a card days afterward, folded in her coat pocket, and the rich aroma, still faintly preserved, would warm her as she waited on cold mornings for the T.

That day, stopping to smell one of the more pleasing cards, Miranda noticed a man standing at one of the counters. He held a slip of paper covered in a precise, feminine hand. A saleswoman took one look at the paper and began to open drawers. She produced an oblong cake of soap in a black case, a hydrating mask, a vial of cell renewal drops, and two tubes of face cream. The man was tanned, with black hair that was visible on his knuckles. He wore a flamingo pink shirt, a navy blue suit, a camel overcoat with gleaming leather buttons. In order to pay he had taken off pigskin gloves. Crisp bills emerged from a burgundy wallet. He didn't wear a wedding ring.

"What can I get you, honey?" the saleswoman asked Miranda. She looked over the tops of her tortoiseshell glasses, assessing Miranda's complexion.

Miranda didn't know what she wanted. All she knew was that she didn't want the man to walk away. He seemed to be lingering, waiting, along with the saleswoman, for her to say something. She stared at some bottles, some short, others tall, arranged on an oval tray, like a family posing for a photograph.

"A cream," Miranda said eventually.

"How old are you?"

"Twenty-two."

The saleswoman nodded, opening a frosted bottle. "This may seem a bit heavier than what you're used to, but I'd start now. All your wrinkles are going to form by twenty-five. After that they just start showing."

While the saleswoman dabbed the cream on Miranda's face, the man stood and watched. While Miranda was told the proper way to apply it, in swift upward strokes beginning at the base of her throat, he spun the lipstick carousel. He pressed a pump that dispensed cellulite gel and massaged it into the back of his ungloved hand. He opened a jar, leaned over, and drew so close that a drop of cream flecked his nose.

Miranda smiled, but her mouth was obscured by a large brush that the saleswoman was sweeping over her face. "This is blusher Number Two," the woman said. "Gives you some color."

Miranda nodded, glancing at her reflection in one of the angled mirrors that lined the counter. She had silver eyes and skin as pale as paper, and the contrast with her hair, as dark and glossy as an espresso bean, caused people to describe her as striking, if not pretty. She had a narrow, egg-shaped head that rose to a prominent point. Her features, too, were narrow, with nostrils so slim that they appeared to have been pinched with a clothespin. Now her face glowed, rosy at the cheeks, smoky below the brow bone. Her lips glistened.

The man was glancing in a mirror, too, quickly wiping the cream from his nose. Miranda wondered where he was from. She thought he might be Spanish, or Lebanese. When he opened another jar, and said, to no one in particular, "This one smells like pineapple," she detected only the hint of an accent.

"Anything else for you today?" the saleswoman asked, accepting Miranda's credit card.

"No thanks."

The woman wrapped the cream in several layers of red tissue. "You'll be very happy with this product." Miranda's hand was unsteady as she signed the receipt. The man hadn't budged.

"I threw in a sample of our new eye gel," the saleswoman added, handing Miranda a small shopping bag. She looked at Miranda's credit card before sliding it across the counter. "Bye-bye, Miranda."

Miranda began walking. At first she sped up. Then, noticing the doors that led to Downtown Crossing, she slowed down.

"Part of your name is Indian," the man said, pacing his steps with hers.

She stopped, as did he, at a circular table piled with sweaters, flanked with pinecones and velvet bows. "Miranda?"

"Mira. I have an aunt named Mira."

His name was Dev. He worked in an investment bank back that way, he said, tilting his head in the direction of South Station. He was the first man with a mustache, Miranda decided, she found handsome.

They walked together toward Park Street station, past the kiosks that sold cheap belts and handbags. A fierce January wind spoiled the part in her hair. As she fished for a token in her coat pocket, her eyes fell to his shopping bag. "And those are for her?"

"Who?"

"Your Aunt Mira."

"They're for my wife." He uttered the words slowly, holding Miranda's gaze. "She's going to India for a few weeks." He rolled his eyes. "She's addicted to this stuff."

Somehow, without the wife there, it didn't seem so wrong. At first Miranda and Dev spent every night together, almost. He explained that he couldn't spend the whole night at her place, because his wife called every day at six in the morning, from India, where it was four in the afternoon. And so he left her apartment at two, three, often as late as four in the morning, driving back to his house in the suburbs. During the day he called her every hour, it seemed, from work, or from his cell phone. Once he learned Miranda's schedule he left her a message each evening at five-thirty, when she was on the T coming back to her apartment, just so, he said, she could hear his voice as soon as she walked through the door. "I'm thinking about you," he'd say on the tape. "I can't wait to see you." He told her he liked spending time in her apartment, with its kitchen counter no wider than a breadbox, and scratchy floors that sloped, and a buzzer in the lobby that always made a slightly embarrassing sound when he pressed it. He said he admired her for moving to Boston, where she knew no one, instead of remaining in Michigan, where she'd grown up and gone to college. When Miranda told him it was nothing to admire, that she'd moved to Boston precisely for that reason, he shook his head. "I know what it's like to be lonely," he said, suddenly serious, and at that moment Miranda felt that he understood her—understood how she felt some nights on the T, after seeing a movie on her own, or going to a bookstore to read magazines, or having drinks with Laxmi, who always had to meet her husband at Alewife station in an hour or two. In less serious moments Dev said he liked that her legs were longer than her torso, something he'd observed the first time she walked across a room naked. "You're the first," he told her, admiring her from the bed. "The first woman I've known with legs this long."

Dev was the first to tell her that. Unlike the boys she dated in college, who were simply taller, heavier versions of the ones she dated in high school, Dev was the first always to pay for things, and hold doors open, and reach across a table in a restaurant to kiss her hand. He was the first to bring her a bouquet of flowers so immense she'd had to split it up into all six of her drinking glasses, and the first to whisper her name again and again when they made love. Within days of meeting him, when she was at work, Miranda began to wish that there were a picture of her and Dev tacked to the inside of her cubicle, like the one of Laxmi and her husband in front of the Taj Mahal. She didn't tell Laxmi about Dev. She didn't tell anyone. Part of her wanted to tell Laxmi, if only because Laxmi was Indian, too. But Laxmi was always on the phone with her cousin these days, who was still in bed, whose husband was still in London, and whose son still wasn't going to school. "You must eat something," Laxmi would urge. "You mustn't lose your health." When she wasn't speaking to her cousin, she spoke to her husband, shorter conversations, in which she ended up arguing about whether to have chicken or lamb for dinner. "I'm sorry," Miranda heard her apologize at one point. "This whole thing just makes me a little paranoid."

Miranda and Dev didn't argue. They went to movies at the Nickelodeon and kissed the whole time. They ate pulled pork and cornbread in Davis Square, a paper napkin tucked like a cravat into the collar of Dev's shirt. They sipped sangria at the bar of a Spanish restaurant, a grinning pig's head presiding over their conversation. They went to the MFA and picked out a poster of water lilies for her bedroom. One Saturday, following an afternoon concert at Symphony Hall, he showed her his favorite place in the city, the Mapparium at the Christian Science center, where they stood inside a room made of glowing stained-glass panels, which was shaped like the inside of a globe, but looked like the outside of one. In the middle of the room was a transparent bridge, so that they felt as if they were standing in the center of the world. Dev pointed to India, which was red, and far more detailed than the map in *The Economist.* He explained that many of the countries, like Siam and Italian Somaliland, no longer existed in the same way; the names had changed by now. The ocean, as blue as a peacock's breast, appeared in two shades, depending on the depth of the water. He showed her the deepest spot on earth, seven miles deep, above the Mariana Islands. They peered over the bridge and saw the Antarctic archipelago at their feet, craned their necks and saw a giant metal star overhead. As Dev spoke, his voice bounced wildly off the glass, sometimes loud, sometimes soft, sometimes seeming to land in Miranda's chest, sometimes eluding her ear altogether. When a group of tourists walked onto the bridge, she could hear them clearing their throats, as if through microphones. Dev explained that it was because of the acoustics.

Miranda found London, where Laxmi's cousin's husband was, with the woman he'd met on the plane. She wondered which of the cities in India Dev's wife was in. The farthest Miranda had ever been was to the Bahamas once when she was a child. She searched but couldn't find it on the glass panels. When the tourists left and she and Dev were alone again, he told her to stand at one end of the bridge. Even though they were thirty feet apart, Dev said, they'd be able to hear each other whisper.

"I don't believe you," Miranda said. It was the first time she'd spoken since they'd entered. She felt as if speakers were embedded in her ears.

"Go ahead," he urged, walking backward to his end of the bridge. His voice dropped to a whisper. "Say something." She watched his lips forming the words; at the same time she heard them so clearly that she felt them under her skin, under her winter coat, so near and full of warmth that she felt herself go hot.

"Hi," she whispered, unsure of what else to say.

"You're sexy," he whispered back.

At work the following week, Laxmi told Miranda that it wasn't the first time her cousin's husband had had an affair. "She's decided to let him come to his senses," Laxmi said one evening as they were getting ready to leave the office. "She says it's for the boy. She's willing to forgive him for the boy." Miranda waited as Laxmi shut off her computer. "He'll come crawling back, and she'll let him," Laxmi said, shaking her head. "Not me. If my husband so much as looked at another woman I'd change the locks." She studied the picture tacked to her cubicle. Laxmi's husband had his arm draped over her shoulder, his knees leaning in toward her on the bench. She turned to Miranda. "Wouldn't you?"

She nodded. Dev's wife was coming back from India the next day. That afternoon he'd called Miranda at work, to say he had to go to the airport to pick her up. He promised he'd call as soon as he could.

"What's the Taj Mahal like?" she asked Laxmi.

"The most romantic spot on earth." Laxmi's face brightened at the memory. "An everlasting monument to love."

While Dev was at the airport, Miranda went to Filene's Basement to buy herself things she thought a mistress should have. She found a pair of black high heels with buckles smaller than a baby's teeth. She found a satin slip with scalloped edges and a knee-length silk robe. Instead of the pantyhose she normally wore to work, she found sheer stockings with a seam. She searched through piles and wandered through racks, pressing back hanger after hanger, until she found a cocktail dress made of a slinky silvery material that matched her eyes, with little chains for straps. As she shopped she thought about Dev, and about what he'd told her in the Mapparium. It was the first time a man had called her sexy, and when she closed her eyes she could still feel his whisper drifting through her body, under her skin. In the fitting room, which was just one big room with mirrors on the walls, she found a spot next to an older woman with a shiny face and coarse frosted hair. The woman stood barefoot in her underwear, pulling the black net of a body stocking taut between her fingers.

"Always check for snags," the woman advised.

Miranda pulled out the satin slip with scalloped edges. She held it to her chest.

The woman nodded with approval. "Oh yes."

"And this?" She held up the silver cocktail dress.

"Absolutely," the woman said. "He'll want to rip it right off you."

Miranda pictured the two of them at a restaurant in the South End they'd been to, where Dev had ordered foie gras and a soup made with champagne and raspberries. She pictured herself in the cocktail dress, and Dev in one of his suits, kissing her hand across the table. Only the next time Dev came to visit her, on a Sunday afternoon several days since the last time they'd seen each other, he was in gym clothes. After his wife came back, that was his excuse: on Sundays he drove into Boston and went running along the Charles. The first Sunday she opened the door in the knee-length robe, but Dev didn't even notice it; he carried her over to the bed, wearing sweatpants and sneakers, and entered her without a word. Later, she slipped on the robe when she walked across the room to get him a saucer for his cigarette ashes, but he complained that she was depriving him of the sight of her long legs, and demanded that she remove it. So the next Sunday she didn't bother. She wore jeans. She kept the lingerie at the back of a drawer, behind her socks and everyday underwear. The silver cocktail dress hung in her closet, the tag dangling from the seam. Often, in the morning, the dress would be in a heap on the floor; the chain straps always slipped off the metal hanger.

Still, Miranda looked forward to Sundays. In the mornings she went to a deli and bought a baguette and little containers of things Dev liked to eat, like pickled herring, and potato salad, and tortes of pesto and mascarpone cheese. They ate in bed, picking up the herring with their fingers and ripping the baguette with their hands. Dev told her stories about his childhood, when he would come home from school and drink mango juice served to him on a tray, and then play cricket by a lake, dressed all in white. He told her about how, at eighteen, he'd been sent to a college in upstate New York during something called the Emergency, and about how it took him years to be able to follow American accents in movies, in spite of the fact that he'd had an English-medium education. As he talked he smoked three cigarettes, crushing them in a saucer by the side of her bed. Sometimes he asked her questions, like how many lovers she'd had (three) and how old she'd been the first time (nineteen). After lunch they made love, on sheets covered with crumbs, and then Dev took a nap for twelve minutes. Miranda had never known an adult who took naps, but Dev said it was something he'd grown up doing in India, where it was so hot that people didn't leave their homes until the sun went down. "Plus it allows us to sleep together," he murmured mischievously, curving his arm like a big bracelet around her body.

Only Miranda never slept. She watched the clock on her bedside table, or pressed her face against Dev's fingers, intertwined with hers, each with its half-dozen hairs at the knuckle. After six minutes she turned to face him, sighing and stretching, to test if he was really sleeping. He always was. His ribs were visible through his skin as he breathed, and yet he was beginning to develop a paunch. He complained about the hair on his shoulders, but Miranda thought him perfect, and refused to imagine him any other way.

At the end of twelve minutes Dev would open his eyes as if he'd been awake all along, smiling at her, full of a contentment she wished she felt herself.

"The best twelve minutes of the week." He'd sigh, running a hand along the backs of her calves. Then he'd spring out of bed, pulling on his sweatpants and lacing up his sneakers. He would go to the bathroom and brush his teeth with his index finger, something he told her all Indians knew how to do, to get rid of the smoke in his mouth. When she kissed him good-bye she smelled herself sometimes in his hair. But she knew that his excuse, that he'd spent the afternoon jogging, allowed him to take a shower when he got home, first thing.

Apart from Laxmi and Dev, the only Indians whom Miranda had known were a family in the neighborhood where she'd grown up, named the Dixits. Much to the amusement of the neighborhood children, including Miranda, but not including the Dixit children, Mr. Dixit would jog each evening along the flat winding streets of their development in his everyday shirt and trousers, his only concession to athletic apparel a pair of cheap Keds. Every weekend, the family—mother, father, two boys, and a girl—piled into their car and went away, to where nobody knew. The fathers complained that Mr. Dixit did not fertilize his lawn properly, did not rake his leaves on time, and agreed that the Dixits' house, the only one with vinyl siding, detracted from the neighborhood's charm. The mothers never invited Mrs. Dixit to join them around the Armstrongs' swimming pool. Waiting for the school bus with the Dixit children standing to one side, the other children would say "The Dixits dig shit," under their breath, and then burst into laughter.

One year, all the neighborhood children were invited to the birthday party of the Dixit girl. Miranda remembered a heavy aroma of incense and onions in the house, and a pile of shoes heaped by the front door. But most of all she remembered a piece of fabric, about the size of a pillowcase, which hung from a wooden dowel at the bottom of the stairs. It was a painting of a naked woman with a red face shaped like a knight's shield. She had enormous white eyes that tilted toward her temples, and mere dots for pupils. Two circles, with the same dots at their centers, indicated her breasts. In one hand she brandished a dagger. With one foot she crushed a struggling man on the ground. Around her body was a necklace composed of bleeding heads, strung together like a popcorn chain. She stuck her tongue out at Miranda.

"It is the goddess Kali," Mrs. Dixit explained brightly, shifting the dowel slightly in order to straighten the image. Mrs. Dixit's hands were painted with henna, an intricate pattern of zigzags and stars. "Come please, time for cake."

Miranda, then nine years old, had been too frightened to eat the cake. For months afterward she'd been too frightened even to walk on the same side of the street as the Dixits' house, which she had to pass twice daily, once to get to the bus stop, and once again to come home. For a while she even held her breath until she reached the next lawn, just as she did when the school bus passed a cemetery.

It shamed her now. Now, when she and Dev made love, Miranda closed her eyes and saw deserts and elephants, and marble pavilions floating on lakes beneath a full moon. One Saturday, having nothing else to do, she walked all the way to Central Square, to an Indian restaurant, and ordered a plate of tandoori chicken. As she ate she tried to memorize phrases printed at the bottom of the menu, for things like "delicious" and "water" and "check, please." The phrases didn't stick in her mind, and so she began to stop from time to time in the foreign-language section of a bookstore in Kenmore Square, where she studied the Bengali alphabet in the Teach Yourself series. Once she went so far as to try to transcribe the Indian part of her name, "Mira," into her Filofax, her hand moving in unfamiliar directions, stopping and turning and picking up her pen when she least expected to. Following the arrows in the book, she drew a bar from left to right from which the letters hung; one looked more like a number than a letter, another looked like a triangle on its side. It had taken her several tries to get the letters of her name to resemble the sample letters in the book, and even then she wasn't sure if she'd written Mira or Mara. It was a scribble to her, but somewhere in the world, she realized with a shock, it meant something.

During the week it wasn't so bad. Work kept her busy, and she and Laxmi had begun having lunch together at a new Indian restaurant around the corner, during which Laxmi reported the latest status of her cousin's marriage. Sometimes Miranda tried to change the topic; it made her feel the way she once felt in college, when she and her boyfriend at the time had walked away from a crowded house of pancakes without paying for their food, just to see if they could get away with it. But Laxmi spoke of nothing else. "If I were her I'd fly straight to London and shoot them both," she announced one day. She snapped a papadum in half and dipped it into chutney. "I don't know how she can just wait this way."

Miranda knew how to wait. In the evenings she sat at her dining table and coated her nails with clear nail polish, and ate salad straight from the salad bowl, and watched television, and waited for Sunday. Saturdays were the worst because by Saturday it seemed that Sunday would never come. One Saturday when Dev called, late at night, she heard people laughing and talking in the background, so many that she asked him if he was at a concert hall. But he was only calling from his house in the suburbs. "I can't hear you that well," he said. "We have guests. Miss me?" She looked at the television screen, a sitcom that she'd muted with the remote control when the phone rang. She pictured him whispering into his cell phone, in a room upstairs, a hand on the doorknob, the hallway filled with guests. "Miranda, do you miss me?" he asked again. She told him that she did.

The next day, when Dev came to visit, Miranda asked him what his wife looked like. She was nervous to ask, waiting until he'd smoked the last of his cigarettes, crushing it with a firm twist into the saucer. She wondered if they'd quarrel. But Dev wasn't surprised by the question. He told her, spreading some smoked whitefish on a cracker, that his wife resembled an actress in Bombay named Madhuri Dixit.

For an instant Miranda's heart stopped. But no, the Dixit girl had been named something else, something that began with P. Still, she wondered if the actress and the Dixit girl were related. She'd been plain, wearing her hair in two braids all through high school.

A few days later Miranda went to an Indian grocery in Central Square which also rented videos. The door opened to a complicated tinkling of bells. It was dinnertime, and she was the only customer. A video was playing on a television hooked up in a corner of the store: a row of young women in harem pants were thrusting their hips in synchrony on a beach.

"Can I help you?" the man standing at the cash register asked. He was eating a samosa, dipping it into some dark brown sauce on a paper plate. Below the glass counter at his waist were trays of more plump samosas, and what looked like pale, diamond-shaped pieces of fudge covered with foil, and some bright orange pastries floating in syrup. "You like some video?"

Miranda opened up her Filofax, where she had written "Mottery Dixit." She looked up at the videos on the shelves behind the counter. She saw women wearing skirts that sat low on the hips and tops that tied like bandannas between their breasts. Some leaned back against a stone wall, or a tree. They were beautiful, the way the women dancing on the beach were beautiful, with kohl-rimmed eyes and long black hair. She knew then that Madhuri Dixit was beautiful, too.

"We have subtitled versions, miss," the man continued. He wiped his fingertips quickly on his shirt and pulled out three titles.

"No," Miranda said. "Thank you, no." She wandered through the store, studying shelves lined with unlabeled packets and tins. The freezer case was stuffed with bags of pita bread and vegetables she didn't recognize. The only thing she recognized was a rack lined with bags and bags of the Hot Mix that Laxmi was always eating. She thought about buying some for Laxmi, then hesitated, wondering how to explain what she'd been doing in an Indian grocery.

"Very spicy," the man said, shaking his head, his eyes traveling across Miranda's body. "Too spicy for you."

By February, Laxmi's cousin's husband still hadn't come to his senses. He had returned to Montreal, argued bitterly with his wife for two weeks, packed two suitcases, and flown back to London. He wanted a divorce.

Miranda sat in her cubicle and listened as Laxmi kept telling her cousin that there were better men in the world, just waiting to come out of the woodwork. The next day the cousin said she and her son were going to her parents' house in California, to try to recuperate. Laxmi convinced her to arrange a weekend layover in Boston. "A quick change of place will do you good," Laxmi insisted gently, "besides which, I haven't seen you in years."

Miranda stared at her own phone, wishing Dev would call. It had been four days since their last conversation. She heard Laxmi dialing directory assistance, asking for the number of a beauty salon. "Something soothing," Laxmi requested. She scheduled massages, facials, manicures, and pedicures. Then she reserved a table for lunch at the Four Seasons. In her determination to cheer up her cousin, Laxmi had forgotten about the boy. She rapped her knuckles on the laminated wall.

"Are you busy Saturday?"

The boy was thin. He wore a yellow knapsack strapped across his back, gray herringbone trousers, a red V-necked sweater, and black leather shoes. His hair was cut in a thick fringe over his eyes, which had dark circles under them. They were the first thing Miranda noticed. They made him look haggard, as if he smoked a great deal and slept very little, in spite of the fact that he was only seven years old. He clasped a large sketch pad with a spiral binding. His name was Rohin.

"Ask me a capital," he said, staring up at Miranda.

She stared back at him. It was eight-thirty on a Saturday morning. She took a sip of coffee. "A what?"

"It's a game he's been playing," Laxmi's cousin explained. She was thin like her son, with a long face and the same dark circles under her eyes. A rust-colored coat hung heavy on her shoulders. Her black hair, with a few strands of gray at the temples, was pulled back like a ballerina's. "You ask him a country and he tells you the capital."

"You should have heard him in the car," Laxmi said. "He's already memorized all of Europe."

"It's not a game," Rohin said. "I'm having a competition with a boy at school. We're competing to memorize all the capitals. I'm going to beat him."

Miranda nodded. "Okay. What's the capital of India?"

"That's no good." He marched away, his arms swinging like a toy soldier. Then he marched back to Laxmi's cousin and tugged at a pocket of her overcoat. "Ask me a hard one."

"Senegal," she said.

"Dakar!" Rohin exclaimed triumphantly, and began running in larger and larger circles. Eventually he ran into the kitchen. Miranda could hear him opening and closing the fridge.

"Rohin, don't touch without asking," Laxmi's cousin called out wearily. She managed a smile for Miranda. "Don't worry, he'll fall asleep in a few hours. And thanks for watching him."

"Back at three," Laxmi said, disappearing with her cousin down the hallway. "We're double-parked."

Miranda fastened the chain on the door. She went to the kitchen to find Rohin, but he was now in the living room, at the dining table, kneeling on one of the director's chairs. He unzipped his knapsack, pushed Miranda's basket of manicure supplies to one side of the table, and spread his crayons over the surface. Miranda stood over his shoulder. She watched as he gripped a blue crayon and drew the outline of an airplane.

"It's lovely," she said. When he didn't reply, she went to the kitchen to pour herself more coffee.

"Some for me, please," Rohin called out.

She returned to the living room. "Some what?"

"Some coffee. There's enough in the pot. I saw."

She walked over to the table and sat opposite him. At times he nearly stood up to reach for a new crayon. He barely made a dent in the director's chair.

"You're too young for coffee."

Rohin leaned over the sketch pad, so that his tiny chest and shoulders almost touched it, his head tilted to one side. "The stewardess let me have coffee," he said. "She made it with milk and lots of sugar." He straightened, revealing a woman's face beside the plane, with long wavy hair and eyes like asterisks. "Her hair was more shiny," he decided, adding, "My father met a pretty woman on a plane, too." He looked at Miranda. His face darkened as he watched her sip. "Can't I have just a little coffee? Please?"

She wondered, in spite of his composed, brooding expression, if he were the type to throw a tantrum. She imagined his kicking her with his leather shoes, screaming for coffee, screaming and crying until his mother and Laxmi came back to fetch him. She went to the kitchen and prepared a cup for him as he'd requested. She selected a mug she didn't care for, in case he dropped it.

"Thank you," he said when she put it on the table. He took short sips, holding the mug securely with both hands.

Miranda sat with him while he drew, but when she attempted to put a coat of clear polish on her nails he protested. Instead he pulled out a paperback world almanac from his knapsack and asked her to quiz him. The countries were arranged by continent, six to a page, with the capitals in boldface, followed by a short entry on the population, government, and other statistics. Miranda turned to a page in the Africa section and went down the list.

"Mali," she asked him.

"Bamako," he replied instantly.

"Malawi."

"Lilongwe."

She remembered looking at Africa in the Mapparium. She remembered the fat part of it was green.

"Go on," Rohin said.

"Mauritania."

"Nouakchott."

"Mauritius."

He paused, squeezed his eyes shut, then opened them, defeated. "I can't remember."

"Port Louis," she told him.

"Port Louis." He began to say it again and again, like a chant under his breath.

When they reached the last of the countries in Africa, Rohin said he wanted to watch cartoons, telling Miranda to watch them with him. When the cartoons ended, he followed her to the kitchen, and stood by her side as she made more coffee. He didn't follow her when she went to the bathroom a few minutes later, but when she opened the door she was startled to find him standing outside.

"Do you need to go?"

He shook his head but walked into the bathroom anyway. He put the cover of the toilet down, climbed on top of it, and surveyed the narrow glass shelf over the sink which held Miranda's toothbrush and makeup.

"What's this for?" he asked, picking up the sample of eye gel she'd gotten the day she met Dev.

"Puffiness."

"What's puffiness?"

"Here," she explained, pointing.

"After you've been crying?"

"I guess so."

Rohin opened the tube and smelled it. He squeezed a drop of it onto a finger, then rubbed it on his hand. "It stings." He inspected the back of his hand closely, as if expecting it to change color. "My mother has puffiness. She says it's a cold, but really she cries, sometimes for hours. Sometimes straight through dinner. Sometimes she cries so hard her eyes puff up like bullfrogs."

Miranda wondered if she ought to feed him. In the kitchen she discovered a bag of rice cakes and some lettuce. She offered to go out, to buy something from the deli, but Rohin said he wasn't very hungry, and accepted one of the rice cakes. "You eat one too," he said. They sat at the table, the rice cakes between them. He turned to a fresh page in his sketch pad. "You draw."

She selected a blue crayon. "What should I draw?"

He thought for a moment. "I know," he said. He asked her to draw things in the living room: the sofa, the director's chairs, the television, the telephone. "This way I can memorize it."

"Memorize what?"

"Our day together." He reached for another rice cake.

"Why do you want to memorize it?"

"Because we're never going to see each other, ever again."

The precision of the phrase startled her. She looked at him, feeling slightly depressed. Rohin didn't look depressed. He tapped the page. "Go on."

And so she drew the items as best as she could—the sofa, the director's chairs, the television, the telephone. He sidled up to her, so close that it was sometimes difficult to see what she was doing. He put his small brown hand over hers. "Now me."

She handed him the crayon.

He shook his head. "No, now draw me."

"I can't," she said. "It won't look like you."

The brooding look began to spread across Rohin's face again, just as it had when she'd refused him coffee. "Please?"

She drew his face, outlining his head and the thick fringe of hair. He sat perfectly still, with a formal, melancholy expression, his gaze fixed to one side. Miranda wished she could draw a good likeness. Her hand moved in conjunction with her eyes, in unknown ways, just as it had that day in the bookstore when she'd transcribed her name in Bengali letters. It looked nothing like him. She was in the middle of drawing his nose when he wriggled away from the table.

"I'm bored," he announced, heading toward her bedroom. She heard him opening the door, opening the drawers of her bureau and closing them.

When she joined him he was inside the closet. After a moment he emerged, his hair disheveled, holding the silver cocktail dress. "This was on the floor."

"It falls off the hanger."

Rohin looked at the dress and then at Miranda's body. "Put it on."

"Excuse me?"

"Put it on."

There was no reason to put it on. Apart from in the fitting room at Filene's she had never worn it, and as long as she was with Dev she knew she never would. She knew they would never go to restaurants, where he would reach across a table and kiss her hand. They would meet in her apartment, on Sundays, he in his sweatpants, she in her jeans. She took the dress from Rohin and shook it out, even though the slinky fabric never wrinkled. She reached into the closet for a free hanger.

"Please put it on," Rohin asked, suddenly standing behind her. He pressed his face against her, clasping her waist with both his thin arms. "Please?"

"All right," she said, surprised by the strength of his grip.

He smiled, satisfied, and sat on the edge of her bed.

"You have to wait out there," she said, pointing to the door. "I'll come out when I'm ready."

"But my mother always takes her clothes off in front of me."

"She does?"

Rohin nodded. "She doesn't even pick them up afterward. She leaves them all on the floor by the bed, all tangled.

"One day she slept in my room," he continued. "She said it felt better than her bed, now that my father's gone."

"I'm not your mother," Miranda said, lifting him by the armpits off her bed. When he refused to stand, she picked him up. He was heavier than she expected, and he clung to her, his legs wrapped firmly around her hips, his head resting against her chest. She set him down in the hallway and shut the door. As an extra precaution she fastened the latch. She changed into the dress, glancing into the full-length mirror nailed to the back of the door. Her ankle socks looked silly, and so she opened a drawer and found the stockings. She searched through the back of the closet and slipped on the high heels with the tiny buckles. The chain straps of the dress were as light as paper clips against her collarbone. It was a bit loose on her. She could not zip it herself.

Rohin began knocking. "May I come in now?"

She opened the door. Rohin was holding his almanac in his hands, muttering something under his breath. His eyes opened wide at the sight of her. "I need help with the zipper," she said. She sat on the edge of the bed.

Rohin fastened the zipper to the top, and then Miranda stood up and twirled. Rohin put down the almanac. "You're sexy," he declared.

"What did you say?"

"You're sexy."

Miranda sat down again. Though she knew it meant nothing, her heart skipped a beat. Rohin probably referred to all women as sexy. He'd probably heard the word on television, or seen it on the cover of a magazine. She remembered the day in the Mapparium, standing across the bridge from Dev. At the time she thought she knew what his words meant. At the time they'd made sense.

Miranda folded her arms across her chest and looked Rohin in the eyes. "Tell me something."

He was silent.

"What does it mean?"

"What?"

"That word. 'Sexy.' What does it mean?"

He looked down, suddenly shy. "I can't tell you."

"Why not?"

"It's a secret." He pressed his lips together, so hard that a bit of them went white.

"Tell me the secret. I want to know."

Rohin sat on the bed beside Miranda and began to kick the edge of the mattress with the backs of his shoes. He giggled nervously, his thin body flinching as if it were being tickled.

"Tell me," Miranda demanded. She leaned over and gripped his ankles, holding his feet still.

Rohin looked at her, his eyes like slits. He struggled to kick the mattress again, but Miranda pressed against him. He fell back on the bed, his back straight as a board. He cupped his hands around his mouth, and then he whispered, "It means loving someone you don't know."

Miranda felt Rohin's words under her skin, the same way she'd felt Dev's. But instead of going hot she felt numb. It reminded her of the way she'd felt at the Indian grocery, the moment she knew, without even looking at a picture, that Madhuri Dixit, whom Dev's wife resembled, was beautiful.

"That's what my father did," Rohin continued. "He sat next to someone he didn't know, someone sexy, and now he loves her instead of my mother."

He took off his shoes and placed them side by side on the floor. Then he peeled back the comforter and crawled into Miranda's bed with the almanac. A minute later the book dropped from his hands, and he closed his eyes. Miranda watched him sleep, the comforter rising and falling as he breathed. He didn't wake up after twelve minutes like Dev, or even twenty. He didn't open his eyes as she stepped out of the silver cocktail dress and back into her jeans, and put the high-heeled shoes in the back of the closet, and rolled up the stockings and put them back in her drawer.

When she had put everything away she sat on the bed. She leaned toward him, close enough to see some white powder from the rice cakes stuck to the corners of his mouth, and picked up the almanac. As she turned the pages she imagined the quarrels Rohin had overheard in his house in Montreal. "Is she pretty?" his mother would have asked his father, wearing the same bathrobe she'd worn for weeks, her own pretty face turning spiteful. "Is she sexy?" His father would deny it at first, try to change the subject. "Tell me," Rohin's mother would shriek, "tell me if she's sexy." In the end his father would admit that she was, and his mother would cry and cry, in a bed surrounded by a tangle of clothes, her eyes puffing up like bullfrogs. "How could you," she'd ask, sobbing, "how could you love a woman you don't even know?"

As Miranda imagined the scene she began to cry a little herself. In the Mapparium that day, all the countries had seemed close enough to touch, and Dev's voice had bounced wildly off the glass. From across the bridge, thirty feet away, his words had reached her ears, so near and full of warmth that they'd drifted for days under her skin. Miranda cried harder, unable to stop. But Rohin still slept. She guessed that he was used to it now, to the sound of a woman crying.

On Sunday, Dev called to tell Miranda he was on his way. "I'm almost ready. I'll be there at two."

She was watching a cooking show on television. A woman pointed to a row of apples, explaining which were best for baking. "You shouldn't come today."

"Why not?"

"I have a cold," she lied. It wasn't far from the truth; crying had left her congested. "I've been in bed all morning."

"You do sound stuffed up." There was a pause. "Do you need anything?"

"I'm all set."

"Drink lots of fluids."

"Dev?"

"Yes, Miranda?"

"Do you remember that day we went to the Mapparium?"

"Of course."

"Do you remember how we whispered to each other?"

"I remember," Dev whispered playfully.

"Do you remember what you said?"

There was a pause. "'Let's go back to your place.'" He laughed quietly. "Next Sunday, then?"

The day before, as she'd cried, Miranda had believed she would never forget anything—not even the way her name looked written in Bengali. She'd fallen asleep beside Rohin and when she woke up he was drawing an airplane on the copy of *The Economist* she'd saved, hidden under the bed. "Who's Devajit Mitra?" he had asked, looking at the address label.

Miranda pictured Dev, in his sweatpants and sneakers, laughing into the phone. In a moment he'd join his wife downstairs, and tell her he wasn't going jogging. He'd pulled a muscle while stretching, he'd say, settling down to read the paper. In spite of herself, she longed for him. She would see him one more Sunday, she decided, perhaps two. Then she would tell him the things she had known all along: that it wasn't fair to her, or to his wife, that they both deserved better, that there was no point in it dragging on.

But the next Sunday it snowed, so much so that Dev couldn't tell his wife he was going running along the Charles. The Sunday after that, the snow had melted, but Miranda made plans to go to the movies with Laxmi, and when she told Dev this over the phone, he didn't ask her to cancel them. The third Sunday she got up early and went out for a walk. It was cold but sunny, and so she walked all the way down Commonwealth Avenue, past the restaurants where Dev had kissed her, and then she walked all the way to the Christian Science center. The Mapparium was closed, but she bought a cup of coffee nearby and sat on one of the benches in the plaza outside the church, gazing at its giant pillars and its massive dome, and at the clear-blue sky spread over the city.

▓ Exercises for Jhumpa Lahiri's "Sexy."

1. Re-create the phone conversation between Laxmi's cousin and her husband, as described in the story's opening paragraph. Write one of the daily phone conversations between Laxmi and her cousin.

2. What role does Miranda's relative isolation play in the story? Give Miranda a roommate, or have her confide in Laxmi about her affair.

3. Consider the flashback to Miranda's childhood neighbors, the Dixits. Write a full story dealing with the Dixits' and Miranda's experience at that birthday party. Delete that flashback, and everything about the Dixits, from "Sexy." What is the effect?

4. Write the same story in first person. Try changing the tone from melancholy to comic.

5. Write a scene in which Dev meets a friend for lunch and discusses his affair.

6. Write a scene portraying Dev and his wife at home.

7. Write a story in your own voice (first person) and strip this situation of all ethnicity—but keep the focus on the thematic issues of fidelity and love.

8. Rewrite the story, changing the ethnicity of Dev, Laxmi, and her cousin. What if Dev and Laxmi's cousin were not from the same country?

9. Write the story of Rohin and his parents' failing marriage, ending with his day at Miranda's apartment. Write the story of Rohin's mother and her failing marriage, ending with her day at the spa with Laxmi.

10. Try to rewrite this story without the character of Rohin.

THE KIND OF LIGHT
THAT SHINES ON TEXAS
by Reginald McKnight

I never liked Marvin Pruitt. Never liked him, never knew him, even though there were only three of us in the class. Three black kids. In our school there were fourteen classrooms of thirty-odd white kids (in '66, they considered Chicanos provisionally white) and three or four black kids. Primary school in primary colors. Neat division. Alphabetized. They didn't stick us in the back, or arrange us by degrees of hue, apartheidlike. This was real integration, a ten-to-one ratio as tidy as upper-class landscaping. If it all worked, you could have ten white kids all to yourself. They could talk to you, get the feel of you, scrutinize you bone deep if they wanted to. They seldom wanted to, and that was fine with me for two reasons. The first was that their scrutiny was irritating. How do you comb your hair—why do you comb your hair—may I please touch your hair—were the kinds of questions they asked. This is no way to feel at home. The second reason was Marvin. He embarrassed me. He smelled bad, was at least two grades behind, was hostile, dark skinned, homely, close-mouthed. I feared him for his size, pitied him for his dress, watched him all the time. Marveled at him, mystified, astonished, uneasy.

He had the habit of spitting on his right arm, juicing it down till it would glisten. He would start in immediately after taking his seat when we'd finished with the Pledge of Allegiance, "The Yellow Rose of Texas," "The Eyes of Texas Are upon You," and "Mistress Shady." Marvin would rub his spit-flecked arm with his left hand, rub and roll as if polishing an ebony pool cue. Then he would rest his head in the crook of his arm, sniffing, huffing deep like black-jacket boys huff bagsful of acrylics. After ten minutes or so, his eyes would close, heavy. He would sleep till recess. Mrs. Wickham would let him.

There was one other black kid in our class. A girl they called Ah-so. I never learned what she did to earn this name. There was nothing Asian about this big-shouldered girl. She was the tallest, heaviest kid in school. She was quiet, but I don't think any one of us was subtle or sophisticated enough to nickname our classmates according to any but physical attributes. Fat kids were called

Porky or Butterball, skinny ones were called Stick or Ichabod. Ah-so was big, thick, and African. She would impassively sit, sullen, silent as Marvin. She wore the same dark blue pleated skirt every day, the same ruffled white blouse every day. Her skin always shone as if worked by Marvin's palms and fingers. I never spoke one word to her, nor she to me.

Of the three of us, Mrs. Wickham called only on Ah-so and me. Ah-so never answered one question, correctly or incorrectly, so far as I can recall. She wasn't stupid. When asked to read aloud she read well, seldom stumbling over long words, reading with humor and expression. But when Wickham asked her about Farmer Brown and how many cows, or the capital of Vermont, or the date of this war or that, Ah-so never spoke. Not one word. But you always felt she could have answered those questions if she'd wanted to. I sensed no tension, embarrassment, or anger in Ah-so's reticence. She simply refused to speak. There was something unshakable about her, some core so impenetrably solid, you got the feeling that if you stood too close to her she could eat your thoughts like a black star eats light. I didn't despise Ah-so as I despised Marvin. There was nothing malevolent about her. She sat like a great icon in the back of the classroom, tranquil, guarded, sealed up, watchful. She was close to sixteen, and it was my guess she'd given up on school. Perhaps she was just obliging the wishes of her family, sticking it out till the law could no longer reach her.

There were at least half a dozen older kids in our class. Besides Marvin and Ah-so there was Oakley, who sat behind me, whispering threats into my ear; Varna Willard with the large breasts; Eddie Limon, who played bass for a high school rock band; and Lawrence Ridderbeck, who everyone said had a kid and a wife. You couldn't expect me to know anything about Texan educational practices of the 1960s, so I never knew why there were so many older kids in my sixth-grade class. After all, I was just a boy and had transferred into the school around midyear. My father, an air force sergeant, had been sent to Viet Nam. The air force sent my mother, my sister, Claire, and me to Connolly Air Force Base, which during the war housed "unaccompanied wives." I'd been to so many different schools in my short life that I ceased wondering about their differences. All I knew about the Texas schools is that they weren't afraid to flunk you.

Yet though I was only twelve then, I had a good idea why Wickham never once called on Marvin, why she let him snooze in the crook of his polished arm. I knew why she would press her lips together, and narrow her eyes at me whenever I correctly answered a question, rare as that was. I know why she badgered Ah-so with questions everyone knew Ah-so would never even consider answering. Wickham didn't like us. She wasn't gross about it, but it was clear she didn't want us around. She would prove her dislike day after day with little stories and jokes. "I just want to share with you all," she would say, "a little riddle my daughter told me at the supper table th'other day. Now, where do you go when you injure your knee?" Then one, two, or all three of her pets would say for the rest of us, "We don't know, Miz Wickham," in that skin-

good shiner. His acne burned red like a fresh abrasion. He snapped the locker open and kicked his shoes off without sitting. Then he pulled off his shorts, revealing two paddle stripes on his ass. They were fresh red bars speckled with white, the white speckles being the reverse impression of the paddle's suction holes. He must not have watched his filthy mouth while in Gilchrest's presence. Behind me, I heard Preston and Nailor pad to their lockers.

Oakley spoke without turning around. "Somebody's gonna git his skinny black ass kicked, right today, right after school." He said it softly. He slipped his jock off, turned around. I looked away. Out the corner of my eye I saw him stride off, his hairy nakedness a weapon clearing the younger boys from his path. Just before he rounded the corner of the shower stalls, I threw my toilet kit to the floor and stammered, "I—I never did nothing to you, Oakley." He stopped, turned, stepped closer to me, wrapping his towel around himself. Sweat streamed down my rib cage. It felt like ice water. "You wanna go at it right now, boy?"

"I never did nothing to you." I felt tears in my eyes. I couldn't stop them even though I was blinking like mad. "Never."

He laughed. "You busted my nose, asshole."

"What about before? What'd I ever do to you?"

"See you after school, Coonie." Then he turned away, flashing his acne-spotted back like a semaphore. "Why?" I shouted. "Why you wanna fight me?" Oakley stopped and turned, folded his arms, leaned against a toilet stall. "Why you wanna fight *me*, Oakley?" I stepped over the bench. "What'd I do? Why me?" And then unconsciously, as if scratching, as if breathing, I walked toward Marvin, who stood a few feet from Oakley, combing his hair at the mirror. "Why not him?" I said. "How come you're after *me* and not *him*?" The room froze. Froze for a moment that was both evanescent and eternal, somewhere between an eye blink and a week in hell. No one moved, nothing happened; there was no sound at all. And then it was as if all of us at the same moment looked at Marvin. He just stood there, combing away, the only body in motion, I think. He combed his hair and combed it, as if seeing only his image, hearing only his comb scraping his scalp. I knew he'd heard me. There's no way he could not have heard me. But all he did was slide the comb into his pocket and walk out the door.

"I got no quarrel with Marvin," I heard Oakley say. I turned toward his voice, but he was already in the shower.

I was able to avoid Oakley at the end of the school day. I made my escape by asking Mrs. Wickham if I could go to the rest room.

"'Rest room,'" Oakley mumbled. "It's a damn toilet, sissy."

"Clinton," said Mrs. Wickham. "Can you *not* wait till the bell rings? It's almost three o'clock."

"No ma'am," I said. "I won't make it."

"Well I should make you wait just to teach you to be more mindful about . . . hygiene . . . uh things." She sucked in her cheeks, squinted. "But I'm feeling charitable today. You may go." I immediately left the building, and got on the bus. "Ain't you a little early?" said the bus driver, swinging the door shut. "Just left the office," I said. The driver nodded, apparently not giving me a second thought. I had no idea why I'd told her I'd come from the office, or why she found it a satisfactory answer. Two minutes later the bus filled, rolled, and shook its way to Connolly Air Base. When I got home, my mother was sitting in the living room, smoking her Slims, watching her soap opera. She absently asked me how my day had gone and I told her fine. "Hear from Dad?" I said.

"No, but I'm sure he's fine." She always said that when we hadn't heard from him in a while. I suppose she thought I was worried about him, or that I felt vulnerable without him. It was neither. I just wanted to discuss something with my mother that we both cared about. If I spoke with her about things that happened at school, or on my weekends, she'd listen with half an ear, say something like, "Is that so?" or "You don't say?" I couldn't stand that sort of thing. But when I mentioned my father, she treated me a bit more like an adult, or at least someone who was worth listening to. I didn't want to feel like a boy that afternoon. As I turned from my mother and walked down the hall I thought about the day my father left for Viet Nam. Sharp in his uniform, sure behind his aviator specs, he slipped a cigar from his pocket and stuck it in mine. "Not till I get back," he said. "We'll have us one when we go fishing. Just you and me, out on the lake all day, smoking and casting and sitting. Don't let Mama see it. Put it in y'back pocket." He hugged me, shook my hand, and told me I was the man of the house now. He told me he was depending on me to take good care of my mother and sister. "Don't you let me down, now, hear?" And he tapped his thick finger on my chest. "You almost as big as me. Boy, you something else." I believed him when he told me those things. My heart swelled big enough to swallow my father, my mother, Claire. I loved, feared, and respected myself, my manhood. That day I could have put all of Waco, Texas, in my heart. And it wasn't till about three months later that I discovered I really wasn't the man of the house, that my mother and sister, as they always had, were taking care of me.

For a brief moment I considered telling my mother about what had happened at school that day, but for one thing, she was deep down in the halls of *General Hospital,* and never paid you much mind till it was over. For another thing, I just wasn't the kind of person—I'm still not, really—to discuss my problems with anyone. Like my father I kept things to myself, talked about my problems only in retrospect. Since my father wasn't around I consciously wanted to be like him, doubly like him, I could say. I wanted to be the man of the house in some respect, even if it had to be in an inward way. I went to my room, changed my clothes, and laid out my homework. I couldn't focus on it. I thought about Marvin, what I'd said about him or done to him—I couldn't tell which. I'd done something to him, said something about him; said something about and done something to myself. *How come you're after* me *and not* him? I kept trying to tell myself I hadn't meant it that way. *That* way. I thought about approaching Marvin, telling him what I really meant was that he was more

Oakley's age and weight than I. I would tell him I meant I was no match for Oakley. *See, Marvin, what I meant was that he wants to fight a colored guy, but is afraid to fight you 'cause you could beat him.* But try as I did, I couldn't for a moment convince myself that Marvin would believe me. I meant it *that* way and no other. Everybody heard. Everybody knew. That afternoon I forced myself to confront the notion that tomorrow I would probably have to fight both Oakley and Marvin. I'd have to be two men.

I rose from my desk and walked to the window. The light made my skin look orange, and I started thinking about what Wickham had told us once about light. She said that oranges and apples, leaves and flowers, the whole multicolored world, was not what it appeared to be. The colors we see, she said, look like they do only because of the light or ray that shines on them. "The color of the thing isn't what you see, but the light that's reflected off it." Then she shut out the lights and shone a white light lamp on a prism. We watched the pale splay of colors on the projector screen; some people oohed and aahed. Suddenly, she switched on a black light and the color of everything changed. The prism colors vanished, Wickham's arms were purple, the buttons of her dress were as orange as hot coals, rather than the blue they had been only seconds before. We were all very quiet. "Nothing," she said, after a while, "is really what it appears to be." I didn't really understand then. But as I stood at the window, gazing at my orange skin, I wondered what kind of light I could shine on Marvin, Oakley, and me that would reveal us as the same.

I sat down and stared at my arms. They were dark brown again. I worked up a bit of saliva under my tongue and spat on my left arm. I spat again, then rubbed the spittle into it, polishing, working till my arm grew warm. As I spat, and rubbed, I wondered why Marvin did this weird, nasty thing to himself, day after day. Was he trying to rub away the black, or deepen it, doll it up? And if he did this weird nasty thing for a hundred years, would he spit-shine himself invisible, rolling away the eggplant skin, revealing the scarlet muscle, blue vein, pink and yellow tendon, white bone? Then disappear? Seen through, all colors, no colors. Spitting and rubbing. Is this the way you do it? I leaned forward, sniffed the arm. It smelled vaguely of mayonnaise. After an hour or so, I fell asleep.

I saw Oakley the second I stepped off the bus the next morning. He stood outside the gym in his usual black penny loafers, white socks, high-water jeans, T-shirt, and black jacket. Nailor stood with him, his big teeth spread across his bottom lip like playing cards. If there was anyone I felt like fighting, that day, it was Nailor. But I wanted to put off fighting for as long as I could. I stepped toward the gymnasium, thinking that I shouldn't run, but if I hurried I could beat Oakley to the door and secure myself near Gilchrest's office. But the moment I stepped into the gym, I felt Oakley's broad palm clap down on my shoulder. "Might as well stay out here, Coonie," he said. "I need me a little target practice." I turned to face him and he slapped me, one-two, with the back, then the palm of his hand, as I'd seen Bogart do to Peter Lorre in *The Maltese Falcon*. My heart went wild. I could scarcely breathe. I couldn't swallow.

"Call me a nigger," I said. I have no idea what made me say this. All I know is that it kept me from crying. "Call me a nigger, Oakley."

"Fuck you, ya black-ass slope." He slapped me again, scratching my eye. "I don't do what coonies tell me."

"Call me a nigger."

"Outside, Coonie."

"Call me one. Go ahead!"

He lifted his hand to slap me again, but before his arm could swing my way, Marvin Pruitt came from behind me and calmly pushed me aside. "Git out my way, boy," he said. And he slugged Oakley on the side of his head. Oakley stumbled back, stiff-legged. His eyes were big. Marvin hit him twice more, once again to the side of the head, once to the nose. Oakley went down and stayed down. Though blood was drawn, whistles blowing, fingers pointing, kids hollering, Marvin just stood there, staring at me with cool eyes. He spat on the ground, licked his lips, and just stared at me, till Coach Gilchrest and Mr. Calderon tackled him and violently carried him away. He never struggled, never took his eyes off me.

Nailor and Mrs. Wickham helped Oakley to his feet. His already fattened nose bled and swelled so that I had to look away. He looked around, bemused, walleyed, maybe scared. It was apparent he had no idea how bad he was hurt. He didn't blink. He didn't even touch his nose. He didn't look like he knew much of anything. He looked at me, looked me dead in the eye, in fact, but didn't seem to recognize me.

That morning, like all other mornings, we said the Pledge of Allegiance, sang "The Yellow Rose of Texas," "The Eyes of Texas Are upon You," and "Mistress Shady." The room stood strangely empty without Oakley, and without Marvin, but at the same time you could feel their presence more intensely somehow. I felt like I did when I'd walk into my mother's room and could smell my father's cigars or cologne. He was more palpable, in certain respects, than when there in actual flesh. For some reason, I turned to look at Ah-so, and just this once I let my eyes linger on her face. She had a very gentle-looking face, really. That surprised me. She must have felt my eyes on her because she glanced up at me for a second and smiled, white teeth, downcast eyes. Such a pretty smile. That surprised me too. She held it for a few seconds, then let it fade. She looked down at her desk, and sat still as a photograph.

■ Exercises for Reginald McKnight's "The Kind of Light That Shines on Texas."

1. Tell the first two pages of this story in third-person, present-tense prose. "Clinton does not like Marvin Pruitt . . ."

2. Have the narrator tell this story to his son or grandson who is taking boxing lessons and wants to sign up for the army.

3. Have him visit Marvin Pruitt in detention after school; write the scene between them as they go home together at day's end.

4. Have Mr. Gilchrest and Mrs. Wickham meet in the Teacher's Common Room and talk about their "problem students" and what happened that afternoon in gym class.

5. Tell the last two pages of "The Kind of Light That Shines on Texas" from Ah-so's point of view. Have her explain why she refuses to offer comments in class.

6. Write a story describing your own act of bravery or cowardice when you were twelve years old; what did you learn on that day?

7. Have Preston and Nailor take Oakley home after Pruitt has beaten him up; describe the house, the conversation, the response of Oakley's mother if she's home.

8. Write the scene of "Dad" returning from Vietnam; father and son go fishing and they smoke cigars and talk about what Clinton's been learning at school.

9. Strip this story of issues of race and class; what would remain?

10. Move this story from Texas to your own hometown; what would change?

FAITH IN THE AFTERNOON
by Grace Paley

A s for you, fellow independent thinker of the Western Bloc, if you have any-thing sensible to say, don't wait. Shout it out loud right this minute. In twenty years, give or take a spring, your grandchildren will be lying in sand-boxes all over the world, their ears to the ground, listening for signals from long ago. In fact, kneeling now on the great plains in a snootful of gray dust, what do you hear? Pigs oinking, potatoes peeling, Indians running, winter coming?

Faith's head is under the pillow nearly any weekday midnight, asweat with dreams, and she is seasick with ocean sounds, the squealing wind stuck in its rearing tail by high tide.

That is because her grandfather, scoring the salty sea, skated for miles along the Baltic's icy beaches, with a frozen herring in his pocket. And she, all ears, was born in Coney Island.

Who are her antecedents? Mama and Papa of course. Her environment? A brother and a sister with their own sorrow to lead by the nose out of this life. All together they would make a goddamn quadruped bilingual hermaphrodite. Even so, proving their excellence, they bear her no rancor and are always anx-ious to see her, to see the boys, to take the poor fatherless boys to a picnic with their boys, for a walk, to an ocean, glad to say, we saw Mama in the Children of Judea, she sends love . . . They never say snidely, as the siblings of others might, It wouldn't hurt you to run over, Faith, it's only a subway ride . . .

Hope and Faith and even Charles—who comes glowering around once a year to see if Faith's capacity for survival has not been overwhelmed by her sus-ceptibility to abuse—begged their parents to reconsider the decision to put money down and move into the Children of Judea. "Mother," said Hope, tak-ing off her eyeglasses, for she did not like even that little window of glass to come between their mother and herself. "Now, Mother, how will you make out with all those *yentas*? Some of them don't even speak English." "I have spoken altogether too much English in my life," said Mrs. Darwin. "If I really liked

English that much, I would move to England." "Why don't you go to Israel?" asked Charles. "That would at least make sense to people." "And leave you?" she asked, tears in her eyes at the thought of them all alone, wrecking their lives on the shoals of every day, without her tearful gaze attending.

When Faith thinks of her mother and father in any year, young or impersonally aged, she notices that they are squatting on the shore, staring with light eyes at the white waves. Then Faith feels herself so damply in the swim of things that she considers crawling Channels and Hellesponts and even taking a master's degree in education in order to exult at last in a profession and get out of the horseshit trades of this lofty land.

Certain facts may become useful. The Darwins moved to Coney Island for the air. There was not enough air in Yorkville, where the grandmother had been planted among German Nazis and Irish bums by Faith's grandfather, who soon departed alone in blue pajamas, for death.

Her grandmother pretended she was German in just the same way that Faith pretends she is an American. Faith's mother flew in the fat face of all that and, once safely among her own kind in Coney Island, learned real Yiddish, helped Faith's father, who was not so good at foreign languages, and as soon as all the verbs and necessary nouns had been collected under the roof of her mouth, she took an oath to expostulate in Yiddish and grieve only in Yiddish, and she has kept that oath to this day.

Faith has only visited her parents once since she began to understand that because of Ricardo she would have to be unhappy for a while. Faith really is an American and she was raised up like everyone else to the true assumption of happiness.

No doubt about it, squinting in any direction she is absolutely miserable. She is ashamed of this before her parents. "You should get help," says Hope. "Psychiatry was invented for people like you, Faithful," says Charles. "My little blondie, life is short. I'll lay out a certain amount of cash," says her father. "When will you be a person," says her mother.

Their minds are on matters. Severed Jerusalem; the Second World War still occupies their arguments; peaceful uses of atomic energy (is it necessary altogether?); new little waves of anti-Semitism lap the quiet beaches of their accomplishment.

They are naturally disgusted with Faith and her ridiculous position right in the middle of prosperous times. They are ashamed of her willful unhappiness.

All right! Shame then! Shame on them all!

That Ricardo, Faith's first husband, was a sophisticated man. He was proud and happy because men liked him. He was really, he said, a man's man. Like any true man's man, he ran after women too. He was often seen running, in fact, after certain young women on West Eighth Street or leaping little fences in Bedford Mews to catch up with some dear little pussycat.

He called them pet names, which generally referred to certain flaws in their appearance. He called Faith Baldy, although she is not and never will be bald. She is fine-haired and fair, and regards it as part of the lightness of her general construction that when she gathers her hair into an ordinary topknot, the stuff escapes around the contour of her face, making her wisp-haired and easy to blush. He is now living with a shapely girl with white round arms and he calls her Fatty.

When in New York, Faith's first husband lives within floating distance of the Green Coq, a prospering bar where he is well known and greeted loudly as he enters, shoving his current woman gallantly before. He introduces her around—hey, this is Fatty or Baldy. Once there was Bugsy, dragged up from the gutter where she loved to roll immies with Russell the bartender. Then Ricardo, to save her from becoming an old tea bag (his joke), hoisted her on the pulpy rods of his paperbacked culture high above her class, and she still administers her troubles from there, poor girl, her knees gallivanting in air.

Bugsy lives forever behind the Horney curtain of Faith's mind, a terrible end, for she used to be an ordinarily reprehensible derelict, but by the time Ricardo had helped her through two abortions and one lousy winter, she became an alcoholic and a whore for money. She soon gave up spreading for the usual rewards, which are an evening's companionship and a weekend of late breakfasts.

Bugsy was before Faith. Ricardo agreed to be Faith's husband for a couple of years anyway, because Faith in happy overindulgence had become pregnant. Almost at once, she suffered a natural miscarriage, but it was too late. They had been securely married by the state for six weeks when that happened, and so, like the gentleman he may very well be, he resigned himself to her love—a medium-sized, beefy-shouldered man, Indian-black hair, straight and coarse to the fingers, lavender eyes—Faith is perfectly willing to say it herself, to any good listener: she loved Ricardo. She began indeed to love herself, to love the properties which, for a couple of years anyway, extracted such heart-warming activity from him.

Well, Faith argues whenever someone says, "Oh really, Faithy, what do you mean—love?" She must have loved Ricardo. She had two boys with him. She had them to honor him and his way of loving when sober. He believed and often shouted out loud in the Green Coq, that Newcastle into which he reeled every night, blind with coal, that she'd had those kids to make him a bloody nine-to-fiver.

Nothing, said Faith in those simple days, was further from her mind. For her public part, she had made reasoned statements in the playground, and in the A&P while queued up for the cashier, that odd jobs were a splendid way of making out if you had together agreed on a substandard way of life. For, she explained to the ladies in whom she had confided her entire life, how can a man know his children if he is always out working? How true, that is the trouble with children today, replied the ladies, wishing to be her friend, they never see their daddies.

"Mama," Faith said, the last time she visited the Children of Judea, "Ricardo and I aren't going to be together so much anymore."

"Faithy!" said her mother. "You have a terrible temper. No, no, listen to me. It happens to many people in their lives. He'll be back in a couple of days. After all, the children . . . just say you're sorry. It isn't even a hill of beans. Nonsense. I thought he was much improved when he was here a couple of months ago. Don't give it a thought. Clean up the house, put in a steak. Tell the children be a little quiet, send them next door for the television. He'll be home before you know it. Don't pay attention. Do up your hair something special. Papa would be more than glad to give you a little cash. We're not poverty-stricken, you know. You only have to tell us you want help. Don't worry. He'll walk in the door tomorrow. When you get home, he'll be turning on the hi-fi."

"Oh, Mama, Mama, he's tone deaf."

"Ai, Faithy, you have to do your life a little better than this."

They sat silently together, their eyes cast down by shame. The doorknob rattled. "My God, Hegel-Shtein," whispered Mrs. Darwin. "Ssh, Faith, don't tell Hegel-Shtein. She thinks everything is her business. Don't even leave a hint."

Mrs. Hegel-Shtein, president of the Grandmothers' Wool Socks Association, rolled in on oiled wheelchair wheels. She brought a lapful of multicolored wool in skeins. She was an old lady. Mrs. Darwin was really not an old lady. Mrs. Hegel-Shtein had organized this Active Association because children today wear cotton socks all winter. The grandmothers who lose heat at their extremities at a terrible clip are naturally more sensitive to these facts than the present avocated generation of mothers.

"Shalom, darling," said Mrs. Darwin to Mrs. Hegel-Shtein. "How's tricks?" she asked bravely.

"Aah," said Mrs. Hegel-Shtein. "Mrs. Essie Shifer resigned on account of her wrists."

"Really? Well, let her come sit with us. Company is healthy."

"Please, please, what's the therapy value if she only sits? Phooey!" said Mrs. Hegel-Shtein. "Excuse me, don't tell me that's Faith. Faith? Imagine that. Hope I know, but this is really Faith. So it turns out you really have a little time to see your mother . . . What luck for her you won't be busy forever."

"Oh, Gittel, I beg you, be quiet," Faith's mortified mother said. "I must beg you. Faith comes when she can. She's a mother. She has two little small boys. She works. Did you forget, Gittel, what it was like in those days when they're little babies? Who comes first? The children . . . the little children, they come first."

"Sure, sure, first, I know all about first. Didn't Archie come first? I had a big honor. I got a Christmas card from Florida from Mr. and Mrs. First. Listen to me, foolish people. I went by them to stay in the summer place, in the woods, near rivers. Only it got no ventilation, the whole place smells from termites and the dog. Please, I beg him, please, Mr. First, I'm a old woman, be sorry for me, I need extra air, leave your door open, I beg, I beg. No, not a word. Bang, every night eleven o'clock, the door gets shut like a rock. For a ten-minute business they close themselves up a whole night long.

"I'm better off in a old ladies' home, I told them. Nobody there is ashamed of a little cross ventilation."

Mrs. Darwin blushed. Faith said, "Don't be such a clock watcher, Mrs. Hegel-Shtein."

Mrs. Hegel-Shtein, who always seemed to know Faith better than Faith knew Mrs. Hegel-Shtein, said, "All right, all right. You're here, Faithy, don't be lazy. Help out. Here. Hold it, this wool on your hands, your mama will make a ball." Faith didn't mind. She held the wool out on her arms. Mrs. Darwin twisted and turned it round and round. Mrs. Hegel-Shtein directed in a loud voice, wheeling back and forth and pointing out serious mistakes. "Celia, Celia," she cried, "it should be rounder, you're making a square. Faithy, be more steadier. Move a little. You got infantile paralysis?"

"More wool, more wool," said Mrs. Darwin, dropping one completed ball into a shopping bag. They were busy as bees in a ladies' murmur about life and lives. They worked. They took vital facts from one another and looked as dedicated as a kibbutz.

The door to Mr. and Mrs. Darwin's room had remained open. Old bearded men walked by, thumbs linked behind their backs, all alike, the leftover army of the Lord. They had stuffed the morning papers under their mattresses, and because of the sorrowful current events they hurried up to the Temple of Judea on the sixth floor, from which they could more easily communicate with God. Ladies leaned on sticks stiffly, their articulations jammed with calcium. They knocked on the open door and said, "Oi, busy . . ." or "Mrs. Hegel-Shtein, don't you ever stop?" No one said much to Faith's mother, the vice-president of the Grandmothers' Wool Socks Association.

Hope had warned her: "Mother, you are only sixty-five years old. You look fifty-five." "Youth is in the heart, Hopey. I feel older than Grandma. It's the way I'm constituted. Anyway Papa is practically seventy, he deserves a rest. We have some advantage that we're young enough to make a good adjustment. By the time we're old and miserable, it'll be like at home here." "Mother, you'll certainly be an object of suspicion, an interloper, you'll have enemies everywhere." Hope had been sent to camp lots of years as a kid; she knew a thing or two about group living.

Opposite Faith, her mother swaddled the fat turquoise balls in more and more turquoise wool. Faith swayed gently back and forth along with her out-stretched wool-wound arms. It hurt her most filial feelings that, in this acute society, Mrs. Hegel-Shtein should be sought after, admired, indulged . . .

"Well, Ma, what do you hear from the neighborhood?" Faith asked. She thought they could pass some cheery moments before the hovering shadow of Ricardo shoved a fat thumb in her eye.

"Ah, nothing much," Mrs. Darwin said.

"Nothing much?" asked Mrs. Hegel-Shtein. "I heard you correctly said nothing much? You got a letter today from Slovinsky family, your heart stuck in your teeth, Celia, you want to hide this from little innocent Faith. Little baby Faithy. Ssh. Don't tell little children? Hah?"

"Gittel, I must beg you. I have reasons. I must beg you, don't mix in. Oh, I must beg you, Gittel, not to push anymore, I want to say nothing much on this subject."

"Idiots!" Mrs. Hegel-Shtein whispered low and harsh.

"Did you really hear from the Slovinskys, Mama, really? Oh, you know I'm always interested in Tessie. Oh, you remember what a lot of fun Tess and I used to have when we were kids. I liked her. I never didn't like her." For some reason Faith addressed Mrs. Hegel-Shtein: "She was a very beautiful girl."

"Oh, yeh, beautiful. Young. Beautiful. Very old story. Naturally. Gittel, you stopped winding? Why? The meeting is tonight. Tell Faithy all about Slovinsky, her pal. Faithy got coddled from life already too much."

"Gittel, I said shut up!" said Mrs. Darwin. "Shut up!"

(Then to all concerned a short dear remembrance arrived. A policeman, thumping after him along the boardwalk, had arrested Mr. Darwin one Saturday afternoon. He had been distributing leaflets for the Sholem Aleichem School and disagreeing reasonably with his second cousin, who had a different opinion about the past and the future. The leaflet cried out in Yiddish: "Parents! A little child's voice calls to you, 'Papa, Mama, what does it mean to be a Jew in the world today?'" Mrs. Darwin watched them from the boardwalk bench, where she sat getting sun with a shopping bag full of leaflets. The policeman shouted furiously at Mr. and Mrs. Darwin and the old cousin, for they were in an illegal place. Then Faith's mother said to him in the Mayflower voice of a disappearing image of life, "Shut up, you Cossack!" "You see," said Mr. Darwin, "to a Jew the word 'shut up' is a terrible expression, a dirty word, like a sin, because in the beginning, if I remember correctly, was the word! It's a great assault. Get it?")

"Celia, if you don't tell this story now, I roll right out and I don't roll in very soon. Life is life. Everybody today is coddlers."

"Mama, I want to hear anything you know about Tess, anyway. Please tell me," Faith asked. "If you don't tell me, I'll call up Hope. I bet you told her."

"All stubborn people," said Mrs. Darwin. "All right. Tess Slovinsky. You know about the first tragedy, Faith? The first tragedy was she had a child born a monster. A real monster. Nobody saw it. They put it in a home. All right. Then the second child. They went right away ahead immediately and they tried and they had a second child. This one was born full of allergies. It had rashes from orange juice. It choked from milk. Its eyes swoll up from going to the country. All right. Then her husband, Arnold Lever, a very pleasant boy, got a cancer. They chopped off a finger. It got worse. They chopped off a hand. It didn't help. Faithy, that was the end of a lovely boy. That's the letter I got this morning just before you came."

Mrs. Darwin stopped. Then she looked up at Mrs. Hegel-Shtein and Faith. "He was an only son," she said. Mrs. Hegel-Shtein gasped. "You said an only son!" On deep tracks, the tears rolled down her old cheeks. But she had smiled so peculiarly for seventy-seven years that they suddenly swerved wildly toward her ears and hung like glass from each lobe.

Faith watched her cry and was indifferent. Then she thought a terrible thought. She thought that if Ricardo had lost a leg or so, that would certainly have kept him home. This cheered her a little, but not for long.

"Oh, Mama, Mama, Tessie never guessed what was going to happen to her. We used to play house and she never guessed."

"Who guesses?" screamed Mrs. Hegel-Shtein. "Archie is laying down this minute in Florida. Sun is shining on him. He's guessing?"

Mrs. Hegel-Shtein fluttered Faith's heart. She rattled her ribs. She squashed her sorrow as though it were actually the least toxic of all the world's great poisons.

However, the first one to live with the facts was Mrs. Hegel-Shtein. Eyes dry, she said, "What about Brauns? The old Braun, the uncle, an idiot, a regular Irgunist, is here."

"June Braun?" Faith asked. "My friend June Braun? From Brighton Beach Avenue? That one?"

"Of course, only, that isn't so bad," Mrs. Darwin said, getting into the spirit of things. "Junie's husband, an engineer in airplanes. Very serious boy. Papa doesn't like him to this day. He was in the movement. They bought a house in Huntington Harbor with a boat, a garage, a garage for the boat. She looked stunning. She had three boys. Brilliant. The husband played golf with the vice-president, a goy. The future was golden. She was active in everything. One morning they woke up. It's midnight. Someone uncovers a little this, a little that. (I mentioned he was in the movement?) In forty-eight hours, he's black-listed. Good night Huntington Harbor. Today the whole bunch live with the Brauns in four rooms. I'm sorry for the old people."

"That's awful, Mama," Faith said. "The whole country's in a bad way."

"Still, Faith, times change. This is an unusual country. You'll travel around the world five times over, you wouldn't see a country like this often. She's up, she's down. It's unusual."

"Well, what else, Mama?" Faith asked. June Braun didn't sorrow her at all. What did June Braun know about pain? If you go in the dark sea over your head, you have to expect drowning cheerfully. Faith believed that June Braun and her husband whatever-his-name-could-be had gone too deeply into the air pocket of America whence all handouts come, and she accepted their suffocation in good spirit.

"What else, Mama? I know, what about Anita Franklin? What about her? God, was she smart in school! The whole senior class was crazy about her. Very chesty. Remember her, she got her period when she was about nine and three-quarters? Or something like that. You knew her mother very well. You were always in cahoots about something. You and Mrs. Franklin. Mama!"

"You sure you really want to hear, Faithy, you won't be so funny after-ward?" She liked telling these stories now, but she was not anxious to tell this one. Still she had warned Faith. "All right. Well, Anita Franklin. Anita Franklin also didn't guess. You remember she was married way ahead of you and Ricardo to a handsome boy from Harvard. Oh, Gittel, you can imagine what hopes her mother and her father had for her happiness. Arthur Mazzano, you know, Sephardic. They lived in Boston and they knew such smart people. Professors, doctors, the finest people. History-book writers, thinking American people. Oh, Faithy darling. I was invited to the house several times, Christmas, Easter. I met their babies. Little blondies like you were, Faith. He got maybe two Ph.D.s, you know, in different subjects. If someone wanted to ask a question, on what subject, they asked Arthur. At eight months their baby walked. I saw it myself. He wrote articles for Jewish magazines you never heard of, Gittel. Then one day, Anita finds out from the horse's mouth itself, he is fooling around with freshmen. Teenagers. In no time it's in the papers, everybody in court, talking talking talking, some say yes, some no, he was only flirting, you know the way a man flirts with youngsters. But it turns out one of the foolish kids is pregnant."

"Spanish people," said Mrs. Hegel-Shtein thoughtfully. "The men don't like their wives so much. They only get married if it's a good idea."

Faith bowed her head in sorrow for Anita Franklin, whose blood when she was nine and three-quarters burst from her to strike life and hope into the busy heads of all the girls in the fifth and sixth grades. Anita Franklin, she said to herself, do you think you'll make it all alone? How do you sleep at night, Anita Franklin, the sexiest girl in New Utrecht High? How is it these days, now you are never getting laid anymore by clever Arthur Mazzano, the brilliant Sephardic Scholar and Lecturer? Now it is time that leans across you and not handsome, fair Arthur's mouth on yours, or his intelligent Boy Scouty conflagrating fingers.

At this very moment, the thumb of Ricardo's hovering shadow jabbed her in her left eye, revealing for all the world the shallowness of her water table. Rice could have been planted at that instant on the terraces of her flesh and sprouted in strength and beauty in the floods that overwhelmed her from that moment on through all the afternoon. For herself and Anita Franklin, Faith bowed her head and wept.

"Going already, Faith?" her father asked. He had poked his darling birdy head with poppy pale eyes into the sun-spotted room. He is not especially good-looking. He is ugly. Faith has often thanked the Germ God and the Gene Goddess and the Great Lords of All Nucleic Acid that none of them looks like him, not even Charles, to whom it would not matter, for Charles has the height for any kind of face. They all look a little bit Teutonish, like their grandmother, who thinks she's German, just kind of light and even-featured, with Charles inclining to considerable jaw. People expect decision from Charles because of that jaw, and he has learned to give it to them—the wit of diagnosis, then inescapable treatment, followed by immediate health. In fact, his important colleagues often refer their wives' lower abdominal distress to Charles. Before he is dead he will be famous. Mr. Darwin hopes he will be famous soon, for in that family people do not live long.

Well, this popeyed, pale-beaked father of Faith's peered through the room into the glassy attack of the afternoon sun, couldn't focus on tears, or bitten lips for that matter, but saw Faith rise to look for her jacket in the closet.

"If you really have to go, I'll walk you, Faithy. Sweetheart, I haven't seen you in a long time," he said. He withdrew to wait in the hallway, well out of the circle of Mrs. Hegel-Shtein's grappling magnetism.

Faith kissed her mother, who whispered into her damp ear, "Be something, don't be a dishrag. You have two babies to raise." She kissed Mrs. Hegel-Shtein, because they had been brought up that way, not to hurt anyone's feelings, particularly if they loathed them, and they were much older.

Faith and her father walked through the light-green halls in silence to the life-giving lobby, where rosy, well-dressed families continued to arrive in order to sit for twenty minutes alongside their used-up elders. Some terrible political arguments about Jews in Russia now were taking place near the information desk. Faith paid no attention but moved toward the door, breathing deeply. She tried to keep her father behind her until she could meet the commitments of her face. "Don't rush, sweetheart," he said. "Don't rush, I'm not like these old cockers here, but I am no chicken definitely."

Gallantly he took her arm. "What's the good word?" he asked. "Well, no news isn't bad news, I hope?"

"So long, Chuck!" he called as they passed the iron gate over which, in stunning steel cursive, a welder had inscribed *The Children of Judea*. "Chuckle, chuckle," said her father, grasping her elbow more firmly, "what a name for a grown-up man!"

She turned to give him a big smile. He deserved an enormous smile, but she had only a big one available.

"Listen, Faithl, I wrote a poem, I want you to hear. Listen. I wrote it in Yiddish, I'll translate it in my head:

Childhood passes
Youth passes
Also the prime of life passes.
Old age passes.
Why do you believe, my daughters,
That old age is different?

"What do you say, Faithy? You know a whole bunch of artists and writers."

"What do I say? Papa." She stopped stock-still. "You're marvelous. That's like a Japanese Psalm of David."

"You think it's good?"

"I love it, Pa. It's marvelous."

"Well . . . you know, I might give up all this political stuff, if you really like it. I'm at a loss these days. It's a transition. Don't laugh at me, Faithy. You'll have to survive just such events someday yourself. Learn from life. Mine. I was going to organize the help. You know, the guards, the elevator boys—colored fellows, mostly. You notice, they're coming up in the world. Regardless of hopes, I never expected it in my lifetime. The war, I suppose, did it. Faith, what do you think? The war made Jews Americans and Negroes Jews. Ha ha. What do you think of that for an article? 'The Negro: Outside In at Last.'"

"Someone wrote something like that."

"Is that a fact? It's in the air. I tell you, I'm full of ideas. I don't have a soul to talk to. I'm used to your mother, only a funny thing happened to her, Faithy. We were so close. We're still friendly, don't take me the wrong way, but I mean a funny thing, she likes to be with the women lately. Loves to be with that insane, persecution, delusions-of-grandeur, paranoical Mrs. Hegel-Shtein. I can't stand her. She isn't a woman men can stand. Still, she got married. Your mother says, Be polite, Sid; I am polite. I always loved the ladies to a flaw, Faithy, but Mrs. Hegel-Shtein knocks at our room at 9 a.m. and I'm an orphan till lunch. She has magic powers. Also she oils up her wheelchair all afternoon so she can sneak around. Did you ever hear of a wheelchair you couldn't hear coming? My child, believe me, what your mother sees in her is a shady mystery. How could I put it? That woman has a whole bag of spitballs for the world. And also a bitter crippled life."

They had come to the subway entrance. "Well, Pa, I guess I have to go now. I left the kids with a friend."

He shut his mouth. Then he laughed. "Aaah, a talky old man . . ."

"Oh no, Pa, not at all. No. I loved talking to you, but I left the kids with a friend, Pa."

"I know how it is when they're little, you're tied down, Faith. Oh, we couldn't go anywhere for years. I went only to meetings, that's all. I didn't like to go to a movie without your mother and enjoy myself. They didn't have babysitters in those days. A wonderful invention, babysitters. With this invention two people could be lovers forever."

"Oh!" he gasped, "my darling girl, excuse me . . ." Faith was surprised at his exclamation because the tears had come to her eyes before she felt their pain.

"Ah, I see now how the land lies. I see you have trouble. You picked yourself out a hard world to raise a family."

"I have to go, Pa."

"Sure."

She kissed him and started down the stairs.

"Faith," he called, "can you come soon?"

"Oh, Pa," she said, four steps below him, looking up, "I can't come until I'm a little happy."

"Happy!" He leaned over the rail and tried to hold her eyes. But that is hard to do, for eyes are born dodgers and know a whole circumference of ways out of a bad spot. "Don't be selfish, Faithy, bring the boys, come."

"They're so noisy, Pa."

"Bring the boys, sweetheart. I love their little goyish faces."

"O.K., O.K.," she said, wanting only to go quickly. "I will, Pa, I will."

Mr. Darwin reached for her fingers through the rail. He held them tightly and touched them to her wet cheeks. Then he said, "Aaah . . ." an explosion of nausea, absolute digestive disgust. And before she could turn away from the old age of his insulted face and run home down the subway stairs, he had dropped her sweating hand out of his own and turned away from her.

Exercises for Grace Paley's "Faith in the Afternoon."

1. Tell Hope's side of the story of childhood; tell Charles's.

2. Describe Ricardo's afternoon while Faith is at the "Children of Judea."

3. Have Pinye Salzman and Leo Finkle—from Bernard Malamud's short story "The Magic Barrel"—visit their relatives also at the "home."

4. Write the story of the courtship with Ricardo, then the marriage ceremony.

5. Write five more poems in Faith's father's voice.

6. Write the ensuing scene: what happens when Faith returns to her apartment.

7. Do a scene from "Fenstad's Mother" by Charles Baxter, or "My Mother" by Jamaica Kincaid, or any of the other stories in Grace Paley's voice.

8. Transpose the first page into dialogue, the conversation of father and daughter into descriptive prose.

9. Propose fifty further exercises—on Cheever, Davies, Diaz, Dybek, and the rest.

10. List a dozen other authors and stories whose work you would choose to "imitate" in a sequel to this course.

THE WAVEMAKER FALTERS

by George Saunders

Halfway up the mountain it's the Center for Wayward Nuns, full of sisters and other religious personnel who've become doubtful. Once a few of them came down to our facility in stern suits and swam cautiously. The singing from up there never exactly knocks your socks off. It's very conditional singing, probably because of all the doubt. A young nun named Sister Viv came unglued there last fall and we gave her a free season pass to come down and meditate near our simulated Spanish trout stream whenever she wanted. The head nun said Viv was from Idaho and sure enough the stream seemed to have a calming effect.

One day she's sitting cross-legged a few feet away from a Dumpster housed in a granite boulder made of a resilient synthetic material. Ned, Tony, and Gerald as usual are dressed as Basques. In Orientation they learned a limited amount of actual Basque so that they can lapse into it whenever Guests are within earshot. Sister Viv's a regular so they don't even bother. I look over to say something supportive and optimistic to her and then I think oh jeez, not another patron death on my hands. She's going downstream fast and her habit's ballooning up. The fake Basques are standing there in a row with their mouths open.

So I dive in and drag her out. It's not very deep and the bottom's rubber-matted. None of the Basques are bright enough to switch off the Leaping Trout Subroutine however, so twice I get scraped with little fiberglass fins. Finally I get her out on the pine needles and she comes to and spits in my face and says I couldn't possibly know the darkness of her heart. Try me, I say. She crawls away and starts bashing her skull against a tree trunk. The trees are synthetic too. But still.

I pin her arms behind her and drag her to the Main Office, where they chain her weeping to the safe. A week later she runs amok in the nun eating hall and stabs a cafeteria worker to death.

So the upshot of it all is more guilt for me, Mr. Guilt.

Once a night Simone puts on the mermaid tail and lipsynchs on a raft in the wave pool while I play spotlights over her and broadcast "Button Up Your Overcoat." Tonight as I'm working the lights I watch Leon, Subquadrant Manager, watch Simone. As he watches her his wet mouth keeps moving. Every time I accidentally light up the Chlorine Shed the Guests start yelling at me. Finally I stop watching Leon watch her and try to concentrate on not getting written up for crappy showmanship.

I can't stand Leon. On the wall of his office he's got a picture of himself Jell-O-wrestling a traveling celebrity Jell-O-wrestler. That's pure Leon. Plus he had her autograph it. First he tried to talk her into dipping her breasts in ink and doing an imprint but she said no way. My point is, even traveling celebrity Jell-O-wrestlers have more class than Leon.

He follows us into Costuming and chats up Simone while helping her pack away her tail. Do I tell him to get lost? No. Do I knock him into a planter to remind him just whose wife Simone is? No. I go out and wait for her by Loco Logjam. I sit on a turnstile. The Italian lights in the trees are nice. The night crew's hard at work applying a wide range of commercial chemicals and cleaning hair balls from the filter. Some exiting guests are brawling in the traffic jam on the access road. Through a federal program we offer discount coupons to the needy, so sometimes our clientele is borderline. Once some bikers trashed the row of boutiques, and once Leon interrupted a gang guy trying to put hydrochloric acid in the Main Feeder.

Finally Simone's ready and we walk over to Employee Underground Parking. Bald Murray logs us out while trying to look down Simone's blouse. On the side of the road a woman's sitting in a shopping cart, wearing a grubby chemise.

For old time's sake I put my hand in Simone's lap.

Promises, promises, she says.

At the roadcut by the self-storage she makes me stop so she can view all the interesting stratification. She's never liked geology before. Leon takes geology at the community college and is always pointing out what's glacial till and what's not, so I suspect there's a connection. We get into a little fight about him and she admires his self-confidence to my face. I ask her is that some kind of a put-down. She's only saying, she says, that in her book a little boldness goes a long way. She asks if I remember the time Leon chased off the frat boy who kept trying to detach her mermaid hairpiece. Where was I? Why didn't I step in? Is she my girl or what?

I remind her that I was busy at the controls.

It gets very awkward and quiet. Me at the controls is a sore subject. Nothing's gone right for us since the day I crushed the boy with the wavemaker. I haven't been able to forget his little white trunks floating out of the inlet port all bloody. Who checks protective-screen mounting screws these days? Not me. Leon does when he wavemakes of course. It's in the protocol. That's how he got to be Subquadrant Manager, attention to detail. Leon's been rising steadily since we went through Orientation together, and all told he's saved three Guests and I've crushed the shit out of one.

The little boy I crushed was named Clive. By all accounts he was a sweet kid. Sometimes at night I sneak over there to do chores in secret and pray for forgiveness at his window. I've changed his dad's oil and painted all their window frames and taken the burrs off their Labrador. If anybody comes out while I'm working I hide in the shrubs. The sister who wears cateye glasses even in this day and age thinks it's Clive's soul doing the mystery errands and lately she's been leaving him notes. Simone says I'm not doing them any big favor by driving their daughter nuts.

But I can't help it. I feel so bad.

We pull up to our unit and I see that once again the Peretti twins have drawn squashed boys all over our windows with soap. Their dad's a bruiser. No way I'm forcing a confrontation.

In the driveway Simone asks did I do my résumé at lunch.

No, I tell her, I had a serious pH difficulty.

Fine, she says, make waves the rest of your life.

The day it happened, an attractive all-girl glee club was lying around on the concrete in Kawabunga Kove in Day-Glo suits, looking for all the world like a bunch of blooms. The president and sergeant at arms were standing with brown ankles in the shallow, favorably comparing my Attraction to real surf. To increase my appeal I had the sea chanteys blaring. I was operating at the prescribed wave-frequency setting but in my lust for the glee club had the magnitude pegged.

Leon came by and told me to turn the music down. So I turned it up. Consequently I never heard Clive screaming or Leon shouting at me to kill the waves. My first clue was looking out the Control Hut porthole and seeing people bolting towards the ladders, choking and with bits of Clive all over them. Guests were weeping while wiping their torsos on the lawn. In the Handicapped Section the chaired guys had their eyes shut tight and their heads turned away as the gore sloshed towards them. The ambulatories were clambering over the ropes, screaming for their physical therapists.

Leon hates to say he told me so but does it all the time anyway. He constantly reminds me of how guilty I am by telling me not to feel guilty and asking about my counseling. My counselor is Mr. Poppet, a gracious and devout man who's always tightening his butt cheeks when he thinks no one's looking. Mr. Poppet makes me sit with my eyes closed and repeat, "A boy is dead because of me," for half an hour for fifty dollars. Then for another fifty dollars he makes me sit with my eyes closed again and repeat, "Still, I'm a person of considerable value," for half an hour. When the session's over I go out into the bright sun like a rodent that lives in the earth, blinking and rubbing my eyes, and Mr. Poppet stands in the doorway, clapping for me and intoning the time of day of our next appointment.

The sessions have done me good. Clive doesn't come into my room at night all hacked up anymore. He comes in pretty much whole. He comes in and sits on my bed and starts talking to me. Since his death he's been hanging around with dead kids from other epochs. One night he showed up swearing in Latin. Another time with a wild story about an ancient African culture that used radio waves to relay tribal myths. He didn't use those exact words of course. Even though he's dead, he's still basically a kid. When he tries to be scary he gets it all wrong. He can't moan for beans. He's scariest when he does real kid things, like picking his nose and wiping it on the side of his sneaker.

He tries to be polite but he's pretty mad about the future I denied him. Tonight's subject is what the Mexico City trip with the perky red-haired tramp would have been like. He dwells on the details of their dinner in the catacombs and describes how her freckles would have looked as daylight streamed in through the cigarette-burned magenta curtains. Wistfully he says he sure would like to have tasted the sauce she would have said was too hot to be believed as they crossed the dirt road lined with begging cripples.

"Forgive me," I say in tears.

"No," he says, also in tears.

Near dawn he sighs, tucks in the parts of his body that have been gradually leaking out over the course of the night, pats my neck with his cold little palm, and tells me to have a nice day. Then he fades, producing farts with a wet hand under his armpit.

Simone sleeps through the whole thing, making little puppy sounds and pushing her rear against my front to remind me even in her sleep of how long it's been. But you try it. You kill a nice little kid via neglect and then enjoy having sex. If you can do it you're demented.

Simone's an innocent victim. Sometimes I think I should give her her space and let her explore various avenues so her personal development won't get stymied. But I could never let her go. I've loved her too long. Once in high school I waited three hours in a locker in the girls' locker room to see her in her panties. Every part of me cramped up, but when she finally came in and showered I resolved to marry her. We once dedicated a whole night to pretending I was a household invader who tied her up. In my shorts I stood outside our sliding-glass door shouting, "Meter man!" At dawn or so I made us eggs but was so high on her I ruined our only pan by leaving it on the burner while I kept running back and forth to look at her nude.

What I'm saying is, we go way back.

I hope she'll wait this thing out. If only Clive would resume living and start dating some nice-smelling cheerleader who has no idea who Benny Goodman is. Then I'd regain my strength and win her back. But no. Instead I wake at night and Simone's either looking over at me with hatred or whisking her privates with her index finger while thinking of God-knows-who, although I doubt very much it's me.

At noon next day a muscleman shows up with four beehives on a dolly. This is Leon's stroke of genius for the Kiper wedding. The Kipers are the natural type. They don't want to eat anything that ever lived or buy any product that even vaguely supports notorious third-world regimes. They asked that we run a check on the ultimate source of the tomatoes in our ketchup and the union status of the group that makes our floaties. They've opted to recite their vows in the Waterfall Grove. They've hired a blind trumpeter to canoe by and a couple of illegal aliens to retrieve the rice so no birds will choke.

At ten Leon arrives, proudly bearing a large shrimp-shaped serving vat full of bagels coated with fresh honey. Over the weekend he studied honey extraction techniques at the local library. He's always calling himself a Renaissance man but the way he says it it rhymes with "rent-a-dance fan." He puts down the vat and takes off the lid. Just then the bride's grandmother falls out of her chair and rolls down the bank. She stops faceup at the water's edge and her wig tips back. One of the rice-retrievers wanders up and addresses her as señora. I look around. I'm the nearest Host. According to the manual I'm supposed to initiate CPR or face a stiff payroll deduction. The week I took the class the dummy was on the fritz. Of course.

I straddle her and timidly start chest-pumping. I can feel her bra clasp under the heel of my hand. Nothing happens. I keep waiting for her to throw up on me or come to life. Then Leon vaults over the shrimp-shaped vat. He shoos me away, checks her pulse, and begins the Heimlich Maneuver.

"When your victim is elderly," he says loudly and remonstratively, "it's natural to assume heart attack. Natural, but, in this case, possibly deadly."

After a few more minutes of Heimlich he takes a pen from his pocket and drives it into her throat. Almost immediately she sits up and readjusts her wig, with the pen still sticking out. Leon kisses her forehead and makes her lie back down, then gives the thumbs-up.

The crowd bursts into applause.

I sneak off and sit for about an hour on the floor of the Control Hut. I keep hoping it'll blow up or a nuclear war will start so I'll die. But I don't die. So I go over and pick up my wife.

Leon wants to terminate me but Simone has a serious chat with him about our mortgage and he lets me stay on in Towel Distribution and Collection. Actually it's a relief. Nobody can get hurt. The worst that could happen is maybe a yeast infection. It's a relief until I go to his office one day with the Usage Statistics and hear moans from inside and hide behind a soda machine until Simone comes out looking flushed and happy. I want to jump out and confront her but I don't. Then Leon comes out and I want to jump out and confront him but I don't.

What I do is wait behind the soda machine until they leave, then climb out a window and hitchhike home. I get a ride from a guy who sells and services

Zambonis. He tells me to confront her forcefully and watch her fall to pieces. If she doesn't fall to pieces I should beat her.

When I get home I confront her forcefully. She doesn't fall to pieces. Not only does she not deny it, she says it's going to continue no matter what. She says I've been absent too long. She says there's more to Leon than meets the eye.

I think of beating her, and my heart breaks, and I give up on everything.

Clive shows up at ten. As he keeps me awake telling me what his senior prom would have been like, Simone calls Leon's name in her sleep and mutters something about his desk calendar leaving a paper cut on her neck. Clive follows me into the kitchen, wanting to know what a nosegay is. Outside, all the corn in the cornfield is bent over and blowing. The moon comes up over Delectable Videos like a fat man withdrawing himself from a lake. I fall asleep at the counter. The phone rings at three. It's Clive's father, saying he's finally shaken himself from his stupor and is coming over to kill me.

I tell him I'll leave the door open.

Clive's been in the bathroom imagining himself some zits. Even though he's one of the undead I have a lot of affection for him. When he comes out I tell him he'll have to go, and that I'll see him tomorrow. He whines a bit but finally fades away.

His dad pulls up in a Land Cruiser and gets out with a big gun. He comes through the door in an alert posture and sees me sitting on the couch. I can tell he's been drinking.

"I don't hate you," he says. "But I can't have you living on this earth while my son isn't."

"I understand," I say.

Looking sheepish, he steps over and puts the gun to my head. The sound of our home's internal ventilation system is suddenly wondrous. The mole on his cheek possesses grace. Children would have been nice.

I close my eyes and wait. Then I urinate myself. Then I wait some more. I wait and wait. Then I open my eyes. He's gone and the front door's wide open.

Jesus, I think, embarrassing, I wet myself and was ready to die.

Then I go for a brisk walk.

I hike into the hills and sit in a graveyard. The stars are blinking like cat's eyes and burned blood is pouring out of the slaughterhouse chimney. My crotch is cold with the pee and the breeze. The moon goes behind a cloud and six pale forms start down from the foothills. At first I think they're ghosts but they're only starving pronghorn come down to lick salt from the headstones. I sit there trying to write Simone off. No more guys ogling her in public and no more dippy theories on world hunger. Then I think of her and Leon watching the test pattern together nude and sweaty and I moan and double over with dread, and a doe bolts away in alarm.

A storm rolls in over the hills and a brochure describing a portrait offer gets plastered across my chest. Lightning strikes the slaughterhouse flagpole and the antelope scatter like minnows as the rain begins to fall, and finally, having lost what was to be lost, my torn and black heart rebels, saying enough already, enough, this is as low as I go.

Exercises for George Saunders's "The Wavemaker Falters."

1. Write the scene of Clive's death from other points of view—Clive's, his parents', other guests'.

2. Draw a promotional-style map of the theme park, indicating all the attractions and quadrants mentioned here and adding others of your own invention.

3. Write the employee manual for the theme park.

4. List every detail this story gives about the town or area outside the theme park. Building upon these details, create a lengthy description of the town.

5. Rewrite the story, changing the tone: eliminate as much of the humor as possible. What is the result?

6. Write a love scene and conversation between Simone and Leon.

7. Create the diary of Simone or Leon or Clive's father or sister.

8. Transpose any of these pages into third-person point of view; then have this "wavemaker" remember how, when he was thirteen years old, he first learned to dive—as in "Forever Overhead"—and compare and contrast the two pools.

9. Set the story in an ordinary theme park, using the actual names of contemporary products, rides, cartoon characters, and brand names. What is the effect?

10. Write the scene that would follow the story's ending.

FOREVER OVERHEAD

by David Foster Wallace

Happy Birthday. Your thirteenth is important. Maybe your first really public day. Your thirteenth is the chance for people to recognize that important things are happening to you.

Things have been happening to you for the past half year. You have seven hairs in your left armpit now. Twelve in your right. Hard dangerous spirals of brittle black hair. Crunchy, animal hair. There are now more of the hard curled hairs around your privates than you can count without losing track. Other things. Your voice is rich and scratchy and moves between octaves without any warning. Your face has begun to get shiny when you don't wash it. And two weeks of a deep and frightening ache this past spring left you with something dropped down from inside: your sack is now full and vulnerable, a commodity to be protected. Hefted and strapped in tight supporters that stripe your buttocks red. You have grown into a new fragility.

And dreams. For months there have been dreams like nothing before: moist and busy and distant, full of yielding curves, frantic pistons, warmth and a great falling; and you have awakened through fluttering lids to a rush and a gush and a toe-curling scalp-snapping jolt of feeling from an inside deeper than you knew you had, spasms of a deep sweet hurt, the streetlights through your window blinds cracking into sharp stars against the black bedroom ceiling, and on you a dense white jam that lisps between legs, trickles and sticks, cools on you, hardens and clears until there is nothing but gnarled knots of pale solid animal hair in the morning shower, and in the wet tangle a clean sweet smell you can't believe comes from anything you made inside you.

The smell is, more than anything, like this swimming pool: a bleached sweet salt, a flower with chemical petals. The pool has a strong clear blue smell, though you know the smell is never as strong when you are actually in the blue water, as you are now, all swum out, resting back along the shallow end, the hip-high water lapping at where it's all changed.

Around the deck of this old public pool on the western edge of Tucson is a Cyclone fence the color of pewter, decorated with a bright tangle of locked bicycles. Beyond this a hot black parking lot full of white lines and glittering cars. A dull field of dry grass and hard weeds, old dandelions' downy heads exploding and snowing up in a rising wind. And past all this, reddened by a round slow September sun, are mountains, jagged, their tops' sharp angles darkening into definition against a deep red tired light. Against the red their sharp connected tops form a spiked line, an EKG of the dying day.

The clouds are taking on color by the rim of the sky. The water is spangles of soft blue, five-o'clock warm, and the pool's smell, like the other smell, connects with a chemical haze inside you, an interior dimness that bends light to its own ends, softens the difference between what leaves off and what begins.

Your party is tonight. This afternoon, on your birthday, you have asked to come to the pool. You wanted to come alone, but a birthday is a family day, your family wants to be with you. This is nice, and you can't talk about why you wanted to come alone, and really truly maybe you didn't want to come alone, so they are here. Sunning. Both your parents sun. Their deck chairs have been marking time all afternoon, rotating, tracking the sun's curve across a desert sky heated to an eggy film. Your sister plays Marco Polo near you in the shallows with a group of thin girls from her grade. She is being blind now, her Marco's being Polo'd. She is shut-eyed and twirling to different cries, spinning at the hub of a wheel of shrill girls in bathing caps. Her cap has raised rubber flowers. There are limp old pink petals that shake as she lunges at blind sound.

There at the other end of the pool is the diving tank and the high board's tower. Back on the deck behind is the SN CK BAR, and on either side, bolted above the cement entrances to dark wet showers and lockers, are gray metal bullhorn speakers that send out the pool's radio music, the jangle flat and tinny thin.

Your family likes you. You are bright and quiet, respectful to elders—though you are not without spine. You are largely good. You look out for your little sister. You are her ally. You were six when she was zero and you had the mumps when they brought her home in a very soft yellow blanket; you kissed her hello on her feet out of concern that she not catch your mumps. Your parents say that this augured well. That it set the tone. They now feel they were right. In all things they are proud of you, satisfied, and they have retreated to the warm distance from which pride and satisfaction travel. You all get along well.

Happy Birthday. It is a big day, big as the roof of the whole southwest sky. You have thought it over. There is the high board. They will want to leave soon. Climb out and do the thing.

Shake off the blue clean. You're half-bleached, loose and soft, tenderized, pads of fingers wrinkled. The mist of the pool's too-clean smell is in your eyes; it breaks light into gentle color. Knock your head with the heel of your hand. One side has a flabby echo. Cock your head to the side and hop—sudden heat in your ear, delicious, and brain-warmed water turns cold on the nautilus of your ear's outside. You can hear harder tinnier music, closer shouts, much movement in much water.

The pool is crowded for this late. Here are thin children, hairy animal men. Disproportionate boys, all necks and legs and knobby joints, shallow-chested, vaguely birdlike. Like you. Here are old people moving tentatively through shallows on stick legs, feeling at the water with their hands, out of every element at once.

And girl-women, women, curved like instruments or fruit, skin burnished brown-bright, suit tops held by delicate knots of fragile colored string against the pull of mysterious weights, suit bottoms riding low over the gentle juts of hips totally unlike your own, immoderate swells and swivels that melt in light into a surrounding space that cups and accommodates the soft curves as things precious. You almost understand.

The pool is a system of movement. Here now there are: laps, splash fights, dives, corner tag, cannonballs, Sharks and Minnows, high fallings, Marco Polo (your sister still It, halfway to tears, too long to be It, the game teetering on the edge of cruelty, not your business to save or embarrass). Two clean little bright-white boys caped in cotton towels run along the poolside until the guard stops them dead with a shout through his bullhorn. The guard is brown as a tree, blond hair in a vertical line on his stomach, his head in a jungle explorer hat, his nose a white triangle of cream. A girl has an arm around a leg of his little tower. He's bored.

Get out now and go past your parents, who are sunning and reading, not looking up. Forget your towel. Stopping for the towel means talking and talking means thinking. You have decided being scared is caused mostly by thinking. Go right by, toward the tank at the deep end. Over the tank is a great iron tower of dirty white. A board protrudes from the top of the tower like a tongue. The pool's concrete deck is rough and hot against your bleached feet. Each of your footprints is thinner and fainter. Each shrinks behind you on the hot stone and disappears.

Lines of plastic wieners bob around the tank, which is entirely its own thing, empty of the rest of the pool's convulsive ballet of heads and arms. The tank is blue as energy, small and deep and perfectly square, flanked by lap lanes and SN CK BAR and rough hot deck and the bent late shadow of the tower and board. The tank is quiet and still and healed smooth between fallings.

There is a rhythm to it. Like breathing. Like a machine. The line for the board curves back from the tower's ladder. The line moves in its curve, straightens as it nears the ladder. One by one, people reach the ladder and climb. One by one, spaced by the beat of hearts, they reach the tongue of the board at the top. And once on the board, they pause, each exactly the same tiny heartbeat pause. And their legs take them to the end, where they all give the same sort of stomping hop, arms curving out as if to describe something circular, total; they come down heavy on the edge of the board and make it throw them up and out.

It's a swooping machine, lines of stuttered movement in a sweet late bleach mist. You can watch from the deck as they hit the cold blue sheet of the tank. Each fall makes a white that plumes and falls into itself and spreads and fizzes. Then blue clean comes up in the middle of the white and spreads like pudding, making it all new. The tank heals itself. Three times as you go by.

You are in line. Look around. Look bored. Few talk in the line. Everyone seems by himself. Most look at the ladder, look bored. You almost all have crossed arms, chilled by a late dry rising wind on the constellations of blue-clean chlorine beads that cover your backs and shoulders. It seems impossible that everybody could really be this bored. Beside you is the edge of the tower's shadow, the tilted black tongue of the board's image. The system of shadow is huge, long, off to the side, joined to the tower's base at a sharp late angle.

Almost everyone in line for the board watches the ladder. Older boys watch older girls' bottoms as they go up. The bottoms are in soft thin cloth, tight nylon stretch. The good bottoms move up the ladder like pendulums in liquid, a gentle uncrackable code. The girls' legs make you think of deer. Look bored.

Look out past it. Look across. You can see so well. Your mother is in her deck chair, reading, squinting, her face tilted up to get light on her cheeks. She hasn't looked to see where you are. She sips something sweet out of a bright can. Your father is on his big stomach, back like the hint of a hump of a whale, shoulders curling with animal spirals, skin oiled and soaked red-brown with too much sun. Your towel is hanging off your chair and a corner of the cloth now moves—your mother hit it as she waved away a sweat bee that likes what she has in the can. The bee is back right away, seeming to hang motionless over the can in a sweet blur. Your towel is one big face of Yogi Bear.

At some point there has gotten to be more line behind you than in front of you. Now no one in front except three on the slender ladder. The woman right before you is on the low rungs, looking up, wearing a tight black nylon suit that is all one piece. She climbs. From above there is a rumble, then a great falling, then a plume and the tank reheals. Now two on the ladder. The pool rules say one on the ladder at a time, but the guard never shouts about it. The guard makes the real rules by shouting or not shouting.

This woman above you should not wear a suit as tight as the suit she is wearing. She is as old as your mother, and as big. She is too big and too white. Her suit is full of her. The backs of her thighs are squeezed by the suit and look like cheese. Her legs have abrupt little squiggles of cold blue shattered vein under the white skin, as if something were broken, hurt, in her legs. Her legs look like they hurt to be squeezed, full of curled Arabic lines of cold broken blue. Her legs make you feel like your own legs hurt.

The rungs are very thin. It's unexpected. Thin round iron rungs laced in slick wet Safe-T felt. You taste metal from the smell of wet iron in shadow. Each rung presses into the bottoms of your feet and dents them. The dents feel deep and they hurt. You feel heavy. How the big woman over you must feel. The handrails along the ladder's sides are also very thin. It's like you might not hold on. You've got to hope the woman holds on, too. And of course it looked like fewer rungs from far away. You are not stupid.

Get halfway up, up in the open, big woman placed above you, a solid bald muscular man on the ladder underneath your feet. The board is still high overhead, invisible from here. But it rumbles and makes a heavy flapping sound, and a boy you can see for a few contained feet through the thin rungs falls in a flash of a line, a knee held to his chest, doing a splasher. There is a huge exclamation point of foam up into your field of sight, then scattered claps into a great fizzing. Then the silent sound of the tank healing to new blue all over again.

More thin rungs. Hold on tight. The radio is loudest here, one speaker at ear-level over a concrete locker room entrance. A cool dank whiff of the locker room inside. Grab the iron bars tight and twist and look down behind you and you can see people buying snacks and refreshments below. You can see down into it: the clean white top of the vendor's cap, tubs of ice cream, steaming brass freezers, scuba tanks of soft drink syrup, snakes of soda hose, bulging boxes of salty popcorn kept hot in the sun. Now that you're overhead you can see the whole thing.

There's wind. It's windier the higher you get. The wind is thin; through the shadow it's cold on your wet skin. On the ladder in the shadow your skin looks very white. The wind makes a thin whistle in your ears. Four more rungs to the top of the tower. The rungs hurt your feet. They are thin and let you know just how much you weigh. You have real weight on the ladder. The ground wants you back.

Now you can see just over the top of the ladder. You can see the board. The woman is there. There are two ridges of red, hurt-looking callus on the backs of her ankles. She stands at the start of the board, your eyes on her ankles. Now you're up above the tower's shadow. The solid man under you is looking through the rungs into the contained space the woman's fall will pass through.

She pauses for just that beat of a pause. There's nothing slow about it at all. It makes you cold. In no time she's at the end of the board, up, down on it, it bends low like it doesn't want her. Then it nods and flaps and throws her violently up and out, her arms opening out to inscribe that circle, and gone. She disappears in a dark blink. And there's time before you hear the hit below.

Listen. It does not seem good, the way she disappears into a time that passes before she sounds. Like a stone down a well. But you think she did not think so. She was part of a rhythm that excludes thinking. And now you have made yourself part of it, too. The rhythm seems blind. Like ants. Like a machine.

You decide this needs to be thought about. It may, after all, be all right to do something scary without thinking, but not when the scariness is the not thinking itself. Not when not thinking turns out to be wrong. At some point the wrongnesses have piled up blind: pretend-boredom, weight, thin rungs, hurt feet, space cut into laddered parts that melt together only in a disappearance that takes time. The wind on the ladder not what anyone would have expected. The way the board protrudes from shadow into light and you can't see past the end. When it all turns out to be different you should get to think. It should be required.

The ladder is full beneath you. Stacked up, everyone a few rungs apart. The ladder is fed by a solid line that stretches back and curves into the dark of the tower's canted shadow. People's arms are crossed in the line. Those on the ladder's feet hurt and they are all looking up. It is a machine that moves only forward.

Climb up onto the tower's tongue. The board turns out to be long. As long as the time you stand there. Time slows. It thickens around you as your heart gets more and more beats out of every second, every movement in the system of the pool below.

The board is long. From where you stand it seems to stretch off into nothing. It's going to send you someplace which its own length keeps you from seeing, which seems wrong to submit to without even thinking.

Looked at another way, the same board is just a long thin flat thing covered with a rough white plastic stuff. The white surface is very rough and is freckled and lined with a pale watered red that is nevertheless still red and not yet pink—drops of old pool water that are catching the light of the late sun over sharp mountains. The rough white stuff of the board is wet. And cold. Your feet are hurt from the thin rungs and have a great ability to feel. They feel your weight. There are handrails running above the beginning of the board. They are not like the ladder's handrails just were. They are thick and set very low, so you almost have to bend over to hold on to them. They are just for show, no one holds them. Holding on takes time and alters the rhythm of the machine.

It is a long cold rough white plastic or fiberglass board, veined with the sad near-pink color of bad candy.

But at the end of the white board, the edge, where you'll come down with your weight to make it send you off, there are two areas of darkness. Two flat shadows in the broad light. Two vague black ovals. The end of the board has two dirty spots.

They are from all the people who've gone before you. Your feet as you stand here are tender and dented, hurt by the rough wet surface, and you see that the two dark spots are from people's skin. They are skin abraded from feet by the violence of the disappearance of people with real weight. More people than you could count without losing track. The weight and abrasion of their disappearance leaves little bits of soft tender feet behind, bits and shards and curls of skin that dirty and darken and tan as they lie tiny and smeared in the sun at the end of the board. They pile up and get smeared and mixed together. They darken in two circles.

No time is passing outside you at all. It is amazing. The late ballet below is slow motion, the overbroad movements of mimes in blue jelly. If you wanted you could really stay here forever, vibrating inside so fast you float motionless in time, like a bee over something sweet.

But they should clean the board. Anybody who thought about it for even a second would see that they should clean the end of the board of people's skin, of two black collections of what's left of before, spots that from back here look like eyes, like blind and cross-eyed eyes.

Where you are now is still and quiet. Wind radio shouting splashing not here. No time and no real sound but your blood squeaking in your head.

Overhead here means sight and smell. The smells are intimate, newly clear. The smell of bleach's special flower, but out of it other things rise to you like a weed's seeded snow. You smell deep yellow popcorn. Sweet tan oil like hot coconut. Either hot dogs or corn dogs. A thin cruel hint of very dark Pepsi in paper cups. And the special smell of tons of water coming off tons of skin, rising like steam off a new bath. Animal heat. From overhead it is more real than anything.

Look at it. You can see the whole complicated thing, blue and white and brown and white, soaked in a watery spangle of deepening red. Everybody. This is what people call a view. And you knew that from below you wouldn't look nearly so high overhead. You see now how high overhead you are. You knew from down there no one could tell.

He says it behind you, his eyes on your ankles, the solid bald man, Hey kid. They want to know. Do your plans up here involve the whole day or what exactly is the story. Hey kid are you okay.

There's been time this whole time. You can't kill time with your heart. Everything takes time. Bees have to move very fast to stay still.

Hey kid he says Hey kid are you okay.

Metal flowers bloom on your tongue. No more time for thinking. Now that there is time you don't have time.

Hey.

Slowly now, out across everything, there's a watching that spreads like hit water's rings. Watch it spread out from the ladder. Your sighted sister and her thin white pack, pointing. Your mother looks to the shallows where you used to be, then makes a visor of her hand. The whale stirs and jiggles. The guard looks up, the girl around his leg looks up, he reaches for his horn.

Forever below is rough deck, snacks, thin metal music, down where you once used to be; the line is solid and has no reverse gear; and the water, of course, is only soft when you're inside it. Look down. Now it moves in the sun, full of hard coins of light that shimmer red as they stretch away into a mist that is your own sweet salt. The coins crack into new moons, long shards of light from the hearts of sad stars. The square tank is a cold blue sheet. Cold is just a kind of hard. A kind of blind. You have been taken off guard. Happy Birthday. Did you think it over. Yes and no. Hey kid.

Two black spots, violence, and disappear into a well of time. Height is not the problem. It all changes when you get back down. When you hit, with your weight.

So which is the lie? Hard or soft? Silence or time?

The lie is that it's one or the other. A still, floating bee is moving faster than it can think. From overhead the sweetness drives it crazy.

The board will nod and you will go, and eyes of skin can cross blind into a cloud-blotched sky, punctured light emptying behind sharp stone that is forever. That is forever. Step into the skin and disappear.

Hello.

▨ Exercises for David Foster Wallace's "Forever Overhead."

1. Rewrite the story, beginning with a different congratulatory opening, such as: "Happy Anniversary. Ten years is a long time." Or, "Congratulations. Your first baby is important!"

2. Revise the early passage describing the protagonist and his happy family ("Your family likes you. You are bright and quiet, respectful to elders . . ."). Change everything; give the boy some fire or make him a "difficult" child. What does this do?

3. Set the story in a different location—a ski lodge, a mall, a "Driver's Ed." class, a church—necessitating a different personal challenge for the protagonist.

4. Rewrite "Forever Overhead," making the protagonist female.

5. Write the same story, using only or primarily dialogue, with minimal **exposition** and introspection.

6. Write the same story in third person or in first person. Make it, however, the story of your own first experience at swimming or sailing or on the diving board . . .

7. Write the scene—in the author's style—of the boy's birthday party, or the family's trip to the pool. Does this remind you of John Barth's "Lost in the Funhouse"? If the answer is no, what's different here; if the answer is yes, in what ways?

8. The conflict of this story is primarily internal, but set in a very public space. What if this story's conflict were external? What if his parents had forbidden him to jump off the high dive, and the action focused on his surreptitious attempt to make the jump? Or what if the boy were alone at a

private pool? Rewrite the story, pursuing either of these options, and discuss the difference.

9. What if the ladder weren't full of people waiting to jump when our hero reaches the top? What if the "solid bald man" hadn't started to ask, "Hey, kid"? Rewrite.

10. "Everything takes time." Trim enough lines from the story to make it half as long. What is the effect? In the end, do you consider any lines or passages inessential?

WHY I LIVE AT THE P.O.

by Eudora Welty

I was getting along fine with Mama, Papa-Daddy and Uncle Rondo until my sister Stella-Rondo just separated from her husband and came back home again. Mr. Whitaker! Of course I went with Mr. Whitaker first, when he first appeared here in China Grove, taking "Pose Yourself" photos, and Stella-Rondo broke us up. Told him I was one-sided. Bigger on one side than the other, which is a deliberate, calculated falsehood: I'm the same. Stella-Rondo is exactly twelve months to the day younger than I am and for that reason she's spoiled.

She's always had anything in the world she wanted and then she'd throw it away. Papa-Daddy gave her this gorgeous Add-a-Pearl necklace when she was eight years old and she threw it away playing baseball when she was nine, with only two pearls.

So as soon as she got married and moved away from home the first thing she did was separate! From Mr. Whitaker! This photographer with the popeyes she said she trusted. Came home from one of those towns up in Illinois and to our complete surprise brought this child of two.

Mama said she like to made her drop dead for a second. "Here you had this marvelous blonde child and never so much as wrote your mother a word about it," says Mama. "I'm thoroughly ashamed of you." But of course she wasn't.

Stella-Rondo just calmly takes off this *hat,* I wish you could see it. She says, "Why, Mama, Shirley-T.'s adopted, I can prove it."

"How?" says Mama, but all I says was, "H'm!" There I was over the hot stove, trying to stretch two chickens over five people and a completely unexpected child into the bargain, without one moment's notice.

"What do you mean—'H'm!'?" says Stella-Rondo, and Mama says, "I heard that, Sister."

I said that oh, I didn't mean a thing, only that whoever Shirley-T. was, she was the spit-image of Papa-Daddy if he'd cut off his beard, which of course he'd never do in the world. Papa-Daddy's Mama's papa and sulks.

Stella-Rondo got furious! She said, "Sister, I don't need to tell you you got a lot of nerve and always did have and I'll thank you to make no future reference to my adopted child whatsoever."

"Very well," I said. "Very well, very well. Of course I noticed at once she looks like Mr. Whitaker's side too. That frown. She looks like a cross between Mr. Whitaker and Papa-Daddy."

"Well, all I can say is she isn't."

"She looks exactly like Shirley Temple to me," says Mama, but Shirley-T. just ran away from her.

So the first thing Stella-Rondo did at the table was turn Papa-Daddy against me.

"Papa-Daddy," she says. He was trying to cut up his meat. "Papa-Daddy!" I was taken completely by surprise. Papa-Daddy is about a million years old and's got this long-long beard. "Papa-Daddy, Sister says she fails to understand why you don't cut off your beard."

So Papa-Daddy l-a-y-s down his knife and fork! He's real rich. Mama says he is, he says he isn't. So he says, "Have I heard correctly? You don't understand why I don't cut off my beard?"

"Why," I says, "Papa-Daddy, of course I understand, I did not say any such of a thing, the idea!"

He says, "Hussy!"

I says, "Papa-Daddy, you know I wouldn't any more want you to cut off your beard than the man in the moon. It was the farthest thing from my mind! Stella-Rondo sat there and made that up while she was eating breast of chicken."

But he says, "So the postmistress fails to understand why I don't cut off my beard. Which job I got you through my influence with the government. 'Bird's nest'—is that what you call it?"

Not that it isn't the next to smallest P.O. in the entire state of Mississippi.

I says, "Oh, Papa-Daddy," I says, "I didn't say any such of a thing, I never dreamed it was a bird's nest, I have always been grateful though this is the next to smallest P.O. in the state of Mississippi, and I do not enjoy being referred to as a hussy by my own grandfather."

But Stella-Rondo says, "Yes, you did say it too. Anybody in the world could of heard you, that had ears."

"Stop right there," says Mama, looking at *me*.

So I pulled my napkin straight back through the napkin ring and left the table.

As soon as I was out of the room Mama says, "Call her back, or she'll starve to death," but Papa-Daddy says, "This is the beard I started growing on the Coast when I was fifteen years old." He would of gone on till nightfall if Shirley-T hadn't lost the Milky Way she ate in Cairo.

So Papa-Daddy says, "I am going out and lie in the hammock, and you can all sit here and remember my words: I'll never cut off my beard as long as I live, even one inch, and I don't appreciate it in you at all." Passed right by me in the hall and went straight out and got in the hammock.

It would be a holiday. It wasn't five minutes before Uncle Rondo suddenly appeared in the hall in one of Stella-Rondo's flesh-colored kimonos, all cut on the bias, like something Mr. Whitaker probably thought was gorgeous.

"Uncle Rondo!" I says. "I didn't know who that was! Where are you going?"

"Sister," he says, "get out of my way, I'm poisoned."

"If you're poisoned stay away from Papa-Daddy," I says. "Keep out of the hammock. Papa-Daddy will certainly beat you on the head if you come within forty miles of him. He thinks I deliberately said he ought to cut off his beard after he got me the P.O., and I've told him and told him and told him, and he acts like he just don't hear me. Papa-Daddy must of gone stone deaf."

"He picked a fine day to do it then," says Uncle Rondo, and before you could say "Jack Robinson" flew out in the yard.

What he'd really done, he'd drunk another bottle of that prescription. He does it every single Fourth of July as sure as shooting, and it's horribly expensive. Then he falls over in the hammock and snores. So he insisted on zigzagging right on out to the hammock, looking like a half-wit.

Papa-Daddy woke up with this horrible yell and right there without moving an inch he tried to turn Uncle Rondo against me. I heard every word he said. Oh, he told Uncle Rondo I didn't learn to read till I was eight years old and he didn't see how in the world I ever got the mail put up at the P.O., much less read it all, and he said if Uncle Rondo could only fathom the lengths he had gone to to get me that job! And he said on the other hand he thought Stella-Rondo had a brilliant mind and deserved credit for getting out of town. All the time he was just lying there swinging as pretty as you please and looping out his beard, and poor Uncle Rondo was *pleading* with him to slow down the hammock, it was making him as dizzy as a witch to watch it. But that's what Papa-Daddy likes about a hammock. So Uncle Rondo was too dizzy to get turned against me for the time being. He's Mama's only brother and is a good case of a one-track mind. Ask anybody. A certified pharmacist.

Just then I heard Stella-Rondo raising the upstairs window. While she was married she got this peculiar idea that it's cooler with the windows shut and locked. So she has to raise the window before she can make a soul hear her outdoors.

So she raises the window and says, "Oh!" You would have thought she was mortally wounded.

Uncle Rondo and Papa-Daddy didn't even look up, but kept right on with what they were doing. I had to laugh.

I flew up the stairs and threw the door open! I says, "What in the wide world's the matter, Stella-Rondo? You mortally wounded?"

"No," she says, "I am not mortally wounded but I wish you would do me the favor of looking out that window there and telling me what you see."

So I shade my eyes and look out the window.

"I see the front yard," I says.

"Don't you see any human beings?" she says.

"I see Uncle Rondo trying to run Papa-Daddy out of the hammock," I says. "Nothing more. Naturally, it's so suffocating-hot in the house, with all the windows shut and locked, everybody who cares to stay in their right mind will have to go out and get in the hammock before the Fourth of July is over."

"Don't you notice anything different about Uncle Rondo?" asks Stella-Rondo.

"Why, no, except he's got on some terrible-looking flesh-colored contraption I wouldn't be found dead in, is all I can see," I says.

"Never mind, you won't be found dead in it, because it happens to be part of my trousseau, and Mr. Whitaker took several dozen photographs of me in it," says Stella-Rondo. "What on earth could Uncle Rondo *mean* by wearing part of my trousseau out in the broad open daylight without saying so much as 'Kiss my foot,' *knowing* I only got home this morning after my separation and hung my negligee up on the bathroom door, just as nervous as I could be?"

"I'm sure I don't know, and what do you expect me to do about it?" I says. "Jump out the window?"

"No, I expect nothing of the kind. I simply declare that Uncle Rondo looks like a fool in it, that's all," she says. "It makes me sick to my stomach."

"Well, he looks as good as he can," I says. "As good as anybody in reason could." I stood up for Uncle Rondo, please remember. And I said to Stella-Rondo, "I think I would do well not to criticize so freely if I were you and came home with a two-year-old child I had never said a word about, and no explanation whatever about my separation."

"I asked you the instant I entered this house not to refer one more time to my adopted child, and you gave me your word of honor you would not," was all Stella-Rondo would say, and started pulling out every one of her eyebrows with some cheap Kress tweezers.

So I merely slammed the door behind me and went down and made some green-tomato pickle. Somebody had to do it. Of course Mama had turned both the Negroes loose; she always said no earthly power could hold one anyway on the Fourth of July, so she wouldn't even try. It turned out that Jaypan fell in the lake and came within a very narrow limit of drowning.

So Mama trots in. Lifts up the lid and says, "H'm! Not very good for your Uncle Rondo in his precarious condition, I must say. Or poor little adopted Shirley-T. Shame on you!"

That made me tired. I says, "Well, Stella-Rondo had better thank her lucky stars it was her instead of me came trotting in with that very peculiar-looking child. Now if it had been me that trotted in from Illinois and brought a peculiar-looking child of two, I shudder to think of the reception I'd of got, much less controlled the diet of an entire family."

"But you must remember, Sister, that you were never married to Mr. Whitaker in the first place and didn't go up to Illinois to live," says Mama, shaking a spoon in my face. "If you had I would of been just as overjoyed to see you and your little adopted girl as I was to see Stella-Rondo, when you wound up with your separation and came on back home."

"You would not," I says.

"Don't contradict me, I would," says Mama.

But I said she couldn't convince me though she talked till she was blue in the face. Then I said, "Besides, you know as well as I do that that child is not adopted."

"She most certainly is adopted," says Mama, stiff as a poker.

I says, "Why, Mama, Stella-Rondo had her just as sure as anything in this world, and just too stuck up to admit it."

"Why, Sister," said Mama. "Here I thought we were going to have a pleasant Fourth of July, and you start right out not believing a word your own baby sister tells you!"

"Just like Cousin Annie Flo. Went to her grave denying the facts of life," I remind Mama.

"I told you if you ever mentioned Annie Flo's name I'd slap your face," says Mama, and slaps my face.

"All right, you wait and see," I says.

"I," says Mama, "*I* prefer to take my children's word for anything when it's humanly possible." You ought to see Mama, she weighs two hundred pounds and has real tiny feet.

Just then something perfectly horrible occurred to me.

"Mama," I says, "can that child talk?" I simply had to whisper! "Mama, I wonder if that child can be—you know—in any way? Do you realize," I says, "that she hasn't spoken one single, solitary word to a human being up to this minute? This is the way she looks," I says, and I looked like this.

Well, Mama and I just stood there and stared at each other. It was horrible!

"I remember well that Joe Whitaker frequently drank like a fish," says Mama. "I believed to my soul he drank *chemicals*." And without another word she marches to the foot of the stairs and calls Stella-Rondo.

"Stella-Rondo? O-o-o-o-o! Stella-Rondo!"

"What?" says Stella-Rondo from upstairs. Not even the grace to get up off the bed.

"Can that child of yours talk?" asks Mama.

Stella-Rondo says, "Can she what?"

"Talk! Talk!" says Mama. "Burdyburdyburdyburdy!"

So Stella-Rondo yells back, "Who says she can't talk?"

"Sister says so," says Mama.

"You didn't have to tell me, I know whose word of honor don't mean a thing in this house," says Stella-Rondo.

And in a minute the loudest Yankee voice I ever heard in my life yells out, "OE'm Pop-OE the Sailor-r-r-r Ma-a-an!" and then somebody jumps up and down in the upstairs hall. In another second the house would of fallen down.

"Not only talks, she can tap-dance!" calls Stella-Rondo. "Which is more than some people I won't name can do."

"Why, the little precious darling thing!" Mama says, so surprised. "Just as smart as she can be!" Starts talking baby talk right there. Then she turns on me.

"Sister, you ought to be thoroughly ashamed! Run upstairs this instant and apologize to Stella-Rondo and Shirley-T."

"Apologize for what?" I says. "I merely wondered if the child was normal, that's all. Now that she's proved she is, why, I have nothing further to say."

But Mama just turned on her heel and flew out, furious. She ran right upstairs and hugged the baby. She believed it was adopted. Stella-Rondo hadn't done a thing but turn her against me from upstairs while I stood there helpless over the hot stove. So that made Mama, Papa-Daddy and the baby all on Stella-Rondo's side.

Next, Uncle Rondo.

I must say that Uncle Rondo has been marvelous to me at various times in the past and I was completely unprepared to be made to jump out of my skin, the way it turned out. Once Stella-Rondo did something perfectly horrible to him—broke a chain letter from Flanders Field—and he took the radio back he had given her and gave it to me. Stella-Rondo was furious! For six months we all had to call her Stella instead of Stella-Rondo, or she wouldn't answer. I always thought Uncle Rondo had all the brains of the entire family. Another time he sent me to Mammoth Cave, with all expenses paid.

But this would be the day he was drinking that prescription, the Fourth of July.

So at supper Stella-Rondo speaks up and says she thinks Uncle Rondo ought to try to eat a little something. So finally Uncle Rondo said he would try a little cold biscuits and ketchup, but that was all. So *she* brought it to him.

"Do you think it wise to disport with ketchup in Stella-Rondo's flesh-colored kimono?" I says. Trying to be considerate! If Stella-Rondo couldn't watch out for her trousseau, somebody had to.

"Any objections?" asks Uncle Rondo, just about to pour out all the ketchup.

"Don't mind what she says, Uncle Rondo," says Stella-Rondo. "Sister has been devoting this solid afternoon to sneering out my bedroom window at the way you look."

"What's that?" says Uncle Rondo. Uncle Rondo has got the most terrible temper in the world. Anything is liable to make him tear the house down if it comes at the wrong time.

So Stella-Rondo says, "Sister says, 'Uncle Rondo certainly does look like a fool in that pink kimono!'"

Do you remember who it was really said that?

Uncle Rondo spills out all the ketchup and jumps out of his chair and tears off the kimono and throws it down on the dirty floor and puts his foot on it. It had to be sent all the way to Jackson to the cleaners and re-pleated.

"So that's your opinion of your Uncle Rondo, is it?" he says. "I look like a fool, do I? Well, that's the last straw. A whole day in this house with nothing to do, and then to hear you come out with a remark like that behind my back!"

"I didn't say any such of a thing, Uncle Rondo," I says, "and I'm not saying who did, either. Why, I think you look all right. Just try to take care of yourself and not talk and eat at the same time," I says. "I think you better go lie down."

"Lie down my foot," says Uncle Rondo. I ought to of known by that he was fixing to do something perfectly horrible.

So he didn't do anything that night in the precarious state he was in—just played Casino with Mama and Stella-Rondo and Shirley-T. and gave Shirley-T. a nickel with a head on both sides. It tickled her nearly to death, and she called him "Papa." But at 6:30 A.M. the next morning, he threw a whole five-cent package of some unsold one-inch firecrackers from the store as hard as he could into my bedroom and they every one went off. Not one bad one in the string. Anybody else, there'd be one that wouldn't go off.

Well, I'm just terribly susceptible to noise of any kind, the doctor has always told me I was the most sensitive person he had ever seen in his whole life, and I was simply prostrated. I couldn't eat! People tell me they heard it as far as the cemetery, and old Aunt Jep Patterson, that had been holding her own so good, thought it was Judgment Day and she was going to meet her whole family. It's usually so quiet here.

And I'll tell you it didn't take me any longer than a minute to make up my mind what to do. There I was with the whole entire house on Stella-Rondo's side and turned against me. If I have anything at all I have pride.

So I just decided I'd go straight down to the P.O. There's plenty of room there in the back, I says to myself.

Well! I made no bones about letting the family catch on to what I was up to. I didn't try to conceal it.

The first thing they knew, I marched in where they were all playing Old Maid and pulled the electric oscillating fan out by the plug, and everything got real hot. Next I snatched the pillow I'd done the needlepoint on right off the davenport from behind Papa-Daddy. He went "Ugh!" I beat Stella-Rondo up the stairs and finally found my charm bracelet in her bureau drawer under a picture of Nelson Eddy.

"So that's the way the land lies," says Uncle Rondo. There he was, piecing on the ham. "Well, Sister, I'll be glad to donate my army cot if you got any place to set it up, providing you'll leave right this minute and let me get some peace." Uncle Rondo was in France.

"Thank you kindly for the cot and 'peace' is hardly the word I would select if I had to resort to firecrackers at 6:30 A.M. in a young girl's bedroom," I says back to him. "And as to where I intend to go, you seem to forget my position as postmistress of China Grove, Mississippi," I says. "I've always got the P.O."

Well, that made them all sit up and take notice.

I went out front and started digging up some four-o'clocks to plant around the P.O.

"Ah-ah-ah!" says Mama, raising the window. "Those happen to be my four-o'clocks. Everything planted in that star is mine. I've never known you to make anything grow in your life."

"Very well," I says. "But I take the fern. Even you, Mama, can't stand there and deny that I'm the one watered that fern. And I happen to know where I can send in a box top and get a packet of one thousand mixed seeds, no two the same kind, free."

"Oh, where?" Mama wants to know.

But I says, "Too late. You 'tend to your house, and I'll 'tend to mine. You hear things like that all the time if you know how to listen to the radio. Perfectly marvelous offers. Get anything you want free."

So I hope to tell you I marched in and got that radio, and they could of all bit a nail in two, especially Stella-Rondo, that it used to belong to, and she well knew she couldn't get it back, I'd sue for it like a shot. And I very politely took the sewing-machine motor I helped pay the most on to give Mama for Christmas back in 1929, and a good big calendar, with the first-aid remedies on it. The thermometer and the Hawaiian ukulele certainly were rightfully mine, and I stood on the step-ladder and got all my watermelon-rind preserves and every fruit and vegetable I'd put up, every jar. Then I began to pull the tacks out of the bluebird wall vases on the archway to the dining room.

"Who told you you could have those, Miss Priss?" says Mama, fanning as hard as she could.

"I bought 'em and I'll keep track of 'em," I says. "I'll tack 'em up one on each side the post-office window, and you can see 'em when you come to ask me for your mail, if you're so dead to see 'em."

"Not I! I'll never darken the door to that post office again if I live to be a hundred," Mama says. "Ungrateful child! After all the money we spent on you at the Normal."

"Me either," says Stella-Rondo. "You can just let my mail lie there and *rot*, for all I care. I'll never come and relieve you of a single, solitary piece."

"I should worry," I says. "And who you think's going to sit down and write you all those big fat letters and postcards, by the way? Mr. Whitaker? Just because he was the only man ever dropped down in China Grove and you got him—unfairly—is he going to sit down and write you a lengthy correspondence after you come home giving no rhyme nor reason whatsoever for your separation and no explanation for the presence of that child? I may not have your brilliant mind, but I fail to see it."

So Mama says, "Sister, I've told you a thousand times that Stella-Rondo simply got homesick, and this child is far too big to be hers," and she says, "Now, why don't you all just sit down and play Casino?"

Then Shirley-T. sticks out her tongue at me in this perfectly horrible way. She has no more manners than the man in the moon. I told her she was going to cross her eyes like that some day and they'd stick.

"It's too late to stop me now," I says. "You should have tried that yesterday. I'm going to the P.O. and the only way you can possibly see me is to visit me there."

So Papa-Daddy says, "You'll never catch me setting foot in that post office, even if I should take a notion into my head to write a letter some place." He says, "I won't have you reachin' out of that little old window with a pair of shears and cuttin' off any beard of mine. I'm too smart for you!"

"We all are," says Stella-Rondo.

But I said, "If you're so smart, where's Mr. Whitaker?"

So then Uncle Rondo says, "I'll thank you from now on to stop reading all the orders I get on postcards and telling everybody in China Grove what you think is the matter with them," but I says, "I draw my own conclusions and will continue in the future to draw them." I says, "If people want to write their inmost secrets on penny postcards, there's nothing in the wide world you can do about it, Uncle Rondo."

"And if you think we'll ever *write* another postcard you're sadly mistaken," says Mama.

"Cutting off your nose to spite your face then," I says. "But if you're all determined to have no more to do with the U.S. mail, think of this: What will Stella-Rondo do now, if she wants to tell Mr. Whitaker to come after her?"

"Wah!" says Stella-Rondo. I knew she'd cry. She had a conniption fit right there in the kitchen.

"It will be interesting to see how long she holds out," I says. "And now—I am leaving."

"Good-bye," says Uncle Rondo.

"Oh, I declare," says Mama, "to think that a family of mine should quarrel on the Fourth of July, or the day after, over Stella-Rondo leaving old Mr. Whitaker and having the sweetest little adopted child! It looks like we'd all be glad!"

"Wah!" says Stella-Rondo, and has a fresh conniption fit.

"*He* left *her*—you mark my words," I says. "That's Mr. Whitaker. I know Mr. Whitaker. After all, I knew him first. I said from the beginning he'd up and leave her. I foretold every single thing that's happened."

"Where did he go?" asks Mama.

"Probably to the North Pole, if he knows what's good for him," I says.

But Stella-Rondo just bawled and wouldn't say another word. She flew to her room and slammed the door.

"Now look what you've gone and done, Sister," says Mama. "You go apologize."

"I haven't got time, I'm leaving," I says.

"Well, what are you waiting around for?" asks Uncle Rondo.

So I just picked up the kitchen clock and marched off, without saying "Kiss my foot" or anything, and never did tell Stella-Rondo good-bye.

There was a girl going along on a little wagon right in front.

"Girl," I says, "come help me haul these things down the hill, I'm going to live in the post office."

Took her nine trips in her express wagon. Uncle Rondo came out on the porch and threw her a nickel.

And that's the last I've laid eyes on any of my family or my family laid eyes on me for five solid days and nights. Stella-Rondo may be telling the most horrible tales in the world about Mr. Whitaker, but I haven't heard them. As I tell everybody, I draw my own conclusions.

But oh, I like it here. It's ideal, as I've been saying. You see, I've got everything cater-cornered, the way I like it. Hear the radio? All the war news. Radio, sewing machine, book ends, ironing board and that great big piano lamp—peace, that's what I like. Butter-bean vines planted all along the front where the strings are.

Of course, there's not much mail. My family are naturally the main people in China Grove, and if they prefer to vanish from the face of the earth, for all the mail they get or the mail they write, why, I'm not going to open my mouth. Some of the folks here in town are taking up for me and some turned against me. I know which is which. There are always people who will quit buying stamps just to get on the right side of Papa-Daddy.

But here I am, and here I'll stay. I want the world to know I'm happy.

And if Stella-Rondo should come to me this minute, on bended knees, and *attempt* to explain the incidents of her life with Mr. Whitaker, I'd simply put my fingers in both my ears and refuse to listen.

▨ Exercises for Eudora Welty's "Why I Live at the P.O."

1. Recast the first two pages of this story in third-person point of view; make "I" into "She."

2. Recast the last two pages of this story as first-person narrative told from two of the following: (a) Mama's point of view, (b) Stella-Rondo's, (c) Uncle Rondo's, (d) Papa-Daddy's.

3. Tell the story—in any point of view you choose—of the failed courtship between Sister and Mr. Whitaker.

4. "And if Stella-Rondo should come to me this minute, on bended knees, and *attempt* to explain the incidents of her life with Mr. Whitaker . . ." what would she say? And if Sister would "simply put my fingers in both my ears and refuse to listen," what would she fail to hear?

5. "I was getting along fine with Mama . . ." Discuss the role of the nontrustworthy narrator here, and how it functions with comic effect; what parts of this story are funny and which parts, if any, are sad? "My family are naturally the main people in China Grove," says Sister; discuss here the evidence of class.

6. Recast the scene at dinner as a screenplay, then a one-act play.

7. Imagine this Southern family's story as told by Flannery O'Connor. What would be constant, what changed?

8. "Stella-Rondo is exactly twelve months to the day younger than I am and for that reason she's spoiled." Describe a birthday party when Sister is seven and Stella-Rondo six.

9. "OE'm Pop-OE the Sailor-r-r-r Ma-a-an!" sings Shirley-T. Who is her father and is she from a single parent or adopted and what does she make of her new relatives?

10. "I must say that Uncle Rondo has been marvelous to me at various times in the past . . ." Write a scene in which Uncle Rondo is marvelous to Sister, and at Papa-Daddy's expense.

Glossary

action The events occurring during the time frame of a narrative.

aesthetics A particular conception of art or beauty which may govern the choices an author makes when writing.

aesthetic or artistic credo A brief statement or creed outlining the approach (stylistic, structural, thematic, etc.) to writing and reading that a writer values.

allegory A narrative in which key elements like characters or settings are intended to be read as symbols conveying universal truths or moral lessons.

anecdote A brief narrative about an amusing or interesting incident.

antagonist The character who opposes or is in conflict with the protagonist, or main character.

anticlimax The opposite of a climax; a point in a narrative that is striking for its *lack* of excitement, intensity, or emphasis.

allusion A reference to another work of art or literature, or to a person, place, or event outside the text.

aphorism A succinct statement of a sentiment, truth, or principle, such as "Love is blind."

Aristotelian narrative Aristotle's definition of narrative as consisting of a single, complete action (rather than a complete time period or theme) with a beginning, middle, and end. Generally associated with a linear plot structure, this type of narrative typically begins with exposition and escalation of the conflict, proceeding by cause and effect toward a climax at the approximate two-thirds point, followed by a resolution of the conflict.

aside In drama, a remark made by an actor to the audience which the other characters do not hear. This convention is sometimes discernable in fiction writing, when a self-conscious narrator breaks the flow of the narrative to make a remark directly to the reader.

backstory Essential information, usually about the past of a character or conflict, that is summarized or inserted in a narrative to contextualize the present action of the story.

ballad A song or poem that tells a lively or tragic story through simple language, using rhyming four-line stanzas.

Baroque A very ornate, extravagant, sometimes grotesque style of art and architecture that flourished in the 17th century.

burlesque A work of drama or literature that ridicules its subject matter through exaggerated mockery and broad comedy.

caricature A portrait that ridicules a person by exaggerating his or her most prominent features.

cadence The inherent melody and rhythm of words or phrases, or of a person's voice or accent.

catalyst In science, a substance that initiates a chemical reaction. In fiction, a character or force that initiates a course of action that would not occur otherwise.

catastrophe The downfall of the hero or the tragic reversal of the hero's fate.

catharsis The purging of emotions which the audience experiences as a result of the powerful climax of a classical tragedy; the sense of relief and renewal experienced through art.

character A person invented by an author to act in a literary text.

characterization The way in which an author creates or exposes a character in a text.

climax The major turning point in a narrative; the point of greatest intensity and significance.

collective first person The first person plural mode of narration in which the narrative voice is a collective *we*.

conflict A struggle between opposing forces in a narrative. A struggle between two or more characters or forces is called an **external conflict;** a struggle occurring within a character is an **internal conflict.**

counterpoint The use of contrasting or complementary elements in a work of art.

counterpointed characterization The use of contrasting characters to intensify the dramatic conflict or to help define each character more precisely.

craft The relatively teachable set of skills authors use to create literary texts.

crisis The climax or turning point in a literary text, generally preceded by a

build-up of tension and followed by resolution.

denouement The resolution of dramatic conflict, or the events following the climax of a literary work.

dialogue A conversation between characters, generally presented in quotation marks.

diction The vocal expression or choice of words of a particular character, narrator, or author in a given text.

digression A passage or commentary that strays from the main flow of ideas or action in a text.

doppelgänger or literary double From the German "double goer," a character who acts as a ghost-like double or a very similar counterpart of another character.

doubling pattern The repetition or echoing of significant elements in a narrative, such as characters, conflicts, images, or settings. This can create a sense of unity in the composition and can guide the reader's attention to what is important in a text.

dramatic encounter A point when conflicting characters or forces are brought together and thus forced to interact or struggle, creating tension and drama.

dramatic license The author's prerogative to alter or embellish the components of a story to enhance its effect on the audience.

dramatic monologue A poem in which the speaker addresses a particular silent listener, giving the reader the sense that he or she is overhearing the speaker's comments.

elide To leave out, omit.

epiphany In religion, the moment when a divine being suddenly appears. In narrative, the moment when a significant truth or the essence of something is suddenly revealed to a character.

episode An event or incident within a longer narrative.

episodic narrative or plot A narrative that seems to pursue a chain of distinct episodes rather than working through one central conflict.

epistolary novel A novel that takes the form of letters between characters.

eros The Greek god of erotic love. In Freudian theory, eros represents the instinctual impulse to satisfy basic human needs (such as sex) to sustain the body and mind. See **thanatos.**

exposition A passage in a narrative devoted to presenting necessary information about the character, setting, or background of the conflict.

fable A short narrative that often uses animals as characters or involves supernatural events to illustrate a moral.

farce A work of drama or literature that uses broad, often physical comedy, exaggerated characters, absurd situations and improbable plot twists to evoke laughter without intending social criticism.

fatalism The belief that all events are predestined and human beings are powerless to change their fate.

fate The final, perhaps inevitable, outcome of a character's life.

form The shape, structure, and style of a literary work, as distinguishable from, but integral to, the content or substance of a literary work.

frame story A narrative that includes another narrative within it.

free verse Verse that has no regular pattern of line length, rhyme scheme, or meter.

genre A literary category or form, such as the short story or novel.

grotesque A style marked by the unsettling combination of incongruous elements or the distortion of what is considered natural, balanced or harmonious.

homage A tribute to another artist or work of art; a respectful imitation intended to acknowledge the influence of another artist or work of art.

hypotaxis See **parataxis.**

idiomatic language Dialect; verbal expressions that reflect a particular cultural affiliation and may deviate from standard grammatical usage or meaning.

image A sensory impression created by language. Not all images are visual pictures; an image can appeal to any of the five senses, the emotions, the intellect, etc.

imagery The pattern of images used in a particular literary work.

imperative In grammar, a command form, such as "Buy this book."

inflected dialogue Dialogue that attempts to replicate the particular sound, accent, cadence, or dialect of a character's speech, such as The Misfit's line, "I wisht I had of been there."

interior monologue Also called "stream of consciousness," a passage in a narrative that presents the disorganized thoughts and fleeting impressions of a character.

irony An incongruity between what is said and what is meant, or between what occurs and what is expected to occur.

juxtaposition The placing of two or more things side by side.

limerick A light, often humorous verse form consisting of five anapestic lines, with a rhyme scheme of *aabba.* The first, second, and fifth lines consist of three feet, while lines three and four consist of two feet.

linear plot A plot that essentially moves forward in chronological sequence, without a complex reordering of the events of the story.

list story A story with the structural form of a list, or a story that makes significant use of lists.

litany A repetitive chant or prayer.

luftmensch A familiar type from Yiddish theater and short stories, a weightless man who lives on air.

lyric, lyrical A mode of writing that expresses the thoughts and feelings of a speaker or character in a subjective, personal way.

mannered Displaying a particular artistic or cultural manner or style that may be more artificial than natural.

magic realism A style of fiction which combines realistic and fantastic elements, as well as the use of dreams, myths, convoluted plots, and surrealistic description.

material The subject matter, raw experience or research an author draws upon to build a narrative.

melodrama A sensational type of drama associated with extremes of emotion and using simplified heroes and villains that represent absolute good and evil.

meta-fiction A work of fiction that self-consciously draws attention to itself as a work of fiction. Rather than upholding the standard pretense, prevalent in realist fiction, that a story creates or refers to a "real world" beyond the text, meta-fiction self-consciously reveals the fact and sometimes the manner of its own construction. Meta-fiction is often associated with postmodernism, but examples of meta-fiction also occur in many other literary movements.

metaphor A comparison between two dissimilar things without the use of *like* or *as*.

mimesis Greek word meaning imitation of reality, or mimicry.

minimalism A style of art or literature in which the work is stripped down to its most essential features. In literature, this can involve extremely economical prose, streamlined structure, and the revelation of only as much information as is absolutely necessary.

mythology The collective term for the myths of a given society.

myth A traditional story dealing with supernatural beings or ancestral heroes that illuminates the origins, beliefs, or customs of a society.

modernism An artistic movement running from the late nineteenth century through the early twentieth century. Modernist literature is quite varied, but some important attributes are: an increased interest in language, experimentation in form, impressionism, and a sense that objective, universal truths could no longer be trusted to represent the world. Perhaps because of this last tendency, modernist authors tended to reject the omniscient narrator in favor of subjective narrators whose means of perception influenced their telling of the story.

narrator The voice or persona telling the story, as distinct from the actual author of the text.

narrative A story as told or constructed by a particular voice.

naturalism A term used loosely to describe works of literature that use realistic means and subject matter and demonstrate a strong interest in and sympathy for nature.

nonlinear plot A plot that does not follow chronological sequence; the events of the plot have been substantially reordered for some artistic purposes. See **linear plot.**

objective point of view A point of view that functions as a kind of roving camera; the narrator can report on everything seen or heard in a scene, but cannot report what goes on in any character's mind. Also called **dramatic point of view.**

omniscient narrator A narrator who knows everything and can report not just the physical actions of each character but also the inner thoughts, emotions, and judgments of each character.

opening beat The first phrase or sentence in a prose passage.

pace The speed at which the events of a narrative seem to unfold.

parataxis A syntactical and rhetorical construction in which clauses or phrases are linked without subordination, such as, "I came, I saw, I conquered." **Hypotaxis,** in contrast, is the use of subordination when linking clauses, such as, "Once we conquered, we rested."

parody A work of art that imitates another artist's style in order to ridicule it or create comic effect.

pastiche A work of art that imitates the style of another work or combines elements of different works in a patchwork form.

pedagogical device A tool or technique used for teaching.

plot The sequence of events that occur in a narrative, as organized by the author.

plot device A strategy or mechanism devised by an author to advance the plot or change the trajectory of a character. Often, this involves introducing a complication, obstacle, or competing force.

point of view The perspective from which the events of the story are observed and reported. The point of view can be **limited** to the vision and insights of one character, or can be **omniscient,** all-knowing.

postmodernism A movement in the arts beginning in the latter part of the twentieth century which is notoriously difficult to define but is often associated, in literature, with the following: fragmentation, parody, pastiche, reflexivity or self-consciousness, a re-

jection of rigid distinctions between genres, and a rejection of the hierarchical division between "high" and "low" culture. Like the modernists, post-modernists are skeptical about whether reality can be objectively or universally represented, but while the modernists seem to lament this circumstance, the post-modernists celebrate it, engaging in the playful manipulation and combination of diverse forms, perspectives, and genres.

précis A summary or shortened version of a work.

prolixity Verboseness, elaborate and unnecessary wordiness.

prose Writing in the form of paragraphs rather than verse. Also, the term used to discuss the style or qualities of an author's word choice, sentence structure, and paragraphs, as in, "Hemingway's prose is very economical."

prosody The study of versification, including meter, rhyme, rhythm, and stanza forms.

protagonist The main character in a narrative.

realism 1. A style of writing that attempts to portray the world in detail as it really seems, i.e., without distortion, sensationalism, or the use of fantastic or supernatural elements. 2. A literary movement that flourished in Europe in the nineteenth century and was marked by this style.

scene In fiction, a passage that presents a particular incident or encounter moment by moment, using detail and dialogue to give the reader the sense that he or she is watching the action unfold in approximately real time.

self-conscious author Found in self-reflexive or meta-fiction, a self-conscious author is one who interrupts the narrative to comment on the text itself or the composition of the text. Although the self-conscious author may share the actual author's name and be closely affiliated with the actual author, he or she is generally a stylized, fictionalized version of the author.

self-reflexive fiction See **meta-fiction.**

simile A comparison between two dissimilar things, generally using *like* or *as.*

solecism An ungrammatical phrase or blunder.

sonnet A poem consisting of fourteen lines, usually written in iambic pentameter. There are different rhyme schemes for different types of sonnets.

sonnet sequence A series of sonnets written on a particular theme.

stock character A familiar, simplified type that recurs in several works of a particular genre, such as the clown, the confidant, or the jealous husband.

structure The way in which the various formal elements of a literary work are organized; the architecture of a story. A play may have a five-act structure; a short story may be structured as a list or as a frame story, etc.

style The characteristic way an author expresses his or her ideas with language and literary techniques.

summary In fiction, a passage that condenses information, action, or dialogue and relates them in brief, rather than presenting them moment by moment in scene.

surreal Exhibiting the intense yet irrational type of reality found in dream states.

symbol An object or image that represents something else.

syntax The way in which words are organized to form sentences or phrases.

tableau In theater, a moment when the actors silently freeze in a particular pose to leave a visual impression on the audience.

thanatos The Greek god of death. In Freudian theory, thanatos represents the instinctual desire for death. See **eros.**

theme The central idea contained in a literary work, distinct from but understood through the plot, subject matter, characters, and stylistic devices.

tone The attitude or atmosphere of a text, as expressed through the author's word choice, selection of details, imagery, prose style, etc.

tragedy A form of drama concerned with the reversal of fortune, typically for the worse. Traditionally tragic heroes were great figures rather than ordinary people, and their downfall seemed inevitable.

transposition Translation. In music, to transpose is to write or perform a piece in a different key.

type See **stock character.**

unreliable narrator A narrator who cannot be trusted to present an accurate or truthful account of the events of the story.

vaudeville A light theatrical work or performance involving comedy, music, or dance.

verbal tic A persistent feature in a person's speech patterns.

vignette A brief, descriptive literary sketch or short scene.

villanelle A nineteen-line lyric poem that consists of five tercets (three-lined stanzas) and one final quatrain (four-lined stanza). The first and third lines of the first stanza alternate as the last line in the stanzas that follow and form a final couplet in the last stanza.

zeugma A figure of speech in which one word governs or modifies two or more words in a way that connotes a different meaning for each. For example: "The thieves made off with our wallets and our pride."

Credits

Text Credits

Andrea Barrett, "The Behavior of the Hawkweeds" from *Ship Fever & Other Stories*. Copyright © 1996 by Andrea Barrett. Used by permission of W.W. Norton & Company, Inc.

John Barth, "Lost in the Funhouse," from *Lost in the Funhouse* by John Barth. Copyright © 1967 by The Atlantic Monthly Company. Used by permission of Doubleday, a division of Random House, Inc.

Dylan Thomas, "In My Craft or Sullen Art" by Dylan Thomas from *The Poems of Dylan Thomas*. Copyright © 1946 by New Directions Publishing Corp. Reprinted by permission of New Directions Publishing Corp. and Dent Publishers.

Charles Baxter, "Fenstad's Mother" from *A Relative Stranger*. Copyright © 1990 by Charles Baxter. Used by permission of W.W. Norton & Company, Inc.

Raymond Carver, "A Small, Good Thing" from *Cathedral*. Copyright © 1983 by Raymond Carver. Used by permission of Alfred A. Knopf, a division of Random House, Inc.

Richard Ford, "Communist" from *Rock Springs*. Copyright © 1987 by Richard Ford. Reprinted by permission of Grove/Atlantic, Inc.

Ernest Hemingway, from *A Farewell to Arms*. Reprinted with permission of Scribner, an imprint of Simon & Schuster Adult Publishing Group. Copyright © 1929 by Charles Scribner's Sons. Copyright renewed © 1957 by Ernest Hemingway.

Ernest Hemingway, from *In Our Time*. Reprinted with permission of Scribner, an imprint of Simon & Schuster Adult Publishing Group. Copyright © 1925 by Charles Scribner's Sons. Copyright renewed 1953 by Ernest Hemingway.

Ernest Hemingway, "In Another Country" from *The Short Stories of Ernest Hemingway*. Reprinted with permission of Scribner, an imprint of Simon & Schuster Adult Publishing Group. Copyright © 1927 by Charles Scribner's Sons. Copyright renewed 1955 by Ernest Hemingway.

Bharati Mukherjee, "The Management of Grief" from *The Middleman and Other Stories*. Copyright © 1988 Bharati Mukherjee. Reprinted by permission of Grove/Atlantic, Inc. and Penguin Books Canada Limited.

Lorrie Moore, "How to Become a Writer" from *Self-Help*. Copyright © 1985 by M.L. Moore. Used by permission of Alfred A. Knopf, a division of Random House, Inc.

Photo Credits

Index